MARVEL COMICS

MARVEL COMICS

The Untold Story

SEAN HOWE

HARPER

An Imprint of HarperCollins*Publishers*

www.harpercollins.com

HarperCollins books may be purchased for educational, business, or sales promotional use. For information, please e-mail the Special Markets Department at SPsales@harpercollins.com.

FIRST EDITION

Library of Congress Cataloging-in-Publication Data

Howe, Sean.
Marvel Comics : the untold story / by Sean Howe.
p.   cm.
ISBN 978-0-06-199210-0
1. Marvel Comics Group. 2. Comic books, strips, etc.—United States—History and criticism. I. Title.
PN6725.H69   2012
741.5'973—dc23   2012015058

12 13 14 15 16   OV/RRD   10 9 8 7 6 5 4 3 2 1

To the Merry Marvel Bullpen

In the beginning Marvel created the Bullpen and the Style.

And the Bullpen was without form, and was void; and darkness was upon the face of the Artists. And the Spirit of Marvel moved upon the face of the Writers.

And Marvel said, Let there be The Fantastic Four. And there was The Fantastic Four.

And Marvel saw The Fantastic Four. And it was good.

—*Stan Lee*

Ideas can never be traced to any one source. They are tossed back and forth between people until the decision makers step in and choose what they think is a success formula.

—*Jack Kirby*

CONTENTS

MARVEL COMICS

PROLOGUE

IN 1961, STANLEY MARTIN LIEBER WAS PUSHING FORTY, WATCHING THE COMIC-book industry, in which he'd toiled for over two decades, fade away. Recently forced to fire his staff of artists, he sat alone in the comics division of publisher Martin Goodman's perfunctorily named Magazine Management Company, where he'd been hired, as a teenager, at eight dollars a week. He'd once wanted to be a novelist, but he never managed to get around to it, and it seemed unlikely that he'd be able to work Big Ideas into the monster, romance, and western comics that were still dribbling out from the vestiges of the company. Tucked away in a quiet corner, the highlights of Lieber's days were writing corny jokes for toss-off humor books like *Blushing Blurbs: A Ribald Reader for the Bon Vivant* and *Golfers Anonymous*. Not wanting to use his real name, he signed them "Stan Lee."

Fate intervened (or so the story went) in the form of a golf game between Martin Goodman and Jack Liebowitz, publisher of rival publisher DC Comics. Liebowitz reportedly told Goodman that DC had thrown together some of its most popular characters—Superman, Batman, Wonder Woman, Green Lantern—into a single supergroup title, *The Justice League of America,* and found itself with a surprise hit. Goodman marched into the office with a mandate for Lee: *steal this idea and create a team of superheroes.* But Lee had been through attempted superhero revivals before. He went home to his wife, Joanie, and announced that he was finally going to quit. She talked him out of it. "Just do it the way you want to," she insisted. "Work your ideas into the comic book. What are they going to do, fire you?"

"It took a few days of jotting down a million notes," Lee would re-member years later, "crossing them out and jotting down a million more until I finally came up with four characters that I thought would work well together as a team. . . . I wrote an outline containing the basic description of the new characters and the somewhat offbeat story line and gave it to my most trusted and dependable artist, the incredibly talented Jack Kirby."

That was how Stan Lee recalled the genesis of *The Fantastic Four*, and how he related it over and over again through the following decades, in his inimitably jaunty manner. Jack Kirby, who'd launched to stardom in the 1940s, when he'd co-created the iconic Captain America for Goodman, would later tell it differently. "Marvel was on its ass, literally, and when I came around, they were practically hauling out the furniture," Kirby said. "They were beginning to move, and Stan Lee was sitting there crying. I told them to hold everything, and I pledged that I would give them the kind of books that would up their sales and keep them in business."

This much is certain: in the middle of 1961, Lee and Kirby threw together twenty-five pages of story and art, attached a crude logo, and thousands of copies of *Fantastic Four #1* were shipped off to take their places on newsstand tables and spinner racks across the country, wedged between the latest issues of *Millie the Model* and *Kid Colt Outlaw*.

The Fantastic Four wasn't quite the *Justice League* rip-off that Goodman had ordered—in the first issue, the protagonists didn't even wear cos-tumes; stranger still, they were constantly bickering. Never before had a comic-book team been shaded with such distinct personalities. In a nearly revolutionary flourish, the Thing was even conceived as "a heavy—not really a good guy," who might go rogue at any moment, a far cry from the upstanding citizenship of Superman and Green Lantern. But copies sold, quickly, and fan letters poured in to the Magazine Management of-fices. The book had sparked something, a fervor unfamiliar to Lee.

Lee and another of the monster-comics regulars, artist Steve Ditko, soon introduced "Spider-Man," who behind his mask was just Peter Parker, an angsty teenage nerd who sometimes struggled to make good choices. A moody, outcast kid as a superhero? It had never been done. But Spider-Man, too, struck a chord with readers.

Magazine Management quickly cranked out more off-kilter creations, heroes with just enough moral ambiguity for Cold War children in the last moments before Lyndon Johnson and the Beatles. In a matter of months, they introduced a test-site researcher metamorphosed by radiation into a violent green beast, a crippled physician transformed into the God of Thunder, an arms dealer with a heart condition who built a metal suit with which to fight communists, and a washed-up, egomaniacal surgeon who found his true calling in the occult. Heroes with feet of clay, many of them were marked by loneliness and self-doubt. Even the more confident among them carried the knowledge that they didn't fit in with the rest of the world.

Lee and the small stable of middle-aged freelance artists, plugging away in a medium that was ignored or ridiculed by most of society, were, in their way, misfits, too. But their work began to attract and foster a dedicated community of admirers. It was a fellowship that existed below the radar of media attention, at first, without even a name to rally around: Goodman's comics line, once best known as Timely Comics, was published under dozens of different nearly anonymous company names, from Atlas to Zenith, visible only in the small print of the copyright notices. Finally, at the end of 1962, Goodman and Lee settled on branding their reinvigorated line as Marvel Comics.

Marvel's colorful creations—the Fantastic Four, Spider-Man, the Incredible Hulk, Thor, Iron Man, and Doctor Strange—built the groundwork for a self-contained fictional construct called "The Marvel Universe," in which all heroes' adventures were intertwined with great complexity. Soon their rapidly expanding world also included the likes of the X-Men, a gang of ostracized mutant schoolchildren whose struggle against discrimination paralleled the civil rights movement, and Daredevil, a blind lawyer whose other senses were heightened to inhuman levels. The Black Widow, Hawkeye, the Silver Surfer, and countless others followed. For twelve cents an issue, Marvel Comics delivered fascinatingly dysfunctional protagonists, literary flourishes, and eye-popping images to little kids, Ivy Leaguers, and hippies alike.

In 1965, Spider-Man and the Hulk both infiltrated *Esquire* magazine's list of twenty-eight college campus heroes, alongside John F. Kennedy and Bob Dylan. "Marvel often stretches the pseudoscientific imagination far into the phantasmagoria of other dimensions, problems of time and space, and even the semi-theological concept of creation," one Cornell student gushed to the magazine. "They are brilliantly illustrated, to a nearly hallucinogenic extent. Even the simple mortal-hero stories are illustrated with every panel as dramatically composed as anything Orson Welles ever put on film."

"Face Front, True Believers!"

Stan Lee addressed Marvel's audience colloquially and excitedly in the comics' back pages, making readers feel like they were part of an exclusive club. Although most of the stories were produced in the silence of freelancers' homes, Lee painted the drab Marvel offices as a crowded and chatty "House of Ideas," a throwback to the bustling, desk-filled rooms that he'd known in earlier years but that now existed only in his mind. With a jazzy string of *didja know*s and all-caps accents and exclamation-point backslaps, Lee's "Bullpen Bulletins" columns could confer excitement even on the very idea of a workplace. "It isn't generally known, but many of our merry Marvel artists are also talented story men in their own right! For example, all Stan has to do with the pros like JACK 'KING' KIRBY, dazzling DON HECK, and darlin' DICK AYERS is give them the germ of an idea, and they make up all the details as they go along, drawing and plotting out the story. Then, our leader simply takes the finished drawings and adds all the dialogue and captions! Sounds complicated? Maybe it is, but it's another reason why no one else can bring you that old Marvel magic!" Entranced readers, poring over every behind-the-scenes glimpse, soon learned the name of each contributor, from the inkers and letterers to the receptionist and production manager. When Lee started an official fan club—"The Merry Marvel Marching Society"—fifty thousand fans paid a dollar each to join. Like one of its own characters, the weakling underdog Marvel Comics had become a great American success story.

"It seems to work out well," Stan Lee once wrote in a letter describing Marvel's working methods, "although it's not a system I'd advise anyone else to try." The arrangement did have its drawbacks, especially as Lee ceded more and more of the plot development to the artists, some of whom began to feel they were doing the heavy lifting for less credit than they deserved. Steve Ditko, who'd imbued Spider-Man with melancholy soul and Doctor Strange with hallucinatory verve, left the company; Spider-Man and Doctor Strange stayed behind. Jack Kirby, who churned out, almost helplessly, a flood of ingenious costume designs, bone-rattling action scenes, and complex fables of secret alien races, exited—but the Hulk, Fantastic Four, and the X-Men remained.

The comic industry was still subject to cyclical downturns, though, and Stan Lee continued working feverishly, determined to never again sit in that corner cubicle. In the early 1970s, he and his deputy, a fan-turned-pro named Roy Thomas, plugged holes in the workforce with a new generation of creators, wide-eyed twenty-somethings who flashed their old Merry Marvel Marching Society badges as though they were licenses for breaking rules. Embracing what they remembered as the spirit of Marvel, they smuggled countercultural dispatches into the four-color newsprint that found its way to drugstore spinner racks affixed with friendly "Hey Kids—Comics!" signs. Lee hardly noticed. Martin Goodman had sold the company, and as soon as the new owners placed Lee in charge, he turned his attention to pursuing television and movie deals, which he saw as Marvel's ticket out of the precipitous comics industry.

Over the following decades, as Lee pressed on with his quest for a Hollywood triumph, the reins of Marvel's publishing passed between editors who struggled to negotiate artistic ambitions and a fickle marketplace, and between owners—from ragtag entertainment consortiums to billionaire corporate raiders—who were progressively hell-bent on maximizing the bottom line at any cost.

———

All the while, a steady stream of writers and artists continued to arrive and depart, each contributing their own creations, or building on the creations of those before them. Everything was absorbed into the snowballing Marvel Universe, which expanded to become the most intricate fictional narrative in the history of the world: thousands upon thousands of interlocking characters and episodes. For generations of readers, Marvel was the great mythology of the modern world.

But the myth creators weren't distant, long-dead Homers and Hesiods. They carted their own proprietary feelings about the characters and stories, and their own emotional and financial entanglements, which made passing through the company's constantly revolving doors an arduous and sometimes painful process. As time wore on, there came a growing tide of failed friendships, professional defections, bitter lawsuits, and untimely deaths.

The universe grew.

PART I

Creations and Myths

$$1$$

LONG BEFORE THERE WAS MARVEL COMICS, THERE WAS MARTIN GOODMAN. Born in Brooklyn in 1908 to Russian immigrants, the ninth of thirteen children, Goodman was such an avid reader as a youth that he would cut up pieces of old magazines and paste them into new creations. But a life of leisurely imagination was not an option: his father's construction jobs ended with a backbreaking rooftop fall, and Isaac Goodman became a peddler. The fifteen members of the Goodman family constantly moved around Brooklyn, trying to stay one step ahead of their landlords. Martin was forced to drop out of school in the fifth grade and worked a series of jobs that failed to excite him. Finally, as he reached the end of his teen years, he resolved to make a bid for freedom: he set out to travel the country by train. By the time the Great Depression hit America, he'd already racked up journals detailing his coast-to-coast experiences on railroads and in hobo camps.

It was his childhood love of magazines that eventually called him home. Returning to New York, he found work singing the praises of pulps as a publisher's representative for Eastern Distributing. Eastern soon fell apart, but Goodman's fortune only rose: he and his coworker Louis Silberkleit joined forces to form Newsstand Publications. From a dingy office in lower Manhattan, they turned out westerns, detective stories, and romance tales at fifteen cents an issue.

Lone Ranger rip-offs may not have been high art, but, somewhat improbably, Martin Goodman had ascended from poor immigrant to rail-hopper to magazine editor. Slight, quiet, his arched eyebrows overwhelming his wire-frame eyeglasses and a bow tie punctuating one of his many crisp pink shirts, Goodman even had prematurely whitened hair that neatly completed his transformation from street kid to businessman. He was twenty-five.

In 1934, Newsstand Publications' distributor went under, costing Goodman and Silberkleit several thousand dollars in lost payments. Newsstand was unable to meet payments to its printer; its assets were seized. Silberkleit abandoned the company, but an eager Goodman convinced the printer that it stood to make back its money if it allowed him to continue publishing some of the titles. Goodman's cunning instincts quickly carried the company back into profitability; within a couple years, he'd moved into the considerably more elegant RKO Building uptown. He'd devised a simple formula for success: "If you get a title that catches on, then add a few more," he told *Literary Digest*, "you're in for a nice profit." It was all about staying on top of trends, not providing anything more than disposable literature. "Fans," he decreed, "are not interested in quality." When the market crashed again, Goodman stayed afloat: he simply filled out his magazines with unlabeled reprints of other publishers' stories.

Now he was in a financial position to set his parents up in a little house in the Crown Heights section of Brooklyn. He could also afford to relax. On a cruise ship to Bermuda, he approached two young women playing Ping-Pong and asked to play the winner. Jean Davis—also a New Yorker, but from a more cultured and sophisticated New York—soon became the apple of Goodman's eye. Back in America, Jean was on-again, off-again about having a serious relationship, but Goodman threw everything he could into the courtship. Once, scraping into his bank account, he flew her to Philadelphia for a dinner and a concert performance. Eventually, he won her over, and she became his bride. They honeymooned in Europe, with plans to return on the fashionable *Hindenburg*—but there were no two seats together, so they changed their plans at the last moment and caught a plane. Martin Goodman's luck just kept improving.

Goodman was publishing more than two dozen magazines by 1939, with names like *Two Gun Western*, *Sex Health*, and *Marvel Science Stories*. (The latter didn't sell especially well, but there was something Goodman liked about that word, *Marvel*. He'd remember that one.) He moved his business into the fashionable McGraw-Hill Building on Forty-Second

Street, where he set about providing steady work for his brothers. Good-man's operation was, in the words of one editor, a "little beehive of nepotism": one brother did bookkeeping; one worked in production; one kept an office where he photographed aspiring starlets for the pulps. Even Jean's uncle Robbie got in on the action. Furthermore, the flood of company names that Goodman shuffled around—advantageous for tax purposes, and for quick maneuvering in the event of legal trouble—were often derived from family members: there was the Margood Publishing Corp., the Marjean Magazine Corp., and soon, when Jean gave birth to sons Chip and Iden, there would be Chipiden.

The company name that stuck, though, was "Timely," taken from Goodman's *Timely* magazine. It was no longer racking up debt, but neither was it setting the world on fire. Pulp sales, crowded by the increased popularity of radio serials, were starting to go flat. Martin Goodman needed a hit.

The American comic book, meanwhile, was beginning to take form. In 1933, the Eastern Color Printing Company used its idle presses at nighttime to publish *Funnies on Parade*, a book of reprints of Sunday newspaper strips. The strips were printed side by side on a single tabloid page, folded in half and stapled, and sold to Procter & Gamble to give away as promotional items. The following year, Eastern Color slapped a ten-cent price on the cover of *Famous Funnies #1*, and sold more than 200,000 copies through newsstands; soon that title was seeing a profit of $30,000 a month. Other publishers gave it a shot. The biggest sellers were re-packaged Sunday newspaper comic strips like *Tarzan*, *Flash Gordon*, and *Popeye*, but *New Fun*, a black-and-white, ten-by-fifteen-inch anthology of unpublished strips, became the first comic book of all-new material. By 1937, a few enterprising men set up packaging services in which comic books were produced by efficient assembly lines, in the tradition of garment factories. A writer would hand his script off to an efficient assembly line of out-of-work veteran illustrators and young art school graduates armed with fourteen-by-twenty-one-inch Bristol board. In turn, they would break the action down into a series of simply rendered panels, flesh out the drawings in pencil, add backgrounds, embellish the artwork with ink, letter the dialogue, and provide color guides for the printer. It wasn't a way to get rich, but in the throes of the Depression, it was steady work.

And then, in 1938, Jerry Siegel and Joe Shuster, two twenty-three-year-olds from Cleveland, sold a thirteen-page story called "Superman" to National Allied Publications for $130. The character was a mix of everything kids liked—pulp heroes, science-fiction stories, classical myths—rolled up into one glorious, primary-colored package. The "champion of the oppressed, the physical marvel who had sworn to devote his existence to helping those in need" fought corporate greed and crooked politicians, and preached for social reform at every turn, a perfect fantasy for the New Deal era. But Superman was more than just a symbol; his secret identity as the mewling Clark Kent offered even the loneliest readers a fellow outsider with whom to identify. Premiering in the cover feature of *Action Comics* #1, Superman became a surprise runaway success, and by its seventh issue, *Action* was selling half a million copies per issue. National's sister company Detective Comics (they'd soon merge and come to be known as DC Comics) introduced Batman, another caped avenger, and gave Superman his own title—just as competitors rolled out a wave of colorfully costumed knockoffs. (Legend claimed that the publisher of Wonder Man, one of the earliest and most blatant imitations, had been an accountant for the head of National until he saw the numbers on *Action* and quickly set up his own company.)

Lloyd Jacquet, a soft-spoken, pipe-smoking ex-colonel, decamped from his position as art director of Centaur Comics and, following the leads of others, went into business as a comic-book packager, churning out stories for trend-hopping publishers. Chief among the artists Jacquet grabbed from Centaur and assigned to develop new superheroes for his new concern—Funnies, Inc.—were Carl Burgos and Bill Everett. Both were twenty-one years old and restless. Burgos had quit the National Academy of Design, impatient with the speed at which he was being taught; Everett, a three-pack-a-day smoker and already a decade into serious drinking, had bounced between Boston, Phoenix, Los Angeles, and Chicago. Now they sat down at a Manhattan bar called the Webster and hammered out their plans for superheroes. They kept it simple: fire and water.

Burgos came up with the idea of a brilliant but avaricious scientist, Professor Phineas T. Horton, who creates a synthetic man within a giant test tube, only to see him burst into flames upon contact with oxygen. The "Human Torch" needs no costume: his featureless face and vague anatomy, both reddened and obscured by wisps of fire, are surrounded by stray, tear-shaped bursts that fly off him like nervous crimson sweat, and the flares at the top of his head suggest demonic intent. He is, in other words, a creature flickering with fear and anger. Upon his inevitable escape, he sets about shooting fireballs from his hands and scaring the bejeezus out of cops and criminals alike; Burgos's low-budget primitivist style only increased the sense that the flimsy buildings, cars, and people the Torch encountered were hastily constructed only to be destroyed in short measure. By the end of his first adventure, the Human Torch learns to control his powers, but he's a man on the run.

Everett's contribution, which borrowed from Jack London's maritime adventure tales, Coleridge's "Rime of the Ancient Mariner," and Giambologna's *Mercury*, was Prince Namor, the Sub-Mariner. After an arctic expedition unknowingly causes destruction to the underwater settlement of an aquatic race, the amphibious emperor sends his daughter to spy on the humans. The princess marries the expedition's commander, gathers intelligence for her homeland, and, before returning to the ocean, conceives a son. Nineteen years later, the pointy-eared, pointy-eyebrowed, widow-peaked Namor, clad only in swimming trunks (and graced with winged feet), is "an ultra-man of the deep . . . flies in the air . . . has the strength of a thousand men"—and he seeks revenge on America. Putting his powers to scary use, he murders two deep-sea divers (one via vicious stabbings, the other via head-crushing) and then shoves their ship into a reef. The faint horizontal lines, lonely bubbles, and levitating objects that Everett administered in ink-wash to convey the subaquatic world gave the proceedings an eerie, theremin-ready ambience, although such subtleties of mood were necessarily temporary.* Pages later, the creepy languor of the saltwater battles gives way to pure action, as Namor hurls a pilot from

---

* Even more than other comics, the delicate line work and ambitious coloring of early Sub-Mariner strips were compromised by cheap printing, which muddled everything into a purple sludge.

a biplane and "dives into the ocean again—on his way to further adventures in his crusade against the white men!" Unredeemingly violent and willfully unassimilated, the sneering Sub-Mariner was the reverse negative of the alien-as-immigrant-hero Superman.

The Sub-Mariner strip was marked for inclusion in *Motion Pictures Funnies Weekly*, a giveaway comic that movie theaters would distribute to moviegoing kids, in hopes that they'd be hooked enough to show up for the following week. But *Motion Pictures Funnies* stalled out, never going to press except for a handful of sample copies that were handed out to theater owners.

Luckily, the Funnies, Inc. sales agent, a compact and balding Irishman named Frank Torpey, had connections, and one of them was Martin Goodman, with whom he'd worked at Eastern Distributing. Torpey grabbed copies of *Superman* and *Amazing Man* (a title that Everett had recently done for Centaur), walked three blocks north from the shabby building that housed the Funnies, Inc. loft, and entered the pristine blue-green Art Deco skyscraper headquarters of Timely, where he made the pitch to his old friend Goodman. Comics, Torpey said, were easy money. They made a deal for Goodman to publish the Human Torch and Sub-Mariner strips in a new comic book anthology. Goodman already had a perfect idea for a title.

Marvel Comics #1, produced entirely by Jacquet's team, covered all the popular bases in its sixty-four pages: Paul Gustavson's mustachioed, Saint-like Angel, Ben Thompson's jungle adventurer Ka-Zar (a Tarzan knockoff, resurrected from one of Goodman's pulps), Al Anders's cowboy the Masked Raider, and gag cartoons to fill it out. Goodman commissioned a cover from veteran pulp illustrator Frank R. Paul, and Timely's first comic book was published on August 31, 1939. Hours later, halfway around the world, Nazi Germany invaded Poland. World War II was in motion.

Marvel Comics #1 sold 80,000 copies in September 1939, and so Goodman went back to press. Eventually it sold 800,000—better than the average DC Comics title. In the years to come, Timely staffers would talk about seeing Frank Torpey darting in and out of Goodman's office, moving so fast they thought he was a messenger. The truth was that he was just collecting twenty-five dollars, a weekly thank-you from Martin Goodman for pulling him into the comic-book industry.

Goodman never missed an opportunity to change a name, and *Marvel Comics* became *Marvel Mystery Comics* with the second issue. The Human Torch started to act like every other costumed crime-fighter; whether the threat he defended against was a Martian or a trigger-happy racketeer, it could just as easily be a job for Superman—indeed, following in Superman's footsteps, the Torch took on an alias (Jim Hamond) along with an upright-citizen day job (policeman). Namor, on the other hand, stayed true to his anger: He kidnapped a high-society woman and killed a cop.

Namor did find one human he liked. Betty Dean was, of course, a pretty girl; less predictably, she was also a policewoman, friendly with the Human Torch's alter ego Jim Hamond and thus in the unique position to act as a go-between for Timely's two most popular characters. And so it was that in *Marvel Mystery Comics #7*, a seemingly throwaway moment—in which Betty warns Namor that the Torch is now on the police force and looking for him—carried the seeds of something revolutionary: the fictional universes of two characters, conceived by two different imaginations, were in fact one and the same.

Or was this a fictional universe at all? Wasn't that the Manhattan skyline behind the Torch? Wasn't that the Hudson River that the Sub-Mariner was diving into? Superman and Batman had smiled together on a few carefree covers, but every kid knew that they were fully tethered to their respective Metropolis and Gotham City, and that never the twain would meet. Who cared if the Acme Skyscraper fell, or the First National Bank had to give up its cash? Timely's New York City, on the other hand, was rife with Real Stuff to Destroy. In *Marvel Mystery Comics #8* and *#9*, which hit newsstands in the spring of 1940, Namor wreaks havoc on the Holland Tunnel, the Empire State Building, the Bronx Zoo, and the George Washington Bridge ("Hah! Another man-made monument!" he shouts, breathlessly aroused at the potential carnage) before the Human

Torch finally confronts him, and the battle rages to the Statue of Liberty and Radio City Music Hall. Was it possible that they'd turn a corner and meet the Angel? Or, better yet, show up at the reader's home?

Maybe they'd bump into the slew of other characters that Funnies, Inc. was now cranking out for Goodman's two new titles: the Blue Blaze and Flexo the Rubber Man, or the Phantom Reporter and Marvex the Super Robot. Alas, *Daring Mystery Comics* and *Mystic Comics* didn't sell anything like *Marvel Mystery Comics*. Flexo the Rubber Man would never get within stretching distance of the Human Torch.

Goodman didn't want to count on Lloyd Jacquet's studio alone, especially if they weren't going to come up with new hits. He quickly realized that it was possible to reduce the role of the profit-eating middleman. When Goodman had requested another hero in the vein of the Human Torch, one of Jacquet's freelancers, Joe Simon, had risen to the occasion, creating the flame-shooting Fiery Mask. Now Goodman asked him to create new characters directly for Timely. Simon, a former newspaper cartoonist from Rochester, New York, was earning seven dollars per page from Funnies, Inc.; Goodman would pay him twelve per page, and still spend less than he paid to Jacquet. Simon, always an astute businessman, took the money. Soon he was, incredibly, balancing the work for Goodman with a job as the editor in chief at Victor Fox's Fox Publications, where he made corrections, assigned stories, cranked out covers, and supervised a staff of low-paid, mostly inexperienced artists.

At Fox, Simon met a twenty-one-year-old artist named Jacob Kurtzberg, a product of the Lower East Side slums. "My mother once wanted to give me a vacation," Kurtzberg said, describing his childhood, "so she put me on a fire escape for two weeks and I was out in the open air sleeping for two weeks on a fire escape and having a grand time." A member of the Suffolk Street Gang, as a youth he was no stranger to the rougher elements of his neighborhood ("I would wait behind a brick wall for three guys to pass and I'd beat the crap out of them and run like hell"), but Kurtzberg found his escape in fantasy: in Shakespeare, in movie matinees. The life-changing moment was the rainy day he saw a pulp magazine with an illustration of a foreign-looking, futuristic object on the cover, floating down the gutter. He picked up the copy of *Wonder Stories* and stood transfixed, staring at this thing called a rocket ship.

Kurtzberg threw himself into drawing his own stories, carefully studying the comic-strip artistry of Milton Caniff's *Terry and the Pirates*, Hal Foster's *Tarzan*, and Billy DeBeck's *Barney Google*. A short stint at the Pratt Institute ended after a week, when his father lost his factory job, but Kurtzberg found an alternate path to his career dreams. After joining the Boys Brotherhood Republic, a local civic club designed to rescue youths from the streets, Kurtzberg began producing a mimeographed cartoon series for the organization's newsletters. Then he enrolled in industrial school, filling out auto mechanic classes with an afternoon art course. At the end of his teens, he was hired to draw for the Fleischer brothers' animation studio, but the assembly-line production of *Popeye* and *Betty Boop* reminded him too much of his father's factory job. Stints at various comic-strip syndicates followed, and by the time he met Joe Simon at Fox, Kurtzberg was ready to create something of his own.

Kurtzberg was skilled, fast, and, because he was the one putting money on the table for his parents and younger brother, eager to earn as much as he could. Impressed with Kurtzberg's talent and work ethic, Simon soon conscripted him as a partner in his freelance endeavors, and in early 1940 they worked together on a new title for Timely called *Red Raven*. Kurtzberg went uncredited for his work on an eight-page story called "Mercury in the 20th Century," in which the fleet-footed god is sent "from High Olympus, Celestial retreat of the ancient gods" to save mankind from itself—and from Mercury's cousin Pluto, who has taken the disguise of "Rudolph Hendler," dictatorial leader of "Prussland." But for another feature, the Flash Gordon–derivative "Comet Pierce," Kurtzberg signed a pseudonymous name that he would soon adopt permanently, and legally: Jack Kirby.

Unfortunately, Simon's title feature in *Red Raven* was inane: an orphaned plane-crash survivor raised by bird-men on a "gravity-free island" is given wings, and later fights a bald, gold-pillaging demon named Zeelmo. The comic sold poorly, and a month later, Goodman replaced *Red Raven* with a new title that starred a proven commodity: *The Human Torch*.

Despite the failure, Goodman kept Simon around as an art director on one of his crime magazines. He liked the idea of generating comics without Funnies, Inc. and encouraged more submissions from Simon and Kirby. Their track record improved immediately. After they introduced Marvel Boy and the Vision, Simon sketched out a variation on MLJ Comics' star-spangled hero the Shield.

"I stayed up all night sketching," Simon remembered. "Mailed armor jersey, bulging arm and chest muscles, skin-hugging tights, gloves, and boots flapping and folded beneath the knee. I drew a star on his chest, stripes from the belt to a line below the star, and colored the costume red, white and blue. I added a shield." At the bottom of the page, he wrote "Super American." Then he reconsidered, and changed the name to "Captain America."*

While Superman, Batman, and other heroes continued battling aliens, costumed villains, and bank robbers, the grittier, louder, angrier Timely stars had already rolled up their sleeves to combat the real-life villains of World War II. In the last weeks of 1939 the Sub-Mariner had taken on a German U-boat off the New York coast; soon Marvel Boy was fighting a dictator named Hiller (Goodman, it was said, was afraid that Adolf might sue), and the Sub-Mariner was joining a French island in resistance to Nazi invaders. These were sporadic battles. But now the war in Europe was ratcheting up: France had fallen, and the threat of Nazi rule spreading across the world finally began to sink in for Americans. Captain America would be focused on his mission: taking down the Third Reich.

Sensing Captain America's great potential, Simon negotiated a special deal with Timely through Maurice Coyne, the company's chief accountant.† "We can't keep putting out this crap for long," Goodman had told Simon on their first meeting, but he too must have recognized something

---

* In a 1966 deposition, Jack Kirby recalled a different origin: "In the course of the discussions we first evolved a main character and then began to build around him."

† "He didn't like them very much," Simon claimed. "He was also part owner of Archie Comics, then known as MLJ. Maurice was the 'M' in 'MLJ.' [Goodman's former boss, Louis Silberkleit, was the 'L.'] It was his idea that we arrange some kind of 25% royalty for me."

special. Not only did he agree to the 25 percent royalty rate (which Simon would split with the artist), but he also asked Simon to come on board full-time, as an editor. Goodman would still need to pay Funnies, Inc. for his two biggest characters, the Human Torch and the Sub-Mariner, but he could get Simon to pad out the line at a huge savings. (Eventually, Goodman would buy those characters outright.)

Simon soon asked Jack Kirby to come work for Goodman full-time. While Simon handed out assignments, brainstormed titles with Goodman, designed logos, and art-directed the pulp magazines, Jack sat and drew, all day. When Simon prepared to assign the penciling of Captain America to a team of freelancers, Kirby told him not to bother. He could get it done on time by himself.

But Goodman was already nervous about the idea that Hitler might be killed before Captain America reached newsstands. Kirby penciled the issue, but Simon had an old cartoonist pal from Syracuse, New York, ink the pages. Also brought in to help was Syd Shores, a quiet art school graduate who'd spent seven years working in a whiskey plant, and would become Timely Comics' third employee. On Shores's first day at work, Simon sat him down at a desk in the room he already shared with Kirby, handed him the cover that Kirby had just drawn, and asked him to ink it. It showed Captain America punching out Adolf Hitler.

While *Captain America* #1 was at the printers, a tall, teenaged cousin of Jean Goodman traveled down from the Bronx to the foot of the McGraw-Hill Building—which, he'd later recall with wonder, "seemed to be made entirely of glass"—and rode the elevator up to the Timely offices for the first time. He opened the door to a tiny waiting room and gave his name, Stanley Lieber, to the secretary at the window.

Circulation manager Robbie Solomon—Jean Goodman's "Uncle Robbie"—was expecting the visit. Stanley's mother, Celia, was Robbie's sister. Celia had explained to Robbie that Stanley wanted to be a writer, but he was floundering—he'd recently been fired from a menial job in trouser manufacturing. Solomon opened a door to the left of the secretary's window and invited Stanley to follow him back. They took a quick left into the eighteen-by-ten room that Simon, Kirby, and Shores shared.

"This is my nephew," Solomon said. "Can you find something for him to do?" Simon interviewed the teenager, who didn't seem to know much about comic books but was very eager. And, of course, he was a relative of the boss. Simon hired him.

On December 20, 1940, *Captain America* #1 hit newsstands. It told the story of a scrawny army-enlistment reject named Steve Rogers who was administered an experimental "super-soldier" serum that bulked him up and allowed him to fight those who would threaten the United States. No bulletproof Superman, he carried a stars-and-stripes shield that matched his patriotic costume. Except for the appearance of actual Nazis, *Captain America* didn't add much to the formula that MLJ Magazines' *The Shield* had introduced: just another scientifically improved, star-spangled enemy of Fifth Columnists. But the ever-shifting angles and fluid action of Kirby's artwork gave it wings. *Captain America* #1 sold a near-*Superman* number of one million copies, exceeding everyone's expectations; the office was deluged with orders for the "Sentinels of Liberty" fan club, which for a dime included a brass badge depicting a smiling Captain America. Simon focused his energy helping Timely to capitalize on its success, brainstorming titles with Goodman—*U.S.A. Comics, All-Winners Comics,* and *Young Allies,* which featured Toro and Bucky, teenage sidekicks of the Human Torch and Captain America—and designing logos. Simon and Kirby held story conferences in the tiny waiting room out front, where they handed out assignments to writers. "And when the script came back," said Simon, "we'd tear it apart, change the dialogue and everything else. When things got really hectic, we'd write the story right on the drawing board." For the second issue of *Captain America,* they sent the hero to Germany, where he and Bucky infiltrated a concentration camp in the Black Forest. "Dot Yankee schwein vood upzet mein plans," Hitler worried, before Bucky kicked him in the stomach.

While Kirby hummed to himself, cranking out pages behind a cloud of cigar smoke, Stanley would empty ashtrays, sweep floors, fetch coffee, and erase pencil marks from inked pages. Sometimes he would get to proofread, and often, to the consternation of his older coworkers, he would break the silence with an ocarina. "Jack sat at a table behind a big cigar," he remembered years later. "Joe stood up behind another big cigar, and he would ask Jack, 'Are you comfortable? Do you want some more ink? Is your brush okay? Is the pencil all right?' And then Joe would go out and yell at me for a while, and that was the way we spent our days."

After a month or two, Simon gave Stanley a break, or maybe it would be better described as busywork—text features were needed to qualify for magazine postal rates, Simon told him to write a short Captain America story that would be accompanied by two panels of illustration. He turned in twenty-six ham-fisted paragraphs, with the title "Captain America Foils the Traitor's Revenge," which he signed with a pseudonym, so as not to derail his future career as a serious writer. The byline read "Stan Lee."

A few months after that, Stan started to get the occasional assignment for actual comics stories, and by the summer he was writing the adventures of characters like the Destroyer (Keen Marlow, American doctor, drinks a serum developed by a German doctor, and fights Nazis across enemy lines) and Jack Frost (an icy avenger comes to New York from "the far North" to fight crime).

When Simon wasn't throwing work to Stan, he was throwing work back at Funnies, Inc., at Goodman's request. "Martin wanted me to make it as hard as possible on Funnies. He was making the stuff in-house for much less than he was paying them. He wanted me to ask for as many corrections as I could come up with in an effort to make them throw up their hands and give up."

Everett and Burgos, meanwhile, were upping the ante: "The Human Torch Battles the Sub-Mariner as the World Faces DESTRUCTION!" shouted the title page of *Human Torch* #5, in which the previous battle between the fire-and-ice heroes was put to shame. This was accompanied by an illustration of the "maddened Sub-Mariner" riding beside Hitler, Mussolini, and Death herself; the Four Horsemen of a four-color apocalypse. The story opened with Namor witnessing the destruction that a German-Russian battle had wrought on his underwater kingdom, and, persuaded by the feminine wiles of a "refugee princess" of another aquatic civilization, vowing to conquer the world above the sea. Over an astonishing sixty pages his rampage unfolded, as he and his forces took Gibraltar from Britain, wiped out an Italian fleet, flooded North Africa, drove a glacier into Moscow, and directed a tornado at Berlin. There was no distinguishing between the Axis and Allied powers. He brainwashed the Human Torch into aiding him, too, until the Torch caught a glimpse of the stars and stripes. "Shocked to the core at the sight of his flag," hummed the narration, "Torch descends, dousing his flame, and salutes." Everything came to a head after Namor flooded New York City with "a mammoth tidal wave so high it surmounts the city's tallest building, so wide it stretches from the battery to the Bronx, so terrific it slams down the world's most famous skyline as if it were built with cards and then, its fury still unspent, spans the Hudson River and roars westward! Goodbye Broadway! So long, Times Square! Down goes the Empire State Building! Down goes the George Washington Bridge!" It all climaxed at the Statue of Liberty, with a showdown between the Human Torch and Namor, who regained his senses and received an unlikely pardon from FDR. Along the way, there were cameos by characters from the pages of *Marvel Mystery Comics*: Angel, the Patriot, Toro, and Ka-Zar.

The whole comic was produced in a matter of days, with nearly a dozen hands on deck, making the story up as they went along, writing dialogue directly onto the pages. "We just stayed there the entire weekend," said Everett. "Nobody left except to go out and get food or more liquor and come back and work." When they ran out of room in the apartment, one artist set up in the bathtub. They slept in shifts, played the radio through the nights, and deflected noise complaints from neighbors.

The issue was a sellout.

With Captain America riding high, and titles multiplying, the daily grind at Timely was demanding. But Simon and Kirby were natural hustlers, and they continued to quietly freelance for other companies, even as they were hiring additional staff at Timely. It was a smooth arrangement—until Maurice Coyne came to Simon and told him that Goodman was shorting him and Kirby on their royalties: nearly all the Timely overhead was being deducted from *Captain America* profits. Instead of confronting

Goodman, Simon and Kirby called Jack Liebowitz at DC Comics, who'd already made clear his interest in them. Liebowitz told them that they could make five hundred dollars a week with DC. They rented a cheap room at a nearby hotel and worked after hours developing projects for Timely's competition. They may have pushed their moonlighting too far, though, when they started going to the hotel room on lunch hours. Stan grew nosy, and then suspicious, and insisted on tagging along to lunch.

"You guys must be working on something of your own!"

They reluctantly let him in on the secret, and soon he was joining them during lunchtimes at the hotel—"getting in the way," as Simon put it.

The extracurricular activity didn't remain a secret for long. Within days, the Goodman brothers surrounded Simon and Kirby for a confrontational firing.

Kirby was convinced that Stan had ratted them out. "The next time I see that little son of a bitch," he told Simon, "I'm going to kill him."

The Goodman brothers decided to take advantage of the eager protégé in their midst, at least until they found someone new. At eighteen years of age, Stan Lee found himself the editor of a major comic-book company. He had a small office off the artists' room, which they now called the Bullpen, and into which the growing staff and their desks were now crammed.

He was still blowing his ocarina, a little more brashly now. "He'd make us wait while he finished blowing whatever tune he was playing," recalled Vince Fago, one of his new hires. "He'd even go into Martin Goodman's office and blow it at him."

Lee's consistent jauntiness belied an upbringing that hadn't been easy. His father, Jack, a dress-cutter, had been unemployed most of Stan's childhood, and Stan's earliest memories were of Jack poring over the want ads and fighting with Celia. Stan slept in the living room of their cramped Bronx apartment. It would be easy to say that his voracious reading and moviegoing were the classic escapism of a hard childhood—except that rather than withdraw into fantasy, Stan was always jovial and outgoing, as interested in learning about public speaking as he was in entering essay contests. Years later, he would often recall being inspired in high school by a visiting newspaper subscription salesman who entranced a class with his pitch. He'd learned to do that job himself, selling for a rival newspaper. Now that upbeat, communicative manner was serving him well: his employees were inspired by his decisiveness and energy. What might have been seen as childish guile by Joe Simon looked now, to the people who worked for Lee, like the qualities of a leader, with or without the propeller beanie he sometimes wore. He was dictating scripts to writers over the phone, making snap decisions about new titles, and himself writing two or three stories a week. "No matter how many new titles were thrown at him at the last minute, he somehow never failed to meet the deadlines," remembered one artist. Goodman was still involved in cover choices—as he would remain for decades—but Stan Lee's leash was getting longer.

And then, Japan bombed Pearl Harbor. Carl Burgos, Syd Shores, and Bill Everett were all drafted. Before long, Lee enlisted. "How would you like my job?" he asked Vince Fago one day in 1942. (Fago was a smart choice: he specialized in "funny animal" comics, which had been quickly gaining in popularity thanks to Dell Comics' Disney tie-ins.) Lee was assigned to the Signal Corps on November 9, reporting to duty in Queens. At first he was climbing telephone poles and stringing wires for radio communications, but eventually word got out that he was a writer. Soon he was writing posters about venereal disease, manuals about tank operation, and cartoons to train payroll officers. Transferred to North Carolina and then to Indiana, he still wrote the occasional *Captain America*—only now, he was credited as Private Stan Lee.

After a German U-boat sank two tankers near Long Island in 1942, Martin Goodman became an air warden, patrolling the neighborhoods surrounding Woodmere, making sure that residents kept their windows blocked at night so that no lights would be visible from the ocean. As Goodman drove around Hewlett Bay, he and his son Iden would stop at all the newsstands to make sure Timely's product was prominently displayed. Goodman wasn't just protecting America—he was looking out for *Captain America*, too.

———

Throughout the war, *Captain America* was the company's best-selling title, a leader in a field that was rapidly growing. In less than two years, the number of comic books sold each month grew from 15 million to 25 million; by 1943 it was a $30 million per year industry. A large percentage of those sales were to overseas GIs, and *Captain America* couldn't have found a better audience, with stories like "Trapped in the Nazi Stronghold," "Blitzkrieg to Berlin," and "Tojo's Terror Masters" guaranteed to fly off PX racks.

The average print run of a Timely book during the war, recalled Vince Fago, approached a half million per issue. "Sometimes we'd put out five books a week or more. You'd see the numbers come back and could tell that Goodman was a millionaire."

Goodman moved into a sprawling colonial mansion, with five fireplaces and four master bedrooms, in the upscale neighborhood of Woodmere, next door to a country club. When he took his father to see the house, Isaac Goodman was astonished. "This," he said, "was the kind of house I was a serf on, in Russia."

After the war, in 1945, Stan returned to a changed Timely. Those funny-animal comics had flourished under Fago, and there was a steady influx of new talent on everything else: for *Jap-Buster Johnson* alone, future novelists Mickey Spillane and Patricia Highsmith were submitting scripts. Goodman had moved his magazine and comic book operations into the fourteenth floor of the Empire State Building, and the staff had swelled. Teams of pencilers, inkers, letterers, and colorists would punch in at 9 a.m. and huddle at their desks. Now there were different departments, with the funny-animals division rivaling the superheroes division. A permanent breeze swept through a permanently stuck window—there was no air conditioner—as the sounds of distant traffic wafted in.

It didn't affect Martin Goodman, though. Every afternoon, after approving covers, surveying the work of new artists, and analyzing his sales charts, Goodman would go to the corner of his office, lie back in a chaise longue near his window that looked out on Thirty-Third Street, and close his eyes, paying heed to the DON'T FORGET TO RELAX sign that hung in his office.

Lee hired a small fleet of sub-editors, each of whom moved into their own offices and worked on their own titles while he quickly adjusted to the new comic trends. He banged out scripts for *Millie the Model, Tessie the Typist*, and *Nellie the Nurse*, and redoubled the superhero line. During the war, Fago had continued Lee's strategy of overassigning and keeping inventory on hand. ("We always had backlog, so I could drop another story in if someone was late or drank and lied about it. Then we'd put ten guys on it to get it done.") At one point, Fago had amassed about $100,000 worth of inventory, just hidden away in cabinets, ready for emergency use. Stan moved it into a closet; he didn't need it. There was a younger wave of talented young artists knocking at the door, eager for anything he'd throw them: Johnny Romita, Gene Colan, John Buscema, Joe Maneely. With his incredible surplus of energy, Stan self-published *Secrets Behind the Comics*, a pamphlet that divulged the ways in which comic books were produced. "He has been in complete charge of more comic magazines than any other living editor," his bio read.

That wasn't all he was in charge of. He moved into a room in the Alamac Hotel and lived the life of a playboy, impressing ladies with his Buick convertible, Sinatra-indebted style, and five-grand bank account. Years later, he reflected about how he'd missed his college experience—"Like you see in the movies—living on campus, having beer parties, getting laid every night." He'd finally started to make up for that in the army. "I was in love a hundred times," he said. "They shipped me to different cities all over the country; every city I'd go to, I'd meet some other gal I thought was terrific." Now he was dating up a storm. Freelancers were stunned by his parade of gorgeous secretaries. "I had three secretaries myself, and I kept them busy. I used to dictate stories in the office. I was a show-off, in my early twenties, as I look back at it. I'd quickly dictate a page of one story to one girl, and while she was transcribing it, I'd dictate a page of another story to another girl, and then maybe a third one to a third girl. I had this great feeling of power, that I was keeping three secretaries busy with three stories, and I knew that occasionally people were watching— and I was so proud. . . . I got a kick out of playing to the crowd."

But the bachelor life reached its end in 1947, when, through a cousin,

Lee met a stunning British hat model named Joan Boocock. A year into her marriage, she was bored already. He convinced her to go to Reno for a divorce; he flew out to Nevada, and they were married on December 5. They took the train back to New York, but skipped a honeymoon. There was work to do.

Comic-book trends were changing at a whiplash speed. Postwar America, suddenly obsessed with the plague of juvenile delinquency, began to pry crime-themed comics from the hands of its youths and, noticing the sultry adulteresses and violent toughs within, figured it had found a smoking gun. (Never mind that approximately 90 percent of all children, hoods and choirboys alike, were reading comics; aberrant behavior might as well have been blamed on chewing gum or tree forts.) Small towns organized comic bonfires, scolding articles ran in *Time* and *Collier's*, and a few towns and cities, including Detroit, introduced legislation to ban the scourge. Sensing the need for preemptive action, a group of publishers huddled and devised a series of content guidelines, just as Hollywood had done with the Hays Code twenty years earlier. Crime comics, strangulated by the new rules, were quickly supplanted by westerns, and then romance comics, and then punch line–heavy gag comics.

Meanwhile, superheroes had waned in popularity, lacking both Axis enemies and a dedicated readership of U.S. servicemen. Lee called for Captain America's sidekick, Bucky Barnes, to be shot ("I always hated sidekicks," he'd say later). By the end of 1949, the Human Torch and Sub-Mariner had vanished, and Captain America remained only in name: *Captain America's Weird Tales* was a bizarre horror title in which the Captain himself was nowhere to be found.

That was okay with Lee, as long as *something* was popular. He needed to keep working. After his mother died, his fifteen-year-old brother, Larry, came to live with him and Joan, who was pregnant with their first child. They moved out of their fourth-floor walk-up with zebra-skin furniture, and into a $13,000 two-story house in the Long Island suburbs, right near Martin Goodman's mansion.

As a boss, Martin Goodman could be difficult. He was magisterial— even his brothers called him "Mr. Goodman"—and he had mastered the art of the awkward silence, which he delivered with a calm stare. But he had a generous streak. Once, when he discovered that one of his magazine employees was taking his sick child to a veterans' hospital, Goodman handed the staffer a blank check. "Use this as you wish," he said. "Don't leave anything undone that could be done with money." He offered to take on one editor's mortgage, and assured another that her job would be waiting for her when she returned from having a child. "The only regret I have," he told her softly, "is that if I'd known how successful I was going to be, I would have had a fourth child." But as with so many autocrats, his largesse was capricious. One employee remembered Goodman offering him a cigar while out for a lunch meeting; when he responded with "No thanks, maybe later," Goodman replied, "Yes, maybe later, but what if I don't offer you one later?" One never knew when the charity would evaporate.

And so when Martin Goodman opened a closet door in the Timely offices and found himself face-to-face with the thousands of dollars' worth of inventoried pages that Lee had been stuffing away, he asked why he was paying for the production of so much new material. He ordered Lee to start trimming the staff. Shortly before Christmas in 1949, a speaker system was installed in the artists' rooms. The artists called it "the bitch box." "Every so often you'd hear Stan yell 'so-and-so come into my office' and you'd know that 'so-and-so' was being fired," remembered one staffer. "It was the voice of doom." Not only did Lee have to tell the artists they were out of work; he had to explain that it was because Goodman wanted to use up the inventory that he himself had stockpiled. By February, nearly everyone but Lee was on the street.

That outdated supply of inventory couldn't hope to fill the need for the latest trends, including war comics (popular in the wake of the Korean War) and horror comics (lucrative following the wild success of EC Comics' *Vault of Horror*, *Crypt of Terror*, and *Haunt of Fear*), and so freelance assignments began trickling down the following year. But for Lee and many of the writers and artists, the firings were a brutal reminder of the lack of security afforded the creative community. When Goodman decided to distribute his publications himself, under the name "Atlas," that word began appearing on comic covers emblazoned majestically across a globe-draping banner—an ironic flourish of triumphalism, given the layoffs.

The days of the bustling, oversized artists' rooms were over. But Lee began to build up a production staff again, as Goodman aggressively jockeyed for space on newsstand racks. While other publishers cut back, Timely added more titles. When *The Adventures of Superman* translated the Man of Steel into a television sensation, Goodman resuscitated his own holy trinity—Captain America, the Human Torch, and the Sub-Mariner—and pitted them against communists, in hopes that he'd capture a little of that old wartime thrill. As though history were repeating itself, men who'd made a splash for Timely in the 1940s, like Bill Everett and Carl Burgos, were now regular visitors to the Timely hallways, alongside a wave of younger talent. Rapidly expanding, Goodman moved operations to Madison Avenue, above the Boyd Chemists drugstore and cafeteria. With a carpeted office and a short walk to Central Park, he was headquartered at ground zero of 1950s consumerism, where legions of well-dressed martini lunchers, responsible for approximately half of the advertising dollars in the country, ducked into newly built towers and straightened their ties at the elevator banks. At 655 Madison, most of Goodman's new office space was dedicated to his magazine line (the creatively titled Magazine Management, Inc.), which had evolved from its pulp roots into a mixture of true confessions, movie gossip, crossword puzzles, and, under the editorial stewardship of Bruce Jay Friedman, mildly smutty action-adventure titles like *Stag,** *Male, For Men Only*, and *Men's World*. But off to the side, Stan Lee was overseeing more than sixty different titles and, in the words of Friedman, "a sea of employees."

In April 1954, just as Goodman's editors were unpacking their boxes and getting settled on Madison Avenue, the furor over comic books returned with a vengeance. Child psychologist Frederic Wertham, who'd been a prominent critic of comics for years, published *Seduction of the Innocent*, a full-throttle attack on the lurid contents of various crime, horror, and

---

* In 1953, a Chicago entrepreneur borrowed from family and friends to launch a new magazine called *Stag Party*. Goodman objected, and the young entrepreneur, Hugh Hefner, changed the name of his magazine to *Playboy*.

even superhero titles (including graphic illustrations of wife-beatings, sadomasochism, and gruesome murders); weeks later, a U.S. Senate subcommittee on juvenile delinquency turned its sights on the same, with Wertham as an expert witness. When Monroe Froehlich Jr., Timely's business manager, was called to testify, he and Martin Goodman loaded a station wagon filled with comics and drove down to Washington, eager to provide wholesome counterexamples. ("May I tell you about Bible tales?" Froehlich helpfully offered from the stand.) But they shouldn't have bothered; the subcommittee had its own supply of four-color thrills. In televised hearings, an interrogator waved a copy of Timely's *Strange Tales* #28 at the audience, noting that it contained "five stories in which 13 people die violently."

Timely got off easy. William Gaines was the publisher of EC Comics, whose war, crime, and horror tales embraced outsiderism and railed against the hypocrisies of conformist American society. But EC's stories also included vile scenarios, like a group of murderers who use the corpse of their victim to play a game of baseball. ("See the long strings of pulpy intestines that mark the base lines," the narration cooed. "The heart that is home plate . . . see the batter come to the plate swinging the legs, the arms, then throwing all but one away and standing in the box waiting for the pitcher to hurl the head in to him.") When Gaines took the stand, he was asked to answer for the cover of *Crime Suspenstories* #22: A killer's left hand held a bloody ax; the right held the blond hair of a decapitated head, with eyes rolled back. Visible in the background were the victim's skirt and lifeless high-heeled legs stretched along a tile floor. "Do you think that is in good taste?" Senator Estes Kefauver of Tennessee asked Gaines. "Yes, sir, I do, for the cover of a horror comic," Gaines replied.

His testimony made the front page of *The New York Times*.

The subcommittee hearings were adjourned and never reconvened, but the damage was done. A few months later, on a weekend in the Catskills, Lee mentioned to a rifle salesman that he was a comic-book editor. "You do comic books?" the man spat at Lee. "That is absolutely criminal— totally reprehensible. You should go to jail for the crime you're committing." Artist Dick Ayers donated an autographed box of comics to his daughter's school fund drive, only to have them returned with a note recommending that they be burned.

In the summer of 1954, fifteen comic publishers went out of business. In September, nearly all the remaining publishers formed the Comics Magazine Association of America, which instituted self-regulating rules that were modeled after Hollywood's Hays Code but even more draconian: according to the new Comics Code, covers could not even include the words *horror* and *terror*; under no circumstances were zombies, vampires, ghouls, or werewolves permitted to appear anywhere in the comics. Furthermore—and this is where the rules tipped into the Orwellian—there could be no sympathy created for criminals, nor disrespect of the sanctity of marriage. "Good," the rules demanded, "must triumph over evil." If a book didn't have a Comics Code seal, distributors wouldn't touch it. EC Comics, with its brilliant but lurid crime and horror titles, shut down its entire comic-book line, although one title, *Mad*, was reformatted into a magazine.

Comic books, defanged just as television sales were skyrocketing and rock and roll was beginning, lost their momentum. In the two years that followed Wertham's crusade, the number of titles produced by the comic industry was halved. Companies folded left and right. Timely Comics cut its budget drastically, paying less and less every month to its freelancers; years later Goodman's secretary would remember Lee repeatedly walking into the publisher's office to fight for higher artists' rates.

And rates were more important than ever to the draftsmen, who were by now scrubbed of the youthfully exuberant curiosity. The honing of craft, the following of whims, and the breaking of rules all took a backseat to the necessity of family-supporting paychecks. "Talk was no longer about work," recalled cartoonist Jules Feiffer. "The men were too old, too bored for that. It was about wives, baseball, kids, broads—or about what a son of a bitch the guy you were working for was: office gas. The same as in any office anywhere, not a means of communication but a ritualistic discharge. The same release could be achieved through clowning: joke phone calls, joke run-around-errands for the office patsy, joke disappearances of the new man's artwork. Everyone passed it off as good fun in order not to be marked as a bad sport."

With lowered morale, they continued to churn out product that shared shelf space with similarly antisepticized comics from industry leaders Dell (which held longtime licenses of Walt Disney and Warner Bros. characters) and DC (which had begun to reintroduce its superheroes as squeaky-clean citizens who worked by day as policemen, scientists, and police scientists in gleaming, modernist urban landscapes).

In late 1956, at the advice of Monroe Froehlich, Goodman abandoned self-distribution and signed with the American News Company. But ANC—reeling from a Department of Justice investigation for monopolistic practices, and fighting lawsuits from its own clients—suddenly ceased its Wholesale Periodical Division in April 1957, leaving Goodman with a magazine and comic-book empire but no way to reach newsstands. Independent News, seeing the profitability of Goodman's magazines, agreed to distribute Goodman's publications. But because Independent News was owned by Timely's rival, DC, there would be a catch: Goodman's comic-book output could not exceed eight titles per month.

The Timely line was decimated instantly. Goodman scheduled himself a vacation in Florida and told Lee to fire the staff once again. "It was the toughest thing I ever did in my life," said Lee. "I had to tell them, and I was friends with these people. So many of them, I had dinner with them at their homes—I knew their wives, their kids, and I had to tell them this. It was, as I say, the most horrible thing I ever had to do." After each conversation with a staff member, Lee left for the bathroom. Then he came back and fired another.

John Romita, already impatient with his dwindling page rates, got a call from one of Stan's lovely, soon-to-depart assistants: *stop work immediately*. He asked to be recompensed for the work he'd already done; she said she'd pass along the message, but he never heard back. "If Stan Lee ever calls," Romita told his wife, "tell him to go to hell."

The artists panicked. Some walked right over to DC Comics and showed their samples, but many ran as far from comics as they could. Bill Everett went to a greeting-card company, Gene Colan moved into advertising, and Don Heck began designing model airplanes. Mike Sekowsky, a cocky and lightning-fast penciler who'd been one of the stars of the Bullpen, got a job bagging groceries.

Stan moved into a cubicle on the other side of Bruce Jay Friedman, a thin partition separating them. "I thought it was very brave of him to stay on, to go from those heights to one little desk and a secretary," said Friedman. "It appeared that he was being pushed out and that he refused to be pushed out." But Goodman had his own reasons for keeping his wife's cousin on board. He'd seen comics rise and fall and rise again, and he was damned if he was going to give up the rack space now, only to be shut out of the game later on.

When the inventory started to run out this time, there was no rehiring of staff. Only about a half-dozen artists stayed on Lee's Rolodex for the required work. One of them, though, was his absolute favorite. Joe Maneely, who was speedy and astonishingly versatile, handling the *Casper the Ghost* facsimile *Melvin the Monster* and the western *Two-Gun Kid* with equal aplomb. Although he lived in New Jersey, Maneely became a regular guest at the Lees' martini parties in Long Island, and by early 1958, Maneely and Lee were doing a syndicated comic strip, *Mrs. Lyons' Cubs,* independently of Goodman. Lee would later say that, if things had gone differently, he might have quit Marvel to go work with Maneely on other projects. But one Friday in June, after drinks with a handful of other Timely alumni, Maneely—who'd lost his glasses earlier in the week—fell between cars of his commuter train. He was thirty-two. A devastated Lee lost not only his friend and collaborator, but also one of his most prolific employees.

That week, in need of new material for Goodman's science-fiction and fantasy titles, a still-shaken Lee got in touch with two artists who'd taken assignments a couple of years earlier, briefly, right before Timely lost its distributor and work dried up. Steve Ditko, a quiet thirty-year-old who'd recently recovered from tuberculosis, got a phone call at the midtown studio he shared with fetish artist Eric Stanton. There was work again; did he want to come back?

Lee also spoke to Jack Kirby. Their paths had taken them in vastly different directions since Kirby left Timely for DC in 1941 with Joe Simon. World War II brought Kirby to Omaha Beach less than two weeks after D-Day, where bodies were still lying in heaps; to the edges of the Siege of Bastogne; even, he'd later recall, to the liberation of a small concentration camp. After the war, a reunited Simon and Kirby moved into houses across the street from one another in Long Island, and bounced around from publisher to publisher, working in the various genres that flitted in and out of vogue.* They did westerns, crime tales, and space adventures; with *Young Romance*, they invented the romance comic book, and when Marvel revived Captain America, they produced *The Fighting American*, a pointed rip-off of their earlier creation.† In 1954, they launched their own comics company, called Mainline—perfect timing for a small publisher to be wiped out amid the furor over comic-book delinquency. Simon & Kirby then ended their fifteen-year partnership, and Kirby went back to DC and cranked out *Green Arrow* and an adventure feature called *Challengers of the Unknown*. By the time Stan Lee was looking for material in 1958, Kirby was also starting work on a syndicated science-fiction comic strip called *Sky Masters*. He was flush with work, but, never having shaken the habits of an impoverished youth, Kirby always wanted to line up more.

The six- and eight-page tales that populated interchangeably finger-wiggling titles like *Journey into Mystery*, *Tales of Suspense*, and *Tales to Astonish* were pure *Twilight Zone* in their twist-ending moral lessons. They featured contributions from several of Lee's longtime stable of artists, but it was the collaborations with Ditko and Kirby that held clues about what was to come. Kirby delivered large-scale visions of awe-inspiring alien technology and brutish monsters, while Ditko depicted jittery, ambitious outcasts humbled by the consequences of their hubris and imprisoned by their own psyches. In both of their work, men endured excruciating scientific transformations and traumatic gains of knowledge that permanently separated them from the civilizations to which they'd once belonged.

---

* In the case of romance comics, Simon and Kirby actually *invented* the genre.

† "We were, of course, I'll say bitter, about not owning Captain America," said Simon. "We thought we'd show them how to do Captain America."

Shortly after *Strange Worlds* and *Tales of Suspense* premiered, though, Kirby's career hit obstacles. The DC editor who'd arranged the *Sky Masters* comic strip deal sued Kirby for not paying him the percentage that the contract stipulated. Although Kirby continued work on *Sky Masters* while the lawsuit played out, there would be no more work from DC. Joe Simon gave Kirby a few assignments when he edited a super-hero line for Archie Comics in 1959, but after only a couple of months, Simon turned to advertising gigs for a steady paycheck. Kirby did not follow. "Jack never liked the advertising field," said his wife, Roz. "I'm sure he could have gone into it, but he never liked it. His heart had always been with comics." That left Kirby dependent on Stan Lee, his onetime errand boy, for work.

Throughout the 1940s and 1950s, while Lee had weathered the storms of the comics industry by holding tightly to Goodman's ship, Kirby had earned top rates thanks to his track record and reputation as a guaranteed creator of hits. Now, with Lee's titles on the wane, and Kirby's disappearing connections, both of them had lost their sense of security.

Along with a few surviving western titles, much of Kirby's output was now movie-matinee-style monsters with names like Monstrom and Titano and Groot and Krang and Droom. Lee would feed plots to his younger brother, Larry Lieber, who would then write them into scripts and send them to Kirby. With every successive cover, they became more hilarious in their repetition: it was always a clutch of tiny, high-tailing humans shrieking, falling down, and pointing fingers as they announced the mind-boggling danger that pursued them. "They warned us—but we didn't believe Monstrom existed!" "Help! Save us! He's alive! He's coming! IT'S DROOM!"

"I would much rather have been drawing *Rawhide Kid*," Kirby lamented. "But I did the monsters. We had Grottu and Kurrgo and it . . . it was a challenge to try to do something—anything with such ridiculous characters." He described his fate as "shipwrecked at Marvel."

Stan Lee felt the same way. "[Martin Goodman] goes by and he doesn't even say hello to me," he told one of his artists. "It's like a ship sinking, and we're the rats. And we've got to get off."

THE EDITORS OF *MEN* AND *MALE* AND *STAG* PAID LITTLE ATTENTION TO THE guy toiling on funnybooks, sitting alone at his corner desk at 655 Madison Avenue. There was no staff surrounding Stan Lee any longer, just the handful of artists who dropped off finished pages, and the occasional visits from *Millie the Model* penciler Stan Goldberg, who would stop by to pitch in on production work. "It was basically him and I on all those books that came out," Goldberg said of Lee. "Jack Kirby would come up, and if I didn't catch him to have a bite to eat or something, he would run home." The click and clack of Lee's two-finger typing continued.

Martin Goodman's fateful game of golf came in the spring of 1961. When Stan Lee rolled up his sleeves and went back to writing about superheroes once again—at the age of thirty-eight, and twenty years into a no-longer-promising career—nobody blinked.

The cover of *The Fantastic Four #1* was nothing like the other superhero titles on the rack. There were no colorful costumes; the protagonists appeared small and helpless; a white background lent the whole scenario an unfinished look. The shakily rendered title logo looked almost like it had been drawn by a child. What it *did* resemble was the monster magazines that Stan and Jack had been churning out for Goodman. In fact, with its scaly skin, mouth agape, and right arm raised, the unnamed creature erupting from the city street and threatening the heroes could have been a relative of Orrgo the Unconquerable, the cover star of that same month's *Strange Tales #90*; the off-balance citizens scurrying away on each cover were identically panicky. Any special appeal of these new heroes was unclear. "I can't turn invisible fast enough!" cried a well-coiffed blond woman in a pink blouse. "It's time for The Thing to take a hand!" shouted an orange lump with his back to the reader. If you didn't know (as you couldn't possibly, yet) that the awkward man in the foreground had the ability to stretch his body as though it was rubber—just like Quality Comics' old Plastic Man character—you might guess that Jack Kirby had simply never learned to draw elbows properly.

The inside of the comic was similarly shambolic, as though the narrative had been improvised. To a degree, it had been: in recent years, Lee had begun providing artists with mere plot synopses, rather than full scripts, to ease his workload and prevent a bottlenecking of the production schedule. As a result, the artists often determined the page-by-page pacing and plot details. When the penciled pages were returned to Lee, he would write the dialogue, sometimes covering up inconsistencies, and sometimes changing the intent of the artist. Over time, this would evolve into an effective conduit for creative synergy; in these early days, it could result in something like confused rambling.

On the opening page of *Fantastic Four* #1, a gray-templed man in a suit fires a flare gun, which gains the attention of most of the generically rendered Central City, but three people in particular: society girl Susan Storm, who turns invisible and sneaks out of afternoon tea; an unnamed figure who discards his trench coat, sunglasses, and fedora and rushes out of a Big and Tall Store, revealing himself to be an orange, clay-like behemoth; and teenaged Johnny Storm, Sue's brother, who abandons his hot rod at a service station when he bursts into flames and flies away. They gather in the man's apartment, and the action flashes back, jarringly . . .

The next panel shows the four gathered at an earlier date. Reed Richards, the gray-templed man, is arguing with a tough-talking bruiser named Benjamin Grimm about the prospect of piloting a ship into space. "Ben, we've got to take that chance," insists Susan Storm, Richards's fiancée, "unless we want the commies to beat us to it!" And so the four of them drive to the local rocket launchpad, and, "before the guard can stop them," take off for the stars. Unfortunately, they're bombarded by cosmic rays, and they make an emergency return to earth. At the rural crash-landing site, the heroes discover their new, radiated physiologies. What's striking about this sequence is the feeling of horror, the absence of joy in becoming super-powered. "You're (gasp) fading away!" someone yells at Sue Storm as her body slowly disappears. "He's turned into a-a— some sort of a thing!" Sue shrieks of Ben, as he grows into an ochreous, bricky mass, angrily attacks Reed, and jealously vows to win Sue. And then she notices her morphing beloved, his body elongating wildly and rubberily. "Reed . . . not you, too!! Not you, too!" Ben is restrained just as Johnny's body ignites with flame and he flies into the air.

Once they adjust to the transparency and the orange rockiness and the stretching and the immolation, their future is clear. "You don't have to make a speech, big shot!" Ben says to Reed. "We understand. We've gotta use that power to help mankind, right?" Thus are born the Invisible Girl, the Thing, Mister Fantastic, and a new version of the Human Torch.

A shift back to the moment of that flare-gun summons provides an anticlimactic twelve-page adventure, involving atomic power plants that have sunken into the earth, thanks to the Mole Man and his army of "underground gargoyles" on Monster Isle. (One of these creatures is recognizable from the issue's cover, but the city streets and bystanders are nowhere to be seen.) The energy of the artwork is undeniably special, but the roaring and snarling three-headed monsters are no longer where Lee's or Kirby's interests lie. We're granted one last look at the creatures that might have been named Mongu or Sporr or Zzutak, before a rock slide seals them off forever and the Fantastic Four, and Marvel Comics, fly into the future.

The issue reached newsstands on August 8, 1961, the same week that East Germany began work on the Berlin Wall. The space-race themes couldn't have been better timed: between the conception and publication of the comic, the Soviets had made cosmonaut Yuri Gagarin the first man in space (although there were no reports of dangerous cosmic rays). Although sales figures wouldn't come in for months, there was an immediate surge in reader mail—not the usual complaints about missing staples, but an engaged audience taken with the complicated characters. "We are trying (perhaps vainly?) to reach a slightly older, more sophisticated group," Lee wrote in a private letter three weeks later. For the first time in years, it looked like Marvel had something special on its hands.

Lee and Kirby improved the comic with every subsequent issue, giving emphasis to the internal struggles of the dysfunctional team, especially Johnny Storm's callow moodiness and Ben Grimm's rage and self-pity (his occasional return to human form was always fleeting, a cruel tease to his hopes for normality). This misery was offset, though, with tricked-out secret headquarters and a sleek flying automobile called a FantasiCar. And although they remained unmasked (in another break from comic-book convention, they were going to keep their identities public), at the urging of letter-writing fans they soon had snappy blue uniforms. "Jack gave them this long underwear with the letter '4' on their chest," said Stan Goldberg, who designed the color schemes of the Marvel comics. "I made the '4' blue and kept a little area around it white, and then when the villains came in—the villains get the burnt umbers, dark greens, purples, grays, things like that—they can bounce off it." The blast of colorful heroics against a murky background world immediately set *Fantastic Four* apart from everything else on the newsstand.

There were immediate signs—a letters page, cliffhangers—that these characters would be sticking around, that Marvel was committed to seeing this through for a while. And soon *Fantastic Four* had company. Goodman canceled *Teen-Age Romance* to clear the way for *The Incredible Hulk,* a Nuclear Age updating of the Dr. Jekyll/Mr. Hyde story, and Marvel had its second superhero title of the 1960s. Again, the scientific frontiers of the Cold War were vital to the story: Dr. Bruce Banner was preparing to test a Gamma Bomb for the U.S. military when a reckless teenager named Rick Jones drove his convertible onto the desert testing site on a dare. Banner called for a delay on the test while he got Jones to safety, but a communist spy on the lab team proceeded anyway, bombarding Banner with radiation. The highlight of the story was the traumatic gamma-blast sequence, which made the Fantastic Four's metamorphoses look relaxing in comparison: "The world seems to stand still, trembling on the brink of infinity, as his ear-splitting scream fills the air," Lee wrote, over Kirby's panels of Banner in a catatonic state, mouth agape and eyes filled with terror, as hours passed and medical professionals tried to bring him back from the edge of insanity. Later, as night fell, Banner's body grew and turned gray, and he began to wreck guns, and jeeps, and all prospects for his own happiness. As the Hulk, he would be relentlessly stalked by General Thunderbolt Ross, whose military-man bullheadedness positioned the monster as an antiauthoritarian rebel. Hip-talking Rick Jones, meanwhile, spent the early issues as Banner's one friend, locking him up at night like he was a violent drunk on detox watch. It all added up to pure misery for the title character, filled with blackouts, fear, guilt, and unrequited love for the general's daughter Betty. You could call the Hulk a superhero, but what was he saving? And from whom?

Kirby and Lee staked out more gradations on the hero-villain continuum. In *Fantastic Four #4*, Prince Namor, the Sub-Mariner, returned for the first time since 1954. In this new context, with romantic designs on Sue Storm and hatred for the rest of the human race, Namor teetered close to villainy. The next issue introduced Victor Von Doom, an old classmate of Reed Richards, who, after being scarred in a scientific experiment, trekked to Tibet to learn the "forbidden secrets of black magic and sorcery" and then took over his Eastern European homeland of Latveria. Doctor Doom was insufferably pompous, but along with his haughty manner came a sort of honorable code; he always kept his word. When Doom and the Sub-Mariner briefly teamed for an uneasy alliance in *Fantastic Four #6*, the Marvel landscape suddenly had some neat shadings: the bickering protagonists versus a tempestuous Byronic sparkplug and a Faustian archenemy.

In early 1962, as the Hulk and Sub-Mariner made their way toward newsstands, Lee and Kirby worked out three more heroes for the summer, each of which would headline a title previously devoted to monsters: *Journey into Mystery* would spotlight their take on Thor, the Norse god of thunder. In the Marvel version, lame physician Don Blake was vacationing in Scandinavia and found a walking stick that, when struck against the ground, became the hammer of legend—and transformed Blake into the long-haired titan with a winged helmet, weather-controlling abilities, and an Old English patois of *verily*s and *methinks*es. *Tales to Astonish*, meanwhile, would be the home of Ant-Man, alter ego of Henry Pym, yet another scientist driven into superheroics by the communist threat. Pym developed a serum that shrank him to a height of six inches, and an oversize helmet that allowed him, via electronic impulses, to command . . . ants.

But the third character—intended for *Amazing Fantasy*, the worst seller of the bunch—had problems. When Lee asked Steve Ditko to ink the first six penciled pages of Kirby's latest feature, Ditko pointed out that the concept—a teenaged orphan with a magic ring that transforms him into an adult superhero—was a retread of the Fly, a character that Kirby had already done for Harvey Comics in 1959. Lee decided that some changes were in order. With the deadlines approaching, he typed up synopses for the Thor and Ant-Man features, and handed them over to his younger brother, Larry Lieber, to write out as full scripts. Then he gave his full attention to the revised *Amazing Fantasy* character. In the new synopsis, a radioactive spider bite replaced the ring as the source of power, and there was no transformation to adulthood for the meek teenager. Instead of giving it to Jack Kirby, Lee asked Ditko, even though Ditko's moody, almost foreboding style hardly seemed to cry out for teen-age superheroics.

Amazing Fantasy #15, featuring the first appearance of Spider-Man, reached newsstands in June 1962. It strayed far from superhero conventions, further even than *The Fantastic Four* had. Unlike Kirby, whose heroes had a stocky majesty, Ditko populated his stories with rail-thin, squinting malcontents, placing the protagonist, Peter Parker, in a constellation of sneers, jabbing fingers, and angry eyebrows. On the very first page, Parker—tie, vest, big round eyeglasses, and tightly combed hair—is ostracized by his sweater-letter classmates, a nightmare vision of high school social life in which Archie, Jughead, Betty, and Veronica have teamed up against one four-eyed weakling. Parker's friends are limited to his elderly Uncle Ben and Aunt May, who dotes on him like he was a small child, and his piles of textbooks. After the science-lab spider bite gives him great strength and agility, and the ability to scale walls (his "spider-sense" intuition will come later), Parker enters a wrestling contest to earn some scratch. (He wrestles with a mask on, because his adolescent insecurities remain—"What if I fail? I don't want to be a laughing stock! I-I'll find some way to disguise myself!"—but makes quick work of his bulky opponent.) His feats land him an appearance on a TV show, for which he sews his own red-and-blue costume, complete with underarm webbing, spider insignias on the chest and back, and a white-eyed balaclava hood. Clothes, however, do not make the hero: after the broadcast, a criminal runs past Parker in the halls of the studio, and he shrugs off the opportunity to intervene. He's looking out for number one—until he comes home one evening to find that a burglar has murdered his saintly Uncle Ben. Parker, dressed as Spider-Man, tracks down and captures the thug before realizing it's the same criminal he allowed to escape from the studio. Rattled and guilt-ridden, he finally understands his fate. "With great power," Lee's narration tells the reader, "there must also be great responsibility!"

The grand melodrama was offset by Lee's snappy patter, Ditko's stunning costume design, and, once again, the primary-color palette choices of Stan Goldberg, who selected for Spider-Man's costume a combination of cherry red and dark cobalt (in deliberate contrast to the more vivacious azure of the Fantastic Four). None of these details mattered to Goodman, who canceled *Amazing Fantasy* immediately.

But readers responded ecstatically to the issue, and the character got its own title—*The Amazing Spider-Man*—by the end of the year. There remained an off-kilter gloom to Parker's world, and when he wasn't worrying about his Aunt May's health, or earning some money to help her pay bills, his face often conveyed the bitterness of an outcast who's finally gained some power, an I'll-show-them madness in his eyes. He became a freelance photographer for the *Daily Bugle*, snapping shots of his alter ego in action; despite the "great responsibility" line, Spider-Man's early crime-fighting adventures were driven more by the promise of lucrative photo ops than by any do-gooder impulse. (Alas, these pictures would inevitably be twisted into propaganda against him by *Bugle* publisher J. Jonah Jameson, who'd embarked on a campaign against the "public menace" of Spider-Man.) The moments in which Parker is receiving payment are among the few that Ditko gives him a smile. At least when Bruce Banner became the Hulk, he was issued a reprieve from self-reflection. But Peter Parker's problems and Spider-Man's problems became one, as evidenced by a litany of neurosis-flooded thought balloons. After one misunderstanding causes a scuffle with police officers, he runs home through the abandoned, shadowy city streets. "Nothing turns out right . . . (sob) . . . I wish I had never gotten my super powers!"

All of this was balanced, brilliantly and precariously, with breezy acrobatic action sequences. Ditko's rendering of athleticism was quite different from Kirby's, more about gymnastic dodging than knockout punches, but it was just as exciting. Lee's brilliant touch was to have Parker deliver a nonstop parade of corny jokes when he was in the Spider-Man costume: a convincing manifestation of obsessive nervous thinking, yes, but more importantly an effective mood-lightener. Despite the taunting teenage jeers, empty wallet, ailing relative, hostile workplace, and criminal threats, *The Amazing Spider-Man* managed to be a whole lot of fun.

Superheroes were now regularly sweeping out the odd, neglected corners of the line. *Strange Tales* was taken over by solo adventures of the Human Torch; on the very same day that *Linda Carter, Student Nurse* was replaced on the schedule by *Amazing Spider-Man*, the last of the monster books, *Tales of Suspense*, got a new cover star: Iron Man. Tony Stark didn't have crippling self-esteem issues, or problems paying rent, or a tough time talking to girls. He was a womanizing industrialist with military contracts and a mustache. Wounded and kidnapped by Wong-Chu, the "Red Guerrilla Tyrant," Stark is ordered to develop a weapon for the communist enemy. Instead he constructs a metal suit that will keep his failing heart in operation, and also serve as armor in which he can escape. Kirby designed a round and clunky gray heap; by the time Don Heck drew the story, it was equipped with suction cups, jets, transistor-powered magnets, and drills but not a lot of aesthetic appeal. Steve Ditko would soon streamline the armor, and a red-and-yellow color scheme would improve the look considerably. The character of Tony Stark would later improve as well, but for now his most compelling problem was that of an oversexed playboy who "can never appear bare-chested" because of the mechanical plate over his heart.

Don Heck became the regular *Iron Man* artist; Kirby just didn't have enough time. "The poor guy only has two hands, and can only draw with one!" Lee wrote to a fan. "I like to have him start as many strips as possible, to get them off on the right foot—but he cannot physically keep 'em all up—in fact, I sometimes wonder how he does as much as he does do."

"Enough of that 'Dear Editor' jazz from now on!" blared the letters column in *Fantastic Four* #10. "Jack Kirby and Stan Lee (that's us!) read every letter personally, and we like to feel that we know you and that you know us!" Thus were planted the seeds for Lee's most important non-super-powered characters: the merry members of the mythical Marvel Bullpen. There *had* been real bullpens, of course—first at the Empire State Building, and then again here at 655 Madison, though that was already five years in the past, before Stan got shuffled off into the corner, crowded in between file cabinets. Now Lee began to paint a picture of a utopian workplace, in which all the jolly artists cracked jokes while they worked away under one happy roof. (Doctor Doom even visited "the studio of Kirby and Lee, on Madison Avenue," in that same issue of *The Fantastic Four*, crashing a plotting session and knocking them out with sleeping gas.) In reality, Kirby only came into the offices about once a week. He worked from a varnished-pine room in the basement of his Long Island home, with a bookshelf of Shakespeare and science fiction for inspiration and a ten-inch black-and-white television for company—and the door shut, to keep the cigar smoke from billowing out to the rest of the house. His name certainly wasn't on any Madison Avenue door. "That was a lot of stuff that Stan Lee put into magazines, but the artists were all over the island," *Iron Man* artist Don Heck told an interviewer. "I could go into the office two times this week, and somebody else could go in two other times . . . you just don't cross paths." But Lee's spirit of cheer was genuine. Things were looking brighter.

"I would see Stan being very convivial out of the corner of my eye, seeming to have fun with his work," said Bruce Jay Friedman, who had watched as the comic kingdom had been stripped from Lee in the late 1950s. "He was sort of like a big kid. I had no idea there was a legend building right in front of my eyes."

Still, Lee needed help. "We seem to exist from crisis to crisis," he wrote in private correspondence with a fan. "You can't possibly imagine how rushed we are. It isn't a question of can't our artists do better (or can't I write better)—it's more a question of how well can we do in the brief time allotted to us? Some day, in some far distant Nirvana, perhaps we will have a chance to produce a strip without a frantic deadline hanging over us." Soon Sol Brodsky, who'd been a production hand for Atlas Comics, returned, as the de facto production manager. "My job was mainly talking to the artists and the writers and telling them how I wanted the stuff done," Lee recalled. "Sol did everything else—corrections, making sure everything looked right, making sure things went to the engraver, and he also talked to the printer. . . . Little by little, we built things back up again."

Lee began sharing more of the writing duties, often with old friends. "Martin Goodman started pressuring Lee to have other writers do some of the stories," said Leon Lazarus, an ex-Timely staffer who was himself recruited to script an issue of *Tales to Astonish*. "He became concerned that Stan would have too much leverage over him, and he worried about what would happen if Stan ever decided to leave the company."

At the end of 1962, Lee moved younger brother Larry back over to the westerns, and assigned "Iron Man," "Thor," and "Ant-Man" scripts to other veterans. "The Human Torch" was passed like a hot potato, finally landing with an artist credited as Joe Carter.

Joe Carter's real name, it turned out, was Jerry Siegel. The co-creator of Superman had been reduced in the late 1950s to pleading for assignments from Superman's copyright holder, DC Comics, and toiling under the abusive watch of editor Mort Weisinger for little pay. (According to industry legend, Weisinger once said to the meek Siegel, who was seated in his office, "I have to go to the can. Do you mind if I use your script to wipe my ass?") In the early 1960s, Siegel started making noise about a Superman lawsuit, and, bracing for DC's wrath, began looking elsewhere for employment. How could Lee *not* give work to one of the creators of the industry?

Unfortunately, Siegel's earnest, old-fashioned scripts didn't meet Lee's standards. Nor, it seemed, did anyone else's. Lee started seizing back "Iron Man" and "Thor" and "Ant-Man." Despite the substantial plotting contributions of Kirby and Heck and Ditko, when it came to the narration and dialogue, he trusted only himself.

Desperate to catch up on deadlines, Lee got Goodman's approval to hire George Roussos, who could ink two dozen pages in a day, for a staff position. But Roussos, wary of Goodman's hiring-and-layoff cycles, passed. Lee had better luck finding an assistant—a "gal Friday," in his words—to at least help with the administrative work. In March 1963, a temp agency sent over Florence Steinberg, a button-cute, bouffant-sporting twenty-five-year-old in pearls and white gloves who'd recently arrived in New York from Boston. Steinberg, a former art history major, was every bit as upbeat and outgoing as Lee—she'd been student council president in high school and later volunteered for campaigns of both Ted and Bobby Kennedy. Now stationed at a desk next to Lee, she answered fan mail (hundreds of pieces arrived every day), called freelancers, and shipped pages to the printer for sixty-five dollars a week, while he sat atop a stool and pounded away on his typewriter, or greeted visiting artists for story conferences.

Their office mates at Magazine Management, including future *Godfather* novelist Mario Puzo, scoffed at how frantically Lee and Steinberg and Brodsky were starting to work. But for Lee, something magical was happening. As the breakneck pace of new character introductions continued—Steve Ditko single-handedly developed the arrogant-surgeon-turned-benevolent-magician Doctor Strange for a backup feature in *Strange Tales**—the existing characters began to generate synergistic relationships with one another. A two-page sequence in *Amazing Spider-Man* #1 showed the web-spinner attempting to join the Fantastic Four (he was greatly disappointed to learn that group membership didn't include a salary); the same month, the Hulk (whose own title had just been canceled)† showed up in *The Fantastic Four* #12. Doctor Doom battled Spider-Man; the Human Torch spoke at an assembly at Peter Parker's

---

* Stephen Strange was part of a Ditko tradition that carried back to the 1950s: the glory-craving bastard whose journeys in a snowcapped East lead him to a comeuppance from a wise and ancient mystic.

† Early fandom had unkind words for the Hulk: "It stinks. A comic-book-length rendition of one of their hack monster stories with a continuing character modeled more or less on The Thing," wrote Don and Maggie Thompson in *Comic Art* #3.

high school; and Doctor Strange ended up in a hospital under the care of Dr. Don Blake, the alter ego of Thor. When Ant-Man showed up in *Fantastic Four* #16, accompanied by an alluring new heroine named the Wasp, a footnote explained all: "Meet the Wasp, Ant-Man's new partner-in-peril, starting with issue #44 of *Tales to Astonish!*"* It was canny cross-promotion, sure, but more important, it had narrative effects that would become a Marvel Comics touchstone: the idea that these characters shared a world, that the actions of each had repercussions on the others, and that each comic was merely a thread of one Marvel-wide mega-story.

It all set the stage for *The Avengers*, which gathered an all-star team of Marvel's marquee names (except for Spider-Man, fated to remain a sulking lone wolf). Iron Man, Ant-Man, the Wasp, Thor, and Hulk joined forces to defeat Thor's enemy Loki, and decided that they should get together more often—for an issue every month, to be precise. "The Avengers are on the march," wrote Lee, "and a new dimension is added to the Marvel galaxy of stars!" It wasn't just bluster. Bringing these heroes together forced Lee to further differentiate their individual personalities and voices, and allowed Kirby to show off his skill with complex visual choreography, balancing multiple characters within the confines of single panels.

Shockingly, Lee and Kirby managed to roll out another super-team comic the same month, with all-new characters. *The X-Men* followed the adventures of a group of super-powered teenage mutants who were enrolled at the private school of Professor Charles Xavier, a wheelchair-bound psychic. Under Xavier's leadership, the valiant but inexperienced X-Men—Scott Summers, the self-serious and laser-eyed Cyclops; Hank McCoy, the acrobatic, simian-shaped whiz-kid Beast; Bobby Drake, the jocky, clowny, snowball-generating Iceman; Jean Grey, the redheaded tele-kinetic Marvel Girl; and Warren Worthington III, the feather-winged scion Angel—used their abnormal abilities to halt the schemes of bad-apple

---

*After spoiled socialite Janet Van Dyne found her father murdered, she turned to Henry Pym (Ant-Man) for help. Pym, obsessed with Van Dyne's resemblance to his late wife ("So much like Maria! If she were not such a child!"), asked her to become his crime-fighting partner. He shared with her his shrinking gas, and implanted cells in her skin tissue: "It will leave no scar, but when you are reduced to the size of a wasp you will grow wings and tiny antennae!" Child or no, the two would soon become lovers.

mutants like the metal-commanding Magneto. On their downtime, the guys practiced combat maneuvers, gathered among bongos and beatniks at Greenwich Village's Coffee A-Go-Go, or panted at an endlessly patient Jean Grey.* But despite the banter that streamed between its adolescent heroes, *The X-Men* was the bête noire of *The Avengers*—like Spider-Man, the mutants were viewed with suspicion by the very society they fought to protect, an angle that became even more pointed as time went on. "Look at the crowd! They're livid with rage! Just like Professor X always warned us . . . normal humans fear and distrust anyone with super-mutant powers!" cried Angel in *X-Men* #5, which was written shortly after the bombing of the Sixteenth Street Baptist Church in Birmingham, Alabama, by white supremacists. A few issues later, after the Beast saved the life of a young boy, a mob chased him down and tore his clothes anyway. Was it a coincidence that the nonviolence-preaching Professor Xavier and his archenemy, the by-any-means-necessary warrior Magneto, lined up so neatly as metaphors for Martin Luther King and Malcolm X? "Remember, we are homo superior," scolded Magneto, plucking the Nietzschean term from an old science-fiction novel. "We are born to rule the earth. . . . Why *should* we love the homo sapiens? They hate us—fear us because of our superior power!" If the casually liberal Lee was laying out for readers where he stood on bigotry, it was also clear that he felt there were appropriate limits to the reaction to that bigotry: the hard-line Magneto and his protégés labeled themselves the Brotherhood of Evil Mutants. "By any means necessary" was hardly a superhero catchphrase.

However subtle it may have been, *The X-Men*'s connection to the civil rights struggle was one of Marvel's earliest acknowledgments of the fissures in American society.† In just a few years, the very concept of patrio-

---

* Eventually, Jean Grey and Scott Summers began to date. The trajectory of their relationship was impossible to gauge; they were never shown embracing until they shared a good-bye kiss in 1975's *X-Men* #94.

† Although in its early years *The X-Men* seldom met the standards set by other Lee and Kirby creations, occasionally it would realize its potential for powerful metaphor. In the spring of 1965, immediately after Alabama state troopers attacked civil rights demonstrators in Selma, the X-Men battled the Sentinels, an army of giant mutant-hunting robots created by a zealous anthropologist. "Beware the fanatic!" Lee wrote at the story's end. "Too often his cure is deadlier by far than the evil he denounces!"

tism would polarize the country, and the idea of reintroducing Captain America—a character known as the "Sentinel of Liberty," and literally wrapped in the United States flag—would have been almost unthinkable for a company courting the kids of America. As it was, the Captain America that returned to comics in 1963 in the pages of *The Avengers #4* was a walking anachronism, a man out of time. The newer heroes found him in the sea, unconscious and encased in a block of ice, his youth preserved. "All those years of being in a state of frozen suspended animation," exclaimed the Captain, "must have prevented me from aging!" But it didn't prevent him from feeling guilt over the fate of his former sidekick Bucky (who, it was explained, had died just before Captain America went into a deep freeze), or a deep longing for the simpler times of the 1940s. The revived Captain America was wholesome and admirable, just like he'd always been, but now he was prone to bouts of melancholy, and confusion about what had happened to his country.

Captain America picked an especially disconcerting moment in history to reemerge. *Avengers #4* was still in production on November 22, when news came that President Kennedy had been shot. "We were coming back from lunch, and people were listening to their car radios with the doors open," Flo Steinberg remembered. "We didn't have a television in the office, so everyone just sort of gravitated to a big room and sat around listening to the radio until they announced that he had died. We all left . . . just wandered."

Everyone, that is, but Stan Lee. "He was still working on the comic books," noted Mario Puzo. "Like that was the most important thing in the world."

Lee, once again scripting virtually the entire Marvel line, got his own office—with a door, and a rug—for the first time in seven years. Brodsky and Steinberg shared a desk nearby and were soon joined by another former Atlas bullpenner, Marie Severin. At Atlas, Severin worked in the coloring department under Stan Goldberg, but she was an extremely skilled artist in her own right, and able to harness her wicked sense of humor into withering caricatures. She might have been a star at *Mad* magazine, had her luck lined up differently. Instead, she was making filmstrips for the Federal Reserve Bank when she decided to drop off her illustration portfolio to Lee. He never looked at her samples, though; he sent her straight to Brodsky for a production job.

He should have hired her to draw comics. Kirby was at his drawing board seven days a week. Even at his uncanny speed—he could burn through three pages in a day—something had to give, and Lee was casting around for reinforcements. As he had with writers, he first looked to the old hands of Atlas. He'd started making phone calls to Syd Shores, the *Captain America* artist of the late 1940s, but Shores was busy doing illustration work for magazines. He'd called John Romita, the *Captain America* artist of the 1950s, but DC was paying him more than Marvel could. It wasn't just a matter of recruiting people who could draw. The "Marvel method," as it would come to be known, required that the artists could break down a basic plot into a finely paced, visually clear story over which Lee would write his dialogue. He wanted the panels to function like silent movies, to minimize the need for verbal exposition. Ideally, the artists would also contribute their own narrative ideas—characters, subplots—to the stories, just as Kirby and Ditko did.

Lee moved around the artists that he did have like chess pieces, trying them out on different titles until things clicked. Dick Ayers settled into comfortable stints on *Sgt. Fury* and *Strange Tales'* Human Torch stories; Don Heck inherited *The X-Men* and *The Avengers* and Giant Man from Kirby; and Ditko briefly took over *Tales of Suspense's* Iron Man from Heck. The Hulk was brought back in *Tales to Astonish*, reimagined by Ditko so that Bruce Banner's transformation into the Hulk was caused by Banner's fits of rage.* Artists were regularly asked to emulate Jack Kirby's style. When new artists started on a title, Lee would ask Kirby to draw basic layouts for the first issue, providing the rookies with visual training wheels. "Stan wanted Kirby to be Kirby, Ditko to be Ditko . . . and everyone else to be Kirby," said Don Heck; indeed, when Heck took over *The Avengers*, Lee wasn't shy about touting what he considered the Platonic ideal. "Don Heck drew this one with Dick Ayers helping out on the inks,"

---

* Ditko was called into Lee's office and given his choice of three characters to revive for a series of solo adventures: the Hulk, Ka-Zar, and Sub-Mariner. Ditko chose the Hulk because he wanted to draw the New Mexico locales.

he roared in the letters pages, "and you'll be amazed how closely it parallels King Kirby's great style!"

During story conferences, Lee repeatedly drilled home the idea of dynamism. Every word, he insisted, should move the story forward. All action should be emphatic; when a fist came down on a desk, it should be thunderous, and when someone was punched, they should be sent through the air. Speaking characters should be drawn with mouths wide open. Discussing a fight scene, he'd act out the action for artists, standing on his desk, or jumping on the couch, or making voices, as they craned their necks up in disbelief at the balding, exuberant, forty-two-year-old human action figure. Despite Lee's enthusiastic calisthenics, some of the artists agonized at the sparseness of the plot outlines, which required them to conjure scene-settings and determine pacing (working in the Marvel Method was "like digging into my insides and pulling it out," one of them groaned, years later). The obvious solution, Lee figured, would be to find artists with writing experience who were used to heavy creative lifting and didn't need everything spelled out for them.

He quickly ran through his options. An attempt to collaborate with original Human Torch creator Carl Burgos on solo adventures of the new, teenage incarnation of the character ended quickly. Lee next enlisted Sub-Mariner creator Bill Everett, now forty-six years old and working as an art director in Massachusetts, to see what he could do with the name "Daredevil," which was once another company's trademark but had since fallen out of use. The concept for the new "Daredevil" was not remarkable: Matt Murdock, the hard-studying son of a down-and-out single-father boxer, saves a blind man from an oncoming Ajax Atomic Labs delivery truck—and is then blinded himself by a radioactive cylinder. This being Marvel, however, the radiation also heightens his other senses, which come in handy later when he has to avenge his father's murder. Murdock grows up to be a defense lawyer, satisfying Lee's somewhat forced "justice is blind" hook and providing Daredevil with easy access to criminal happenings.

But Everett didn't come through on the deadline, even after getting a hand from Kirby on the character design. "I was putting in 14 or 15 hours a day," he said later, "and then to come home and try to do comics at night was just too much." He delivered the two-thirds of *Daredevil* #1 that he'd completed to a panicked Sol Brodsky; as luck would have it, Steve Ditko was in the Marvel offices, and Brodsky corralled him into finishing the issue at an available desk. It would be another year before Everett would work for Marvel again.

The second issue of *Daredevil* was given to Joe Orlando, who'd done impressive science-fiction and horror comics for EC. "The problem," admitted Orlando, "was that I wasn't Jack Kirby. Jack—or Ditko, or just a couple of others—could take a couple sentences of plot and bring in 20 pages that Stan could dialogue in an afternoon or two. When I drew out the story my way, Stan would go over it and say, 'this panel needs to be changed' and 'this whole page needs to be changed' and on and on. I didn't plot it out the way he wanted the story told so I wound up drawing at least half of every story twice. They weren't paying enough for that so I quit."

Now *Daredevil* went to Orlando's mentor, the brilliant but mercurial Wally Wood. His slick space tales in *Weird Science* and parodies in *Mad* had made him one of the brightest lights of the EC Comics stable, and Jack Kirby had personally chosen him to ink his work on the *Sky Masters* comic strip. Like Kirby, he was a workhorse. But it wasn't just a punishing schedule that was wearing on Wood. He suffered from a chronic migraine, battled depression, drank heavily, and pulled all-nighters in his studio, subsisting on caffeine and cigarettes.

Shortly before Marvel came calling, Wood had angrily quit *Mad* for good after an editor rejected one of his stories. He needed the money, and he'd quit drinking, but that didn't mean he would just fall into line for the company. He was stubborn, and given to playing little games. "Even though there were ashtrays in Stan's office," said Flo Steinberg, "he'd always drop ashes on Stan's carpet. And that would drive Stan bananas. So when Woody would go into Stan's office, I would walk with him and then very deftly take away his cigarette at the last minute. And it worked a few times. But as soon as he was in Stan's office, he'd light up another one."

Lee trumpeted his new star with a cover blurb, something that even Kirby and Ditko weren't afforded. "Under the brilliant artistic craftsmanship of famous illustrator Wally Wood, Daredevil reaches new heights of glory!" screamed the front of *Daredevil #5*. The cover itself, though, was drawn by Jack Kirby. Lee could always count on Kirby.

Stan had been ramping up his hip, alliterative, carnival-barker-as-beatnik style for a couple of years now, assigning nicknames to everyone who worked on the comics and delivering letters-page news updates in a voice that was a unique cocktail of impossible bluster and blushing self-deprecation. In 1964's *Marvel Tales Annual #1*, he'd run black-and-white photos of "Merry Marty Goodman," "Smilin' Stan Lee," "Sparkling Solly Brodsky," "Jolly ol' Jack Kirby," and sixteen others. There was one particularly notable absence: "Sturdy" Steve Ditko was nowhere to be seen. "A few of our bullpen buddies were out of town when these pix were taken," the text cheerily explained, "so we'll try to print their pans later on."

In fact, Ditko was quietly distancing himself from the Marvel pep rally. On July 27, 1964, a group of fans rented out a meeting hall near Union Square and invited writers, artists, and collectors (and one dealer) of old comic books to meet. Ditko showed up at this, the first comic-book convention, but he was hardly an ambassador of good cheer. One fan, Ethan Roberts, called it "the most depressing exchange I ever had with a comics pro." Ditko—"tall, thin, balding, dour, with glasses"—responded to Roberts's pursuit of a career in comics by telling him "how hard the job was, and that it paid too little and had few lasting rewards. It was a real downer." Ditko never appeared at another convention. When drawings he'd given to fans were published on the covers of their mimeographed fanzines, he responded with angry letters ("This isn't the first time I've been treated inconsiderately by members of fandom") and stopped giving away his artwork.

Two weeks after the convention, *Amazing Spider-Man #18* appeared. It was entirely plotted by Ditko, who'd been having disagreements with Lee about the direction of the comic and gradually taking more control of story lines. Ditko thought Lee was afraid to go with his instincts, too eager to please the letter-writing fans, with "the tendency to take write-in complaints too literally." Ditko resisted Lee's requests to soften the harsh edges of the supporting characters that surrounded Spider-Man. He also argued against overwhelming the title with fantastic or mystical elements, preferring to keep the stories "grounded more in a teenager's credible world." Lee called for a maximum of costumed fight scenes; Ditko pushed for more scenes of Peter Parker. The eighteenth issue brought their conflict to a head: there were a few panels of the Sandman swinging at Spider-Man, but for the most part, it was a superhero comic without an adventure, just a broke, picked-on, lovelorn teenager and his crummy problems. Lee's letters-page description in other Marvel comics that month threw Ditko under the bus even as it made its sales pitch. "A lot of readers are sure to hate it," he promised of the issue, "so if you want to know what all the criticism is about, be sure to buy a copy!"

These fissures started to show just as Lee's cheerleading reached fever pitch. Bard College invited him for a speaking engagement, and other schools quickly followed. Lee was so taken by this interest from the world of higher learning that when he decided to start a Marvel fan club—the Merry Marvel Marching Society, or M.M.M.S.—membership targeted college students more than ten-year-old kids. For a dollar, one could purchase an M.M.M.S. kit that included, along with stickers and a membership card, a button "designed to look great when worn next to your Phi Beta Kappa key!"

A flexi-disc 33 rpm record was also included in the kit. For "The Voices of Marvel," Lee wrote a script filled with corny jokes, booked time at a midtown studio, and gathered staff and freelancers at the offices to practice. "Stan treated it like he was producing the Academy Awards," said Kirby. "He'd written it and rewritten it . . . we all went into the office, more people than there was room for. When you weren't rehearsing your part, you had to go out in the hall and wait. No work was done that day on comics. It was all about the record. We rehearsed all morning. We were supposed to go to lunch and then over to the recording studio . . . but when lunchtime came, Stan said, 'no, no, we're not ready,' so most of us skipped lunch and stayed there to rehearse more. Then we took cabs over to the recording studio and we were supposed to be in and out in an hour or two but we were there well into the evening. I don't know how many takes we did."*

"The Voices of Marvel" featured nearly all of Marvel's boldfaced names, giving charmingly inept deliveries to punch lines that perhaps could not be delivered any other way. Lee, Kirby, Ayers, Heck, Steinberg, Brodsky, Goldberg, inker Chic Stone, letterers Artie Simek and Sam Rosen, and brand-new Marvel superstar Wally Wood were all packed into the five-minute recording. Missing again was Steve Ditko. Lee made it into a gag:

STAN: Hey, what's all that commotion out there, Sol?
SOL: Why, it's shy Steve Ditko. He heard you're making a record and he's got mike fright! Whoops! There he goes!
STAN: Out the window *again*? You know, I'm beginning to think he *is* Spider-Man.

The month the record was announced, a notice ran on the first page of *Amazing Spider-Man*. "Many readers have asked why Stan's name is always first on the credits! And so big-hearted Lee agreed to put Stevey's name first this time! How about that?!!" The joke was that Lee's name was below Ditko's—and twice the size.

Ditko wasn't laughing. As an increasingly devoted adherent of the works of the novelist and philosopher Ayn Rand—whose Objectivist philosophy stressed self-interest, individual rights, and cold, hard logic—he was hardly the picture of a docile employee. Stan Lee, meanwhile, was a magnet for acclaim, eager to please, and beholden to Goodman's demands—practically a made-to-order Rand villain.† "I don't know what he did, or where he lived, or who his friends were, or what he did with himself," Stan Lee would say

---

* In his autobiography, Lee remembered it this way: "In a moment of inspiration, I marched the whole gang out of the office one day to a recording studio about five blocks away . . . we made a record for our fans, ad-libbing the whole thing."

† "The creator stands on his own judgment," Rand wrote in *The Fountainhead*. "The parasite follows the opinions of others. The creator thinks, the parasite copies. The creator produces, the parasite loots. The creator's concern is the conquest of nature. The parasite's concern is the conquest of Man. The creator requires independence—he neither serves nor rules. He deals with men by free exchange and voluntary choice. The parasite seeks power. He wants to bind all men together in common action and common slavery."

years later about Steve Ditko. By the beginning of 1965, the two were no longer speaking. Ditko came up with his own plots, drew his pages, and dropped off his artwork with Sol Brodsky to pass along to Lee.

The M.M.M.S. was an immediate smash; chapters opened at Princeton, Oxford, and Cambridge. Flo Steinberg came into the office on weekends to process the orders that were pouring in. "We had to write down everybody's name and make labels for each one, and pull out all these hundreds of dollar bills. We were throwing them at each other there were so many!" The mania wasn't confined to the mail, either—teenage fans started calling the office, wanting to have long telephone conversations with Fabulous Flo Steinberg, the pretty young lady who'd answered their mail so kindly and whose lovely picture they'd seen in the comics. Before long, they were showing up in the dimly lit hallways of 625 Madison, wanting to meet Stan and Jack and Steve and Flo and the others.

There was no time for that. Lee had an entire fictional universe to manage. He'd vigilantly kept a consistent continuity between all the titles, so that, for instance, when the Hulk was captured in *Tales to Astonish*, Reed Richards wondered about his whereabouts in a *Fantastic Four Annual*. If Tony Stark went missing from *Tales of Suspense*, he was also AWOL in the next issue of *The Avengers*. One issue of the World War II–set *Sgt. Fury and His Howling Commandos*, which had previously been isolated from the superhero characters, featured a crossover appearance from Captain America.* Eventually, the demands of such choreography became so tangled that Lee removed Thor, Iron Man, Giant-Man, and the Wasp from *The Avengers*, replacing them with Hawkeye, a former Iron Man foe, and Quicksilver and the Scarlet Witch, erstwhile X-Men nemeses.† Captain America remained in *The Avengers*, but his solo ad-

---

*Soon afterward, Kirby conceived a contemporary, superspy version of Nick Fury. Fury's existence in two different time frames was considerately explained by giving him a super-serum that kept him young. He thus joined Captain America in the ranks of World War II veterans who'd found a way to battle the aging process, a gimmick that allowed Greatest Generation heroism to carry on into the 1960s; the years of experience lent the characters an additional gravitas.

†This sent a message of unlimited possibility: in the Marvel Universe, team lineups could change, and criminals could reform.

ventures in *Tales of Suspense* now exclusively covered his World War II past, which didn't have to be so tightly synchronized.

Lee was also still trying to plug holes in the workforce. Throughout 1965, more Atlas veterans returned: George Tuska started drawing Captain America in *Tales of Suspense* over Kirby's layouts; Gene Colan started a Sub-Mariner feature in *Tales to Astonish*; John Severin (Marie's older brother) penciled "Nick Fury, Agent of S.H.I.E.L.D." for *Strange Tales*. Kirby briefly reclaimed the Hulk from the incommunicado Ditko before turning it over to a merry-go-round of trial-basis artists who'd eventually include the still-deadline-resistant Bill Everett.

Lee continued to court John Romita, who'd been unceremoniously laid off in 1957. Romita had resisted Lee's persistent overtures throughout the early 1960s, doubting claims about Marvel's changed fortunes. He'd seen enough boom-and-bust cycles to know to stick with the sure thing: DC still paid higher rates. Why take the risk?

In 1965, Romita finally told Lee he was leaving the comic business altogether, and taking a job doing storyboards for the ad agency BBDO. "After eight years of penciling romance comics, I was burned out," Romita said. "I couldn't pencil another thing." Lee insisted they get together and talk.

"You have no idea how popular these guys are," Lee said over lunch, pulling out issues of *Fantastic Four* and *Amazing Spider-Man*. Romita thought *Spider-Man* looked terrible, but Lee insisted that the superheroes were connecting with readers, that this was the future. Romita hesitantly agreed to work with Marvel again, on the condition that he would only be inking work that had been already penciled.

Three weeks later, Lee asked Romita for a sample illustration of Daredevil. He didn't mention that the current *Daredevil* artist, Wally Wood, was headed out the door. To Wood, the so-called Marvel Method—drawing an issue before there was a script—meant that he was plotting the story without being paid or credited. So for the tenth issue of *Daredevil*, Lee turned over the reins completely, and provided a setup for the reader that had a familiarly insinuating ring. "Wally Wood has always wanted to try his hand at *writing* a story as well as drawing it, and bighearted Stan (who wanted a rest anyway) said okay! So, what follows next is anybody's guess! You may like it or not, but you can be sure of this . . . it's gonna be *different!*"

A frustrated Wood immediately decamped to the fledgling Tower Comics to edit a line of superhero titles, and Lee assigned Romita to *Daredevil*, based on his illustration of the hero swinging through the air. When Romita turned in his pages, though, Lee told him his style still betrayed too much of his romance-comics background. Lee told Romita he'd get another artist to break down the story into rough layouts, to show him how it was done. Then he called Jack Kirby.

Wood was already working at Tower Comics when he saw Lee's letters-page remarks for *Daredevil* #10: "Wonderful Wally decided he doesn't have time to write the conclusion next ish, and he's forgotten most of the answers we'll be needing! So, Sorrowful Stan has inherited the job of tying the whole yarn together and finding a way to make it all come out in the wash! And you think you've got troubles!" Wood turned to his Tower colleagues and fumed about Stan Lee. He'd hold on to his rage for years to come.

The truth was that Lee—writing at home in Hewlett Harbor all day on Tuesdays, Thursdays, Saturdays, and Sundays, and coming into the midtown offices the other three days—was still desperate for help with the writing workload. When Steve Skeates, an Iron Man fan preparing to graduate from Alfred University in upstate New York, wrote Marvel a letter in comic-book form, Lee called him personally and hired him, over the phone, as an assistant editor. When Skeates arrived at the offices, he was moved around from desk to desk, where he looked over scripts and tried to help with the production process. But Lee quickly realized that the nervous college graduate knew nothing about how comic books were made and was more adept at bumming cigarettes from Marie Severin than correcting scripts. Asked to redirect word balloon pointers, Skeates could only respond with shakily drawn lines.

It was at this moment that Lee got a note from letters-column regular Roy Thomas, announcing that he'd just moved to New York and would like to meet in person. Thomas was twenty-four years old. He'd spent the last few years teaching high school English in his native Missouri, but he lived and breathed comic books, writing letters to DC and Marvel and editing the fanzine *Alter Ego*. He'd come to New York to work for Mort Weisinger at DC—the same editor who had made Jerry Siegel's life so miserable. But when Thomas arrived, Weisinger promptly shaved 10 percent from the promised salary, and informed him that he was on staff for a trial period of two weeks. Then Weisinger introduced Thomas to his previous assistant, explaining that he'd already been fired but was going to train Thomas. When Weisinger needed Thomas for something, he summoned him into his office with a buzzer, then muttered profanities under his breath. Within two weeks, Thomas was tearing up in his lonely Twenty-Third Street hotel, wondering if pursuing a career in comic books had been a terrible mistake.

Lee called Thomas's hotel and asked him to take a writing test, adding dialogue and captions to pages of *Fantastic Four Annual #2*. On July 9, just two weeks after moving to the city, Thomas was in Stan Lee's office. Lee, tired of conducting his young-talent search and impressed by Thomas, did not want to let him get away. He swiveled away in his chair, gazed out the window, and asked, "What it would take to hire you away from DC?"

Lee sent Thomas home that weekend with instructions to script an issue's worth of *Millie and the Model* pages; when Thomas returned on Monday, he was shoehorned into Brodsky and Steinberg's office, a typewriter atop his corrugated metal desk. He'd been hired to sit there and write for forty hours a week—"staff writer" was his title—but with the phone ringing, freelancers coming and going, and Sol and Flo and Marie hurrying around, he couldn't concentrate, and, before long, he was staying at work until 8 or 9 p.m., clicking off the last lights in the darkened building. Lee revised the terms of the job so that Thomas could work as an editorial assistant during the day and write scripts at home. There was frenzied rewriting from Lee at first, but before long, Thomas's uncanny ability to mimic the boss's style earned him a free hand in his collaborations with the artists of *Sgt. Fury* and *The X-Men*. Finally, after nearly three years of searching, there was someone that Lee trusted to not only script, but also co-plot, Marvel's superhero comics. Lee could devote more time to his secondary position—comics' ambassador to the world.*

By now, Marvel's newsprint masterpieces were being referenced in Cornell physics classes and Colgate student newspapers, and Lee was fielding regular requests for campus speaking. Newspapers, slowly at first, sat up and took notice: the *Wall Street Journal* noted the sales increases, while the *Village Voice* pointed out beatniks' embrace of the kooky, hip stories. "Marvel Comics are the first comic books in history in which a post-adolescent escapist can get involved," the *Voice* gushed. "For Marvel Comics are the first comic books to evoke, even metaphorically, the Real World." Lee's snappy, self-conscious patter was singled out, as was the verisimilitude of the New York City settings. "There are approximately 15 superheroes in the Marvel Group, and nearly all of them live in the New York area. Midtown Manhattan is full of their landmarks. On Madison Avenue the Baxter building houses the Fantastic Four and their various self-protective devices. . . . Doctor Strange is a master of occult knowledge and often walks around in ectoplasmic form; his creators imply that he lives in the Village because no one there is likely to become alarmed at being jostled by a wraith."† Meanwhile, in San Francisco, poet Michael McClure featured a Doctor Strange monologue from *Strange Tales* #130 as a centerpiece in his controversial 1965 play *The Beard.*

A similar infatuation gripped the art world. Roy Lichtenstein appropriated one of Kirby's *X-Men* panels for his painting *Image Duplicator*, and future Warhol collaborator Paul Morrissey made a ten-minute experimental film, *The Origin of Captain America*, in which an actor read from *Tales of Suspense* #63. There were scattered other comics in the

---

* Lee was hardly blowing off the writing. Roy Thomas saw him the Monday morning after the November 9, 1965, blackout and learned that he'd typed ten pages of *Thor* by candlelight. Lee hadn't been able to get to scripting *Sgt. Fury* that weekend, though—which is how Thomas ended up taking over the title.

† The *Voice*'s Sally Kempton packed in an impressive amount of Psych 101 jargon, a sure sign that the characters were matters of serious discussion. "Spiderman has a terrible identity problem, a marked inferiority complex, and a fear of women," she wrote. "He is anti-social, castration-ridden, racked with Oedipal guilt, and accident-prone." Mention was also made of "phallic-looking skyscraper towers" and Peter Parker's submission toward Aunt May.

background of Morrissey's film—and all of them were from Marvel. Lee seized the opportunity and slapped a "Marvel Pop Art Productions" logo on the corners of the covers. Kirby found resonances with modern art as well: he experimented with *grisaille* photocollages in his *Fantastic Four* stories, lending grandiosity to outer-space (and interdimensional) sequences.

The comics also caught the attention of Robert Lawrence, a partner in Grantray-Lawrence Animation, who spied them on the newsstands and made the connection to the Pop Art movement. He contacted Martin Goodman, who by now was teaching his younger son, Chip, the ins and outs of the family business. Grantray-Lawrence made a sweetheart deal to produce an animated series, *The Marvel Super Heroes*, taking all its images directly from published comic panels. The studio secured a continuing interest in merchandising profits related to the show. "We wrote an unbelievable contract with the Goodmans," Lawrence boasted, "because they didn't know what they had and where to go."*

None of this impressed the guys at Magazine Management, who couldn't understand all the sudden attention being paid to so much kids' stuff. When Marvel fan Federico Fellini, in New York to promote *Juliet of the Spirits*, swept into 625 Madison Avenue to meet Stan Lee, *Men* magazine editor Mel Shestack scoffed that Lee didn't even know who Fellini was; years later, Shestack insisted that the director had quickly lost interest in Lee and cottoned instead to the more colorful magazine editors, who were themselves like "living comic books."

Such condescension was the norm. "They were always making jokes about us. They'd come in and giggle," remembered Flo Steinberg. "Mario Puzo would look in and would see us all working on his way to the office and he would say, 'Work faster, little elves. Christmas is coming.'"

In truth, the magazines were still Martin Goodman's bread and butter.

---

* Steve Krantz, who sold the syndication rights to television stations (and foreign markets such as Japan, South America, and Australia), also claimed credit for coming across the comics on newsstands. Krantz told Stan Lee biographer Tom Spurgeon that the Goodmans secured a percentage of profits, and that "Marvel made a great deal of money on the basis of the shows I produced."

"The big sellers were the men's magazines," said Ivan Prashker, another editor. "It wasn't the comic books. The guys who worked at the men's magazines all thought Stan Lee was a schmuck." In the fall of 1965, Roy Thomas recruited fellow Missourian Dennis O'Neil to work as Marvel's second editorial assistant; within a matter of weeks, one of the magazine editors tried to enlist O'Neil in a scheme to dose Stan Lee with LSD. "He was going to supply a sugar cube of acid," said O'Neil. "My mission, should I have chosen to accept it, would have been to drop it into his coffee." O'Neil, a self-described "hippie liberal rebel" who had been lectured by Lee for wearing a T-shirt depicting a cannabis plant to the office, nonetheless declined.

In *Amazing Spider-Man*, Peter Parker graduated from high school, and broke up with the *Daily Bugle*'s Betty Brant, the first girl who'd been kind to him—he realized she could never be happy living with a constantly endangered crime-fighter. He went to college, where he met Gwen Stacy, Harry Osborn, and Professor Miles Warren—all of whom would become significant characters.

All of this happened without Steve Ditko and Stan Lee speaking to each other.

The communication gap was one of the first things that Roy Thomas learned at his new job. After Ditko dropped off an issue and announced that he was headed home to work on the next one, Thomas made a joke: Oh, really? There's going to be another one?

"I was just kidding him, but Sol pulled me aside and said, 'Listen, you have to be careful what you say to a guy like Steve, because he'll be going home on the subway and suddenly start thinking if you meant anything by that, or know something he didn't.' Everyone was walking on eggshells about the situation. How Stan always knew never to be out there when Steve was there, I don't know."

Even when they weren't speaking, they managed to disagree. When Lee added a caption to *Strange Tales* trumpeting, "This series was voted 'Most Likely to Succeed' (By Stan and Steve)," Ditko objected that he hadn't been part of any voting process, and so Lee changed it to "(By Stan and Baron Mordo)."* Ditko's continued devotion to the principles of Ayn Rand, and his desire to fill his comics with references to those principles, didn't make things any smoother. Ditko took the Randian term *looter* and named a villain after it; he took the idea that men "must deal by trade and give value for value" and had Peter Parker demand "equal value trade" from J. Jonah Jameson. It was a relief to see Parker stick up for himself, but he also began acting like a bit of a creep. He used passive-aggressive behavior to end his relationship with Betty Brant, and when he came upon campus protesters in *Amazing Spider-Man* #38, he told them off. "Another student protest! What are they after THIS time?" he seethed. When a letter-writer from Students for a Democratic Society called Lee out on it, he scrambled to make nice. "We never in a million years thought anyone was gonna take our silly protest-marchers seriously!"

At the end of 1965, when a reporter named Nat Freedland visited the Marvel offices for a three-thousand-word profile for the *New York Herald Tribune*, he found Lee in an unusually candid mood. "I don't plot *Spider-Man* any more," he said. "Steve Ditko, the artist, has been doing the stories. I guess I'll leave him alone until sales start to slip. Since Spidey got so popular, Ditko thinks he's the genius of the world. We were arguing so much over plot lines I told him to start making up his own stories. He won't let anybody else ink his drawings either. He just drops off the finished pages with notes at the margins and I fill in the dialogue. I never know what he'll come up with next, but it's interesting to work that way."

Freedland was impressed with Lee. He painted him as an "ultra-Madison Avenue, rangy lookalike of Rex Harrison" responsible for tripling the comics' circulation to 35 million copies a year, selling 40,000 memberships to the Merry Marvel Marching Society, and inspiring 500 fan letters a day. Freedland depicted Lee wearing out his eyes from reading fan mail and fretting over the choice of exactly the right sound effect for a page of *Fantastic Four* #50. Charmed by Lee's self-deprecating quips and Fellini anecdotes, the reporter barely made mention of Martin Goodman,

* "Baron Mordo" was an enemy of Doctor Strange.

and skimmed over Ditko's contributions, referring to Spider-Man as Lee's masterpiece—"the most offbeat character he could think of."

Freedland arranged to sit in on one of Lee and Kirby's Friday morning plotting sessions—and his timing couldn't have been better. They were hashing out the *Fantastic Four*, which was approaching a firing-on-all-cylinders peak, tying together the subplots they'd been weaving for months.

"The Thing finally beats the Silver Surfer," Lee pitched to Kirby, as Freedland jotted notes. "But then Alicia makes him realize he's made a terrible mistake. This is what the Thing has always feared more than anything else, that he would lose control and really clobber somebody." The effusive Lee gained momentum as he went forward, with Kirby simply interjecting with nods and *right*s and *ummh*s. "The Thing is brokenhearted. He wanders off by himself. He's too ashamed to face Alicia or go back home to the Fantastic Four. He doesn't realize how he's failing for the second time. . . . How much the F.F. needs him."

Freedland cut to Kirby, "a middle-aged man with baggy eyes and a baggy Robert Hall-ish suit. He is sucking a huge green cigar and if you stood next to him on the subway you would peg him for the assistant foreman in a girdle factory."

"Great," Freedland quoted Kirby as saying, in a "high-pitched voice." "Great."

Many months later, when an account of the Thing's fight with the Silver Surfer finally emerged, Kirby had changed it, and expanded it, significantly. It appeared as the coda to a grand space opera, a brew of existentialism and high adventure for which he had done the heavy lifting—despite his perpetual freelancer status, Kirby not only generated plots with Lee but was also the primary force when it came to designing characters and pacing stories. By now he was, in a sense, the director of the films they made together, composing each shot and driving the narrative with the momentum of his images. "I don't see him for a week," Lee told one interviewer. "He comes back a week later and the whole strip is drawn. And nobody knows what I'm going to see on those pages. He may have come up with a dozen new ideas, you see. . . . Then I take it, and I write it, on the basis of what Jack has drawn. He's broken it down to continuity for me. He's drawn the whole thing, actually. I put in the dialogue and the captions. So he doesn't know exactly what I'm going to write, what words I'm going to put in their mouths. I don't know what he's going to draw." In fact, the Silver Surfer, who had yet to debut at the time of Freedland's article, was wholly Kirby's creation, a surprise to Lee when the completed pages arrived.

Occasionally when Kirby came into the office, he and Romita would catch a ride home to Long Island with Lee. Romita would crawl into the back of Lee's Cadillac and listen while Lee and Kirby discussed plots. As the convertible dodged in and out of Queens Boulevard traffic, they would volley ideas, each oblivious to the other.

"It's almost like I was watching Laurel and Hardy," Romita said. "These two guys are in the front, two giants, and Jack is saying, 'Well, Stanley, what are we going to make the kid like? Is he going to be a wizard? Is he going to be a genius? Is he going to be super-powered, or is he going to be a normal kid in the midst of a crazy family?' Stan would say, 'Well, let's try this,' and 'Let's try that.' So Stan would go off on a tangent and Jack would be talking about what he thought should happen. Jack would go home and do what he thought Stan was expecting. And when Stan got the script, I could hear him say, 'Jack forgot everything we were talking about!' And that's what led to making slight changes in Jack's stories, because Stan was under the impression that Jack had forgotten what he said."

Early in the morning of January 9, 1966, Stan Lee got a phone call from Roz Kirby. The *Herald Tribune* story was out. "She was almost hysterical," he said, "and she shouted, 'How could you do this? How could you have done this to Jack?'"

When Lee finally got his hands on the article, he said later, he could understand her outrage. "She had every right to be upset. About four-fifths of the article was about me, and made me out to be the most glamorous, wonderful human being that ever lived, and the very last few paragraphs were about Jack and made him sound like a jerk." Lee pleaded his innocence to the Kirbys.

Before long, the credits on *Fantastic Four* and *Thor* regularly read "A

Stan Lee and Jack Kirby Production." There would be no more "written by Stan Lee" on the Kirby books. Tempers cooled, but Kirby would remember the slight for the rest of his life.

Shortly after the *Herald Tribune* piece appeared, Ditko dropped off his pages with Sol Brodsky and announced that when he finished his current assignment, he would not be doing any more work for Marvel Comics. Brodsky rushed into Lee's office to tell him, but Ditko had made up his mind. He even wrote a letter to the still-bruised Jack Kirby, encouraging him to join him in the exodus. Kirby, though, had a wife and four children to support. He couldn't leave the steady gig at Marvel, not yet.

"I've had theories advanced by other guys in the office," Lee said later of speculation as to what was causing Ditko such consternation. It wasn't, apparently, just the fighting about plots. "Letterers who said he hated me putting in sound effects. Sometimes I would add speed lines to his artwork and he hated that. He thought I was doing too much dialogue or too little dialogue. Maybe he felt . . . I don't really know."

Another time, though, Lee hinted at an altogether different kind of tension. The *Herald Tribune* article, published three days before the premiere of the *Batman* television show instigated a mainstream revival of superhero interest, broke the news of Marvel's expanded merchandising plans, including the forthcoming Grantray-Lawrence show. "In the works are plastic models, games, a Spider-Man jazz record and a television cartoon series." Someone was about to make a lot of money, it seemed, and it wasn't anyone who sat at a drawing board. When Lee asked Ditko, years later, if he would return for one last Spider-Man story, Ditko replied, "Not until Goodman pays me the royalties he owes me."

Visiting Princeton University for a speaking engagement in March, Lee sheepishly announced Ditko's departure. "We've just lost the artist who does Doctor Strange, Steve Ditko," he managed, before groans, boos, and hisses drowned him out. "I feel as badly about it as you do. He's a very peculiar guy. He's a great talent, but he's a little eccentric. Anyway, I haven't spoken to this guy for over a year. He mails in the work, and

I write the stories and that's the way he liked to work. One day he just phoned, and he said, 'I'm leaving.' So this is the acid test now, because he was such a popular artist. I *think* we've managed to find people to replace him, where those boos will change to a chorus of cheers."

3

IN 1966, MARTIN GOODMAN MOVED HIS EXPANDING COMIC-BOOK OPERATIONS
out of the cramped offices at 625 Madison, just down the block to 635.
Goodman stayed behind with his magazines; from now on, Stan Lee would
have a little more room to breathe, a little less attention from the boss.

Marvel's old address continued to run in the letter columns, to confuse
the overzealous kids who'd started showing up and trying to sneak by Flo
Steinberg to meet their heroes. (Lee stopped taking the elevator, where
he might be stuck with nutty fans; now he bounded his lean frame up the
stairs every day.) They wouldn't have been treated to much of a spectacle
anyway, certainly nothing like the madcap Bullpen that Lee had planted
in their imaginations, but there was, at last, a real staff. John "the Mountain" Verpoorten, a pipe-smoking, art-school-educated, six-foot-six bear
of a man who collected 16 mm films, and Morrie Kuramoto, a Japanese-
American, chain-smoking health-food advocate who'd been one of the
1957 layoff casualties, were hired to help with production.

But even as Marvel was growing bigger, and ever more popular, DC
Comics was still on top. The writing was consistently professional, and the
artwork—Gil Kane on *Green Lantern*, Carmine Infantino on *The Flash* and
Batman, Timely alumnus Mike Sekowsky on the *Justice League of America*,
Curt Swan on *Superman*—was polished and elegant. But to Marvel readers, the personalities of the DC characters were interchangeable, their lives
static and flat. Neither charge was entirely true: Aquaman and the Flash
both got married, and Superman's lachrymose longings for Krypton carried
a real weight. Still, most of the DC world seemed earnestly homogeneous,
rendered with polite draftsmanship that radiated a kind of complacency.

Although they were, in truth, charming and inventive in their own right, they couldn't hold a candle to the blend of humor and pathos and grandeur that Lee, Kirby, and Ditko had concocted.

The suit-wearing editors at DC discussed Marvel in their meetings, and finally decided that it must be the crude artwork, and the bad puns, that the kids liked. There's no accounting for taste, they grumbled, and tried to get hip by pasting so-called go-go checkerboard patterns at the tops of each comic. Instead of Lee's snappy "Bullpen Bulletins," DC instituted a news update page called "Direct Currents" that might as well have been written by accountants. They introduced a "New Look" version of the dying-on-the-vine *Batman*, replacing horrendous alien-invader stories with horrendous self-parody that Susan Sontag, in *The New York Times*, singled out as a textbook example of "low camp." It was Marvel gone wrong, with only Stan Lee's puns and none of his heart: Spider-Man had Aunt May, and so now Batman got an Aunt Harriet, but instead of familial drama there was only arch, idiot-savant modishness.

Marvel was still scrappier, with a faster-growing fan base. Marvel was more Mets than Yankees, more Rolling Stones than Pat Boone (whom, in fact, DC had immortalized in a comic book); it was the Pepsi Generation challenger to DC's Coca-Cola giant. Where Marvel had the interest of Fellini and the editor of *Existential Psychiatry*, DC had the songwriters of *Bye Bye Birdie* staging *It's A Bird, It's A Plane, It's Superman!* on Broadway.

But DC also had Batman. More specifically, they had *Batman*, star of ABC-TV, an instant Top 10 Nielsen hit, which caused the sales of the comic book to suddenly increase multifold, the first comic book in years to break the one-million-copies mark. New episodes of the show ran an unprecedented twice a week and precipitated a merchandising bonanza, a windfall in junky plastic tie-ins.

The new, campy version of the *Batman* comic had attracted Hollywood's attention; DC's very failure to re-create the Marvel style resulted in its biggest hit. Martin Goodman might have wished he'd waited a little longer to sell the rights to his own characters—but for a magazine publisher whose comic books were a fraction of the business, it was all gravy anyway. Marvel's own success had already catalyzed other publishers to trot out superheroes, and now *Batman* translated into a popularity surge for everybody in the again-growing field.

Much of the new competition employed exiles from Marvel itself: in addition to the Tower Comics books edited by the disgruntled Wally Wood, by 1965 the field also included Archie Comics' imitatively titled "Mighty Comics Group" line, created by Superman co-creator (and former *Strange Tales* writer) Jerry Siegel, and Paul Reinman, the Timely artist who'd inked much of Kirby's early 1960s Marvel work. Mighty Comics tried to have it both ways, with covers that were actionable mimicries of Marvel and a tone as groan-inducingly dopey as *Batman*'s. "*Dig* their crazy costumes—*marvel* at their *stupor* deeds!" read the cover copy on a paperback collection of Mighty stories, titled *High Camp Superheroes*. "Some will say this book is so bad it's GREAT." Charlton Comics' more straight-faced new "Action Heroes" line was home to Steve Ditko, who eventually used the platform to introduce the Question, a right-wing vigilante unfettered by Stan Lee's pesky moral relativism.* And Harvey Comics hired Jack Kirby's old partner, Joe Simon.

With news of Simon's "Harvey Thriller" line in the works, Martin Goodman told Lee to leap into action. "I came in one day," said Kirby, "and Stan said, 'Martin says we have to add more books.' They were afraid Al Harvey, who had pretty good distribution, was going to crowd them off the stands." In the space of a week, Lee and Kirby came up with a misfit group of heroes called the Inhumans and a handsome black hero called the Coal Tiger. But it turned out that DC, which still controlled Marvel's distribution, wouldn't allow Goodman to publish the extra titles anyway. So the new characters were set aside until they could be worked into the *Fantastic Four*, as players in what would be the most adventurous stories that Marvel had ever attempted.

The Marvel heroes populated every corner of the world. The Fantastic Four, Spider-Man, Daredevil, and the Avengers were based in New York

---

* Ditko now had a free hand to insert Randian platitudes in his comics without Goodman and Lee's interference. A sample, from *Mysterious Suspense #1*: "The greatest battle a person must constantly fight is to uphold proper principles, known truths, against everyone he deals with! A truth cannot be defeated!"

City; the X-Men made their home in nearby Westchester County. The Hulk wandered the southwestern United States; Iron Man went to Ireland, battled a Norwegian menace, and visited Vietnam. There was a cavalcade of alien visitations, and Doctor Strange could always be counted on to visit the astral plane. But now Lee and Kirby would really push the boundaries, revving up the mythological grandeur of the Marvel Universe. Kirby freed his inner Edith Hamilton by supplementing Thor's modern-day adventures in *Journey into Mystery* with "Tales of Asgard," in which Norse gods vied for power among themselves. It wasn't just the awe-striking powers that made these stories operatic. There was also the classicism of the narratives—quests for mystical objects, preparations for battle—and themes of duty, heritage, and mortality that seemed wholly unrelated to the alien-punching stories from the newsstand competition. Before now, superhero comics weren't about approval from your king father—that was strictly Shakespeare. Now, in the Marvel version of things, Thor always had to answer to angry dad Odin, and his chief nemesis, Loki, was also his half brother—an enemy-sibling dynamic that would be repeated with characters in *The X-Men* and the *Fantastic Four*.

Journey into Mystery may have been the most explicitly mythological of the Lee and Kirby books, but the stories in *Fantastic Four* were becoming more philosophical, and more ceremonious, with every issue. In the mid–1960s, the psychodrama of the First Family of Marvel Comics reached new levels. For more than six months, Ben Grimm, the Thing, stalked around in a sustained rage, still unable to accept the permanence of his mutated state. Reed and Sue Richards, Mr. Fantastic and the Invisible Girl, followed their nuptials with icy tension, as Reed became more and more withdrawn, obsessed with his scientific pursuits. And everything converged when Johnny Storm, the Human Torch, fell under the spell of doomed love for a doe-eyed beauty named Crystal. It turned out she was a member of the Inhumans, the strange-powered family of exiled royalty who lived hidden in the Swiss Alps but had come to New York City pursuing one of their own, a runaway.

The Inhumans were like nothing that had come before. Their intentions were ambiguous, and their bodies—one had earthquake-inducing hooves, another tentacle-like hair, another gills and fins—verged on the grotesque. Black Bolt, their leader, had a voice that literally shattered the earth around him—and so he remained mute. Lockjaw, the family pet, was a massive mustachioed dog with antennae.

With the introduction of the Inhumans, it was suddenly apparent that the Marvel Universe was infinite, that there could be whole civilizations in every corner of the entire cosmos: as each issue tumbled into the next, picking up momentum, expanding the cast, the grand space opera absorbed forgotten characters and established the relationships between them all. Overlapping with the Inhumans adventure was the threat of Galactus, a twenty-foot-tall humanoid alien who wore purple headgear and drained life from entire planets for sustenance, his arrival heralded by a sterling, speechless being on a flying surfboard—the Silver Surfer—who scouted ahead like an angel of death. The Fantastic Four returned from their latest adventure to find a red-skied New York City in flames, its screaming citizens dropping belongings and falling on one another as they wandered through empty intersections. Even the FF's old enemies, the shape-shifting alien Skrulls, were shown panicking in their spaceships far away. The Watcher, a cosmic deity sworn to observe the galaxies but never interfere, was dusted off from early issues; understanding the threat of Galactus, he broke his oath and offered assistance to the heroes. There was the sense that something big was coming, something scary, something secret—something that didn't belong in comic books.

Kirby, no longer satisfied with air-cars and gamma rays, introduced Atmo-Guns and Matter Mobilizers and Elemental Converters. The Watcher sent the Human Torch into the Negative Zone, an unexplored realm of antimatter, to retrieve a weapon called the Ultimate Nullifier. Lee and Kirby knew better than to explain these concepts in great detail. Readers couldn't possibly understand; even the heroes themselves couldn't process what was going on. The Silver Surfer, the Watcher, Galactus—they were all bigger than the helpless Fantastic Four, who were relegated to sitting on the sidelines. The Watcher commanded them to show humility: "Stand and observe! Try to fathom the cataclysmic forces which have been unleashed!" Two years before *2001: A Space Odyssey*, before the cinema could hope to approach the psychedelic imagination, the Human Torch emerged from an epiphanic trip in the laser-light show that was the Negative Zone, the Ultimate Nullifier finally in hand, but stricken with something like cosmic trauma, stammering in shock: "I traveled through worlds . . . so big . . . so *big* . . . there . . . there aren't words! We're like ants . . . just ants . . . *ants*!!!"

The Fantastic Four nervously brandished the exotic weapon, and the conscience-stricken Silver Surfer turned against his master, but Galactus was more annoyed than intimidated. He agreed to spare the planet in exchange for the surrender of the Ultimate Nullifier and casually sentenced his former messenger to imprisonment on Earth. ("I remove your space-time powers! Henceforth, the Silver Surfer shall roam the galaxies no more!") The devourer of planets finally departed, but it didn't feel like a clean triumph for the heroes, just a loss of innocence. Letter-writers wiped their brows, caught their breath, tried to reason it out: clearly the Galactus saga was a justification for Vietnam, with Galactus as the Viet Cong, the Fantastic Four as South Vietnam, and the Silver Surfer as America . . . right? Lee responded with wry, expert deflection: "Two'll getcha ten that our next mail contains a whole kaboodle of letters from equally imaginative fans who are utterly convinced that Galactus represented Robert McNamara, while the Silver Surfer was Wayne Morse—with Alicia symbolizing Lady Bird!"

He had a point: it was beyond metaphor. And it wasn't just *Fantastic Four* that could no longer be reduced to Joseph Campbell schematics or English Lit 101 symbolisms. Suddenly almost everything in the Marvel Universe was reaching some kind of critical juncture, a point of no return. Nick Fury's modern-day S.H.I.E.L.D. adventures in *Strange Tales* merged with Captain America's missions in *Tales of Suspense* as the heroes teamed against high-tech organizations like A.I.M. (Advanced Idea Mechanics) and HYDRA* for a kind of sci-fi paramilitary feedback loop. Here, too, science bounded forward at a dizzying, almost alarming rate—

---

* "Cut off a limb, and two more shall take its place" was HYDRA's pledge, a concise summary of guerrilla terrorism's chilling power.

even the flurry of good-guy gadgets like Life Model Decoys carried dis-concerting post-atomic associations of *that which humanity is not ready to harness*. A.I.M.—which consisted of shady industrialists outfitted like futuristic beekeepers—created the Super-Adaptoid and brandished a tal-isman known as the Cosmic Cube ("The ultimate weapon! The ultimate source of power! The only such artifact known to man—which can con-vert thought waves—into material action!"), which fell into the hands of the Red Skull, who'd just reemerged from the rubble of the *Führerbunker* after two decades. All you could pray for was to have the Orion Missile, or the Matter Transmitter, on your side.

Thor encountered a simultaneous crisis. The thunder god's own name finally replaced *Journey into Mystery* as the title of his comic, but—as if in ironic commemoration—the "Tales of Asgard" story tucked in the back of the latest issue featured a nightmare vision of Ragnarok, the end of the world. Ragnarok was presented in a sort of premonition-daydream sequence, but it was assuredly an outcome that could not be avoided, a fait accompli: "As chaos and carnage envelop the realm; as a fury akin to madness sweeps the very soul of Asgard; there are those who crumble beneath the strain—who join the ranks of the forces of evil. . . ." Fire and devastation unfolded over two issues, depopulated panels given over to fallen swords, steel-beam crosses, and smoking debris. The prophecy was staved off, but there was the nagging knowledge that this was only a temporary stall from "that which no force in all the universe can prevent." Galactus, the Cosmic Cube, and Ragnarok were all closing in on the skies, a conspiracy of doom. Armageddon was nigh.

It was at this eschatological juncture that Steve Ditko's last *Amazing Spider-Man* and "Doctor Strange" stories were finally published, months after Ditko's actual departure and thus carrying the import of a last will and testament. A conflict between Strange and his rival Dormammu, which had extended over an unprecedented seventeen issues, came to an apocalyptic climax of its own, as Dormammu held hostage a cosmic entity known as . . . *Eternity*. Once again, planets shook, stars screamed, and our hero narrowly avoided insanity. "No human mind can retain the things I have seen!" Strange proclaimed. "Already, the memories begin to fade. . . ." In the final panel, the Sorcerer Supreme turns his back and takes leave of the extradimensional battle site to return home, "his greatest battle won." With that, Ditko was gone from Marvel.

Carl Burgos and Joe Simon, now in their fifties, watched from the sidelines. As the initial twenty-eight-year terms of Marvel's initial copyrights on the Human Torch and Captain America approached expiration, creators Burgos and Simon consulted lawyers and prepared to wrest back ownership of the heroes upon which Marvel had built its comics empire.* While the paperwork was completed, they also saw another way to stick it to Goodman: they'd roll out pointedly competing comic books.

Burgos teamed up with Myron Fass, who'd drawn stories for Timely in the early 1950s and was now a publisher of sleazy magazines, in a gambit to snatch the Captain Marvel trademark. To Goodman's chagrin, the name Captain Marvel had never been his property—it had belonged to Fawcett in the 1940s and 1950s, until the settlement of a DC Comics suit that claimed that the caped and flying character of Captain Marvel infringed on its Superman. The Captain Marvel name had been abandoned along with the character, and now Fass pounced, knowing he'd get a reaction from Goodman. Burgos's new version of Captain Marvel was, like his old creation the Human Torch, a red-costumed android; if Marvel didn't get the message, Burgos also soon introduced a villain named Dr. Doom. The comic, launched in early 1966, bombed, but when an irritated Goodman offered six thousand dollars for the copyright in July, Fass refused.

Burgos was also at that time pursuing legal action against Marvel Comics over the Human Torch copyright. Then, one day in the summer of 1966, his daughter, Susan, watched as he destroyed every trace of his

* In 1966 Bill Everett, who hadn't worked for Marvel since the *Daredevil* #1 fiasco, was suddenly flush with work from Martin Goodman. He was first sated with a regular assignment on the Hulk (in *Tales to Astonish*); when Ditko departed Marvel, Everett was immediately offered work on Dr. Strange (in *Strange Tales*) and received a loan from Goodman that, according to Roy Thomas, "wasn't going to have to be paid back, so he wouldn't sue."

Marvel Comics career—which had to that point been hidden away from her. "I never saw his collection until the day he threw it all out. I just happened to be in the backyard this summer day and there was a whole pile of stuff in the yard. I took as many of the comics as I could carry back to my room, like they were some treasure. He came in and demanded that I give him my comics. . . . I got the impression that he either lost the case or something else had happened pertaining to it." Again Burgos withheld details from his daughter, but over the years she learned the source of his ire. "I grew up believing that he came up with this fabulous idea," she said, "and that Stan Lee took it from him."

In fact, Burgos's claims may have never made it to court; his dark ritual on that summer day may have instead been reaction to a new Marvel comic book. In early August, Lee and Kirby's *Fantastic Four Annual #4* featured Burgos's original Human Torch, battling the new teenage Human Torch and the rest of the Fantastic Four. Cover-dated October 1968, it appeared exactly twenty-eight years after *Marvel Comics #1*—in other words, exactly as the initial twenty-eight-year copyright was expiring. The original Torch had been revived just long enough to ensure their copyright claim—only to be killed again, pages later. "Well, let's face it," mused the Thing when Burgos's creation had been extinguished, "ya win a few . . .'n ya lose a few!" Lee had Johnny Storm, the last Human Torch standing, eulogizing his fallen predecessor this way: "He tried to defeat me . . . and yet, I can't find it in my heart to hate him!"

Burgos quietly registered some copyright claims in 1967 that went nowhere, and then disappeared from Marvel's radar entirely. In the early 1970s, artist Batton Lash tracked down Burgos and asked the veteran for advice. But Burgos had left comics behind for good, and advised Lash to stay away from that "terrible field" as well, citing his own disappointment over the Human Torch. "If I'd known how much trouble and heartbreak the Torch would bring me," he told the young artist, "I would never have created him."

Joe Simon, meanwhile, was about to pursue a copyright claim of his own, on Captain America. Captain America had been—along with Iron Man, Thor, Sub-Mariner, and the Hulk—one of five characters announced for the *Marvel Super Heroes* animated show.* By the spring of 1966, as the series began production, there was already a bonanza of licensing in place: paperbacks, LPs, model kits, costumes, buttons, pins, trading cards, board games, T-shirts and sweatshirts, toys, and stickers. "We've had movie offers for just about all our characters," Lee bragged. Simon would file suit against not only Goodman's Magazine Management, but also Krantz Films (distributor of the cartoon show) and Weston Merchandising (which had developed Captain Action, a figure that included Captain America paraphernalia).† Simon, a businessman as well as an artist, was a greater legal threat than Burgos. He'd kept extensive records—including the original sketches he'd done of Captain America in 1940.

As he had with the Human Torch, Goodman took measures to reestablish Marvel's ownership of Captain America. *Fantasy Masterpieces*, a double-sized title that had run reprints of 1950s Atlas stories, suddenly shifted gears and re-presented Golden Age Captain America. But the credits—"art and editorial by Joe Simon and Jack Kirby"—were removed.

Kirby protested, but he was in a tough spot. "Simon said he created Captain America," Goodman told him. "He wants the copyright and it looks like you're out." Goodman offered a deal: if Kirby would side with Marvel in the dispute, the company would pay him an amount to match any future settlement with Simon. On July 12, 1966, Kirby signed a deposition describing the creation of Captain America. "I felt that whatever I did for Timely belonged to Timely as was the practice in those days. When I left Timely, all of my work was left with them."

As Simon plotted his next legal move, he continued editing superhero books for Harvey Comics, best known for such little-kid fare as *Casper the Friendly Ghost* and *Richie Rich*. Happy to poach from Martin Goodman, he commissioned work from Marvel artists Dick Ayers and George

---

* The rights to the Fantastic Four had been otherwise secured. Spider-Man was originally going to be a part of *Marvel Super Heroes*, but apparently Marvel and Grantay-Lawrence decided to save him for bigger things—after storyboards were drawn up, he was replaced by the Sub-Mariner.

† The side-by-side pictures of Sgt. Fury and Captain America on the back of Captain Action's toy packaging were soon appropriated as anti-imperialist images in Jean-Luc Godard's 1967 film, *La Chinoise*.

Tuska; he also hired Wally Wood.* He recruited newer talent as well: at a Manhattan comic convention, he approached an artist with James Dean hair and a million-dollar smile and invited him to Long Island to help create characters. *I want to compete with Marvel,* Simon told the artist.

The artist's name was Jim Steranko, and he was the twenty-seven-year-old art director at a Shillington, Pennsylvania, ad agency. If there weren't a trail of newspaper clippings to confirm it, one would never believe what Steranko had packed into his early years. He was born into poverty, with a father who struggled to support his family by gathering bootleg coal, digging homemade mines, and taking serious risks in unsafe, rickety shafts. The young Steranko, obsessed with the danger and claustrophobia of his father's daily routine, dedicated himself to the art of escape. By the age of sixteen, he was putting on Houdini-like public performances, showing off to local police that he could escape from their jails. He also slipped out of straitjackets, leg irons, handcuffs, safes, and vaults.

Other performances were less thrilling to the local authorities: The teenaged Steranko began stealing an arsenal's worth of guns and a small parking lot's worth of motor vehicles. In February 1956, Steranko and a partner were arrested for the thefts, committed throughout eastern Pennsylvania, of twenty-five cars and two trucks. (He was careful to avoid criminal activity in his hometown. "None of the things we did were done in Reading, maybe one or two. I stole a submachine gun in Reading, but that was all.") They burglarized gas stations, but a sole, thwarted attempt at armed robbery—the victim sized up Steranko, realized he wouldn't shoot the gun, and refused to hand over any money—showed the limits of his transgressive inclinations. By the early 1960s, Steranko had moved on to playing rock-and-roll guitar (his band shared bills with Bill Haley and His Comets), card tricks (he was nationally ranked and published a book), and fire-eating, before he finally settled into advertising.

Through it all, Steranko found constant inspiration in comic books. But for once, it seemed like instant mastery of a craft was beyond his

---

* Wally Wood, reportedly, was still stinging from his Marvel experience. He told stories—somewhat unlikely stories—about Stan Lee sitting on a file cabinet and lording above freelancers while he threw their checks down to them.

grasp. He'd been turned away by Marvel in the summer of 1965, and now he regaled Simon with silly-named heroes like Spyman and Magicmaster. Steranko not only wrote the scripts and designed the characters; he also included elaborate diagrams that delineated the heroes' powers. But Simon told him that he didn't have the proper artistic skills to draw the stories. And so the prodigy went across town, to the very company that Simon had hired him to challenge.

When Steranko entered the Marvel offices in the summer of 1966, he'd just sold a pitch that very day for an animated series to Paramount Pictures, and had even more swagger than usual. He needed that swagger to get through all the proper channels: he didn't have an appointment. Flo Steinberg called back to Sol Brodsky, who in turn sent Roy Thomas out to the reception area for the formality of humoring yet another amateur comic-book artist. The expected brush-off never happened. Thomas, impressed with what he saw, sent Steranko into Lee's office. Lee was in his usual high-octane mode—as Steranko described it, "equal parts actor, editor, charmer, and showman." The samples, he said, were crude. But there was something he liked about them.

"What's that?" asked Steranko.

"Raw energy!" Lee practically shouted. He pointed to a rack of comics. "What would you like to do for us?" he said. "Pick one!"

Steranko walked out with an art assignment on "Nick Fury." After a few months of drawing over Kirby's layouts, Steranko was handed the reins—solely generating not just the art, but the scripts as well. For the first time since Wally Wood's *Daredevil* #10 fiasco, Lee allowed someone else to write and draw everything in a comic. Jack Kirby, unsatisfied with his own lack of writing credits, took notice.

Stan Lee's mind was elsewhere that summer. The *Marvel Super Heroes* cartoon was getting ready to air on dozens of television stations across the country, five nights a week, and so the show's producer, Robert Lawrence, put Lee up in a midtown penthouse apartment, where after hours he scribbled extensive notes in blue pencil: *We've got to let viewer know who Bucky IS!* . . . *Shapanka is a scientist—doesn't use slang!* . . . *The final frame is weak!* It was Lee's first taste of showbiz, and he wasn't going to let it slide.

When the show began airing, Lawrence accompanied Lee on a tour of college campuses. "The kids were unbelievable," Lawrence marveled. "I think we spent three days at Chapel Hill with them. They'd stay up all night drinking beers, speaking to Stan Lee." *Esquire*'s annual college issue featured the Marvel characters in a full-color, six-page spread, and reported that the company had already "sold 50,000 printed t-shirts and 30,000 sweat shirts, and it has run out of adult sizes of both." College student fans weighed in for the magazine, proving they were digging what Lee and Co. were laying down: "Marvel often stretches the pseudo-scientific imagination far into the phantasmagoria of other dimensions, problems of time and space, and even the semi-technological concept of creation. They are brilliantly illustrated, to a nearly hallucinogenic extent." Before long, Marvel Comics was selling ads for shaving cream and cars. Lee had even earned the respect of Goodman's magazine editors. "For Stan Lee," Mario Puzo inscribed in a copy of his latest novel, "Whose imagination I cannot hope to equal."

Even as he was tending to the animated show, visiting campuses, and scripting a big chunk of the comics line, Lee was also, with Sol Brodsky, spending a lot of his energy shifting writers and artists around—this was the biggest stable of talent they'd had since the 1950s. (A nice side effect of the competition from Tower, Harvey, and Archie superhero lines was that Lee convinced Goodman that Marvel needed to raise page rates to keep their creative edge.) Roy Thomas—goateed now, with a Russian hat, alligator shoes, and a Nehru jacket—offered more writer recommendations, helping to relieve some of Lee's burden. Thomas's high school pal Gary Friedrich scripted westerns and war titles, and bumped the quality level of *Sgt. Fury* above anything Lee had done on the title. It quickly became, ironically, the book with the most explicit criticism of foreign wars, at a time when Lee's characters were occasionally still spouting exclamations like "No one has the right to defy the wishes of his government! Not even Iron Man!"

Before long, Lee handed "Iron Man" over to another Thomas recommendation. Archie Goodwin, a bespectacled EC Comics fan, had graduated from cartooning school just in time for the collapsed comic-book economy of the late 1950s. He'd toiled in the art department of *Redbook* (where he'd rejected Andy Warhol's portfolio, and then lectured Warhol about tracing other people's work), and edited EC-like black-and-white horror publications for the infamously cheap and hot-tempered publisher Jim Warren. At Marvel, Goodwin scaled back the hawkishness of "Iron Man," moving Tony Stark further away from Cold War antagonism and into the spy/technology milieu that had come to define Captain America and Nick Fury.

Thomas's nose for talent helped enormously. But Lee remained the de facto art director, and maintaining the look of Marvel comics fell on his shoulders alone. Near the end of 1965, Lee had asked John Romita to feature Spider-Man in a two-part *Daredevil* story. Romita didn't realize it at the time, but it was an audition to replace Steve Ditko on *Amazing Spider-Man*. When Ditko's inevitable departure finally happened, the new team hit the ground running. Their very first issue together featured the shocking revelation that the Green Goblin's secret identity was Norman Osborn, the wealthy industrialist father of Peter Parker's classmate Harry Osborn. (Rumors circulated that Ditko's refusal to go along with this dramatic plot twist had been the final point of contention between Lee and Ditko.)

Romita had preferred working on *Daredevil*. But he was a team player, a consummate professional happily wearing a crisp white shirt and tie every time he stepped into the office, and anyway he figured the stint was temporary. "I couldn't believe that a guy would walk away from a successful book that was the second-highest seller at Marvel," Romita explained to Thomas years later. "I didn't know Ditko. I assumed he'd do what I would have done—he'd think about how he had given up a top character, and he'd be back. And I was sort of counting the days until I could get back on *Daredevil*." Romita was conscientious about making it a smooth transition, copying Ditko's style as best he could, even using a technical pen for the most faithful mimicry possible.

He failed at his Ditko impression. But Romita's experience with romance comics had advantages. Peter Parker's jaw strengthened, his hair moved into place, and he bulked up slightly. His next-door neighbor, Mary Jane

Watson—whom Lee and Ditko had been coyly hiding in shadows for a year and a half—finally showed her face, and she was a gorgeous, sassy, raven-haired party girl. Gwen Stacy got even prettier; she and Mary Jane began competing for Peter's attentions like they were go-go versions of Betty and Veronica. And everyone, even Flash Thompson, started smiling more. According to Romita, at first Lee admonished him for his glamorous-looking characters, for extinguishing Ditko's moodiness. But before long, Lee himself was asking for changes to soften Peter Parker: longer hair, less of a square, jeans, boots, miniskirted girls all around him. He began dropping copies of *Women's Wear Daily* on Romita's drawing table, instructing him to incorporate the latest fashions. Any temporary concerns he had must have been assuaged by the sales figures—*Spider-Man* was selling better than ever.

Daredevil now belonged to Atlas alumnus Gene Colan, an anxious blond movie buff whom Lee lured back from a soul-crushing job making educational filmstrips. Colan's moody chiaroscuro renderings gave the character a weight that hadn't existed with Wood or Romita, and, more important, finally differentiated him from Spider-Man. Pacing wasn't Colan's strong suit—he had a dangerous habit of drawing breathtaking large-panel scenes, only to realize that he needed to cram the second half of the story into the final few pages—but for Lee, the gain in dramatic range outweighed the logistical headaches. In *Tales of Suspense*, Colan even managed to lend emotional heft to Iron Man, subtly changing the angles of the metal helmet's eye and mouth openings into something resembling facial expressions.

Another Atlas veteran rejoining Marvel was John Buscema, who was gruff, fortyish, with a Robert Mitchum vibe. Like Colan and Romita, Buscema had thoroughly hated the Madison Avenue job he'd had in recent years. But he couldn't help expressing, to almost comic effect, his indifference toward superheroes. He was more concerned with the human form and open landscapes than with colored costumes and gadgetry. He wanted to channel the ancient and fantastic, and hated "goddamn automobiles and skyscrapers"—fixtures, of course, in Marvel Comics.

Roy Thomas, who collaborated with him on *The Avengers*, was so taken with Buscema's richly illustrative style that he tailored his scripts accordingly, resulting in a succession of mythological adventures for the Scarlet Witch, Quicksilver, Hawkeye, and Goliath.

Unfortunately, Colan's "Iron Man" assignment and Buscema's *Avengers* had once belonged to Don Heck, one of the core artists of the early superhero titles. Heck was slowly eased from both, and shifted over to the mediocre-selling *X-Men*. Work was work, and he didn't have strong feelings about which character he was drawing, but he could sense that something was changing. Heck, a longtime pro and illustrator of the prettiest women of anyone at Marvel, now sheepishly visited Jack Kirby at home and asked for drawing advice.* It was becoming clear that Marvel Comics could move ahead with or without any one individual.

Meanwhile, Jim Steranko enjoyed a luxury that Heck (and Kirby, and Ditko, and Wood, and everyone else at Marvel, for that matter) never did: he was already pulling down a lucrative full-time job outside of comics. Making comics essentially as a hobby meant that the financial compensation didn't loom as large. He had no family to support, no children to spend time with. The work, and his romantic notions of the artist's life, were everything. "I believe that happiness is nothing," he told an interviewer. "I don't think people were put here to be happy. I think if you decide to be an artist or a writer, you automatically accept the responsibility of being alone. However, after your 50 or 60 years are up you'll be able to look back and see this output that you've done that will endure long after you're gone, and will continue to fill the minds of millions of people."

So he threw himself into experimenting with the form—slowly, at first, and then relentlessly. He followed Kirby's lead with collage work, which he supplemented with the strobing and shimmying effects of cutting-edge Op Art. He approached his pages more like a designer than an illustrator, paying special attention to the functions of the panel grids

---

* Syd Shores, the onetime Captain America artist, was supposed to relieve Kirby on the title in 1967, after a brief period of inking over Kirby's pencils. But Lee was unsatisfied with Shores's Marvel Method attempts, and Kirby was once again put in the role of pep talker and mentor to his own peers.

and spatial shifts. Concentric circles, perspective-plane diagrams, and other geometric trickery conspired to make *Nick Fury* Marvel's most psychedelic comic since Ditko's *Doctor Strange*. Steranko reached back to Will Eisner's *Spirit* and Johnny Craig's EC horror comics for inspiration, and the futurist bent of the series allowed for high-tech toys on every page, rendered in the intensively elaborate Kirby style. But where Kirby had full-page drawings, Steranko had double-page spreads—and then quadruple-page spreads, for which you'd have to buy two copies and lay them together if you wanted to take in the full vista. There were nods to Salvador Dali, Eadweard Muybridge, Richard Avedon, and the films of Robert Siodmak and Michael Curtiz, and contemporary commercial artists like Richard M. Powers and Bob Peak. It was Positively Postmodernism, in the Merry Marvel Way.

The combination of knowing winks and dazzling, nearly mathematically perfect artwork betrayed a certain emotional distance, but Steranko's work never devolved into camp. Nor did it sell tremendously. To a dedicated readership of gearheads, pot smokers, and art students, "Nick Fury, Agent of S.H.I.E.L.D." was the apex of an art form. But despite a few token guest appearances from Captain America early on, Steranko's world existed mostly on the side, sealed away from everything else.

Increasingly, that was how Jack Kirby felt he existed, too—"a lonely sort of guy." No one would suspect this, of course. Every week he'd come into the office, enjoy a hero's welcome, and chat up the newer Bullpen employees—Herb Trimpe, Stu Schwartzberg, Linda Fite—who gushed with admiration. He told the *Merry Marvel Messenger* that he and that "rascal" Stan Lee liked to "share ideas, laughs, and stubby cigars." "Marvel's been very kind to me and I like the people," he told an audience at the 1966 New York comics convention. "I've been working there seven years and I've been very happy at it." But privately, he was growing irritated that Lee was spending so much time on the college circuit while he was spending seven days a week at the desk in the one-window basement of his home, which he'd taken to calling "the Dungeon." When new artists came to Marvel, they were handed a stack of Kirby's books or, better yet, a stack of Kirby's rough layouts over which to draw. He was, in effect, training others to keep him from becoming too valuable to the company. Kirby waited for Goodman to give him a piece of the earnings that his creations were generating. Lee threw up his hands and said that he couldn't make those decisions. Goodman stalled.

"In the minds and hearts of those of us who have come of age intellectually in the psychedelic sixties," William David Sherman and Leon Lewis rhapsodized in their 1967 survey *Landscape of Contemporary Cinema*, "SNCC supersedes the NAACP, *Ramparts* supersedes *The New Republic*, Sun Ra supersedes Duke Ellington, and all forms of expression from a comic book by Stan Lee and Jack Kirby to a performance by the Fugs become accessible as works of art." Lee and Kirby continued turning out breathtakingly imaginative work, expanding the scope of the Marvel Universe and resonating with the zeitgeist via a menu of token liberal signifiers and general trippiness. Shortly before *Fantastic Four #52* went into production, *The New York Times* ran an article about the Lowndes County Freedom Organization, a political party that had formed in Alabama under the leadership of Stokely Carmichael and the Student Non-Violent Coordinating Committee. The LCFO's logo, a black panther, was so striking that reports began calling the group the Black Panther party. When *Fantastic Four #52* hit the stands, the Coal Tiger—the African adventurer whom Lee and Kirby had kept in cold storage for months—had a new name.* Even with the delay, the Black Panther still managed to make history as the first black superhero to reach a wide audience.

As with so many other totems of the late 1960s counterculture, Marvel trafficked in mind-bending sci-fi grandiosity. Out of costume, the Black Panther was an African prince named T'Challa who led the fictional country of Wakanda, not a Dark Continent noble savage but a scientific

---

*There may have been some internal hand-wringing about the Black Panther. The first version of the cover had shown the Panther's black skin; the published version did not. Previews in other titles that month suggest Marvel couldn't decide how much of him to show—or how to characterize him. "Don't miss the mystery villain of the month!" read the ads, which blocked out the cover art. (Once Marvel committed to a policy of representing black characters, however, change came quickly. The cover of the following month's romance comic *Modeling with Millie* proudly introduced a black British model named Jill Jerold to its cast.)

genius who impressed even the Fantastic Four's Reed Richards. Forget gamma blasts and radioactive spiders; Marvel's creations now reflected a growing interest in the collision of ancient civilizations and futuristic technologies. "As a preliminary to understanding the present, one must be capable of projecting one's intelligence far into the past and far into the future," Jacques Bergier wrote in *The Morning of the Magicians*, a million-selling volume of pseudoscience that kicked off a 1960s fascination with the idea that aliens had visited our planet and bestowed advanced technology. Given Kirby's later dedication to exploring this idea, it's likely that he was the one most responsible for threading it through Marvel's adventures in the mid- and late 1960s. Thor arrived in the old-fashioned Eastern European country of Wundagore and met the High Evolutionary, a genetic scientist with a Faust complex who'd tried to create his own race (later, he'd clone life on a larger scale, fabricating an entire planet in the image of Earth). The Fantastic Four discovered an alien warrior race known as the Kree—who'd communed with the Incas in Peru, just like the ancient astronauts in *The Morning of the Magicians*—and confronted a golden Golem-like being named Him, artificially created by the mysterious enclave at the Citadel of Science. The Negative Zone kept opening up to reveal new psychedelic horrors, rendered by Kirby with rainbow prisms, hectagonal globes, and masses of black dots, sometimes accompanied by his increasingly experimental collage work. Every time a Marvel hero turned over a stone, it seemed, a new, energy-crackling mythology awaited.

But even as Kirby's Promethean concepts spun in all directions, he was, by the summer of 1967, all but finished creating new Marvel heroes. "I'm not going to give them another Silver Surfer" was the oft-repeated reasoning he gave to friends. When Goodman decided to challenge Myron Fass's Captain Marvel trademark by launching a character with that name, Gene Colan drew it—but the origin story of this new Captain Marvel drew on the Kree mythology Kirby had established in *Fantastic Four*. Marvel quickly crashed this Captain Marvel story into the next issue of *Fantasy Masterpieces*, along with the usual Captain America, Human Torch, and Sub-Mariner reprints. For good measure, Goodman renamed the comic *Marvel Super Heroes*, and just in case anyone missed the point, it was all there on the cover: *Marvel Super Heroes* featuring Captain Marvel, published by the Marvel Comics Group. After that, the title began spotlighting other characters for potential stardom and spin-off titles. But Kirby was not involved, even when his characters, such as Doctor Doom and Medusa, were involved. The work fell to Colan, or George Tuska, or Larry Lieber, or bullpenner Herb Trimpe, who was outgrowing a staff job of making corrections and starting to make his own mark as an artist.

The one new title that Kirby did contribute to was *Not Brand Echh*, in which Marvel, showing just how hip it was, satirized its very own characters. Five of the first seven issues of *Not Brand Echh* provided a rare showcase for Kirby's surprisingly daffy sense of humor. By the end of 1967, though, he'd done the last of his wacky cartooning for Marvel. Maybe things just didn't seem so funny anymore.

No one could have known it at the time, but the first flush of the Marvel Age was coming to an end. That winter, leaving a Christmas party, Stan Lee jumped up and clicked his heels in the air—and then fell, breaking his ankle. He spent the last weeks of 1967 in bed.

The popularity of the *Batman* TV show had faded, and with it the idea that publishers could cash in on a comic-book craze. Harvey's Thriller line and Archie's Mighty Comics both fell by the wayside. The American Comics Group folded entirely. Most of Charlton's best talent followed editor Dick Giordano when he was hired at DC Comics. Tower Comics started to crumble, plagued by poor distribution that was, according to Wally Wood, a result of Independent News' bullying tactics toward wholesalers. (Wood would commemorate the company's demise with a fanzine cover that depicted Marvel's Daredevil throwing Tower Comics' Dynamo off the side of a building.) Myron Fass, who'd so proudly refused a $6,000 settlement the previous year, now agreed to drop the *Captain Marvel* suit for $4,500. It was still a good deal. "He was selling lousy, anyway," Fass said.

DC Comics was going through its own changes. In the summer of 1967, president Jack Liebowitz had begun negotiations to merge with the

Kinney National conglomerate, a business-gobbling behemoth that was eyeing not just *Superman* and *Batman*, but also DC's lucrative Independent News, which distributed *Playboy* and *Family Circle*. By the time the deal was completed, nearly a year later, the editorial staff at DC had been thoroughly upended. While DC's forty-eight titles had a monthly circulation of 7 million, Marvel, limited to a third of the output, was pulling in 6 million. DC set out on a mission to compete with Marvel for the hip-youth dollar. Work started drying up for older longtime writers and artists, a process that accelerated when a clutch of veteran writers started piping up about profit-sharing and health benefits. (Ironically, one of those outgoing writers had written a seven-page memo excoriating DC's antiquated, by-the-numbers comics, and warning that Stan Lee would "eventually outstrip us.") Carmine Infantino, the artist who'd been coaching DC on how to liven up its covers, became editorial director and replaced most of the editors under him. Now many of their comics were being written by Denny O'Neil and Steve Skeates—both of whom had been fired by Stan Lee. Skeates sneaked drug references into *Aquaman*, and briefly collaborated on *Hawk & Dove* with Steve Ditko (now also at DC) until their political beliefs proved irreconcilable.

The most notable new arrival at DC was Neal Adams, whose painstaking renderings were the closest thing to photo-realism that comics had ever seen. Like Jim Steranko (virtually the only other comic artist under the age of forty), Adams was a confident young man who utilized his background in commercial illustration to create innovative page layouts. Adams's focus on hyperarticulated anatomy and facial expressions— furrowed brows, curled lips in mid-sentence expressions, foreshortened, pointing fingers—was the flip side to Steranko's streamlined design.* Adams was the most visible break from tradition at DC, and his influence— and Infantino's mandates—soon changed the look of just about everyone's art at the company. The hard-core fans—the letters-column regulars, the fanzine writers, the burgeoning conventioneers—were ecstatic.

Although this hubbub did not have much impact on DC's bottom line,

---

* In one issue of *Strange Adventures*, Adams tweaked his peer in a panel of outrageous wavy lines that spelled out, when the comic was tilted, *Hey! A Jim Steranko effect!*

it didn't go unnoticed at Marvel, where more time was now spent meeting about cover designs. DC was still the biggest fish, and Marvel was the fastest-growing fish, but the pond was running out of water, and every splash counted. Even as Marvel's sales gained on DC's, even as it continued turning a profit, its rate of increase was slowing.

Martin Goodman kept a close watch on every trend. He had seen bubbles burst before. As ABC prepared the premiere of Saturday morning cartoons of *Spider-Man* and *Fantastic Four*, Goodman took out ads in news dealer trades trumpeting Marvel's success with don't-miss-out exclamations:

THE HOUSE OF MARVEL CONTINUES TO GROW . . .

. . . And we do mean GROW! Like, from 22,530,000 copies sold in 1963—to 27,709,000 in 1964—to 34,000,000 in 1965—to a mind-staggering 40,500,000 in 1965! But that's just for OPENERS! We're on our way to over 50,000,000 circulation!

Goodman's magazines, single copy sales: 25 million

+

Marvel Comics, single copy sales: 40 million

=

65 million single copy sales every year

**OVER 175,000 GOODMAN PUBLICATIONS
SOLD EVERY DAY**

Independent News—under Kinney ownership, and with a new perspective on exploiting profits—finally allowed Marvel to begin to expand its line. After years being held hostage to the distributor's limitations, the superheroes still ghettoized as ten-page features in *Tales of Suspense*, *Strange Tales*, and *Tales to Astonish* would finally get their own full-length titles. *Captain America*; *Iron Man*; *Doctor Strange*; *Nick Fury, Agent of S.H.I.E.L.D.*; *The Incredible Hulk*; and *Prince Namor, The Sub-Mariner* began rolling onto racks in the early months of 1968, joined by *Captain Marvel* and even a new, conspicuously derivative war title, *Captain Savage and His Leatherneck Raiders. The Silver Surfer, Ka-Zar,* and *Dr. Doom,* it was announced, would soon follow.

Of these titles, Lee would script only *Captain America* and *The Silver Surfer.* Roy Thomas and Gary Friedrich had taken on more responsibilities as associate editor and assistant editor, respectively, and while Lee was still a very hands-on boss for three days a week, the roles of showman and emissary increasingly dominated his time. He'd taken to writing half-serious editorials on the "Bullpen Bulletins" page, for something he called "Stan's Soapbox." Aside from a handful of generalized denunciations of bigotry, it mostly served as one more platform to hype the goods. "I guess I treated the whole thing like a big advertising campaign," he said later. "I wanted to give the product—which was Marvel Comics, and myself in a way—a certain personality." He grew a beard to complement the toupee he'd starting wearing. He posed for a snapshot in his office; eight-by-ten glossies—"Excelsior!" he signed at the bottom—were printed and sold from the classified ads in the backs of the comics. "Collect an entire series of Bullpen blow-ups," the ad shouted. "Watch for our next nutty announcement!"

No further Bullpen photos were published.

Lee started work on *The Silver Surfer.* He and Kirby had already attempted one solo adventure for the character, intended at first as its own comic but shuffled into a *Fantastic Four* annual. They'd disagreed about the direction of the character. Now, instead of hiring Jack Kirby—who'd created the Surfer on his own—Lee went to John Buscema, and continued to push the character away from the original concept of Spock-like alien coldness. Pining for the spaceways but grounded on our planet by Galactus, the Surfer was forever hurling himself in vain against the earth's atmosphere, Sisyphus recast as a fallen angel. So he became a hyperempathetic wanderer, encountering human foibles and spouting homilies with puppy-dog eyes. (Like the X-Men and Spider-Man, he was misunderstood and feared by the citizenry; he just got tearier about it.) Buscema's imagery was grand and imposing, with monumental panels that ran a quarter or a third of each page, but there was a lachrymose drudgery to the Surfer's constant shoulder-hunching re-creations of *Le Penseur.*

Lee didn't know it, but Kirby, anticipating involvement in the *Silver Surfer* series, had worked out a very different origin story of his own for the character, which he'd even started drawing. Frustrated, Kirby put the pages aside, and wondered what his career options were. Jack Schiff, the DC editor who'd been the reason for Kirby's departure (and continued absence) from Marvel's chief competitor, was no longer around. DC's new editorial director, Carmine Infantino, who had known Kirby for years, got in touch. Maybe they could work something out. Or maybe, Kirby thought, he could finally get Goodman to improve the terms of his employment at Marvel.

Either way, he didn't want to end up like the sixty-three-year-old proofreader working quietly at the corner desk at the Marvel offices, thrown a job because Lee couldn't bear to see him so down on his luck, spat out by the industry he'd helped to build. Although Jerry Siegel didn't bring it up with people, a swirl of whispers followed as he made his way in and out of the office: *That guy co-created Superman. DC Comics won't even let him in their offices anymore.* Kirby refused to meet such a fate.

In June 1968, Martin Goodman's lawyer was approached by a hyperfocused, five-foot-eight, cigar-chomping lawyer named Martin Ackerman, who ran a Manhasset, Long Island–based concern called the Perfect Film & Chemical Corporation. Ackerman was a minor-league version of the new moguls that were beginning to gobble businesses in the 1960s, men like Gulf + Western's Charlie Bluhdorn, ITT's Harold Geneen, and Kinney National's Steve Ross. But even a minor-league conglomerate was formidable: Perfect Film was itself a snowballing amalgam of photofinishing stores, pharmacies, and other smaller companies. Ackerman's specialty was to buy properties, dismantle them, absorb what he liked, and sell off the rest. (*The Gallagher Report*, noting that he'd once been a major shareholder in a chain of Kansas cemeteries, nicknamed him "Marty the Mortician.") In April, when Curtis Publishing was floundering, Perfect had swooped in with a $5 million loan—with the understanding that Ackerman would become Curtis's president. "Good evening," he'd addressed the Curtis staff in his first meeting with them, "I'm Marty Ackerman. I am 36 years old and I am very rich." As president, he spun off the publishing company's distribution arm, Curtis Circulation, and annexed it to Perfect Film. Of course, there was no better way to maximize a magazine distributor's profits than to own some more publications to go with it, and that's where Goodman's Magazine Management came in. If comic books were part of the deal, well, that was fine, too.

Martin Goodman was conflicted about selling the company, according to his son Iden. "It was a difficult thing for my dad to do. I think he felt, on one hand, extremely proud that he'd created this thing that could bring him so much money. And really pleased that he felt he could provide for a couple of generations of Goodmans through the sale of it. The business and golf and his family—that was really his life. He'd built this thing that was paying a lot of bills for a lot of people." Once Goodman made up his mind, though, the sale happened quickly. He wanted everything in cash. Ackerman came back with an offer for just under $15 million—roughly the amount that the company pulled in annually in sales—and threw in some Perfect Film bonds. Goodman signed a contract to remain on board as Marvel's publisher. His younger son, Chip, signed a contract as editorial director, with the idea that he'd eventually replace his retiring father as publisher. *One thing, though*, Ackerman said—*we need to know that Stan Lee, the public face of Marvel Comics, will stay, too.* So Goodman drew up a five-year contract for his star editor, with a provision for a raise. According to a member of Goodman's legal team, Lee was disappointed. "All the employees, Stan Lee included, didn't understand why they didn't get a significant proportion of the sales. Martin very quickly disabused them of that notion. I was shocked—Martin had taken all the risk publishing, they had taken none of the risk, and here they thought they should profit from the sale." But what could Lee do about it? He signed in July. The next night, after dinner at the Goodman home, Goodman put his arm around his wife's cousin. "Stan," he said, "I'll see to it that you and Joanie will never have to want for anything as long as you live."

"We're going to make a fortune in publishing," Ackerman predicted. He spent $1.5 million on a corporate jet, and moved his office into a fancy

Park Avenue spread that he termed "the Town House," where he did business behind a polished antique desk. An oil painting of Ackerman clutching the *Wall Street Journal* hung in the foyer. Across town, though, in the cramped spaces of Marvel's offices, where smudged pages were tacked up over yellow-painted walls, the divides between labor and management seemed greater than ever. Flo Steinberg had quit in the spring, when the Goodmans refused to raise her hourly wage. "They didn't believe in giving raises to people in certain jobs," she said, "because they could be so easily replaced." In May, instead of a contract, or residuals, Jack Kirby had received a loan from Magazine Management, with a 6 percent interest rate. When Roy Thomas added a day to a vacation to elope with his girlfriend, he returned to a lecture from Lee and Brodsky and the news that they'd removed him from "Doctor Strange" and hired Archie Goodwin to replace him.

The strain between Marvel's freewheeling image and its business reality showed in other ways. After painstakingly cultivating a collegiate, even intellectual, audience, Lee was now faced with the uncomfortable widening of the generation gap. His beard and Sol Brodsky's new sideburns weren't enough to mask it. The phone calls from drug-addled Doctor Strange fans had given way to weirder visits, like the appearance at 635 Madison Avenue of two members of the Process Church. As usual, Lee was gracious, and if he had any discomfort when he figured out his guests praised both Jesus Christ and Satan, he masked it well. "He was predictably thrilled by our garb," the Process Church's Timothy Wylie remembered, "and, if I remember rightly, listened intently to our spiel about the reconciliation of opposites. He was both intelligent and funny and kindly agreed for us to use some Marvel material in one of our magazine cartoon pastiches."

Meanwhile, the letters coming in were almost evenly split between support for and opposition to the Vietnam War. It was fiscally advisable for Marvel to hedge, but there was strong criticism when the stories avoided social issues entirely. Stan Lee's middle-of-the-road liberalism was, in its own way, unmovable. He'd happily preach tolerance, but he was not going to get caught taking an unpopular stance. "I don't think we'll be sending him to Vietnam," Lee told a radio interviewer, when asked about plans for Captain America. "We treat these characters sort of tongue-in-cheek and we get a lot of laughs out of them, we have a lot of fun with them. I don't know if it's in good taste to take something as serious as the situation in Vietnam and put a character like Captain America . . . we would have to start treating him differently and taking the whole thing more seriously, which we're not prepared to do."* When makereadies of the first issue of *Not Brand Echh* landed on his desk, he noticed a panel in which a character wore a button that read, "All the Way With LBJ!"—and showed a mushroom cloud. He yelled for Thomas to come into his office, pointed at the illustration, and accused him of sneaking in propaganda at the last minute. But it was on the black-and-white proofs, Thomas said—it was already there when you saw them. Lee insisted it had not been. If you're accusing me of lying, Thomas said, *I quit*. He stormed out.

Lee called him back in, shut the door, and launched into a quiet apology, explaining that the downbeat portrayal of combat in Timely's 1950s war comics, though hardly radical in their politics, had resulted in a Timely ban at the PXs on army bases, a notable source of revenue for the company. Lee had flashed back to the decade before, the decade of Frederic Wertham, of the congressional testimonies, of the layoffs that he'd administered in 1957. Those lean, cruel days all blurred together for Stan Lee, and he didn't want them coming back. For years he'd been a master of the middle ground, crafting stories that were so ambiguous in their political subtext that Marvel was embraced by both the far left and the far right. An editorial in the *New Guard*, the journal of the conservative Young Americans for Freedom, praised Marvel for "the fact that the heroes run to being such capitalistic types as arms manufacturers (Tony Stark, whose alter ego is Iron Man), while the villains are often Communists (and plainly labeled as such, in less than complimentary terms)." Roy Thomas responded to the *New Guard* in evenhanded terms

---

* The question about Captain America in Vietnam had actually been posed to Kirby, during a March 3, 1967, joint interview with Mike Hodel on New York radio station WBAI. "That's Stan Lee's department, and he can answer that," Kirby deferred. "The editor always has the last word on that."

worthy of his mentor, complimenting the article but stressing that the communist villains had started to fade: "We've preferred lately to rely on a more subtle and symbolic method of getting across any potential 'message' that might be read into the books, letting our readers draw their own conclusions."*

But 1968 changed everything. In a span of six months, the fallout from the Tet Offensive, the assassinations of Robert Kennedy and Martin Luther King, and a nationwide rash of protests and riots made it virtually impossible for hip publications to remain uncommitted. The vaguely Judeo-Christian humanitarian sermons of the Silver Surfer weren't doing the trick. After an even more breathless than usual hype campaign, and an impressive-selling, double-sized, double-priced first issue—Marvel even planted a *New York Times* mention that credited the title with a company-wide upturn—sales steadily dropped. Lee had a crisis of faith, unsure what direction to take.†

A few weeks after Columbia University student protesters took over Hamilton Hall, Lee appeared on *The Dick Cavett Show* and rushed to qualify the depiction of longhairs in a recent issue of *Thor*: "We had one sequence where he meets some hippies on the street. And this was done a few months ago, quite a while ago, when hippiedom was perhaps more of a problem than it is today. But we were concerned about all the young people dropping out, and we had him deliver a little lecture in his own ridiculous way of speaking, mentioning that it is far better to plunge in than to drop out. If there are problems, the way to solve them isn't by ignoring them. And at the time the little page was written, it was a good little sermon. Today, fortunately, I don't think it is as necessary. Youth

---

*The author of the *New Guard* article, twenty-two-year-old David Nolan, would go on to cofound the Libertarian Party.

† Lee's panic was contagious. John Buscema decided to break from the Kirby style for *Silver Surfer #4*, and swelled with pride when he turned in the pages. "People were congratulating me on this particular issue. Stan tore the book to pieces! He started with the first page: 'Well, okay, not bad.' On and on and on. Every second page he ripped to shreds. 'This is not good, this should be done this way . . .' I walked out of that damn office of his; I didn't know which way was up or down." Demoralized, Buscema wandered into John Romita's office and asked, "John, how the hell do you do comics?"

today seem to be so much more activist, which I think is a very healthy thing. This business of dropping out has seemed to have gone by the boards for the most part."

During a convention panel Q&A, a fan confronted Lee about Marvel's waffling on social issues. "Our thinking," Lee responded, "is that the pages of our comics magazines may not be the right place for getting too heavy handed with social messages of any sort. We may be wrong. Maybe we should come out more forcibly and maybe we will." Shortly afterward, Marvel finally became more explicit in its incorporation of specific current events, even as the thrust of its commentary remained vague. It wasn't an entirely comfortable mix. "Crisis on Campus!" screamed the cover of *Amazing Spider-Man* #68. Inside, Empire State University student Peter Parker wrestled, almost schizophrenically, with the concept of civil disobedience. As at Columbia, there was a conflict about the use of college-owned real estate. At first Parker is cautiously sympathetic with the plans of revolt he overhears: "Sounds like trouble brewing! Josh is spokesman for a lot of angry cats. . . . And I guess they've got a right to be. . . . Wish I had time to get more involved in this thing!" But pages later, he snaps at his peers, just like he had in the Ditko days: "Anyone can paint a sign, mister! That doesn't make you right!" Then, in a strange collision of headlines and superheroes, Spider-Man's enemy, the Kingpin, furiously destroys college property—and frames the students, who are carted away by police in the final panels. "They'll all have a chance to cool off!" Spider-Man chirps as he swings off. The disconnect between Romita's downbeat pictures and the shoehorned optimism of Lee's words suggested that Marvel might have vacillated on what, if any, stance to take, that there was some second-guessing between the time the pages were drawn and dialogued. As Lee worked on the next two issues, the violent confrontations in Chicago at the Democratic National Convention further changed the national mood. The three-issue story arc concluded with a can't-we-all-just-get-along rap session in which the contrite protesters learn that the ESU dean had been fighting the school's trustees behind the scenes, on their behalf, the whole while. For his part, the dean admits, "I thought students should be seen and not heard."

To present one's progressive bona fides, it was perhaps easier to simply populate the comics with black characters, usually non-super-powered civilians. To its credit, Marvel had been at the vanguard of such casual representation for a couple years now. (As early as 1963, Lee and Kirby had placed a black soldier, Gabe Jones, in Sgt. Fury's team of Howling Commandoes, and protested when the printers tried to color him as a Caucasian.) Two months after the Black Panther debuted in 1966, black biophysicist Bill Foster started popping up in *The Avengers*; a year later, black newspaper editor Joe Robertson joined the *Daily Bugle* staff in *Amazing Spider-Man*. Most notably, the profile of the Black Panther (his name now gaining associations Lee and Kirby could never have guessed) had risen when he joined the cast of *The Avengers* in early 1968. Now the black population of the Marvel Universe started to expand. There was admittedly a clumsiness to some of the renderings—the window-washer-turned-villain Hobie Brown, the militancy-resisting Vietnam vet Billy Carver, and the martyred physicist Al B. Harper, taken all at once, provide a portrait of white-liberal cluelessness—but still there was the sense that Stan Lee was seizing an opportunity rather than just exploiting a trend.

Of course, Lee was also happy to play to an audience. When the *East Village Other* ran an article bemoaning the lack of black characters in both DC and Marvel publications, Lee had an assistant editor write a letter pointing out the scant examples, in a delicate mix of backpedaling and time-buying:

> You implied that the Panther was a token Negro. When we became aware of the lack of Negroes in our magazines, and decided to introduce them in our stories, don't you think it would have looked rather foolish to suddenly have fifteen colored personalities appear and barnstorm through the books? As it is, we have T'Challa (the Panther), Joe Robertson and his son, Willie Lincoln, Sam Wilson (The Falcon), Gabe Jones, Dr. Noah Black (Centurius), and even a super-villain—The Man-Ape. In short, we think that we have approached a decent start with these characters.

Marvel stood on shaky ground: Willie Lincoln was a blind Vietnam vet, Centurius was a villain who'd turned himself into "protoplasmic slime" while trying to make himself a "superior being," and . . . Man-Ape? And no character named the Falcon had, in fact, yet appeared. Lee huddled with Gene Colan, who based the Falcon's look on college football star O. J. Simpson; they quickly stuck him in the pages of *Captain America*. Three months after the *Other* article appeared, the first African-American superhero appeared in a major comic book. The Falcon maintained a rooftop pigeon coop in Harlem, seemingly unemployed, and had no super powers. It was hardly the stuff of revolution—"sort of a Sidney Poitier in supergarb," in the words of one academic observer—but it was a start.

Another way to maintain credibility was by employing whatever artists were exciting fandom. Neal Adams heard from Jim Steranko that Marvel was giving its artists free rein, and arranged a meeting with Stan Lee. "You can do any title you want," Lee told him, just like he'd told Steranko two years earlier. Adams picked *X-Men*, figuring he would be completely left alone to overhaul the company's lowest-selling title as he saw fit. Sure, sure, he was told—just work it out with the title's writer, Roy Thomas.

While Lee was attempting to navigate the social and aesthetic trends of the late 1960s, Thomas was closely following the template of his boss's work, fleshing out the narrative tapestries, building on and sometimes improving on what had come before him. Still in his twenties, he had not just Lee's love for the classics, but also a feel for the cultural touchstones of the younger generation; he peppered his stories with references to everything from Aeschylus to Wonder Wart Hog. Instead of creating new characters, Thomas filled in the backstories of what already existed. While working on *The Avengers*, Lee asked Thomas to add a new member. Thomas wanted to resurrect the Timely character the Vision, unused since Kirby had drawn it in the early 1940s. When Lee insisted that the character had to be an android, Thomas simply sent John Buscema an old picture of the Vision and suggested they appropriate the name and elements of the costume, and describe him as an android. Furthermore, this new Vision would contain circuits that possessed the "brain patterns" of

Lee and Kirby's Wonder Man, who'd died in *Avengers #9*. Thus Thomas was able to efficiently recycle two earlier castoffs into a popular "new" member of the Avengers.

Part of this secondhand tendency was just Thomas's sentimental inclination toward the heroes of his youth, and part of it was an awareness of the way the comic business worked, especially after the problems Siegel and Shuster—and Simon and Burgos and Ditko—had with ownership. He knew Marvel would own whatever character he generated. "I started thinking about how someday they might make a movie or TV show out of one of these characters and how I'd hate the hell out of it if I didn't get money or credit out of it." Instead, what Thomas offered was a more straight-faced take on Lee's characters. The heroes of *The Avengers*, for instance, had begun moving further into adult relationships, although sometimes in odd ways. Henry Pym, who'd already donned costumes as both Ant-Man and Giant-Man, now changed his identity to Yellowjacket after a lab accident caused his id to take over; only through this subconscious transformation was he able to trade his workaholic ways for a long-promised marriage to the Wasp. (Thomas may have invested some of his own grown-up dilemmas into the proceedings; he finished writing the story on his honeymoon.)

The X-Men issues that Adams and Thomas produced, then, weren't just sleek—they were serious, with dark brooding that replaced Lee and Kirby's grand philosophizing. There was domestic tension between Cyclops and Marvel Girl, and a love triangle between Cyclops's brother Havok, the beautiful, green-haired Polaris, and Iceman. Nearly every face that Adams drew looked to be on the verge of tears or paroxysms, and Thomas's dialogue mined the drama of adults lecturing and shouting at one another.

Adams's unconventional page layouts and kineticized fight sequences— with action overflowing between panels—kept *The X-Men* from falling into gloomy melodrama; even the conversational longueurs were spiced with elegantly *contrapposto* figures and odd angles. When Stan Lee expressed concern about the ability of readers to decipher a story from the rampant experimentation, Thomas assured him that the final product would make sense. But after Martin Goodman, still okaying the cover of every Marvel publication, saw the front of Adams's first issue, in which the defeated heroes were bound to the *X-Men* logo, he demanded that the cover be redone—and Adams quickly realized the limits of his freedom.

One of the first to witness the reaction to the team of Adams and Thomas was a political theory major at Bard College named Chris Claremont, who was interning at Marvel. "I was there when Neal and Roy's run on *X-Men* started. I thought it was wonderful, but I had to deal with the mail, a lot of which was from outraged fans of Don Heck." The raves followed in time, but like Nick Fury, *The X-Men* was unable to attract more than a cult following. The series was canceled, and Adams was back at DC within a year.

When Marvel's distribution contract with Independent News expired, the Perfect Film & Chemical–owned Curtis Circulation took over and gave Marvel the freedom, for the first time since 1958, to publish as many titles as it liked. The only problem was that, ironically, the market would no longer bear aggressive expansion.

Martin Goodman, confronted by flat comic sales, started talking about how to cut expenses. He didn't want to lose rack space, but all these new stories were costing money. So he canceled *Doctor Strange* and had the Bullpen prepare reprints of westerns like *Ringo Kid*, and children's comics like *Homer the Happy Ghost* and *Peter the Little Pest*. Stan Lee started making preparations for layoffs, wondering aloud to Roy Thomas if he should fire some of his best artists—among them Buscema, the second-highest-paid after Kirby, and John Severin—because they'd stand the best chance of landing on their feet. Jim Steranko was told that he couldn't do a western-themed comic because his page rate was too high to make it cost-effective. Although Goodman ultimately refrained from calling for payroll cuts, he reduced the number of pages of story in each issue from twenty to nineteen—not a lot, but a noticeable difference to a freelancer depending on a steady check.

Goodman kept handing down decrees. There was a ban on the rockets, ray guns, and robots of classic science fiction. The stories had to cease continuing from one issue to the next, lest new readers become confused by intricate story lines. "You lose the very young kids who just can't follow the whole damn thing," Goodman complained. "I read some stories sometimes and I can't even understand them." No more cosmic sagas, no more cliffhangers. For the last year or two, Lee had conveyed to his writers that Marvel's stories should have only "the illusion of change," that the characters should never evolve too much, lest their portrayals conflict with what licensees had planned for other media. With the ban on multi-issue epics, that illusion would be even harder to maintain, as the final page of each "adventure" saw a return to the status quo, carefully reset for the following month's tale.

While Goodman held back on allowing new directions, Thomas continued holding back on delivering new creations. He seemed almost gleeful in his reappropriations, his oeuvre fast becoming a metatextual commentary on ownership and copyright. From Fawcett's old Captain Marvel character, he borrowed the teen-who-switches-places-with-a-hero shtick (Billy Batson uttered "Shazam!") and used it in Marvel's own *Captain Marvel* (the Hulk's old sidekick Rick Jones clanged together metal wristbands). The very same month, in *The Avengers*, he reimagined Superman, Batman, the Green Lantern, and Flash as "The Squadron Sinister" (Hyperion, Nighthawk, Dr. Spectrum, and the Whizzer). What was intellectual property in the face of good old-fashioned entertainment?

The realities of business were shaping everything about Marvel Comics. The *Spider-Man* and *Fantastic Four* cartoons, airing as the *Batman* craze was sputtering to an end, had been only mild successes.* Looking to squeeze residuals from the company's holdings, Chip Goodman deactivated the Merry Marvel Marching Society, the fan club that had excited the most dedicated segment of the audience, and sold the licensing of Marvel merchandise for ten thousand dollars to a mail-order businessman in California named Don Wallace. Wallace called his enterprise Marvelmania, and although he advertised in the backs of the comics, he operated independently of the publisher. From a post office box in Culver

---

* "Everything we felt made Marvel Marvel were the things that they felt made the stories not really suitable for the very immature television audiences," Lee said in 1968. "We just moved away from it, said, 'You've got the show; put it out any way you want,' so they've been writing their own stories, which I don't watch."

City, Marvelmania rolled out a line of posters, buttons, stickers, stationery, and art portfolios. The vast majority of these images were drawn by Jack Kirby. He wasn't paid for them.

Still, Kirby remained a team player. When Jim Steranko "killed" Captain America for a cliffhanger, and then missed the deadline for the following issue, Lee called Kirby in a panic. He needed a whole comic produced over the weekend. "You want me to bring him back to life?" Kirby asked. "No, keep him dead!" Lee said. Kirby complied, and turned in *Captain America* #112, minus its title hero, that Monday.

In the beginning of 1969, Kirby relocated his family, and his drawing board, to Irvine, California. His youngest daughter had asthma, and the warm air was a big reason for the move. But Kirby was also happy to put more distance between himself and his employer. He had no more luck negotiating with Marvel now that Perfect Film owned it and so, his financial requests ignored by Marvel, he tried to find other ways to supplement his income. When he'd finish a particularly impressive page, he'd have Roz set it aside to sell, and dash off a substitute page to send to Marvel. He began drawing images for use by Marvelmania, which was already reproducing his work from original art provided by Marvel. According to Mark Evanier, who worked as an assistant at Marvelmania, Wallace would use Kirby's original art as payment to people who helped in the offices. Evanier repossessed as many pages as he could and returned them to Kirby.

Meanwhile, Kirby waited to start work on an Inhumans comic. He'd begun drawing their solo adventures two years earlier, only to see them cut into ten-page featurettes and shunted into the back of *Thor*. Now there was talk once again of giving them their own title. Stan Lee teased it in nearly every edition of his "Bullpen Bulletins," and then kept explaining that it would be just a little bit longer. While Goodman kept delaying the green light on *The Inhumans*, Kirby kept throwing drawings of new characters into a pile by his desk. He'd been doing this for months now: variations on Captain America and Thor and other Asgardians, as well as brand-new heroes. These were the next Silver Surfers, not to be given away so lightly. When Carmine Infantino came to visit in April, Jack and Roz invited him over for a Passover dinner, after which Jack showed him the drawings and floated the idea of bringing the characters to DC in exchange for a three-year contract. Infantino liked the sound of that.

Infantino had trouble convincing DC to go along with the plan, however. A decade after the *Sky Masters* fiasco, Jack Schiff's friends still held a grudge. Infantino would have to keep working on them.

Kirby was getting increasingly restless with his new creations, eager to exert more power over these new stories than he did working with Stan Lee. He addressed a group of convention attendees about his vision for the future of comics. "You fellas think of comics in terms of comic books, but you're wrong. I think you fellas should think of comics in terms of drugs, in terms of war, in terms of journalism, in terms of selling, in terms of business. And if you have a viewpoint on drugs, or if you have a viewpoint on war, or if you have a viewpoint on the economy, I think you can tell it more effectively in comics than you can in words. I think nobody is doing it. Comics is journalism. But now it's restricted to soap opera."

Back in New York, Stan Lee was feeling restless, too. "I can't understand people who read comics! I wouldn't read them if I had the time and wasn't in the business," he told the French film director Alain Resnais over dinner and cocktails one night. He complained about how much of his salary went to taxes, and, worse, the fact that he didn't own any of his creations. "Everything I've written, nothing belongs to me." The five-year contract he'd signed the previous summer was easily broken, though, and with Goodman gone, he didn't have a sense of familial loyalty to keep him there.

"Now I figure, for the first time, at my age, it's time I started thinking of other things," he confided. "I've been thinking of trying to write a play, or—I know some producers in this country—trying to do a movie scenario. I was even thinking of writing some poems, like Rod McKuen and people like that, with some philosophy and some satire in them. The type of thing I put in the comics, like the Silver Surfer, you know, or Spider-Man. I think my name may be well-known enough that maybe these poems would sell. The only problem is, as long as I'm here I don't have the time to write them. And if I leave I don't get the income, which I need to keep living! So I've got to figure out how to do this."

But what about the artists, Resnais asked. What about Jack Kirby and John Buscema?

"Well, I thought of that," Lee said. "The thing is, these men are so talented that I think if I do movie work, I could take them with me. Jack is great at set design and things like that. And they're good at storyboards." Lee showed Resnais a package he'd just received, of production designs Kirby had done for a staging of *Julius Caesar* at the University of California, Santa Cruz. Kirby and Buscema could probably get by even if they stayed in the comics industry, Lee told Resnais. "But I would like to take them."

Perfect Film's Marty Ackerman, facing lawsuits and impatient lenders, resigned from the presidency of Curtis. "I'm out," he told *The New York Times*. "Who needs the aggravation?" In June, eager to leave the executive life completely behind, he stepped down from Perfect Film & Chemical, set himself up with a $750,000 consultancy contract, and went off to write a book about his perceived mistreatment at the hands of Curtis.

The Perfect Film board named thirty-eight-year-old Sheldon Feinberg, the former CFO of Revlon, as Ackerman's replacement. Feinberg was, like Ackerman, a brash cigar chomper. He'd been born into poverty, put himself through law school night classes, and learned from Revlon founder Charles Revson how to run a business: with an iron fist and zero guilt. Brought in with the goal of paying off debt to banks, Feinberg announced his arrival at Perfect by relieving Ackerman of the jet plane, multiple automobiles, and personal staff that he'd retained for his town house office. Unable to afford more experienced executives, Feinberg then surrounded himself with young, ambitious advisors—and cultivated an environment of trepidation for everyone else at the company. "With Shelly, you only spoke when spoken to," said one former employee. "My first week on the job, he wanted to meet me, so he called me up said, 'Can you stop by my office?' The suite I was a part of was next door to his huge suite. I said, 'I'll be there in five minutes, I'm just finishing something up.' Within thirty seconds, my direct boss, the VP of Marketing, came in and said, 'Are you an asshole? You do not tell him *one* second. You're there by the time he hangs up the phone.'" Another longtime associate described Feinberg's management style this way: "'Pit your executives against each other, make them fight each other, and then, somehow they should do better. And try to humiliate your subordinates.' He was a real piece of work."

Feinberg was not thrilled with what he'd inherited. It was a "messy conglomerate," he grumbled, hardly the business he'd been led to believe it was. When *The New York Times* asked if he'd have taken the job had he known what he was getting into, Feinberg refused to answer. He began selling off pieces of Perfect Film, an action not unnoticed at Marvel. "Magazines were dying, and we thought comics were next, and we were always disturbed by those kind of things," said John Romita. "They destroyed *Saturday Evening Post*, didn't they? It was terrible. They had nobody with taste in that whole organization."

It was in this climate that Jack Kirby decided to press for a contract. He'd been cheated out of money by Marvelmania, was frustrated with Stan Lee, and felt ignored by both Goodman and Ackerman—even after he'd agreed to take Marvel's side in the Captain America dispute with Joe Simon. When Simon received a settlement on November 20, Kirby waited for Marvel to pay him a matching amount (according to one report, a mere $7,500), as had been promised. Kirby and his lawyer flew to New York in December 1969, hoping for a satisfying sit-down with Perfect Film. But who was Jack Kirby to Sheldon Feinberg or his young executives? Stan Lee, they'd heard of. Still, if Kirby wanted a contract, they would send him a contract.

Kirby finally got the go-ahead for an *Inhumans* series—and because Lee didn't have time to add dialogue, Kirby would write as well as draw it. He was also given an assignment for a new series starring the old Timely pulp character Ka-Zar. But there was a catch: with comic sales down, Goodman figured this was not an ideal time to suddenly expand the line—in fact, he'd just canceled the low-selling *X-Men*, which joined *Doctor Strange* and *Captain Marvel* in the scrap heap. So in a cautious waters-testing return to the early 1960s, the Inhumans and Ka-Zar would be parsed out in ten-page segments, each in new anthology titles. The Inhumans would share *Amazing Adventures* with Black Widow, a re-formed Iron Man villainess; Ka-Zar would share *Astonishing Tales* with Dr. Doom. If sales merited it, maybe one of those characters would get their own book.

Kirby headed home and waited for his contract. While he began figuring out how to chop in half the Inhumans stories he'd already drawn, Lee called him to ask if he'd fill in for an issue of the floundering *Silver Surfer*, in which the title character would be recast as an angry vindicator. It would be called *The Savage Silver Surfer*. (Ironically, this was how Kirby had intended to portray the character all along, ever since he added him to the pages of *Fantastic Four* #48 just before deadline.) Kirby took the assignment, although it was salt in the wound to pinch-hit on the character he'd created himself but been denied control of.

And then the contract arrived. Kirby's heart sank as he read the terms. He could take it or leave it. Kirby's mood came through on the final, frighteningly intense pages of *Silver Surfer* #18. The Surfer flew away from a fight, streaked to a mountaintop, and briefly kneeled down before turning to directly address the reader, his face boiling with rage. "Too long have I displayed restraint! Too long have I refused to flaunt my power!" screamed the Surfer. "I'll have done with reason—and with love—or mercy! To men they're only words—to be uttered and ignored!"*

The next time Carmine Infantino visited California, he brought a contract with him. Kirby went over to Infantino's hotel room and signed a three-year deal with DC Comics.

Through all of this, the atmosphere in the cramped Bullpen had remained, by and large, playful. Maybe it was never quite the utopian elves' workshop depicted in the letter columns, but the *Sorry, No Visitors* sign outside the unlocked front office door was really just to ward off the creepier fans. According to Robin Green, who replaced Flo Steinberg as Marvel's secretary, "the bullpen had become a kind of men's den, with pictures of naked women, some playboy types and some drawings of comic book

---

* The irony, of course, is that the dialogue was by Lee and not by the voiceless Kirby.

characters as they will never appear in *Spider-Man*. Some of them were downright pornographic, and you couldn't talk to [inker] Tony Mortellaro without a tit or an ass staring you in the face." The key to the bathroom was called "the shithouse pass."

The short New York University student film *We Love You Herb Trimpe*, shot at the office at the time, provides visual evidence of this men's den: Trimpe, an Alan Alda lookalike, has decorated his station with a poster of General George S. Patton (World War II biplane models linger just above the shot). John Verpoorten and Marie Severin chat and tease as they work but never look up, the desks pushed together so tightly that everyone would have to stop working in order for anyone to squeeze out of the room. They lament what's happened to their audience, which was once made up of thrilled children and is now dominated by increasingly one-track-minded teenagers. "That word *fan* is just that," says Trimpe. "They're fanatics."

Marie Severin, wide brown eyes hidden behind her glasses, dressed in what Robin Green described as "very Peck & Peck," held her own against both the boys' club and the fans, all of whom she targeted in brilliant, wicked caricatures that were pinned up all around the office. Her cartooning had been given a chance to shine in *Not Brand Echh*; now that it had been canceled, most of her best work was privately circulated, excoriating in-jokes about her coworkers. But behind the cigarette smoke and the wisecracks, there was a familial softness to the Bullpen as well. Kuramoto would paint nature watercolors during his lunch hour. Freelancers would regularly stop in, pull up a chair, and work. When artist Barry Smith visited the Bullpen, he witnessed a spontaneous, collaborative rendition of the Beatles' "Hey Jude," which was playing on the radio: "As it came into the long, chanting coda, one by one each person began singing along—Herb, John Romita, Morrie Kuramoto, Tony Mortellaro, Marie and a few others—all singing at the top of their lungs."

March 6, 1970, was a Friday. The ghosts of the sixties still clung. The Beatles, publicly together but having already broken up behind closed doors, released the single "Let It Be" that morning. In Greenwich Village, a few minutes after 12 noon, members of the radical group the

Weathermen accidentally detonated a bomb they were building, razing their town house headquarters. Uptown, in Marvel's offices, *Captain America* #128, in which a biker gang named Satan's Angels provided security for an Altamont-like rock festival, was in production. Shortly after Jack Kirby's pages for *Fantastic Four* #102 were delivered into Lee's hands, the phone rang at 635 Madison Avenue. "Jack's on line two," Stan Lee's receptionist called out.

A few minutes later, a stunned Lee called in Sol Brodsky, and then Roy Thomas. The just-delivered *Fantastic Four* pages sat on Lee's desk, still carrying the scent of the Roi-Tan Falcon cigars that Kirby smoked at his drawing board.

The King was leaving Marvel.

As soon as the news reached John Romita, he walked into Lee's office and asked if they'd be canceling the *Fantastic Four*. No, said Lee—you're going to do it. "Are you crazy?" Romita asked, but finally accepted. "I did it under extreme duress because I felt inadequate," he recalled later. "It was like trying to raise somebody else's child." John Buscema had an even stronger reaction. "I thought they were going to close up," he recalled. "As far as I was concerned, Jack was the backbone of Marvel."

Somebody found one of the cigar butts that Kirby had left behind on his last visit to the Bullpen. "Marie Severin made a very elaborate plaque out of it," Trimpe later recalled, "labeling it 'Jack Kirby's Last Cigar at Marvel,' with fancy scroll work on it." She hung the plaque on the wall. It read, "Kirby Was Here."

PART II

The Next Generation

4

NINETEEN SEVENTY WAS A STRESSFUL YEAR FOR STAN LEE—"FRENZIED, FRAN-tic, and frenetic," as he put it in a letter to one friend. He was still reeling from Kirby's departure, and in the process of moving his family from Hewlett Harbor to a midtown apartment, when Sol Brodsky sat down and told him he'd been offered the chance to lead a black-and-white comic start-up. Lee resignedly gave Brodsky his blessing and named John Verpoorten the new head of production.

There were reminders everywhere that things had changed since the early days of the Fantastic Four and Spider-Man and the Merry Marvel Marching Society. Every time that Lee walked down the corridor and into his office, he passed a life-size poster of Spider-Man from years ago, drawn by the long-departed Steve Ditko. Flo was gone; Jack was gone; Sol was gone. Stan Goldberg, who'd chosen the colors for the superheroes and drew *Millie the Model* for a decade, had recently left to work for DC, as had longtime artist John Severin. Only Martin Goodman still remained from those halcyon days of the early 1960s, and although he still looked at the covers, and approved new titles, he was halfway out the door already, having arranged for Chip—who was more focused on the magazine line anyway—to take his place. Even Marvel's mysterious owner, Perfect Film & Chemical, changed its name to the still-more-ambiguous Cadence Industries and moved out to New Jersey. And sales were down.

It wasn't the first time Lee had watched as the people who'd helped to build Marvel left him: it had happened in 1941, when Joe Simon and Jack Kirby left; in 1949, when he'd had to fire the freelancers; in 1957, when he'd had to fire the staff. The difference now was that he had some power to determine what would happen next. Throughout 1970, as he prepared to enter his fourth decade as an employee of Marvel Comics, he started eyeing the publishing strategies more closely, and pushing for changes. He made plans with the poet Kenneth Koch to create comics about "which congressmen to vote for, who might help end the war in Vietnam a little sooner."* He huddled with Carmine Infantino at DC to start the Academy of Comic Book Arts, in a bid to gain more widespread acceptance for the industry. "We'll have exhibits in world-famous galleries," he wrote, "a lecture bureau to provide speakers to interested groups here and overseas; and an annual awards ceremony in which we, the pros, will recognize and reward the finest artistic and literary contributions from within our field." (The organization succeeded, at least, in giving out awards.) With Chip Goodman's help, Lee campaigned for the Comics Code Authority to allow depictions of narcotics use. The measure was voted down, but when Lee later received a letter from the U.S. Department of Health, Education, and Welfare asking him to address drug abuse in the comics, he convinced Martin Goodman to bypass the code—and Marvel published a *Spider-Man* story in which Peter Parker's roommate Harry Osborn couldn't stop popping pills. The newspaper coverage easily outweighed the slap on the wrist from the Code Authority.

Marvel won the battle. Within a matter of months the authority, sensing that it was on the wrong side of history, not only began to allow depictions of drug abuse, but also lifted some of its horror-content bans.† Marvel acted quickly to capitalize on the new guidelines, developing *Werewolf by Night, The Tomb of Dracula*, and almost—Lee was talked out of it—a title called *The Mark of Satan*, which would follow the adventures of the devil himself.

---

*This project was ultimately abandoned when the Marvel higher-ups deemed its politics too radical.

†Denny O'Neil and Neal Adams, who'd been shoving every kind of social commentary into *Green Lantern/Green Arrow* for the past year, responded by giving Green Lantern's former sidekick, Speedy, a heroin habit. At the New York Creation Con that year, Gerry Conway promised an upcoming Sub-Mariner story in which the hero "meets up with a New Orleans hooker, goes into a New Orleans cathouse, and does the whole routine with the pimp there. We felt that that was a little strong, so we changed that into something that's cleaner . . . they're all drug addicts now. The Comics Code accepted that."

But Lee had not worked this long and hard just to return to crank out monster comics in a repeatedly endangered industry. For all his campaigning to improve the standing of comic books in the eyes of the world, he wasn't willing to go down with the ship. Rumors swirled that Lee was just waiting out his contract;* such speculation only gained traction when his frustrations surfaced in public. "The comic book market is the worst market that there is on the face of the earth for creative talent and the reasons are numberless and legion," he told a gathering of industry colleagues.

> I have had many talented people ask me how to get into the comic book business. If they were talented enough the first answer I would give them is, "Why would you want to get into the comic book business?" Because even if you succeed, even if you reach what might be considered the pinnacle of success in comics, you will be less successful, less secure and less effective than if you are just an average practitioner of your art in television, radio, movies or what have you. It is a business in which the creator . . . owns nothing of his creation. The publisher owns it. . . . Isn't it pathetic to be in a business where the most you can say for the creative person in the business is that he's serving an apprenticeship to enter a better field? Why not go to the other field directly?

"I would tell any cartoonist who has an idea," Lee concluded, "think twice before you give it to a publisher."

He looked for a way to sample life outside the confines of not just Goodman's rule, but of comic books entirely. He'd solidified his friendship with Alain Resnais, the director of acclaimed art-house films like *Hiroshima Mon Amour* and *Last Year at Marienbad*, who was, like Fellini before him, an avowed Marvel Comics fan. Unlike Fellini, Resnais wanted more than to just pay his respects. He wanted to collaborate on a screenplay.

---

* The mimeographed fanzine *Newfangles* reported that Lee had been letting slip to college audiences that "when his contract is up in three years, no one will see anything of him but dust clouds."

"The Monster Maker is a realistic fantasy about a frustrated movie producer who overcomes his frustrations through trying to solve the problems of pollution," Lee told *The New York Times* about the ecologically focused film. "There will be lots of symbolism—and garbage." With a junk-culture-toiling protagonist nudged into a higher calling on the advice of his wife, it would be difficult not to see *The Monster Maker* as autobiographical. This, perhaps, was how Lee saw his own journey, as a man who'd gone from churning out schlocky product to taking an honorable place in the world and speaking against societal ills. In order to devote more time to working on *The Monster Maker*, Stan Lee took a sabbatical from writing comic books for the first time in his life.

At first it was hard for Lee to let go of the flagship titles, the ones he'd never entrusted to anyone else. Just as no one's artwork seemed to please him like Jack Kirby's did, no one's scripts seemed to please him like his own. But he'd poured everything he had into the *Silver Surfer* series, just to see it canceled. What did it matter anymore? So he handed over the keys to those who'd most thoroughly absorbed his style and could most seamlessly generate simulacra of past glories: *The Amazing Spider-Man* went to Roy Thomas, *Fantastic Four* to Archie Goodwin, *Captain America* to Gary Friedrich. And, most surprising to Marvel fans, *Thor* went to a teenager named Gerry Conway.

Born in Brooklyn, Conway was eight years old when *Fantastic Four* #1 hit the stands. By the time he was sixteen, he was writing scripts for DC Comics; soon after, he met Roy Thomas, who assigned him a Marvel writers' test. But Lee was, as usual, less than impressed with the way another writer handled the characters he shepherded.

"He writes really well for a seventeen-year-old kid," Thomas reasoned.

Lee, who himself had first walked into Marvel's offices at that age, paused. "Well, can't we get someone who writes really well for a *twenty-five*-year-old kid?"

After writing a single Ka-Zar story in *Astonishing Tales*, though, Conway earned a gig writing *Daredevil*. He soon became Marvel's new utility player. Just as Thomas had been picking up slack on titles Lee didn't have time for, Conway swooped in and covered *Iron Man, The Sub-Mariner,* and *The Incredible Hulk*. Conway managed to shake up *Daredevil* by partnering him with the Black Widow, whom Gene Colan rendered as something like an acrobatic Ann-Margret, a skintight-suited siren with long, red hair.* ("There seemed to be some natural chemistry between them," Conway said. "I think Gene's Black Widow was comics' first empowered sexy babe.")

But Conway's *Thor*, illustrated by John Buscema and his younger brother Sal in a faux-Kirby style, faced the same uphill climb as Thomas's *Amazing Spider-Man* and Goodwin's *Fantastic Four*. There were not just the long shadows cast by Lee and Kirby, but also the mandates to preserve status quo; character development was replaced by dramatized public service announcements. The low-selling *Captain America* became *Captain America and the Falcon*, and the new African-American costar began warily dating, and debating, a shrill black militant named Leila. The Avengers tackled women's lib, the Sub-Mariner addressed ecological concerns, and the Incredible Hulk, Thor, and the Inhumans visited the ghetto. Where was the fun in that?†

There hadn't been any new superhero titles in a year or two now—launches were limited to low-cost genre-dabbling like *Western Gun-fighters*, *Lil' Kids*, *Our Love Story*, *Spoof*, *Harvey*, and *Fear*. There was a growing sense, among the letter-writers and fanzine publishers, that Marvel was simply becoming a copy of itself. An issue of *The Fantastic Four* included art appropriated from an unpublished Kirby story. In an attempt to encourage Marvel's writers and artists to keep creating new characters while he was away, Lee suggested new anthology titles like *Marvel Feature*, *Marvel Spotlight*, and *Marvel Premiere*. But *Marvel*

---

* The Black Widow's new costume, designed by John Romita, was based on Tarpe Mills's early 1940s comic strip heroine and series *Miss Fury*, which Timely had reprinted.

† Where Marvel had once revealed campus riots to be the result of dastardly plans by the Kingpin (*Amazing Spider-Man* #68, January 1969) or Modok (*Captain America*, December 1969), now racial discord was also explained away by supervillains. Both the Sons of the Serpent (*Avengers* 73, February 1970) and the Red Skull (*Captain America* 143, November 1971) fomented race riots by disguising themselves as militant blacks. The disenchanted-peace-activist-turned-supervillain Firebrand ("anything the man puts up, I'm ready to tear down!"; *Iron Man* 27, July 1970) wore a raised-fist emblem and stoked anger in the ghettos. He, too, was later revealed to be white.

Feature's the Defenders, the first super-team in eight years, included no new characters—it simply threw together Doctor Strange, the Sub-Mariner, and the Hulk. *Marvel Premiere* starred a character named Adam Warlock—but he was a renamed version of a character that Kirby had introduced in 1967, updated by Roy Thomas and Gil Kane as a kind of cosmic-peacenik *Jesus Christ Superstar* who wandered around with zany longhairs, fighting authority figures of every stripe. The most exciting Marvel comic of 1971, by fan consensus, was an *Avengers* story arc called "The Kree-Skrull War," in which Thomas and Neal Adams reteamed for a welcome return to the tradition of multi-issue space epics. It was an ambitious, often thrilling tour through various Marvel mythologies, featuring not just the two battling alien races, and the Negative Zone, and Captain Marvel, and the Inhumans, but also appearances by Timely-era heroes like the Angel, the Blazing Skull, the Fin, the Patriot, and the original Vision. Paying tribute to what had come before him, with "The Kree-Skrull War" Thomas seemed to be touring disparate corners of the Marvel universe with a dustbin and craft glue, picking up the detritus left in Lee and Kirby's wake and fitting it all together. You could argue that it reached new levels of intertextual ecstasy, or you could wonder if it was just a final, grand echo of past glories, intoxicating fumes from an empty tank.

As the comics coasted along without Lee and Kirby, Martin Goodman hatched a devious plan to conquer DC once and for all. When Marvel and DC agreed to hike the price of comics (which had previously been raised from 10 to 12 cents in 1962, and to 15 cents in 1969), their handshake deal called for the books to expand from 36 to 52 pages—but at a whopping 25 cents apiece. But after a month, Goodman immediately cut back to fewer pages at 20 cents, and offered newsstand proprietors a bigger cut of the profits, ensuring that Marvel would get better rack space. The slow-footed DC tried to make a go of their higher-price, thicker comics, but they took a bath on the maneuver, and by the time they crawled back to the 20-cent price point, they'd lost the battle and the war. For the first time in its history, Marvel Comics was the number-one comic book company in the world. When Goodman got the news, he took the Marvel staff out to dinner at the after-work hangout of DC Comics employees, whose offices were directly across the street.

Unfortunately, leading the comic-book industry was a dubious distinction. Both Marvel and DC had managed to attract media coverage because of the so-called relevance of their social-issues coverage—a *New York* magazine cover story trumpeted, somewhat misleadingly, "The Radicalization of the Superheroes"—but the impact on the bottom line was minimal. Marvel had lost even its underdog status now. In industry circles, the grumblings of Ditko and Wally Wood had been common knowledge for a while, and many others objected to the lack of creative control that DC and Marvel afforded. But with Kirby's departure— and the growth of an organized network of fandom, rife with zines and conventions—gossip and accusations began to spread like wildfire.

The hired hands, given a platform at last, were happy to have the curtain pulled back. Neal Adams, currently working on DC's *Green Lantern* and Marvel's *Avengers*, was a rarity, an artist popular enough to refuse to work exclusively for either company. To a New York convention audience, he candidly offered his take on his employers' business strategies. DC's goal, he said, "probably has more to do with raising the prices even a bit higher, trying to build a market of 50-cent books. Marvel feels it can flood the market with 20-cent books and therefore take over the whole market, and they may be right. They are two very large companies and there is a very heavy competition. I hope neither of them wins."

Lee and Resnais's *Monster Maker* script sold for $25,000, although it would never be filmed. Lee returned from his sabbatical to find Marvel on top and profiled in *Rolling Stone*, where an illustration of the Hulk graced the cover. Lee's former secretary Robin Green, who wrote the feature, found him in a somewhat sensitive state when she approached him. He asked if she would be "nice," noting that "the world is a hostile place." There were rumors that he was unhappy at Marvel, even entertaining offers to move to DC when his contract expired. "Stan's alone in the corner, still Facing Front and smiling, but a little down sometimes," Green wrote. He was manic, nervous: "I asked him where he'd like to sit," she wrote, "and he said, 'You do what's best for you! Have a sourball! You're my guest!' We talked for a while, then played back the tape recorder to see if we were picking everything up, and Stan said, 'You know, that sounds so icky, I wouldn't like me if I met me and I sounded like that. I've gotta try to sound more rugged.'" Lee talked about the loneliness of writing and his wife and daughter's disinterest in comic books, and adjusted his toupee.

Over at DC, Kirby's new creations—*The New Gods*, *Mister Miracle*, and *The Forever People*, which constituted a so-called Fourth World mythology—had begun appearing. These were the next-generation heroes with which Kirby wanted to replace Thor and the other "old gods" after that story about Ragnarok five years ago; this was the direction that Lee had not allowed him to take. To many readers, Kirby's new work was all overgeared: the figures were even blockier than before, and the dialogue was stilted. But unlike Marvel, he was trying something new.

The Marvel staff awaited Kirby's DC work with bated breath. They loved Kirby but guiltily prayed for his new projects to fail. If DC was able to capitalize on Kirby's talent like Marvel had . . . well, the results were unthinkable. Marvel would never survive such competition. Inker Vince Colletta photocopied Kirby pages at the DC offices and carted them over to Marvel, where they went up on the walls. Marvel summoned in its own cover artists for meetings, holding up Kirby's work for analysis.

Kirby wasn't shy about comparing his new employer to his old one. "I don't have the feeling of repression that I had at Marvel," he told an interviewer. "I was never given credit for the writing I did. Most of the writing at Marvel is done by the artist from the script." *The Fantastic Four*, he said, "was my idea. It was my idea to do it the way it was; my idea to develop it the way it was. I'm not saying that Stan had nothing to do with it. Of course he did. We talked things out. As things went on, I began to work at home and I no longer came up to the office. I developed all the stuff at home and just sent it in. I had to come up with new ideas to help the strip sell. I was faced with the frustration of having to come up with new ideas and then having them taken from me."

The harshest barbs, though, were soon to come. In *Mister Miracle #6*, Kirby introduced Funky Flashman, a smooth-talking, fast-hustling promoter who bore more than a passing resemblance to Stan Lee. Funky

Flashman, clean-shaven and bald, began his day by donning a toupee-and-beard mask, and then jumped around speaking in alliterative phrases and making promises he didn't intend to keep. "All the great words and quotations and clichés ever written are at my beck and call!! Even if I say them sideways, the little people will listen!—in wonder! In awe! In reverence!!!—to their Funky!" Tailing him closely was Houseroy, a simpering assistant ("Master Funky! My leader!") who looked suspiciously like Roy Thomas. At story's end, Funky Flashman blithely sacrificed Houseroy to a quartet of angry warriors and made his slippery escape.

Roy Thomas shot back at the portrayal, and at Kirby's "near-paranoid delusions that he created all the Marvel heroes solely by himself and even wrote the stuff." Lee kept quiet about Funky Flashman, but privately he was hurt and angry. He shaved off his beard and put a little distance between himself and his caricature.

It was an especially inopportune time for Marvel to have PR problems. With the Marvelmania fiasco behind him, Chip Goodman had licensed the Marvel characters in the fall of 1971 to a shaggy-haired concert promoter named Steve Lemberg, who planned to adapt their adventures for stage musicals, radio plays, and films. The first part of Lemberg's promotional campaign was turning Stan Lee into an honest-to-God celebrity. He quickly organized a Carnegie Hall event around him. "An erudite evening of cataclysmic culture with your friendly neighborhood bullpen gang!" Spider-Man shouted from a *New York Times* ad for the January 5, 1972, event. At a cost of twenty-five thousand dollars, even a sold-out show wouldn't make Lemberg his money back—the show was a calculated loss leader, designed simply to enhance Lee's notoriety beyond comic circles. Sporting a mustache and sunglasses—he couldn't help being a little funky, and a little flashy—Stan the Man gave his best effort. But the proceedings were a directionless mess, with failed improvisations and low-rent superhero costumes crafted from Magic Markers and Lycra. The guest stars that gathered to perform dramatic readings or musical numbers could not have been a more random collection: Alain Resnais; actors René Auberjonois, Peter Boyle, and Chuck McCann; writer Tom Wolfe; Beach Boy Dennis Wilson; jazz drummer Chico Hamilton; and

Eddie Carmel, holder of the *Guinness Book of World Records* title for the world's tallest man. Lee's wife and daughter recited a poem Lee had written, "God Woke." A slide show spilled onto two screens, where crude projections clashed with the brightly colored Carnegie Hall drapes; a rock-and-roll trio of Roy Thomas, Herb Trimpe, and Barry Smith covered Elvis songs; and, according to reports, bored audience members ripped up their comic books and fashioned them into paper airplanes to direct at the stage. When it was all over, Gerry Conway went backstage to congratulate Lee and saw that his boss's face was ashen. He looked, Conway said, "like a deer in headlights."

Lee took a vacation shortly afterward. He visited Martin Goodman's turquoise-carpeted condominium in Palm Beach, Florida, where they sat on the terrace overlooking the Atlantic and talked with a reporter about selling 50 million comics a year in more than a hundred countries. But all that Lee wanted to discuss, it seemed, was the Kirby-created character that he had failed to turn into a success. "While the Surfer scored highest on our college and high school polls, it left the little kids cold. Perhaps there wasn't enough motion, or enough nonsense. Perhaps the fact that the Surfer was all white, no costume. Or that he was baldheaded. Or that he had no earthly hideout and no double identity."

"I think that psychologically the potential reader didn't care enough about surfing," Goodman wryly added. "So we got the thumbs down."

"The Surfer will return," Lee insisted. "Maybe with some changes. We're thinking about some changes. But we've gotten thousands of letters about his going and I can now say definitely that the Surfer will return."

They looked back out on the ocean. The reporter in Palm Beach didn't know it, but Martin Goodman, at sixty-four years old, was only weeks away from retiring.

Soon after his father left the company that he'd founded, Chip brought his wife, Roberta, to a dinner where Cadence Industries CEO Sheldon Feinberg was being honored. "He said we couldn't leave before he did," remembered Roberta. "And that was the first time we came to the idea that this was going to be different than working for Martin."

Feinberg was no expert on comic books, but even he recognized the threatening implications if Stan Lee were to jump over to DC. In a surprise twist, Feinberg gave Lee a double promotion, to president and publisher of Marvel Comics. Lee would no longer have his hands tied by the Goodmans. He could publish black-and-white comic magazines; he could have final say on covers; he could bring back the Silver Surfer.

On the day that Lee got the news, an old friend of his came by the Marvel offices.

"But who's going to become the editor?" the friend asked.

Lee shrugged his shoulders. "Oh, some guy back there."

"Stan tried to give me the job in a kind of half-assed way," Roy Thomas remembered years later. "He didn't really want to relinquish his major claim to fame, which of course was being the creative force behind Marvel Comics." At first, Lee wanted his old job divided between production manager John Verpoorten, Frank Giacoia (as assistant art director), and Thomas, who'd get a mere "story editor" title. Only after Lee realized that the ambiguous hierarchy of such a triangulated structure would cause him management headaches did he yield the editor in chief title to Thomas.

Meanwhile, Chip Goodman, who'd been preparing to take over his father's business since leaving grad school in the mid–1960s, would remain ensconced with the men's magazines—out of sight and out of mind, as far as Lee was concerned.

Of course, Chip had already left a legacy at Marvel—he'd sold nearly all of the film rights. Steve Lemberg was, like Robert Lawrence (*Marvel Super Heroes*) and Don Wallace (Marvelmania) before him, amazed at how much he'd been given for a minimal cost. "I owned more rights to Marvel than Marvel had," Lemberg mused. After an initial price of $2,500, he could renew indefinitely, with full, exclusive creative control of all characters. "The only decision that Chip ever made was to give me all the rights to his comic books. They gave me a twenty-page contract with interlocking rights and options; I could do anything I wanted. I could make movies, records, anything. It was really a trip." There was talk of a Thor radio series, to run in sixty-five, five-minute installments, a $2.5 million arena-rock show based on various characters, and a Silver Surfer film starring Beach Boy Dennis Wilson. But all of this went on the back burner while Lemberg put together a rock musical LP called *Spider-Man: From Beyond the Grave*, featuring the former lead singer of the Archies. Marvel's world domination would have to wait a little longer.

"It's time for Phase Two to begin," Lee proclaimed in his "Bullpen Bulletins" column. "No man, no group of men, no publishing company can rest on its laurels—and Marvel's still much too young, too zingy, too bright-eyed and bushy-tailed to settle back and bask in the sun of yesterday's success. . . . If you think we turned you on before, the best is yet to be—wait'll you see what's coming! Hang loose! Face front! Marvel's on the move again!" Restless from all the time spent in Martin Goodman's shadow, Lee quickly began casting around for new, more sophisticated ventures. He started to line up luminaries like Anthony Burgess, Kurt Vonnegut, and Vaclav Havel to write a line of adult comic books (Tom Stoppard expressed interest as well). He asked former *Mad* editor (and father figure to the underground comix scene) Harvey Kurtzman to edit a satirical magazine called *Bedlam*.* Lee also turned to the legendary Will Eisner, who wrote to prospective contributors that he'd be publishing a Marvel-funded magazine that was "neither sophomoric, nor foulmouthed or tasteless." Lee invited underground publisher Denis Kitchen to New York to discuss packaging an anthology title that would feature left-of-center artists like Kim Deitch, Art Spiegelman, and Basil Wolverton. Kitchen demanded that artists would retain trademarks to their characters and their original artwork.

Lee decided that he needed to play along with Kitchen's rules if Marvel was going to hold sway with hipper audiences. "One of Marvel's major assets," read an internal marketing memo, "has always been the large number of high school and college students who read our publications. However, each day a new crop of sexy movies and raunchy underground comix, as well as a proliferation of nudie magazines vies with us for this fickle audience." The memo went on to suggest that the company's

---

* "To label it as another 'Marvel Magazine,'" Kurtzman wrote in a June 22, 1972, letter to Lee, "to advertise it as one of a line—can you imagine what it would have done to the uniqueness of Life, Fortune, and Sports Illustrated if their covers had been labeled 'a TIME magazine'?"

product should be available in gas stations, record shops, bookstores, and "youth boutiques." Marvel had lost its edge, though—it didn't even realize that even the underground scene had peaked.

Of all Lee's attempts to reach a "sophisticated" audience, only the Kitchen project would reach fruition, but when *Comix Book #1* was finally published, it was without Marvel's logo. The final product, which allowed for partial nudity and a negotiated selection of profanities, occupied an uncomfortable limbo between its artists' usual sex-and-drug hijinks and the relatively innocuous Marvel style. Lee canceled it after three issues, citing poor sales, but Kitchen wondered if it had also rocked the corporate boat too much. One underground cartoonist who visited the Marvel offices heard employees asking why "the hippies" were getting special treatment. "All the other people who worked for Marvel—in the bullpen and the freelancers—all started giving him a lot of shit about it," said Denis Kitchen, "because they resented that these newcomers had a different deal than they did."

Marvel's comics were steadily dropping in circulation along with those of every other publisher. Marvel maintained its number-one position through a war of attrition, continuing to expand its line of titles despite weak sales, taking up more rack space at the newsstand and attempting to crowd out DC. Stan Lee plotted the return of black-and-white magazines, which had been on his mind since Goodman's cancellation of *Savage Tales*. Because recent changes to the Comics Code allowed for vampires and werewolves, *Dracula Lives, Monsters Unleashed, Tales of the Zombie*, and *Vampire Tales*, each with seventy-six pages of content per month, started rolling off presses.

Along with an ever-growing lineup of reprints of Lee and Kirby's 1960s work, a number of new superhero concepts, most of them delegated by Lee, also began rolling out steadily, ending the R&D drought of the last few years. But these new titles were more transparently tied to trends and business strategies (and loosened Comics Code restrictions) than, say, *Thor* and *Iron Man* had been. "Wherever there is a trend that has been spotted," read a marketing objectives plan, "wherever there is a reading need to be satisfied amongst the 'now-generation' readership, Marvel will make every effort to capture such trends and to fill such needs." Public-domain monsters were recast as trademark-ready supervillains and anti-heroes (*Tomb of Dracula* and *Werewolf by Night*); even the former X-Men member the Beast was reimagined as a furry, monster-like character. Shortly after Evel Knievel announced plans to jump the Snake River Canyon, Roy Thomas, Gary Friedrich, and artist Mike Ploog developed Ghost Rider, a motorcycle daredevil with a flaming skull. *Luke Cage, Hero for Hire* chronicled the exploits of a jive-talking, *Shaft*-inspired ex-con from Harlem who charged a fee for good deeds.

There were now about forty titles coming out monthly. "If we even talked about an idea for a book," Thomas said, "it immediately had to go onto a schedule and be out a few months later." Marvel quickly moved into bigger offices down the street, at 575 Madison Avenue. One visitor described the space as it was still being finished: "The waiting room was frigid modern, pastel plush furniture and not a hint of the comic book source. The home of Spiderman, Thor, and the Fantastic Four might just as well have been the reception room of an accounting firm."

But corporate sterility had its limits: there was a real bullpen again, a space where the production team could stretch out, with comics tacked up on walls and spilling off bookshelves. John Romita was made the official art director, a title that Lee had kept for himself until now. The staffers and freelancers who swarmed around Romita and John Verpoorten in the Bullpen—Frank Giacoia, Mike Esposito, Jack Abel, Danny Crespi, Morrie Kuramoto, Vince Colletta, George Roussos—had, between them, about two centuries of comic book experience; many of them had worked for Atlas in the 1950s. They were the remaining links to the comic industry of the past, a world of Pall Malls and neckties and corned beef sandwiches and baseball on the radio. Onto their desks came a steady stream of pages from veteran freelancers, who, thanks to Marvel's expansion, found themselves in greater demand than they'd been in decades.

Increasingly, though, comics were becoming a young man's game. Lee had returned to writing *Amazing Spider-Man* and *The Fantastic Four* after his sabbatical, but with his promotion to publisher and president, he left them again, this time for good. Gerry Conway, not yet twenty years old, took over *Spider-Man*, Marvel's most popular title. After a few months under Roy Thomas, *Fantastic Four* also passed to Conway.

Thomas was busy recruiting new talent from the world of fanzines and conventions. He knew a whole network of guys who'd grown up absorbing Lee's style and who were now out of college and eager for work. What did Marvel have to lose by letting them take a crack at turning sales around? It was, in a more modest way, a repeat of what Hollywood had been experiencing for a few years, after a conflation of big-budget disasters and the successes of *Easy Rider* and *Bonnie and Clyde* convinced the studios that they might as well throw money at scrappy film school graduates and hope for the best. The hard-core comic readers came from all over the country, although there were certain pockets—St. Louis, Indianapolis, Detroit—where organized fandom had most effectively incubated their obsessions. They'd move to New York and come to one of the monthly "First Friday" industry gatherings held at Roy Thomas's apartment. Bill Everett might be there, or Neal Adams, or Denny O'Neil, or Archie Goodwin, ready with advice and contacts.

This kind of networking had been going on for a couple of years already, and the results were showing up in Jim Warren's black-and-white horror magazines and DC's color horror comics. But by 1972, the influx had reached a critical mass. Artist Jeff Jones had taken over, and expanded, the First Friday parties, and Neal Adams and Dick Giordano had started their own studio, Continuity, providing many an aspiring professional with early experience. The fledgling Skywald had begun hiring for its publications. And, finally, Marvel opened its gates. In the five years since Steranko and Adams, hardly anyone had managed to break in at the House of Ideas, and those who did so, struggled—Barry Smith arrived from England and lived out of a suitcase; Rich Buckler, from Detroit, subsisted on graham crackers and grilled-cheese sandwiches. But in the months after Roy Thomas's promotion to editor in chief, as Marvel's line expanded, pages were filled with the work of more than a dozen new artists who synthesized their forerunners' visual trademarks into ever more intricate styles.

There was a new crop of writers as well, many of whom came up through a revolving door of staff positions. After Steve Englehart, a bearded and bespectacled conscientious objector from Indianapolis, took over Gary Friedrich's assistant editor job,* he became the scripter for *The Defenders*, and then the floundering *Captain America*. When he landed *The Avengers* as well, he convinced Thomas to let him continue an eight-part story, back and forth, between that title and *The Defenders*. It was the first Marvel crossover. Englehart decided to write full-time.

Steve Gerber, a quick-witted, chain-smoking Camus obsessive who'd known Roy Thomas in Missouri, took Englehart's place on staff. Gerber had worked as a salesman for his uncle's used-car lot in St. Louis, but his compulsive honesty, he claimed, got him fired. He and his young family lived on food stamps until he got a job as DJ, and then at an ad agency, where he toiled under fluorescent lights writing copy for savings-and-loan commercials. "You must help me. I am dying," he wrote to Thomas. Six months later he was in New York, and on the Marvel staff for $125 a month. He supplemented this salary by writing *Adventure into Fear*, which starred the *Savage Tales* castoff Man-Thing.

Marv Wolfman, a native New Yorker, came in next. Wolfman and his childhood best friend, Len Wein, were so inseparable, and so much alike, that other fans had taken to calling them "LenMarv." They'd made a pact to break into the industry together, and starting in junior high, they dutifully checked off every box on the fan-to-pro trajectory list: they'd taken tours of the DC Comics offices, made mimeographed zines (Wolfman published Stephen King's first story in one of them), organized conventions, even visited Jack Kirby's house after school and watched him draw while Roz brought them sandwiches and milk. When they showed up at Marvel, Flo Steinberg said, "I'd wish them well and tell them to finish high school." After graduation, they did sporadic work for DC, including the creation of a black superhero that editor Carmine Infantino nixed at the eleventh hour. Now they'd decided to strike out on their own: Wein lived with Gerry Conway and wrote horror comics for DC, and Wolfman, who'd been working at Warren, came on staff at Marvel to help them launch their black-and-white magazines.

---

* Friedrich left New York after his upstairs neighbor was strangled in her apartment by serial killer Rodney Alcala, and Friedrich's wife suggested that a move back to Missouri might be in order.

Don McGregor—a diminutive, fast-talking, aspiring filmmaker from Rhode Island whose commentary had appeared regularly in Marvel's letter pages, and whose stories had run in Warren magazines—sold his house, moved his wife and baby daughter to the Bronx, started proofreading, and waited for his shot at writing.

Tony Isabella, a devout Catholic and a copyboy at the *Cleveland Plain Dealer*, moved to New York to assist Sol Brodsky, who'd returned to Marvel and was overseeing repackaging comics for the British market. Isabella also began helping out with the monster magazines.

"It felt like when you watch a movie from thirty years ago," recalled Jim Salicrup, who at fifteen years of age became an unofficial Marvel intern in 1972, "and it has an old star from decades earlier, and in small supporting parts it has these new people who would become big stars years later. I remember being starstruck by people like Bill Everett, who would be back in the office working with Steve Gerber on a very odd bunch of issues of *The Sub-Mariner*. It was these strange combinations of people coming in and out."

But Bill Everett's health had been diminished from years of heavy drinking. Although he'd been sober for three years, he suffered a heart attack in late 1972; he died the following February at the age of fifty-five. Shortly afterward, Syd Shores, fifty-nine, died of a heart seizure. As Stan Lee turned fifty years old, the average age of the artists of the flagship superhero titles—*The Amazing Spider-Man*, *The Avengers*, *Captain America*, *Daredevil*, *The Fantastic Four*, *The Incredible Hulk*, *Iron Man*, *The Sub-Mariner*, and *Thor*—was forty-three. The average age of the writers was twenty-three.

Change was coming to Marvel Comics.

5

STAN LEE CAME INTO THE OFFICE A FEW DAYS A WEEK, AND STILL LOOKED AT the covers. But when he wasn't blinking his eyes at balance sheets and charts and annual reports, signing off on thousand-dollar merchandise licensing deals for Marvel characters,* or getting called into meetings with Cadence chief Sheldon Feinberg, he was speaking at college campuses, or meeting with producers, hoping to get Spider-Man and the Hulk on the big screen. It wasn't long before he grew tired of all the boardroom stuffiness and realized he didn't want to remain president.

It was around that time that Albert Einstein Landau came on the scene. The son of Jewish Telegraphic Agency founder Jacob Landau, and the godson of Albert Einstein, Al Landau ran a photo agency and news syndicate called Transworld Features, which had over the years provided material to Martin Goodman's magazines. Lately he'd been socializing with Chip—they were neighbors on Fire Island—and as soon as Chip introduced him to Feinberg, he worked to ingratiate himself. Landau invited Feinberg to his home for a game of tennis, listed his accomplishments, and proposed ways in which he could improve the business. Perhaps Feinberg saw his own reflection in the short, abrupt, and aggressive Landau. By the time Chip got the news that Stan Lee was stepping down as president, Feinberg had already hired Landau. It was a done deal, and Chip was one step further down the chain of command.

"Chip was very upset about this, as were Martin and Jean," remembered Chip's wife, Roberta. "They thought Al was a total bullshitter. He

---

*Among the 1973 highlights, thanks to arrangements with two different merchandising reps: bubble bath, paint-by-numbers sets, Halloween costumes, walkie-talkies, calendars, rubber balloons, and bicycle horns.

didn't know anything about the business at all; it wasn't his background. He'd used Chip as a way to get to Shelly [Feinberg], and snuck in between the two of them."

Chip's contract soon expired. The next time that he and Landau had a disagreement, Landau's solution was clear.

"Do you want to be fired or do you want to quit?" he asked Chip.

Although he was no longer president, Lee remained publisher of Marvel Comics—and, once Chip was gone, publisher of the magazines, too. Increasingly, though, it fell to Roy Thomas to bridge the widening gap between business and editorial interests. One of Thomas's first responsibilities as the new editor in chief had been to bring further diversification to the Marvel Universe. As the company's initial attempts to entice a black readership (the Falcon, Luke Cage) sputtered along with middling sales, now a similarly clumsy effort was made to reach female readers, with the launch of three comics ostensibly about feminist empowerment.* For added authenticity (or gimmickry, depending on one's level of cynicism), each of the three new titles was to be written by a woman. Unfortunately, there was none presently writing for Marvel, so Thomas improvised. He drafted his wife, Jeanie, *Hulk* artist Herb Trimpe's new wife, Linda Fite, and comic conventioneer Phil Seuling's wife, Carole. Lee came up with all three concepts the same day, and the titles spoke for themselves: *Night Nurse*, *The Claws of the Cat*, and *Shanna the She-Devil*. In the year of Helen Reddy's "I Am Woman" and the launch of *Ms.* magazine, Marvel's tales of candy stripers, cat-suited sexpots, and jungle queens could hardly be called revolutionary.† (Lee later suggested that

---

* The new attitude was reflected in the existing titles as well. In *Daredevil* #91, a group of women voice their admiration of Black Widow: "Now there's a woman with her own mind," they cheer, "*definitely* the Gloria Steinem of the jump-suit set!"

† Marvel was soon back to its old tricks: in *My Love* #25 (September, 1973, "No Man Is My Master," written by Lee) a young woman named Bev explores feminism but realizes she misses being condescended to; after dating respectful milquetoasts, she returns to a louse who bosses her around and actually utters the words "Me, Tarzan—you, Jane!" In the last panel, she says, "And that's the way it was meant to be!" The final caption reads "The Start—of something lovely!" A 1974 internal memo vowed to use a noncomic format "should we ever again attempt to reach the female market in the future."

the title *Night Nurse* was a final legacy of his former boss: "Martin Goodman always thought there was something inherently sexy about nurses. I could never get inside his thinking there.") It was a disappointing lineup from the beginning. For Fite, a former Marvel secretary and the only one of the three with writing experience, the problems began with the name of the series she was writing. "Why do we have to name it *The Cat*, Roy?" she asked. "Is it a *catfight*?"

Like Luke Cage, the Cat was subjected to medical experiments that gave her super powers. Instead of just super-strength, though, Greer Grant, formerly a docile homemaker, was given an intensified "women's intuition." (Two years later, the character was subjected to radiation, which transformed her into a furry, striped feline named Tigra. Her costume was simply a bikini.) Alas, the message of empowerment was lost on Wally Wood, whom Stan Lee hired to ink the cover of *The Cat* #1. Wood sent back Marie Severin's pencil art with the heroine's clothes completely removed, and Severin—who'd had more than her fill of boys' club shenanigans over the years—had to white out the Cat's nipples and pubic hair.

Carole Seuling departed *Shanna the She-Devil* after only a few months, and Thomas handed the reins to Steve Gerber. By the last issue, it seemed that Gerber was using the comic as a platform to question the point of its own existence. Sprawled on a bed in her leopard-skin bikini, reading from Camus' *The Stranger*, Shanna wonders: "What am I doing here—prancing through the jungle like some 1940s B-movie goddess? I came here to escape the city . . . its violence . . . its plastic landscape. So what do I do? Build a treehouse to rival the Plaza—foster a teen-age malt-shop relationship with Patrick! It's too civilized. I should just walk away from it—try living out in the elements—test myself to the limits. At least we'd see if I'm really the superhuman 'she-devil' they call me!"

Night Nurse was saddled with its own problems: At the end of October, upon returning from a weekend in Vermont, Jean Thomas told Roy that she was leaving him. The seeds of marital tensions had been sown early the previous year, when Jean was graduating from Hunter College and looking for work. Lee dangled the idea of a secretarial job and then quickly withdrew the offer. "There were some people at Marvel, never totally revealed to me, who'd felt she'd be a 'spy' for me on the couple of days I wrote at home, so she was frozen out," said Thomas. "Jeanie felt I should've quit. But I had wanted to defer the decision till I'd talked it over with her, and by that time my moment to 'play hero' had passed. I guess, in her mind, I had failed the test by not standing up for her." And in Thomas's mind, his coworkers had failed the test of loyalty. The bloom was off the rose. His feelings about Marvel would never fully recover.

Within nine months, all three of the distaff titles had gotten the ax. "It's kind of a shame," Thomas lamented. "You could get blacks to buy comics about whites, but it was hard to get whites to buy comics in which the main character was black. And it was even harder to get boys to buy comics about women."* After the initial campaign had failed, the female characters that were introduced in the pages of other titles—Thundra, an angry Femizon in *The Fantastic Four*; Mantis, a Vietnamese ex-prostitute in *The Avengers*; and, in *Marvel Team-Up*, a villainess named Man-Hater—seemed unlikely to emerge as role models.†

Nonetheless, the mandate was to go for "minority" appeal, so in the summer of 1973, as the last issues of *Night Nurse* and *The Cat* slunk quietly from the newsstands, they were quickly replaced by redoubled efforts toward a surge in blackness. Luke Cage became a high-profile guest star in *Amazing Spider-Man*, while in his own title, Marvel delicately reported, "much of Cage's jivin' slang will be eliminated." African-American bad girl Nightshade battled *Captain America and the Falcon*; Jim Wilson returned to the pages of *The Incredible Hulk*. For *Tomb of Dracula*, Marv

---

*There may have been a credibility deficiency to begin with: Stan and Romita were soon (very quietly) working on a proposal for *Playboy* that included characters named Lord Peckerton and Clitanna the High Priestess; the first issue was to open with a shot of the ruler of "a sensual empire" using "chicks as footstools." *Playboy*, trying to compete with *Penthouse*'s "Wicked Wanda," demanded more S&M. Romita balked, and Stan followed him in solidarity. "That's the only time I can point to Stan passing up a chance to make money," Romita later said.

†At Marvel, militant feminists served the same purpose as black militants had a few years before: destructive forces that endangered the achievements of moderates. Compare the words of the Cat in 1973's *Marvel Team-Up* #8 ("If she isn't stopped, she'll destroy everything women have fought for . . . the precious little we've gained!") to Falcon's in 1970's *Captain America* #126: "They're like a black version of the Klan! All they preach is hate Whitey! They can set our progress back a hundred years!"

Wolfman dusted off Blade, a black tinted-goggles-and-bandolier-sporting vampire hunter he'd conceived in the 1960s.* The biracial buddy western comic *Reno Jones and Kid Cassidy: Gunhawks* became *Reno Jones, Gunhawk* when the white half of the team was murdered. The final issues of *Shanna the She-Devil* introduced Nekra, a mutant albino daughter born to an African-American cleaning lady; her criminality was, unsurprisingly, tied up with heavy identity issues. Other new black characters were filtered through the scrim of international exoticism: In *Supernatural Thrillers*, Steve Gerber and Rich Buckler introduced N'Kantu, the Living Mummy; Len Wein and John Romita's Haitian witch doctor Brother Voodoo began starring in *Strange Tales*; and Don McGregor and Rich Buckler brought Black Panther back to his native Wakanda in *Jungle Action*, a title previously devoted to reprints of white imperialist fantasies from the 1950s.

McGregor had been at his proofreading job for a few months, waiting for a chance at writing a title. One that regularly landed on his desk made him wince. "At that time," he said, "*Jungle Action* was basically blond jungle gods and goddesses saving the native populace from whatever threat. It was pretty racist stuff, and I couldn't believe Marvel was publishing it." And then suddenly, he was informed that the twenty-year-old potboilers starring Lo-Zar, Tharn the Magnificent, and Jann of the Jungle would be replaced. *Jungle Action* would now run new adventures of the Black Panther in his native African country of Wakanda—and McGregor would be the writer. "Jungle books didn't sell. I think they figured, 'Well, we'll give Don a jungle book, it'll die and we'll have given him a chance.'"

But the disregarded *Jungle Action* turned out to be the perfect venue for McGregor's idiosyncratic vision—because it was a lower-tier book, no higher-ups were looking at his work until it was just about out the door, too close to deadline for major changes. With artist Rich Buckler (later replaced by the African-American Billy Graham), McGregor immediately embarked on a dense, thirteen-chapter saga called "Panther's Rage,"

---

* Blade was born in an English brothel and trained in hand-to-hand combat by a jazz trumpeter.

in which the Black Panther's alter ego, T'Challa, returns to his homeland and faces revolting countrymen who see him as a sellout for hanging out with the Avengers.

Only two years earlier, in an issue of *The Fantastic Four*, Marvel briefly tried to put distance between the Black Panther and his politically charged namesakes by renaming him Black Leopard. "I neither condemn nor condone those who have taken up the name," T'Challa told the Thing, in a carefully measured bit of expository dialogue. Now McGregor edged the character further into political territory than ever before, and tackled issues of masculinity and patriotism. The gold-chain outfit that T'Challa sometimes paraded around in recalled Isaac Hayes's *Wattstax* getup, but that had more to do with black America's trendy early 1970s appropriation of traditional African garb than with *Jungle Action* becoming one more winking blaxploitation farce. McGregor invested deeply in his characters; the gravitas (and extreme wordiness) that he brought to the comic was typified by the description of the Panther's American girlfriend, Monica Lynne ("once she was a songstress . . . a minor-grade Aretha Franklin . . . and more recently she spent her days as a social worker . . . until the words of this quiet, eloquent man convinced her she might learn more about different lifestyles and herself here in this jungle paradise"). But McGregor could also have fun: corralling generous volunteers from the Bullpen, he filled out the back of the book with maps, pinup galleries, and text pieces—otherwise, he knew, that space would be tainted by reprints of the old jungle strips.

The characteristic that most immediately set *Jungle Action* apart, however, was McGregor's resistance to including white supporting characters, including superhero guest stars. "My feeling was, 'You're dealing with an isolated, hidden African culture. So where were these white people supposed to come from?'" It was the only mainstream American comic book to feature an all-black cast. When the book's sales remained low, that was not a distinction that Marvel had much use for. For a while, though, McGregor's staff position afforded him an extra advantage in greasing the editorial wheels. He even had a deal with his fellow proof-reader, Steve Gerber: "You don't edit my books," McGregor said, "and I won't edit yours."

Steve Gerber gladly accepted the offer. He was happy not to be edited; he was virtually unable to work from a staid template. "Oh, great!" he had a teenager snap in the first Marvel comic he wrote. "It's those guys who were bothering us at the head shop!" Dialogue like that never would have made its way into *Spider-Man*. Gerber got his start toiling in the horror genre, which he found "a crashing bore," but working on the nonsuperhero periphery enabled him to experiment. The tagline for *Adventures into Fear*—"Whatever knows fear . . . burns at the touch of the Man-Thing!"— summed up the extent of motivation for its protagonist, a personality-free monster that simply wandered around the swamps of Citrusville, Florida, causing agony to frightened individuals. So when the title was assigned to Gerber, he was forced to look elsewhere for characterization. After establishing that the Citrusville swamp was the "Crossroads of the Universe," he went about building an extensive, and increasingly bizarre, supporting cast: teenagers Jennifer and Andrew Kale; their grandfather Joshua, who belonged to an Atlantean-worshipping cult called Zhered-Na; a sorcerer named Dakimh; a crew of angry construction workers; and Korrek, a barbarian who emerged from a jar of peanut butter. There was Wundarr, a send-up of Superman so dead-on that DC threatened to sue (Lee, frustrated, nearly removed Gerber from the book). And there was a talking duck named Howard, whom Gerber would later describe as having come to him in a trance as he typed at his home in Brooklyn, the sounds of a salsa record wafting from a neighbor's apartment.

Amazingly, this was all conceived without the help of psychedelics. "He was one of those guys who was militant about not altering his consciousness," said Steve Englehart. "Gerber's weirdness came directly from his id." In his early twenties, in St. Louis, Gerber had been on the sidelines of hippie culture, an observer. "I was always too academic, too conscientiously critical, to throw myself into it totally. There seemed to be a certain shallowness of philosophy, somehow, and beyond that, even, there was a lot of violence associated with that culture." This outsider perspective meant that no ideology, left, right, or center, was safe. The Foolkiller, religious-nut vigilante with a "ray of purity" gun; Holden Crane, an obnoxious, rhetoric-spewing student radical; and F. A. Schist, a money-grubbing industrialist—they each met an early doom at Gerber's hands. Where McGregor's writing was passionately serious, Gerber was a born satirist, almost helplessly lampooning every segment of the population. Filling in on an issue of *Captain America*, he created the Viper, a bad guy whose day job in advertising had left him bitter. "For years," shouted the Viper, "I labored in anonymity, selling other men's products, making other men's fortunes—laying waste to the values and environment of a nation from the privacy of my office . . . now I've left that grey flannel world behind!" After all the relentlessly earnest civic lectures of the past few years, readers encountering Gerber's weird societal critiques were inclined to do a double take—was this for real?

Before long, he was trying his hand at *Iron Man* and the *Sub-Mariner*, and *Daredevil*, where one story line featured *Rolling Stone* editor Jann Wenner and an angry-hippie villain named Angar who blasted people with bad trips and primal screams. In *Marvel Two-in-One*, a series that teamed the Thing with various guest stars, Gerber demonstrated that he'd staked out his own corner of the Marvel universe, where he could have Daredevil and Wundarr coexist. Still, Gerber was at his best when he was freed from the constraints of closely watched properties.

When it became clear that Gerber would make a better full-time freelance writer than staffer—his sleep apnea led to restless nights, and so he regularly dozed off at his desk—McGregor welcomed a revolving door of proofreading partners: first Tony Isabella, and then Doug Moench, from Chicago, and then David Anthony Kraft, a seventeen-year-old from Georgia.* Each of them was a writer as well, and each of them shared an understanding: you leave alone my stuff, and I'll leave alone yours.

Roy Thomas's hands-off, see-what-sticks approach had ushered in Marvel's most unpredictable—and often downright subversive—era. Young creators, eager to refract the superhero world through a prism of boomer values, kept parading through. "It wasn't a corporate environment," said one former Cadence Industries lawyer who'd occasionally

---

* In 1973, Roy Thomas offered one of these positions to nineteen-year-old Gary Groth, who would go on to become one of Marvel's most outspoken critics as the editor of the *Comics Journal*. The idea of Groth as a Marvel employee brings to mind the apocryphal story of a young Fidel Castro trying out as a pitcher for the Washington Senators.

visit the offices. "I remember stepping over people sitting in the hall, smoking pot, 'getting inspiration.'"

Artist Jim Starlin, a Detroit-raised greaser and Vietnam veteran who'd survived a helicopter crash in Sicily and explosions in Southeast Asia, created unsmiling, violent superheroes as a form of "anger management" and stuck them in his freelance work. Steve Englehart, who'd buried his best friend from basic training, marinated the stories he wrote in lefty politics. Where Stan Lee, a master fence-sitter, had managed to always stake out a safe middle ground, Starlin, Englehart, and their peers couldn't help but have stronger, and angrier, convictions.

Of course, the new guys weren't going to be allowed anywhere near *Amazing Spider-Man* or *Fantastic Four* or *The Incredible Hulk* or *The Mighty Thor*—those best-selling titles were reserved for Thomas himself, or for wunderkind Gerry Conway. Those comics were going to stick to their formulas, professionally executed to the point of monotony—and there was no longer any doubt that that was exactly how Stan wanted it. Conway learned this the hard way.

Casting for a way to shake up *Amazing Spider-Man*, Thomas and Conway had discussed the idea of killing off a member of the supporting cast. Aunt May—elderly, generically kindly, and seemingly always at death's door anyway—was the logical nominee. But when John Romita got wind of the plans, he suggested a different victim: Peter Parker's girlfriend, the lovely Gwen Stacy. Conway thought it was a stroke of genius.

"She was a nonentity, a pretty face," he said. "She brought nothing to the mix. It made no sense to me that Peter Parker would end up with a babe like that who had no problems. Only a damaged person would end up with a damaged guy like Peter Parker. And Gwen Stacy was perfect! It was basically Stan fulfilling Stan's own fantasy. Stan married a woman who was pretty much a babe—Joan Lee was a very attractive blond who was obviously Stan's ideal female. And I think Gwen was simply Stan replicating his wife, just like Sue Storm was a replication of his wife. And that's where his blind spot was. The amazing thing was that he created a character like Mary Jane Watson, who was probably the most interesting female character in comics, and he never used her to the extent that he could have. Instead of Peter Parker's girlfriend, he made her Peter Parker's *best friend*'s girlfriend. Which is so wrong, and so stupid, and such a waste. So killing Gwen was a totally logical if not inevitable choice."

Thomas then cleared the plans with Lee. "He was okay with it to the extent that Stan paid attention to anything," said Conway. "At that time he was primarily interested in expanding the line, asserting his authority as publisher to the higher-ups that owned Marvel, and promoting his own brand and his own career. Once he stopped writing a given comic he stopped thinking about it. And so when he stopped writing *Spider-Man*, even though he had a proprietary interest in it, really, it was 'Yeah, whatever you want to do.'"

Conway, Romita, and Gil Kane worked out a story in which Green Goblin kidnapped Gwen Stacy and threw her off the top of the George Washington Bridge; in a perverse twist, someone added a "snap!" to the panel in which Spider-Man's web catches Gwen, implying that it was not the fall but whiplash from the catch that caused her neck to snap, that Spider-Man was implicated in the death.

The readership started hyperventilating as soon as the issue hit stands.

"Stan didn't think about it until he went to a college campus and got yelled at by fans," Conway said. "Instead of acting like he was in charge, he said, 'Oh, they must have done it while I was out of town—I would never have done that!' The pretty horrendous backlash that I received from the fan press, and the lack of support I got from Stan, who said we did it behind his back, had a huge impact on me in terms of my emotional state. He basically threw me to the wolves. This was the first time a beloved character had been killed off in comics. I couldn't go to conventions."

"The idea that the three of us together, or even separately, would have tried to sneak in the death of Gwen Stacy without Stan approving it is just so absurd," said Roy Thomas. "Besides, he was never out of town that long." It came back to what Stan had told Roy Thomas, years before: he didn't want to fix what wasn't broken; he only wanted "the *illusion* of change."

During a speaking engagement at Penn State, Lee was again

surprised to learn of a character death; this time, Len Wein had killed a member of *The Incredible Hulk*'s supporting cast. "I told them not to kill too many people," Lee assured the crowd, and promised that Gwen Stacy would return.

Just as Conway was getting used to the idea that he couldn't tweak Marvel's intellectual property, he was also asked to whip up some merchandising synergy. After toy company Azrak-Hamway offered Marvel a licensing deal for a Spider-Man car, Lee handed down a decree to create something called the Spider-Mobile. Conway thought the idea was ridiculous. Why have a hero who could swing through the city on webs get stuck in New York City traffic? In *Amazing Spider-Man* #126, Conway, annoyed, had a pair of sleazy suits approach Spider-Man and ask him to drive their prototype, for publicity. They looked a little bit like Lee and Thomas, and the address on the business card they handed Spider-Man was 575 Madison Avenue—Marvel's address.

Conway had hardly been the picture of the rebel—while Jim Starlin and Steve Englehart were trying to translate their psychedelic experiences into four-color adventures, Conway blamed Norman Osborn's relapse into his Green Goblin identity (and his subsequent murder of Gwen Stacy) on his son Harry's bad LSD trips. But Conway began sliding a patina of political content into his work. Drawing inspiration from Don Pendleton's popular *Executioner* novels, Conway created a new character called the Punisher. Like Pendleton's Mack Bolan, the Punisher was a Vietnam War veteran who exacted revenge on the mob after it murdered members of his family. But where Bolan—lusty, unrepentantly vicious, and charmless—was cast as a hero, Conway framed the Punisher as a paranoid and dangerous, if somewhat sympathetic, antagonist. It was the vigilante adventure as cautionary tale.

Conway reserved his greatest scorn not for Doctor Octopus or the Kingpin but for newly created bad guys who'd sold out their left-wing compatriots, like Ethiopian supervillain Moses Magnum (who, a caption revealed, had once made a deal with Mussolini), the onetime South American revolutionary known as the Tarantula (who betrayed his fellow rebels to a dictator's army), and the French villain Cyclone, a NATO engineer who'd begun developing weapons on the side.

These flourishes may have sailed over the heads of *Spider-Man's* adolescent readership. But soon after Stan Lee rapped his knuckles for writing Gwen Stacy's death, the twenty-year-old Conway found the next-best way to traumatize legions of twelve-year-olds, this time in the pages of *The Fantastic Four*: divorce proceedings for Reed and Sue Storm. Decades later, novelist Rick Moody would describe the story line in *The Ice Storm*, his roman à clef about familial disintegration: "Sue Richards, nee Storm, the Invisible Girl, had been estranged from her husband, Reed Richards. With Franklin, their mysteriously equipped son, she was in seclusion in the country. She would return only when Reed learned to understand the obligations of family, those paramount bonds that lay beneath the surface of his work."* (They would later reconcile.)

Just as the furor of Gwen Stacy was starting to die down, Roy Thomas saw Howard, the talking duck that Gerber and artist Val Mayerik had placed in *Adventure into Fear*. The book's scary vibe, he thought, was compromised by the inclusion of a funny animal. "Get it out of there as fast as you can," he told Gerber. In his next appearance, Howard made a clumsy step off a rock and fell into oblivion.

The fans reacted instantly. "The office was flooded with letters," Gerber recalled. "There was the one wacko who sent a duck carcass from Canada, saying, 'Murderers, how dare you kill off this duck?' There was the incident at a San Diego Comics Convention where somebody asked Roy whether Howard would ever be coming back, and the entire auditorium stood up and applauded. Stan was being asked about it every place he went on the college circuit."†

---

* Mr. Fantastic and the Invisible Girl had welcomed their son into the world in 1968, a year after Sue Storm's pregnancy was first revealed. Such anomalous domesticity only made *The Fantastic Four* seem that much more exotic.

† This caused further trouble and embarrassment: Stan Lee, the public face of the company, could only respond, "Howard the Who?"

This time, the fans were on the side of the writer. Marvel would bring Howard back.

"I don't have time to edit," Roy had told Steve Englehart on an early assignment, "so we're hiring you to write this book. If you can turn it in on time and can make it sell, you can keep doing it. If you can't, then we'll fire you and hire somebody else."

In this sink-or-swim spirit, Jim Starlin was tapped to plot and draw an issue of *Iron Man*, a comic that his roommate, Mike Friedrich, had been writing for six months. Figuring he might never get another shot, he convinced Friedrich that they should stuff the issue with the characters Starlin had dreamed up while taking psych classes at a Detroit community college after his Navy stint.* Thomas was pleased, and paired Starlin with Steve Gerber for the following issue; however, Lee happened to see that story, deemed the results terrible, and immediately removed Starlin from the title. Then Starlin and Alan Weiss were offered a quick-turnaround art job on the final issue of *The Claws of the Cat*. For two days, Starlin's girlfriend kept them supplied with wine and pot; in a celebratory mood, they filled the margins with smart-alecky comments and in-jokes. By the night before deadline, though, the fading duo had to recruit a third artist, who snuck in his own unsolicited suggestion to the narration: *The Cat gets an ovarian cyst!* After the pages came back to Linda Fite to add her dialogue, she went straight to Lee and complained. The next day, Starlin got an angry call from the office.

But Thomas thought Starlin had promise. He offered him a chance to work on *Captain Marvel,* a faltering title that Thomas had written himself, before editorial duties pulled him away. The conveniently named Mar-Vell, a warrior of the alien Kree race, had defied his own people to protect Earth; now he worked in tandem with Rick Jones, the former teenage sidekick to the Hulk, who had blossomed into an annoying wannabe rock star. The characters had agonizingly bland personalities—but that turned out to be just the blank slate Starlin

---

* They also hinted at plans to realign the political thrust of *Iron Man*: announced that Stark Industries would shift "priorities from weaponry to ecological research."

needed. At first, as he found his footing, he larded the comic with guest stars and big fight scenes, just to make sure it would sell enough to keep going. Then he got adventurous.

"We had different points of view, different attitudes, and different things we wanted to convey, and it was a time of turmoil in the world," said Al Milgrom, a wisecracking, self-described "frat boy" who'd known Starlin growing up in Detroit, and who collaborated with him on *Captain Marvel*. "So when we were given these characters, we went off on some tangents." Indeed: Starlin decided to explore "enlightenment through discipline and training," a concept he still believed in, even though it had eluded him in his own military experiences. In Starlin's hands, *Captain Marvel* was not so much about how much power and charisma its hero had, but about how many limits he had—he was an unenlightened mope who didn't know how to live up to his potential. Within a few issues, Captain Marvel would become "cosmically aware," a process described in words that might have been gleaned from the Dhammapada, fortified with a generous supply of exclamation points: "This *man* has *conquered*! He's beaten *vanity* and *pride* by seeing the *universe* as it is! He knows what must be done and does it, but does it with a *great sorrow*! For this man knows *truth* and *peace*!" Starlin transplanted his characters from that failed issue of *Iron Man*—Thanos, Drax the Destroyer, Mentor, Kronos, Eros—and added several more, turning the book into the kind of vast, multigenerational space opera that would soon make George Lucas a rich man. Of course, *Star Wars* never blew the hinges off the doors of perception.

"I was just as crazy as everybody else post-Watergate, post-Vietnam," said Starlin, whose hobbies included motorcycles, chess, and lysergic acid diethylamide–25. "Each one of those stories was me taking that stuff that had gone before and trying to put my personal slant on it. Mar-Vell was a warrior who decided he was going to become a god, and that's where his trip was." In the pages of *Captain Marvel*, existence itself might be altered several times in the course of an issue. "There is a moment of *change*, then *reality* becomes a thing of the *past*!" howls the evil ruler Thanos, before everything morphs into funhouse-mirror images. His sworn enemy Drax responds: "My *mind* and my *soul* are one . . . my soul . . . an immortal *intangible*, nothing and everything! That which cannot *die* cannot be *enslaved*, for only with *fear* is servitude rendered!" On the following page, Drax's shifting realities are represented by thirty-five panels of warped faces, skulls, eyes, stars, and lizards. *Captain Marvel* had practically become a black-light poster with dialogue. Its sales kept increasing. Soon Starlin was opening his fan mail and finding complimentary joints sent by grateful, mind-blown readers.

Englehart, meanwhile, was humming along on a slightly less psychedelic scale. He'd revamped the dormant Beast for a few issues of *Amazing Adventures*, then landed stints on *The Defenders, Luke Cage,** and *Captain America*, which despite its hero's thirty years of history was barely selling. "It was taking place during the Vietnam War," Englehart scoffed, "and here was this guy wearing a flag on his chest, and everybody was embarrassed." Englehart did away with the character's more reactionary rhetoric, and added a liberal-humanist charge. The first issues of Englehart's *Captain America* explained why, if the character had been encased in a block of ice since the end of World War II, the 1950s revival comics showed him fighting communists: the fifties Cap, it turned out, was an imposter, a superpatriot turned insane by side effects of the super-serum. This retroactive continuity didn't exactly thrill John Romita, who'd actually drawn those 1950s adventures, but readers were electrified. Within six months *Captain America* was Marvel's number-one title, and Englehart was entrusted with *The Avengers*. These young, opinionated rabble-rousers were getting closer and closer to the marquee properties.

It was during this ascendancy that Englehart met Frank Brunner, a Brooklyn artist with long blond hair, a buckskin jacket, and a library of Carlos Castaneda and H. P. Lovecraft paperbacks. Brunner had recently quit Marvel's token occult-superhero comic, *Doctor Strange,* because he didn't like the scripts that sexagenarian DC veteran Gardner Fox was writing—"monster of the month" was his disparaging description of Fox's

---

*In a story that appeared in *Luke Cage, Hero for Hire* #8, Englehart said that artist George Tuska—who would ignore Englehart's subplots and send back artwork with the explanation "I didn't feel like drawing that"—tricked him into referring to Luke Cage as a nice "schvartze" boy. Englehart didn't realize that *schvartze* was a derogatory Yiddish term for a black person. An awkward apology appeared three issues later. "What can I tell you?" Englehart shrugs. "I'm from Indiana."

plotting style, which incorporated a revolving door of inhuman villains. But now Fox was off the book, and Roy wanted Brunner back. When Roy asked him whom he would want on board as a writer, Brunner remembered the guy he'd talked to at parties about kabbalah, astrology, and Satanism. Englehart jumped at the opportunity to bring *Doctor Strange* back to the trippy, Day-Glo heights of the Lee and Ditko era. They got right to work.

"We would get together every two months, have dinner, get loaded about 10 o'clock, and stay there until 3 or 4," said Englehart. "He would be thinking about what would *look* really cool, and I would talk about where I could go with Dr. Strange's consciousness, and we would come up with a summation that was greater than the parts."

When they weren't at each other's apartments getting high, they were rampaging around with Starlin, Al Milgrom, and artist Alan Weiss, a Las Vegas–bred ladies' man who shared a Queens apartment with a rotating cast of five stewardesses. Together, they'd ingest LSD and wander *Death Wish*–era Manhattan at all hours. "We sort of took New York as this vast stage set," said Weiss. "We would launch ourselves to some part we hadn't seen yet, and go explore, day or night." There was the time they traipsed by security guards and wandered through the World Trade Center while it was being built. On one July night they went to Lincoln Center for a screening of Disney's *Alice in Wonderland* and hatched a *Doctor Strange* plot that included a hookah-smoking caterpillar. Then they walked to the U.S. Customs House in lower Manhattan and climbed around on Daniel Chester French's four statues of the continents, where they envisioned a *Defenders* story in which Doctor Strange transformed each statue into thousands of living soldiers to battle hordes of Atlantean invaders.

In Rutland, Vermont, where the annual Halloween parade organized by comics fan Tom Fagan drew swarms of industry professionals, Starlin and Weiss and Englehart sat under a waterfall, opened their minds, and discussed that hoary stoners' concept: God. In a matter of months, their respective visions—informed by such occult touchstones as the Knights Templar, Atlantis, the Illuminati, Druidry, and Aleister Crowley—would turn up in simultaneous issues of *Captain Marvel* and *Doctor Strange*. The evil megalomaniac Thanos captured the all-powerful Cosmic Cube and turned himself into God, but was defeated on a technicality (nobody worshipped Thanos, the heroes helpfully explained at the end—and a god needs worshippers). In *Doctor Strange*, a thirty-first-century magician named Sise-Neg found that by moving backward in time, he could absorb energy from Cagliostro, Merlin, and priests of Sodom and Gomorrah, gathering power until he reached the beginning of time, and became God.

"When the book came out," Brunner said, "Stan finally got a hold of it, and he wrote us a letter saying, 'We can't do God. You're going to have to print, in the letters column, a retraction, saying this is not *the* God, this is just *a* god.' Steve and I said, 'Oh, come on! This is the whole point of the story! If we did that retraction of God, this is meaningless!' So, we cooked up this plot—we wrote a letter from a Reverend Billingsley in Texas, a fictional person, saying that one of the children in his parish brought him the comic book, and he was astounded and thrilled by it, and he said, 'Wow, this is the best comic book I've ever read.'" Englehart had a Christmastime layover in Dallas, and mailed it from there, ensuring a proper postmark. "We got a phone call from Roy, and he said, 'Hey, about that retraction, I'm going to send you a letter, and instead of the retraction, I want you to print this letter.' We printed *our* letter! We later found out that Jim Starlin was in New York at that time, up in the Marvel offices, and he was reading the *Doctor Strange* fan mail, and he was the one who actually saw the letter, believed it was the real thing, and gave it to Roy, who gave it to Stan."

The *real* letters they got, from college students and freaks, were accompanied by baggies of Wowie Maui and said things like, "I like to smoke a bowl, put on ELO or ELP or Pink Floyd and read the latest issue of *Doctor Strange*." Those weren't printed.

On Friday nights, Englehart and Starlin stayed in and watched television. They had become rabid fans of ABC's *Kung Fu*, which starred David Carradine as a Shaolin monk in the Old West who alternated between Eastern philosophizing and ass-kicking. They approached Roy Thomas about doing a *Kung Fu* adaptation for Marvel, but the show was produced by Warner Bros.—DC Comics' corporate parent—so they created their own concept: *Shang-Chi, Master of Kung Fu*. "I was already doing

Doctor Strange, which represented the Western mystical philosophy," Englehart recalled. "I really saw *Shang-Chi* as a chance to do the Eastern mystical philosophy, albeit with a more action-oriented hero than Doctor Strange." In that spirit, he and Alan Weiss settled on Shang-Chi's name, which meant "the rising advancing of the spirit," by throwing the *I Ching* and mixing and matching hexagrams. Then Thomas, who'd secured the rights to Sax Rohmer's pulp-novel Fu Manchu character, suggested they incorporate martial arts into a Fu Manchu comic. So Shang-Chi became the son of Fu Manchu, who learns his father's evil secret and dedicates himself to fighting him.* The mix of philosophy and ass-kicking was perfect for an era that embraced *Passages* and *Walking Tall*.

The plotting was the easy part—party all day; rest; drop more acid. "We saw a movie and came out at 9 or 10, not tired. We started out in midtown and walked all the way to South Ferry. I don't know that we would have walked that far if we hadn't been chemically altered. About two in the morning, we came to the AT&T Long Lines building. A monolith, with monitored underwater cables to Europe, and no windows—a huge monument in a neighborhood of 1940s warehouses. There's construction going on the other side of the street, with guys bent over acetylene torches throwing six-story shadows on the building." They had their model for Fu Manchu's headquarters. When they turned and saw abandoned construction vehicles, they had their scene for a climactic martial-arts fight. The comic was practically writing itself. As Weiss said, "Some of it was chemically fueled. But it was always fodder for creativity. We got very . . . enhanced. We were *extremely* enhanced."†

When the time came to draw the comic, though, things got rocky. Starlin created dozens of sketches for Shang-Chi, whom he rendered with a

---

* With Shang-Chi and *Son of Satan's* Damian Hellstrom, post Vietnam Marvel writers replaced Stan Lee's longing orphans (Peter Parker, Matt Murdock, Johnny Storm) with righteous Oedipal anger.

† Not everyone was enamored of the lysergic-intensive lifestyle: Gerry Conway said he feared for his sanity when he tripped with Englehart and Weiss, and that one member of the acid coterie—he won't say who—"went around the bend" permanently. "He was dating an ex-girlfriend of mine who told me, 'All he wants to do is drop acid and fuck! He won't take me anywhere!' Later, he did my horoscope at a party, decided he was my enemy, and that was it."

Chinese face—except when drafting different costume designs. "I did just this generic face on top of the figures and Stan said 'That's the face you've gotta go with.'" Starlin tried to explain the misunderstanding, but Lee held his ground. Making matters worse, Starlin finally read the Sax Rohmer source material and was aghast at the pervasive racism. "By the time we finally got done with it," Starlin said, "I had a friend who was Oriental who looked at it—he told me flat out he found the whole thing insulting. That was enough for me." When the first issue came out, fans wrote in to complain about Fu Manchu's bright yellow skin, prompting a laborious explanation about the color printing process. By then, Starlin had walked.

Englehart soon followed. "I got five issues into it and they called me up and said, 'Stan rode up on an elevator today and heard two guys talking. One guy said, "what's the hottest thing in movies these days?" and the other guy said, "Kung fu movies and the reason why is because it's wall-to-wall violence."' Stan got off the elevator, walked to Marvel Comics and said, 'Let's do wall-to-wall violence.' They called me up and said, 'We don't want any more of this philosophy. We just want kung fu fights.'"* The series continued on without him, with cover lines like "The Fortune Cookie Says: DEATH!"

Englehart focused his attention on *Captain America*, which, at the time of the Watergate scandal, suddenly seemed like the richest opportunity at Marvel. He crafted a conspiracy story line with thinly veiled correlations to actual headlines: the Committee to Reelect the President (C.R.E.E.P.) became the Committee to Regain America's Principles (C.R.A.P.), with the real world's ex-adman H. R. Haldeman replaced in the comics by ex-adman Quentin Harderman. It all climaxed with Captain America tracing the shadowy "Secret Empire" straight to the Oval Office—where a disgraced commander in chief committed suicide by gunshot.

Englehart never showed the president's face, but Marvel called him when the pages arrived, asking for reassurance that it was not intended to be Nixon. "I swore up and down that it wasn't," he said. "But once it was in print, I had no problem admitting it."

* Perhaps feeling he had nothing to lose, in his final issue Englehart included a character that looked and talked exactly like the original inspiration for Shang-Chi: David Carradine's Caine.

Starlin, on the other hand, felt like he was getting a hard time. After the Shang-Chi fiasco, he began turning his work in at the last moment, to avoid editorial interference. John Romita, who'd been given the title of art director, offered Starlin a regular gig on the flagship *Fantastic Four* but found that the young superstar was no longer yearning to be a team player. "Starlin turned down the *FF*, and that was the first time I ever heard of a professional comic artist—they used to be so grateful to get a steady book that they would crawl on their bellies—turn down a book. He said he didn't want to be 'tied down' to it."

When Mike Friedrich, Starlin's old *Iron Man* writing partner, moved out to Hayward, California, and started independently publishing his own anthology comic book, Starlin jumped at the chance to contribute. The first issue of *Star*Reach* opened with Starlin's seven-page tale about an artist who enters a slick "death building," drops acid as he rides the elevator, boasts that he's a "being of imagination," and beheads a cloaked figure of Death. But the artist is then himself slain. As the story ends, another acid-eating artist enters the building—"My name is Starlin, Jim Starlin!"—one more lamb for the slaughter. The slick office building, revealed upon further inspection of the artwork, was at Fifty-Fifth and Madison—the address of Marvel Comics. Just as "Death Building" was going to press, Starlin threw a fit about an inking substitution in *Captain Marvel*, told Marvel he was quitting, and took off for California.

Brunner quit, too, finding the pace too grueling when rising sales of *Doctor Strange* convinced Marvel to push it from every other month to a monthly title instead. "It was definitely an Oscar and Felix kind of relationship," Englehart said of the collaboration. "I smoked dope, and dropped acid, and ate mushrooms—and I made my deadlines. Brunner was also into that stuff, and in the end couldn't keep up. He would be saying 'We could do this, we could do that,' and I would be saying, 'Yeah, but we *have to get it into seventeen pages.*'" Brunner had started to lose interest anyway—he was more excited about a new project he'd been working on with Gerber, a short story that featured the return of Howard the Duck.

———

In the summer of 1974, news started to surface that Martin and Chip Goodman were planning a return to comics—with the specific goal of exacting revenge on Marvel and Al Landau, whose crowding out of Chip they considered an unforgivable act of betrayal. They created cover designs that blatantly imitated Marvel's branding, right down to the thin horizontal banners at the top of each magazine. They called themselves Atlas Comics, but people in the industry almost immediately began calling them "Vengeance, Incorporated."

The Goodmans spread the word that Atlas would pay higher page rates than Marvel or DC; it would return original artwork; it would even offer the creators ownership of their characters. One artist set up shop outside Marvel's Madison Avenue offices, enthusiastically redirecting other freelancers to Atlas's headquarters, a block away. Before long, many significant Marvel alumni, including John Severin, Wally Wood, Gary Friedrich, Gerry Conway, and Steve Ditko, had signed up; even Lee's own brother, Larry Lieber, was hired as an editor.

In desperation, Lee sat down and typed up a letter to freelancers. "Recently, a number of smaller companies—some already established, some in the process of attempting a launch—have decided that the only way to match Marvel's success is to lure away as many of our people as possible." Then he ramped up the drama considerably.

It's like Nazi Germany and the Allies in World War II. Hitler, being a dictator and having no one to answer to, could do as he wished whenever the mood struck him, and could make the most extravagant promises to his captive people, while being completely heedless to the consequences. The U.S., however, had to move slowly, following firmly established principles of law and government. Marvel, like the Allies, simply cannot counter-react with impetuous pie-in-the-sky offers and promises.

Being aware of this situation, certain competitors are making increasingly frenzied efforts to decimate Marvel's staff, with more and more such offers being dangled before the eyes of almost anyone who can use a pencil, brush, or typewriter. Offers which could ultimately become sand beneath your feet—but their purpose will have been achieved.

Lee emphasized that Marvel was the largest employer of comic freelancers, that its rates had continually risen over the last fifteen years, and that it had instituted a hospitalization and life insurance plan for exclusive freelancers. He emphasized that it was he himself who'd introduced prominent credits in the comics, and that it had been Martin Goodman who had not allowed the return of original artwork. "Marvel has never lied to you," he wrote, in closing. "Marvel never will. Stay with us. You won't regret it."

Lee threatened Archie Goodwin, who'd been writing for Marvel, that working for Atlas would be a bridge-burner, and Thomas advised freelancers that there would be no guarantee of future work with Marvel if they strayed. But in August, Thomas himself went to dinner with Chip, and talked things over—just wanting to feel things out. He was burning out at Marvel, leaving work and beginning all-night writing sessions at ten or eleven at night. Jeanie had come back to him—for now—but things with her felt tenuous, irreparable, and the stress of the job wasn't helping things. He was defending company policies he didn't agree with, constantly caught between labor and management. According to Romita, many of the older Bullpen members had never cottoned to Thomas, or accorded him respect. "When you're used to working with Stan, a lot of them had trouble taking orders from Roy. They felt like he was a kid who shouldn't be in charge." When veteran inker Vince Colletta learned that Roy was planning to remove him from inking duties on *Thor*, he marched into Roy's office and threatened to throw him out the window.

Now Thomas was also feeling unfriendly pressure from above, in the person of Al Landau. They'd gotten off to a bad start: When there had been the threat of an industry-wide artists' union, Thomas wanted to fly to the Philippines to recruit artists who'd work at cheaper rates. Landau vetoed the trip on the ground that it would be "too much like a vacation," despite the revolutionary war raging near Manila at the time. When Thomas broached the idea of selling comics directly to comic stores at a discount, Thomas said, Landau "would look at me as if I were an idiot, tell me that that would just make the wholesalers and retailers mad, and change the subject." A quarter century later, Thomas could remember only one or two times that he and Landau agreed on anything.

Even Stan Lee had started to grow distant—he'd encourage Thomas to push for policies like returning original art to freelancers, or paying royalties on reprints, or distributing directly to specialty comic shops, but if Landau resisted, Lee would stay quiet. "By becoming publisher," Thomas said, "he had gone from being creative force to total company man, which was what he wanted—but I didn't want to follow him along that path as I had before." For his part, Lee told people that he and Thomas were no longer seeing eye to eye.

The comics themselves, at least, were the best they'd been since Kirby left—in fact, Thomas had even had conversations with Kirby about coming back from DC. "Roy was very open to ideas, and allowed you to do almost anything. He managed to find ways to get you into the company before you knew you were there," said Marv Wolfman. "Len had no intention of ever coming over, but slowly found himself working full-time for Marvel. . . . Roy knew how to handle people." Thomas was also talking to Starlin about returning, maybe taking over the superhero-as-Christ parable *Warlock*, with stories so far-out they'd make *Captain Marvel* look like *Marmaduke*. Steve Englehart followed the Watergate story in *Captain America* with adventures based on the Symbionese Liberation Army's Los Angeles siege and the People's Revolutionary Army's kidnapping of an Exxon executive in Argentina; in *The Avengers*, he embarked on a weird epic that involved time travel and telepathic trees.

But Thomas wouldn't be around to see these stories reach fruition. The final straw came, at last, after a freelancer was caught trying to drive up his Marvel income by lying about his page rate with DC. A seething Stan Lee went out to lunch with DC president Carmine Infantino and hammered out an agreement to share information about how much each freelance writer or artist was getting.

When Thomas heard the news, he was appalled—this was collusion, and he wanted no part of it. Jeanie had wanted him to quit all along, ever since Stan had rescinded that job offer to her—hell, he *had* quit once, over the phone, but Stan had talked him out of it. That wouldn't happen again. Before leaving the office that night, he sat down, took out a sheet of paper, and in a one-paragraph memo decried Lee and Infantino's plan as "unethical, immoral, and quite possibly illegal." He would not enforce it. The next day, Thomas wrote from home; and when he returned to Marvel the following day, Lee summoned him into his office. "I suppose that you consider this your letter of resignation," Lee said, before trying to explain his position on freelancer rates. "It doesn't matter," Thomas said. "It's probably best if I leave Marvel."

6

THE STAFF WAS SUMMONED IN FOR THE ANNOUNCEMENT THAT THOMAS—THE second-longest-tenured Marvel employee—was stepping down. The reaction was stunned silence. "Roy was there, sitting rather quietly, and Stan didn't seem happy about it either," remembered Jim Salicrup, who at the time was seventeen years old and working at Marvel as a messenger. "I don't think there was ever any real animosity; I think Stan may not have realized how much more was involved from the days when he had to run the comics line. He may have just thought that Roy was going nuts or something, or demanding too much. I think Roy wanted to put in a structure that would better cope with the expanding workload, and I don't think they realized that this isn't a job for just one person—you have to have x amount of editors handling x amount of titles."

Privately, Lee and Thomas worked out the details of his departure from staff. Carmine Infantino had offered Thomas the chance to write *Superman* at DC, but Lee certainly didn't want his protégé working for the competition, and so he offered Roy a contract that allowed him to continue writing from home, editing himself and answering directly to Lee. Thomas would stay on at the office for a few weeks, oversee a transition, and then, as a sort of going-away present, he'd get a new title called *The Invaders*, featuring World War II–era adventures of his beloved Golden Age characters. He'd also stay on *Conan the Barbarian*, the comic adaptation of Robert E. Howard's pulp character that he'd convinced Marvel to license, and which had become a surprise hit. Lee and Thomas decided that the future editorship should be split up, with Len Wein, recently hired as Thomas's assistant, taking over the color comics and

Marv Wolfman the black-and-whites. With the inseparable "LenMarv" running things, Marvel could get two minds in perfect sync.* Thomas flew down to Washington, D.C., where they were attending a science-fiction convention, to make the offer.

At first Wein was ambivalent. "I've been assistant editor for three months, and now you want me to run the company?" he asked. But Thomas, eager to settle the matter, reassured Wein that he was a capable successor. "He wanted out," recalled Wein. "It took me a year to understand why he left: It was an impossible job. And as long as we kept doing that impossible job, they wouldn't believe it was impossible."

Chris Claremont, a twenty-four-year-old former intern who'd been writing and proofreading part-time while trying to get his acting career off the ground, was named Wein's associate editor: Scott Edelman and Roger Slifer, both nineteen, served as assistant editors. As everyone was figuring out their new duties, there were fifty-four color comics a month that needed to be published. Wein had no choice but to decrease his writing workload, and since he wanted to continue on *The Incredible Hulk*, he'd have to find someone else to write the new *X-Men* series, which was finally in production after many months of development.

The return of the X-Men had been plotted during Roy Thomas's tenure. Marvel president Al Landau still had a hand in the Transworld Features Syndicate, which had begun repackaging Marvel comics for foreign markets; when Landau realized that European and Asian characters would have great international value, he charged Thomas with devising a super-team of non-Americans. Thomas, who'd been already itching for a few years to revive Marvel's mutant team, saw a way for the discontinued title to fill Landau's order.

Thomas, Mike Friedrich, and artist Dave Cockrum went out to lunch at the Autopub, a car-themed restaurant in the bowels of the General

---

* "The story," said Jim Shooter, "was that when Roy left, Len and Marv went together to Stan and told him that everybody hated Gerry, and if he hired Gerry, everyone would quit. And Stan decided, for whatever reason, to go with that theory, and he hired Len as editor in chief. And Gerry quit and went to DC. Stan finally thought it was time to fulfill the old promise."

Motors building, to brainstorm. Sitting at a table made from car chassis, surrounded by monuments to assembly line production, the trio discussed the idea of replacing the old X-Men members with a multi-ethnic team of mutant heroes. Cockrum, who filled his notebooks with sketches of original costume designs, ideas for hire at the ready, was a one-man character machine. He went home and perused his files, selecting characters he'd kicked around over the years, while in college, while in the army, and while working on DC's *Superboy and the Legion of Superheroes*: Typhoon. Black Cat. Mr. Steel. Thunderbird. Nightcrawler. The project went into limbo for months, however, and by the time the title was on the schedule in late 1974, Wein had replaced Friedrich; Typhoon and Black Cat were combined into "Storm"; Mr. Steel was "Colossus"; and Nightcrawler had evolved from an actual demon into a mutant German acrobat with a pointed tail.

The X-Men lineup also included the Canadian mutant Wolverine, whom Len Wein and John Romita had created when Thomas detected a need to exploit the Canadian market. Wolverine had appeared in one *Incredible Hulk* story and quickly made an impression as one of a trend in new characters, including Conway and Romita's Punisher and Rich Buckler's Deathlok, who were angry, violent, and defined by their weapons.

Giant-Size X-Men #1 begins by introducing five individuals, in turn, as they display their powers. Kurt Wagner (Nightcrawler) is hunted by a Bavarian mob as he leaps around and scales buildings; Canadian special agent Wolverine unsheathes a metal claw as he confronts his commanding officer on a military base; in Kenya, Ororo Munroe (Storm) is praised as a goddess for controlling wind and rain; Siberian farmer Peter Rasputin (Colossus) transforms into a powerful man of steel in order to save his sister from an errant tractor; Apache John Proudstar (Thunderbird) tackles a buffalo on an Arizona reservation. Each of them, along with past X-Men associates Banshee and Sunfire, are visited in turn by Professor X, who appeals to their consciences with a sales pitch on power and responsibility. He gathers them at his mansion in Westchester County, where he furnishes them with costumes, and where a condescending Cyclops explains that the X-Men—Iceman, Angel, Marvel Girl, Havok, and Polaris—have gone missing on Krakoa, an island in the South Pacific.

Exchanging threats and insults all the while, these eight set forth for Krakoa, which turns out to be itself a sentient being ("Krakoa . . . the island that walks like a man!"). The rescue mission itself is unremarkable; once the X-Men are freed from captivity (they've been captured by the island itself), it is they, and not the new recruits, who win the battle and earn escape. In fact, nearly everything about *Giant-Size X-Men #1* is a familiar echo of *Fantastic Four #1*: the *Magnificent Seven*–like gathering of the team, the dysfunctional bickering, the mysterious island to which they are summoned, even the dramatic escape by plane as the island explodes behind them.

With the final word balloon of the issue—"what are we going to do with thirteen X-Men?" someone in the plane asks—the transition begins. The old X-Men will be put out to pasture; the new X-Men will have a shot at capturing a younger audience.

Shortly after the issue was finished, it became clear that Wein's workload would force him to abandon the title—not that the decision caused him much distress. "It was just another book," he said. "It was no different to me than 'Brother Voodoo' or a couple of other new series that I was involved in." But for Chris Claremont, who'd been listening in on story meetings from his desk outside Wein's office and chiming in with ideas, it was a golden opportunity. He eagerly volunteered to take over the writing. "I said, 'Shit, yes!' But it was a mid-list title—we figured six issues, and out." Instead, it would change his life.

Wein struggled with the constant cycle of cancellations and launches ordered by Lee and Landau. Iron Fist, a kung-fu hero whose origin was mostly lifted from an old Bill Everett creation that predated Timely, was given his own title, as was Black Goliath, in another attempt at an African-American audience . . . and also Red Sonja, and the Scarecrow, and Skull the Slayer, and Bloodstone, and on and on. "You'd go into the office one day," said one assistant, "and the thirty books you'd edited last week would all be canceled, and even though they were in various stages of production, none of them was published yet, and thirty new books would be there for you to work on."

There was also the chance that Lee would swoop in, look at a page, and offer an offhand remark that would send the office scrambling. Near the end of Roy Thomas's tenure, Lee had taken a look at Iron Man pages in which the hero's faceplate was so flat that it didn't look like Tony Stark's nose would fit. "Shouldn't he have a nose?" he asked Thomas. In the decade since his creation, Iron Man's faceplate had *never* included a nose, but Lee was the boss. In the next issue, Stark redesigned his helmet to include a big metal triangle in the front. Months later, *Iron Man* pages by Mike Esposito landed on the desk of Production Manager John Verpoorten's brand-new assistant, Bill Mantlo. "I'm looking at this book and thinking, 'Jesus Christ, I must be *hallucinating!*'" said Mantlo. "'Iron Man doesn't have a *nose.*' So I sat there, very innocently, with a tube of white-out, and painted out all the noses, and maybe an hour later, I hear screaming. 'Esposito, are you out of your mind?! *What happened to his nose?*' . . . Mike comes in and he's raging, 'Goddamn it, the nose is there!! You can see the little dot of white over each nose!'" Mantlo went through and dutifully scraped the Wite-Out from every panel.

To help writers keep track of the flood of new and changing characters, Thomas had kept a plastic box of index cards noting where characters had last appeared, and what their powers were. That would no longer do. Now there was a gigantic database, an alphabetized list on five pounds of perforated computer paper printouts.

Coordinating the increasingly complex story continuity between titles was also becoming a burden. One of the Marvel Universe's hallmarks was that it was all one grand narrative, that everything that happened in one title had a potential impact on all the others. This was manageable when Stan Lee had personal oversight of eight comics a month, but nearly impossible when a cadre of excitable twenty-somethings wanted to let their imaginations wander—or when the bottom line called for franchise expansion. How could Spider-Man be everywhere at once? "The problem at Marvel," said Wein, "was that we suddenly became a business with a bunch of books that Stan, I don't think, ever in his heart expected to last more than a couple of years." Complicating matters further were the proprietary battles for character use. "Gerber would want to have Hulk do one thing in *The Defenders*," said Claremont, "but Englehart would say, 'I've got him doing this other thing in the *Avengers*. Who has priority?'"

"There was a definite hierarchy," said Bill Mantlo, who was drafted from the production office to write during a deadline crunch, and began getting regular assignments. "It seemed at that time that the key to being a successful Marvel writer was that you had worked for two companies, that made you better than all the hacks like me and Claremont and Moench who'd begun at Marvel, stayed with Marvel, and were loyal to Marvel. In fact, financially, if you quit Marvel and went to DC, you could come back to Marvel at a higher rate than somebody who stayed at Marvel. It was a sign of success to shit on the company, go somewhere else, and then come back, and Chris, Doug, and I, and maybe Tony [Isabella] at that point, were left cleaning up the manure, without thanks, without reward. That went on for quite a while. There was also a theory that if you were Editor, you were supposed to write The Hulk, Spider-Man, and Thor. Maybe Fantastic Four. It fluctuated, depending on who your favorite characters were when you were fifteen. That was what 'Editor' meant at Marvel. Not that you were someone who was officious, not that you were someone who was efficient, who was a good administrator, or who was an excellent writer in his own stead—being an editor at Marvel meant that now you should be able to write whatever the top books were considered to be, and everybody else got what was considered the dregs."*

Over the years, Stan Lee, and then Roy Thomas, had learned how to cede some of the supervision over content. Lee's policy was, according to Claremont, "They miss deadlines, you give them a warning, then you fire them. If the book doesn't sell, you fix it or you cancel the book and fire their ass. If it sells, you shut up and get out of the way. You don't micromanage. There isn't time. There's too much to do."

---

* "Whatever anybody else did was meaningless," Mantlo told *Comics Feature*. "Your job was to come on to a book, and create it out of whole cloth. Marvel history meant nothing, but not *because* of Marvel history—just that you were so intent on being better than the past writer, or showing how stupid the past writer was, that you went to great lengths to negate everything he said. . . . Whoever took over was starting all over."

It wasn't quite as easy for Wein and Wolfman. "It's not that I think that Len and Marv didn't want to do the same thing, but they seemed more willing to step in," said Thomas. "They might have been more nervous about letting a writer of a not particularly successful book do something that they didn't feel comfortable with. They might have worried that they would be out there and get the limb sawed off." A new title called *The Champions* was proposed by Tony Isabella as a vehicle for the discarded X-Men Angel and Iceman, a two-guys-on-the-road serial in the spirit of *Route 66*. But according to Isabella, Wein began applying a succession of rules that called for changes: it had to be a team of five characters; it had to include a woman; it had to include a character that already has its own title as well; it had to include someone with super-strength. *The Champions* eventually became a weird mutt of a comic, in which the thoroughly mismatched Angel, Iceman, Black Widow, Ghost Rider, and Hercules teamed up to fight villains like the bankrupted "Recession Raiders" in Los Angeles.

This kind of fussing put Wein on a collision course with production manager John Verpoorten, who saw the tweaking as frivolous. If a book was in danger of missing its shipping deadline—and thus incurring hundreds of dollars in late fees—Verpoorten's six-foot-seven shadow would darken a desk. A proofreader's protests would fall on deaf ears. "You'll read it when it comes out," he'd bellow as he leaned in to grab the pages.

This, perhaps, is the best way to explain the free rein given to certain titles. As long as sales weren't dropping, so what if a comic was a little bit loose, a little bit off the rails—why bother telling Stan? Why bother telling Len?

A proofreader could be a writer's greatest friend. "Gerber would plot a great story, hook you with a cliffhanger, and have no clue what the hell he was going to do with the next issue," said David Anthony Kraft. "And the deadline would come for the plot, and people would get desperate; you would see the whites of their eyes. And that's when we would go out to dinner and kick around ideas. I did that with a bunch of *Howard the Duck* and *Defenders* issues. It made for interesting stories—if you didn't know where you were going, the readers couldn't outguess you. On the other hand, you could have a mess and never tie your stories up and nothing would pull together. It didn't always turn out for the best." Still, he says, "I tended to like that stuff. So it would just go straight out."

With the lack of oversight came more opportunities for experimentation. Gerber, Englehart, and Starlin chased their whims and colored even further outside the lines, mixing and matching scattershot ideas from older Marvel comic books with current news headlines and pop psychology and spinning them into Dadaist mini-masterpieces that landed every month at the feet of boggled adolescents. They tackled sexual politics, nudged their protagonists into countercultural pursuits, and even offered sly commentary on Marvel Comics itself.

Gerber's *Defenders* consisted of founding members Doctor Strange and the Hulk, plus Valkyrie, a sword-wielding demigoddess who'd taken over the body of naïve twenty-something occultist Barbara Norriss, and Nighthawk, aka Kyle Richmond, a playboy-turned-criminal-turned-hero with Batman-like gadgetry. But superheroics were clearly what interested Gerber the least. As he had with *Man-Thing*, he populated the book with deeply flawed but sympathetic hoi polloi, given to crushingly low self-esteem. And so the icy Valkyrie was destined to endure the needy overtures of not only Kyle Richmond but also the somewhat schmucky Jack Norriss, the estranged husband of her host-body.

Gerber truly began pushing *The Defenders* into ecstatic absurdity at the beginning of 1975, with the introduction of the Headmen, a dastardly trio whose individual exploits had appeared in forgotten one-off 1950s Atlas Comics stories: Dr. Arthur Nagan, a surgeon whose harvesting of gorilla organs led some angry gorillas to transplant his head onto a simian body; Chondu the Mystic, a yoga-advocating caster of spells; and Dr. Jerold Morgan, whose experiments in cellular compression resulted in the shrinking of his bones and loose, doughy skin hanging everywhere. Now gathered in suburban Connecticut, they plotted to take over the world . . . and while that subplot simmered, Gerber added a battle against the KKK-like Serpent Squad, which turned out to be led by Kyle Richmond's butler Pennyworth—a self-loathing, middle-aged African American—and bankrolled by funds siphoned from Richmond's millions.

And while all of this was unfolding, every few issues would include a random murder committed upon ordinary, usually pathetic citizenry, by an unnamed elf with a gun. There was no apparent connection between these murders and anything else in the comic . . . or, in fact, the whole of the Marvel universe.

The young editors just kept shuffling the pages through production.

In *The Avengers*, Steve Englehart shaped a twenty-issue story arc about Mantis, the Vietnamese prostitute who had become the "Celestial Madonna."* She and her lover, the Avengers' onetime foe the Swordsman, had appeared at Avengers Mansion and successfully petitioned for membership. Alas, her potent sexuality—her "death grip" involved wrapping her legs around male victims—disrupted the order of things. "Basically, Mantis was supposed to be a hooker who would join the Avengers and cause dissension amongst all the male members by coming on to each of them in turn," said Englehart. "She was introduced to be a slut. I've always been a big fan of sex, and I would see these grown-up superhero guys fight supervillains, then they'd meet a woman, they'd blush and stammer. They were like big teenage boys, which always seemed dumb to me, because I was accepting them as grown-up men, so why didn't they act like grown-up men?" Englehart eventually backed off from the strumpet angle, although a Scarlet Witch–Vision–Mantis–Swordsman love quadrangle yielded tearful melodrama, alleviated only when the Swordsman died in action.

The mysterious origins of both Mantis and the Vision unfolded over many months. It turned out that she'd been raised by a race of psychic alien cruciferous vegetables named the Cotari, who'd been brought to earth by a sect of Kree pacifists. After Mantis regained her memory of this, the Cotari tree that overlooked the Swordsman's grave took his form, and proposed that Mantis bear its child. "By the end, because it was a cosmic time," said Englehart, "somehow, she just turned herself into the Celestial Madonna and married a tree! And in order to marry the tree, you had to know the history of the universe, you know?"

---

* "I never liked Mantis," said Dave Cockrum. "Most of the Marvel staff at the time hated Mantis' guts. I think it was mostly that 'this one' crap. The one thing I did like about her was the skirt of the costume. In the *Giant Size Avengers* I drew her leaping about, and occasionally showed just a glimpse of her ass. . . . Mantis, however, didn't wear underwear." When Englehart received Cockrum's pages, he claimed that they didn't reflect his instructions, cut up the pages, and rearranged the panels to his liking.

Englehart's retrofitted backstory for the Vision was slightly less insane, but it carried a metatextual wallop. He revealed that the Vision's android body had been repurposed from that of the original Human Torch (absent from the Marvel Universe since his sudden demise amid creator Carl Burgos's 1966 copyright battle). A flashback showed the villainous robot Ultron kidnapping the Human Torch's inventor, Phineas Horton, and forcing him to resurrect his invention. Through Horton, Englehart gave voice to the regret that the embittered Burgos himself felt about the Human Torch: "I thought he'd be my crowning achievement—and my meal-ticket—but my colleagues feared him—hounded me to destroy him—and when he escaped, I was ostracized . . . and he never, ever returned to me! . . . Don't make me face him again—not now, when I'm so old!" Ultron murdered Horton, who slowly uttered his last sentiments as he died cradled in the Vision's arms: "I wanted an issue, creation, some part of me to live on . . ." Life would imitate art when Burgos's own death was not acknowledged in the pages of Marvel Comics, but the Vision—"some part of me"—lived on.

Englehart then turned his attention to the Beast, formerly of the original X-Men, who'd mostly disappeared since Englehart turned him blue and furry a few years earlier. The Beast joined the Avengers, and became the first Marvel weedhead. "The Beast was a product, in his second incarnation here, of my life in California," Englehart said. "He got older, and he started listening to rock and roll, and—quite frankly—he started smoking dope, although we couldn't say that in the books." What he did instead was show the Beast reading Carlos Castaneda and playing Stevie Wonder records, signifiers that "he was a young, intellectual guy who'd gotten hip."

Captain Marvel's struggling-musician sidekick Rick Jones was getting hip, too. In Englehart's *Captain Marvel* #37, Jones's tourmate Dandy hands him a capsule, which she coyly refers to as "Vitamin C": "a present, in case your 'personal thing' gets boring!" Rick Jones's 'personal thing' at this point was that he would switch places with Captain Marvel every time he banged together the metal "Nega-Bands" on his wrists; this meant he spent a lot of time biding time in the Negative Zone, where one of them had to remain at all times. The next time Jones is floating idly in the Negative Zone, he pops the pill and begins hallucinating about his childhood in the suburbs; meanwhile, Captain Marvel's jaw starts tingling, his head pulses, and his surroundings take on the properties of an Escher drawing. When the Watcher shows up and attacks Captain Marvel, our hero breaks out in a cold sweat; fortunately, by the next issue, he and Rick both have their bearings. Captain Marvel lauds Rick for the growth of his mind. Psychedelic drugs have made them even more "cosmically aware"; all ends well.

For all of Gerber and Englehart's subversive invention, though, it was the willful provocation of Jim Starlin's *Warlock* that tested the limits of Marvel's corporate inattention to low-selling content. Roy Thomas had made the character a Christ figure; now Starlin, the recovering Catholic, used him to deliver a critique of organized religion, as well as a protest against systemized stiflings of creative voices.

Wandering space, Adam Warlock comes upon a "non-believer" who's being pursued by armed soldiers; he tries to save her, but fails. Using the "dread power" of his mysterious Soul Gem, he revives her just long enough to learn that her killers were from the Universal Church of Truth, an iron-fisted group with intergalactic reach, led by a being called the Magus—who, Warlock is shocked to learn, is his own future self.

As Warlock journeys to find the Magus, he gains unlikely allies (the foulmouthed troll Pip; the green-skinned, fishnet-wearing alien assassin Gamora) and several more enemies (including Captain Marvel's old foe Thanos). But the greatest threat to his survival, and to his sanity, is the powerful crystal on his forehead—the vampiric Soul Gem—which, he slowly realizes, is thirstily absorbing the spirits of his enemies.

Adam Warlock's adventures were perfect vehicles for Starlin's meditations on the price of power, and for the suspicions he harbored toward rigid institutionalism. Plotting, scripting, penciling, inking, and coloring, Starlin was, in a sense, the first auteur that Marvel had seen since Steranko's early carte blanche days. But even the slightest editorial interferences set off Starlin's inner rebel, and before long, the authority that he questioned so relentlessly was no longer limited to the church.

"Stan always had trouble with the stuff I did," Starlin said, pointing to "The Infinity Formula," a Nick Fury story he wrote while he was also working on *Warlock*. "I had Fury embezzling funds so he could get this formula that would extend his life. Stan was so upset by it he said it would never be used in Marvel continuity, or ever reprinted."

At first there were sneaky little under-the-radar jokes in *Warlock*—altering the Comics Code seal to read as the "Cosmic Code" on the cover of one issue, or having Pip walk into a bar and order a "merde stinger" in the next. And then, the stakes were raised. In the fourth issue of Starlin's saga, Warlock is brainwashed by a pair of clowns, intent on making him conform. "Now take it easy, true believer!" says Len Teans, the first clown. "This is where you shed those dark aspects that set you apart from your fellow clowns!" The second clown, Jan Hatroomi, paints a clown face on Warlock, who is then taken to see another "renegade" being pummeled with pies. "He used to be one of the best," Teans says. "But he tried to buck the system! He began to think people were more important than things!" A child buying this comic from the local drugstore would find this all very wild, of course—even if he didn't notice that "Len Teans" and "Jan Hatroomi" were anagrams for Stan Lee and John Romita, or that the pummeled clown looked a lot like Roy Thomas.

Adam Warlock is led to a swaying tower of trash, to which clowns are busy adding wheelbarrows of garbage. When the tower collapses, he finds a diamond in the wreckage. "Oh, that stuff!" says Len Teans. "We just can't seem to keep it out of our refuse! Someone keeps putting it in while we're not looking!" Jim Starlin was painting Marvel Comics as a delirious purveyor of junk.

The next issue of *Warlock* credited Len Wein with not editing, but instead with "fussing." No one even bothered to change it.

In California, Jack Kirby was miserable. After a promising start, his relationship with DC had quickly turned sour. Shortly after he'd signed with the company, its sales had ceded first place, to Marvel, in an industry that was failing. The comics that made up Kirby's mythological "Fourth World" universe—*The New Gods*, *The Forever People*, and *Mister Miracle*—were canceled. Kirby's stilted dialogue met resistance; his rendering of Superman was repeatedly corrected to match DC's house style; his nonsuperhero concepts failed to impress editors. He was ready and willing to develop new titles—*Omac, Kamandi, The Demon*—but none seemed to carry a spark. Kirby knew there was still a home for him at Marvel; Stan Lee had made it clear in interviews. "We never had a fight," Lee told one reporter. "We got along beautifully. I have the utmost respect for his ability and I wish he'd come back." Tentative overtures were made, phone calls were exchanged, and Lee and Kirby began talking again.

The Mighty Marvel Convention was held on a Saturday through Monday, March 22–24, 1975, at the Hotel Commodore. Thrilling announcements made throughout the weekend suggested that Marvel might reach new audiences: a deluxe-edition *Superman vs. Spider-Man* comic, co-published with DC, would be the first meeting between the two iconic characters, and a deal was being finalized, at last, for a live-action *Spider-Man* movie. But the coup de grâce would wait until the final day of the convention.

Kirby quietly flew into New York, and, art samples in hand, sneaked into Stan's office on Monday before heading over to the convention. Marie Severin spotted him. "I came up to the office and I saw Jack," she said, "and Stan put a page in front of my face and said, 'You did not see any of this!' and I went out in the hall and yelled, 'Kirby's back!'"

Kirby's three-year contract called for him to produce thirteen pages a week, at the rate of $1,100 a week—or $57,200 a year, or $85 per page. He declined to revisit *Fantastic Four* or *Thor*, or any of the titles he'd created with Lee. Instead, he would take back *Captain America*, as the sole writer, artist, and editor. He'd do an adaptation of *2001: A Space Odyssey*; and he'd introduce a new creation, yet another ancient-secrets-of-alien-visitors concept, *The Eternals*.

On Sunday afternoon, at a *Fantastic Four* panel, Lee introduced the surprise guest. There was rapturous applause, and a standing ovation as Kirby stalked down the aisle and took the podium. The company wasn't yet ready to announce which comics Kirby would be working on, but, he promised one audience member during a Q&A, "Whatever I do at Marvel, I can assure you that it'll electrocute you in the mind!"

As usual, Lee didn't hesitate to step in and rewrite Kirby's dialogue. "'Electrify,' Jack!" he corrected. "'Electrify!'"

In 1974, Gerry Conway had not been happy to hear about Wein and Wolfman's promotions. In fact, he'd been furious. He'd been at Marvel longer than either of them, writing the superstar characters, pinch-hitting as an editor when Thomas was out of the office. And he had been promised, many months before, that his turn would come next. "Stan told me, 'Well, Ger,' in the kind of friendly, glad-hand sort of way Stan has, 'if it ever worked out that Roy leaves the company, we want you to take over as editor.'" But that earlier conversation, it seemed, was quickly forgotten. Conway felt betrayed. If the main criterion for the job was familiarity and understanding of the Marvel universe, he wondered, why hire two DC guys who had just come on board in the last year? He was tired of not being taken seriously, and now suspected Marv and Len of playing political games. Apparently his achievements meant nothing to Lee, to Marvel.

So Conway was stuck with orders from Lee to bring back Gwen Stacy, somehow, if only for one issue. (Steve Gerber cheerily offered to introduce her reanimated corpse in the pages of *Tales of the Zombie*, as "Graveyard Gwen.") Annoyed with the mandate,* Conway nonetheless wrote a six-part story in which Gwen returned, re-traumatized Peter Parker (and his new girlfriend, Mary Jane Watson) with her presence, and then discovered that she was, in fact, only a *clone* of Gwen Stacy, created by the Jackal. The Jackal, it turned out, was their onetime biology professor, Professor Warren, who'd been insanely jealous of Parker's relationship with Gwen and later discovered he still had her DNA samples from an old science project. (Further complicating things, Warren also cloned Peter Parker, a minor subplot that would come back to haunt Marvel years later.)

At the end of the story arc, the cloned Gwen—a sad, innocent naïf who shared the memories of the real one—bid a tearful good-bye to Peter Parker, the love of her life, and walked with a packed suitcase into the sunset. Despite the silly contrivances, Conway and artist Ross Andru had produced a genuinely moving, thought-provoking story.

---

* The eighth issue of Marvel's in-house fanzine, *Foom*, quoted Conway as saying, "I was forced to bring back Gwen Stacy, so I'm turning her into a [sexual reference deleted]."

When Lee finally saw the story he'd forced Conway to write, he shrugged. "This doesn't really work, does it?" Conway simmered.

"You're going to have to take care of Gerry," Thomas had warned Lee, knowing that Conway felt he'd earned a heightened level of respect from the company. But now Conway felt he was being treated as just another scribbler, answering to the indivisible team of LenMarv, who, the way he saw it, "really didn't feel that they wanted to fragment their authority." When it was decided that Conway's increasingly popular *Spider-Man* villain the Punisher would get a solo spotlight in the black-and-white magazines, Conway remembered that Thomas had promised him the opportunity to edit the book himself. But the magazines were Marv Wolfman's kingdom now. Conway would have to settle for just scripting, once again. Incensed, he began taking freelance work from Martin and Chip Goodman's Atlas Comics, and then took a staff job writing—and editing—for DC Comics. His first assignment was to tinker with the last issues of *Kamandi* that Kirby had submitted before his abrupt departure. And before long, Conway found himself writing the character to which he'd just bid farewell.

Marvel and DC's *Superman vs. Spider-Man* crossover was going to be oversized, eight times the price of a regular comic, and heavily promoted: a guaranteed blockbuster. For writer Gerry Conway and artist Ross Andru, it was a wonderful payday. For Len Wein, it was the breaking point. At a meeting in Lee's office, sitting around the coffee table, Wein questioned Al Landau's decision to remove Andru from his regular *Amazing Spider-Man* gig to work on the project. *Spider-Man*, after all, was Marvel's number-one title.

"I'm the editor in chief," Wein said. "Why didn't you discuss this with me first?"

Landau looked at him. "Because it was *none of your fucking business.*"

Wein hurled himself at Landau. Marv Wolfman, who'd been sitting between the two, dove into the middle of the melee and tried to push Wein back. As Stan frantically tried to make peace between everyone, Wein realized that the pressure was finally getting to him. The more time he'd spent with the business side, the more he hated the job. "I'm not all that great at running something," said Wein. "I spent all my time up on the ninth floor fighting with the accountants about getting people more money, or not canceling the book, or giving us more pages . . . the comic books were going on by themselves." When he wasn't checking in and out of the hospital with kidney problems, he was frantically trying to catch up with the relentless stream of product being churned out. ("Len was taking a lot of tranquilizers in those days," recalled Dave Cockrum.)

On April 9, 1975, Marvel announced that Wein was stepping down. Marv Wolfman would assume the editor in chief duties, and Archie Goodwin would fill Wolfman's position overseeing the black-and-whites. "I basically cut the same deal Roy had cut," said Wein, "to take my books and just edit those." Those books, as it turned out, included *Amazing Spider-Man* and *Thor*, which Gerry Conway had recently abandoned when he'd been unable to secure the same editor/writer title.

"We're presently undergoing a period of very heavy dramatics," Wolfman admitted in a 1975 interview, but he was fiercely determined not to fall victim to the pressures that had overtaken Wein. For all the similarities between the two old friends, Wolfman had a greater interest in being in charge, and more of an ability not to get hung up on details. One of the biggest problems, as he saw it, was the number of blown deadlines. ("I was just speaking to our printer," John Verpoorten once informed a gathering of the editorial staff. "He was wondering if we were still in business.") This would result in a reader buying, say, the latest issue of *Avengers*, complete with brand-new cover, only to find a reprint of an old story on the inside. But what could an editor do? There wasn't enough good talent to fire all the delinquent contributors. Rolling up his sleeves, Wolfman had John Verpoorten add a new title on the schedule: *Marvel Fill-In Comics* would be written by Bill Mantlo, who'd begun his writing career by volunteering to script a deadline-crunched comic when nobody else was available. Now Mantlo would be a preemptive strike. *Marvel Fill-In*, drawn by workhorse Sal Buscema, would feature two or three characters from whichever titles were in greatest danger of falling behind. When the inevitable Dreaded Deadline Doom struck, the story could easily be slotted in to one of the titles in which those characters were regularly featured.

Once that was out of the way, Wolfman was the recipient of a nice bit of luck: the threat of Martin and Chip Goodman's Atlas Comics—which had been launched while Wein was running ragged—fizzled. Atlas was hindered by a number of second-rate creations and poor organization; even the best titles faced distribution troubles. According to one report, the publisher's Los Angeles distributor immediately returned 2,200 of the 2,500 it had ordered—never even bothering to unpack them. Getting work with Atlas was like hitting a small jackpot—it paid handsomely, but then the money stopped for good. Artist Jack Abel turned in his pages for *Wulf*, used his fee to pay for a vacation to Florida, and returned to find them out of business. David Anthony Kraft, who'd left Marvel for a 50 percent pay hike writing at Atlas, rode cross-country on his motorcycle, with visions of writing issue after issue of Atlas's *Demon Hunter* on the beach. By the time he arrived on the West Coast, Atlas Comics had collapsed.

In the spring, Al Landau had sent out a memo demanding that someone go through the Atlas comics and take notes on possible plagiarisms. It was certainly moot now: Atlas castoffs were simply absorbed into Marvel's empire. Kraft and Rich Buckler reworked "Demon Hunter" as "Devil-Slayer," and wrote him into *Astonishing Tales*. Howard Chaykin walked directly from the Atlas offices and sold a reworked "Scorpion" to Marvel as "Dominic Fortune."

Of course, none of this solved the problem that *no* company's comics were selling. "We were just a bunch of punk kids working in the back end of Magazine Management," said Chris Claremont. "Nobody bought comics. It was a dying industry, and we knew it. Nobody cared. We were just there to have fun. We all figured by 1980 we'd all be out looking for a real job."

Across the nation, supermarkets were replacing mom-and-pop stores, and few had interest in maintaining spinner racks filled with low-profit-margin comics. Worse, the fact that comics were sold to distributors on a returnable basis made publishers extremely vulnerable to unfair business practices. Stories proliferated about unsold copies sitting in warehouses and then stripped of their covers, which were returned in exchange for credit. The coverless comics were then sold at a reduced price—all at a profit to the distributor.

So in 1973, Phil Sculing, a loud-talking high school English teacher and convention organizer from Coney Island, approached Marvel and DC about getting the same 60 percent discount that the wholesalers enjoyed. In return for such a low rate, Seuling would agree to pay for all unsold copies. After all, he could sell the back issues to collectors. For the publishers, it was an improvement on the old business model of printing two or three copies for every one sold, but it wasn't a sustainable alternative, not yet. In 1974, this method of "direct distribution" accounted for only $300,000 of Marvel's sales. The newsstand problem had to be fixed.

For a while, Al Landau managed to give Cadence Industries the illusion that he'd turned Marvel around. Because the comics were returnable, profit reports were based on monthly estimates of "sell-through" copies, not on the quantity shipped. "He had a bit of a Ponzi scheme," one Cadence executive explained. "If you distribute 100,000 copies, and estimate 50% sales, and the next month you distribute two books—print 200,000, and estimate 50%—you have 150,000 in reserve. He kept publishing more every month, so he hid the fact that his estimates were way overblown. He was running the company right into the ground."

When Sheldon Feinberg began to grow suspicious of Landau's numbers, he dispatched two Cadence employees from New Jersey, installing them at Marvel: first, an accountant named Barry Kaplan became chief financial officer, and then a recently hired Curtis Circulation consultant named Jim Galton became a vice president. They went through the profit-and-loss statements and didn't like what they saw.

When Landau returned from a vacation, he found Galton sitting in his office chair.

"What are you doing here?" Landau asked.

"Didn't Shelly tell you?" Galton asked.

Galton and Kaplan took Landau out to the Players Club for lunch. At the table, Galton broke the news that he was personally replacing Landau as president of Marvel and Magazine Management. Landau grabbed his chest and fell to the floor as Galton and Kaplan looked on.

———

If Galton couldn't turn things around in a year or two, there would be no more Marvel Comics. In fact, Sheldon Feinberg was itching to shut down Cadence's entire publishing operation. "I think by June 30th of the year I arrived, Marvel had lost two million dollars," said Galton. "The first thing I had to do was put some order into the organization and stop the bleeding. It was bleeding profusely. That took about six months. In the process, we killed a lot of magazines, and pared down the staff, which had been allowed to just grow with no rhyme or reason." Shortly after Landau left, Galton also gave Landau's number two, Ivan Snyder, the heave-ho, but with a unique sort of severance package: $39,000 worth of Marvel toys and apparel, sold to him at cost. "Ivan was spending a great deal of time trying to build a mail-order company within the company," said Kaplan. "There was a room set up for all the licensed product that Marvel bought from its licensees, which they advertised in the comics." Kaplan pointed out to Galton that Snyder's little project was requiring a large amount of office space, and the shipping-and-handling services of three full-time employees, and not making money for the company. By making a deal with Snyder, Marvel could both get rid of the inventory and gain an ad revenue stream. Snyder agreed to buy advertising space, at a preferential rate.

Snyder put up shelves in the basement of his Randolph, New Jersey, home and called his new company Superhero Enterprises. Within three years, he'd own stores in three cities, and an extremely successful mail-order business. He would cross Marvel's path again.

Stan Lee, meanwhile, had been busying himself on the magazine side since Chip Goodman had exited, to the chagrin of the editors there. They saw Lee as a meddler who swooped in and asked for unnecessary changes, asking out loud who these younger celebrities on the covers were.

At the launch party for Magazine Management's *Film International* (on the first issue's cover was nude *Emmanuelle* star Sylvia Kristal; reviews of several X-rated films ran inside), Stan and Joanie flew to Los Angeles and hobnobbed with C-listers like Arte Johnson and Victoria Principal, and retired directors like King Vidor and Vincente Minnelli, at the Greystone

Mansion. It wasn't as hip as having Fellini and Alain Resnais swing by the office, but it was Hollywood.

Lee's name also appeared on the top of the masthead of *Celebrity*, a *People* knockoff that inserted Lee into the action, posing for photos with story subjects. The vintage of the stars—Mae West, Mickey Cohen, Robert Wagner, Lucille Ball, F. Lee Bailey—gave it the feel of an episode of *Love Boat*. The articles fawned over all of them. "If *Celebrity*'s attitude to the phenomenon [of stardom-obsessed culture] seems diffident," wrote one observer, "that may be because it is published by Stan Lee of Marvel Comics fame, and primarily devoted to the exploits of Lee, the first comic book author to gain celebrity status."

Now Lee enjoyed an exquisitely appointed office—five windows that overlooked Madison Avenue, a boomerang-shaped, glass-topped coffee table, and ample space for three chrome-and-leather chairs and two plush sofas. He still wrote the "Stan's Soapbox" column once a month, but it was Hollywood that called to him. Not only were there movie stars with whom to mingle, but there was also an industry that didn't seem on the verge of collapse. "No matter how successful everything became," said one writer, "he always had the horrible feeling that everybody would disappear and he'd have to step in and write everything again."

As it was, he barely looked at the comics. He took a look at *Iron Man* for the first time in over a year, saw the triangular nose that had been added to the helmet on his own orders, and said, "What's this—why is this here?"

"You don't want that?"

"Well, it looks kind of strange, doesn't it?" Lee zoomed away, on to the next thing.

Everything was big-picture now: synergy, demographics, partnerships. Lee called at least one meeting to remind writers not to make major changes to characters, lest those changes jeopardize deals with licensees. Decisions were being made, Steve Englehart said, "not by Stan Lee as the top of a bunch of creative people, but by Stan Lee as the bottom of a bunch of businessmen. And he began to really put his energy up into the business end of it rather than down into the creative end below."

———

As out of touch as he was with the creative process, by now even Stan Lee knew that fans were clamoring for more of Howard the Duck. Howard's sporadic appearances, in the back pages of the tremendously titled *Giant-Size Man-Thing*, produced an avalanche of mail, and Steve Gerber found himself meeting with Lee about Howard getting his own title. Accompanying Gerber was Mary Skrenes, a college friend of Alan Weiss who'd moved to New York and easily fallen into freelance comic writing. Skrenes found that she loved comics, but it took some time getting used to the man-child comic pros that surrounded her. Gerber, whom she met on a visit to the Marvel offices, was an exception: "I came in," she said, "and everybody clustered around me. Some of these guys weren't used to girls. So they were all around me, saying things like, 'I've been having trouble . . . I hate to go to sleep . . . I hate to wake up,' and I looked up and I saw this big head bouncing toward me from the other room. It was Steve Gerber. He took my hand, and led me out of the room. All these guys are like, 'What?'"

She quickly became Gerber's muse—the inspiration for Howard the Duck's go-go dancing girlfriend, Beverly Switzler—and writing partner. They began dating and soon moved in together. Her sensibility was every bit as skewed as his. When she was asked to take a crack at conceptualizing a superheroine with the name of Ms. Marvel, she turned in a proposal about Loretta Petta, a petite, dyslexic waitress who'd moved from a trailer park to the big city. "When she would get pissed—in the first issue, somebody robbed her diner—she would get super-adrenaline strength. They didn't want her to be tiny and dyslexic; they wanted her to be statuesque. Stan just didn't like it."*

But she and Gerber had better luck together. In the pitch meeting for *Howard*, they'd also brought along their idea for another comic, about a character named James-Michael—"a *real* twelve-year-old," as he put it, "a *human being* poised on the edge of puberty, facing all the enormous

---

* A different version of Ms. Marvel would eventually see the light of day, written by Gerry Conway: Carol Danvers, a security agent at Cape Kennedy Space Center, was a bystander during a battle between Captain Marvel and his Kree enemy; when an exploding piece of Kree technology radiated her, she gained the strength of ten men and "the knowledge and instincts of a Kree warrior." She left her security job to edit *Woman* magazine for the *Daily Bugle*'s J. Jonah Jameson.

(and enormous seeming) problems adolescence would bring." Not, in other words, another stupid kid sidekick.

Of course, it wasn't quite vérité—in the first issue, James-Michael's parents die in a horrible auto accident and are revealed to be robots. James-Michael, hyperintelligent and nearly autistic in his cold manner, is adopted by a kind nurse and her hip roommate, who live in the Hell's Kitchen section of Manhattan, and he's haunted by dreams of a mute, caped alien who shoots lasers from his palms and leaves a trail of destruction that's still there when James-Michael awakes. But what would they call it?

"Omega the Unknown!" Lee shot back. He put both titles on the schedule.

Things were looking up for Chris Claremont, too—the first few issues of the new *X-Men* series had been popular with the fans, as had *Iron Fist*, which he was also writing. In both titles he'd immediately set to building supporting casts of ordinary folks to surround the heroes, surrogate families for the exceptional outcasts with whom an audience of adolescents and aging fans were likely to identify. There was also the artwork: on *X-Men*, Dave Cockrum's colorful costume designs and science-fiction gloss; on *Iron Fist*, the fluid energy and Dutch-angled dynamism of a young Canadian artist named John Byrne. Byrne was an immediate fan favorite. His characters were infallibly vivacious, his panels were filled with minutiae for trainspotting readers, and his page layouts flowed invitingly. He and Claremont immediately hatched plans to collaborate on further projects.*

At the end of 1975, Claremont left his editorial post, as Englehart, Gerber, and McGregor had before him, to devote himself full-time to writing. To replace Claremont in the associate editor position, Wolfman tapped a former DC writer with a decade of industry experience under his belt.

His name was Jim Shooter. He'd just turned twenty-four.

---

* Byrne got his first break at Marvel thanks to Duffy Vohland, a large, flamboyant, red-bearded, velvet-shoulder-bag-toting puck who was an assistant in the Marvel offices. According to David Kraft, "Whenever there was any assignment and people would say, 'Who can we get to do this?' Duffy would be there, going *Johhhhnn Byyyyrne* in his owl-like monotone. All over Marvel, there would be this voice going *Johhhhnn Byyyyrne*, pointing in every direction for everything."

$$7$$

IN THE SUMMER OF 1964, WHEN JIM SHOOTER WAS TWELVE YEARS OLD, HE
spent a week in the children's ward of Mercy Hospital in Pittsburgh, re-
cuperating from minor surgery. From his hospital bed, he worked his way
through the nearby piles of comic books.

"The DC comics were pristine, and the Marvel comics were ratty and
dog-eared," said Shooter. "And so I read a couple DCs and I read a couple
of Marvels and I found out why everyone was reading the Marvels: because they were way, way better."

This gave the boy an idea. "My family had no money, and they won't let
you work at a steel mill if you're twelve. I thought if I could learn to write
like this Stan Lee guy, I could sell stuff to these people at DC—because
they clearly needed help."

For a year, the young Shooter studied every comic he could get his
hands on, figuring out what was good, and what was bad, but above all
else, he wanted to figure out the formula. "I guess I was canny enough
to know that if I just wrote some comic book or everything I had ever
wanted to do in a comic book that they wouldn't buy that. They weren't
going to buy something that was too different."

In the summer of 1965, he wrote a *Superboy and the Legion of Superheroes* story on spec, and gave it to his mother to send to DC. A mail correspondence followed, and within a matter of months, Shooter got a call
from Mort Weisinger, the same "malevolent toad" who only a few months
earlier had scared Roy Thomas away to Marvel. Weisinger invited him to
meet at the DC offices. Shooter, by now fourteen, was accompanied by
his mother.

He got the regular gig, and just in time. "My father had a beat-up old car and the engine died," he said. "That first check bought a rebuilt engine for his car so he didn't have to walk to work anymore."

For four years, Shooter worked for Weisinger on various iterations of the Superman mythos—Superboy, Supergirl, etc.—not only writing scripts, but providing cover designs as well. He also won the good graces of artists Gil Kane and Wally Wood by providing stick-figure layouts for each page. But as high school wore on, the allure of the money began to wear off—it never seemed to be enough for his family anyway. What mattered now was the accolades.*

Unfortunately, praise was limited to the occasional article in the Pittsburgh newspaper or segment on the local TV news. "My father probably said four or five words to me the whole time I was growing up," said Shooter. "One of the greatest men to ever walk the earth . . . but not at connecting with people. He made no comment whatsoever." And Weisinger didn't just withhold praise—he cruelly berated his teenage employee, calling from New York every Thursday night, following the weekly *Batman* television broadcast, with a litany of complaints: *It's not on time. It's over the page limit. How the hell can we get a cover out of this? Why can't you write like you used to?* He referred to Shooter as his "charity case." "He caused a kind of pathological fear of telephones in me," Shooter once told an interviewer. "I felt more and more inadequate . . . and my last chance to be a kid was slipping by."

Holding down an adult job—and, at six feet seven inches, now towering above his classmates—scarcely anything about him, save a serious case of acne, marked him as a teenager. He tried to fit it all in, to "get good grades so I could nail down a scholarship, and have a little fun, like football games, dances, parties and stuff. But it was too much, and it all suffered." He missed sixty days of his senior year of high school, his grades fell, and his productivity for Weisinger decreased.

He managed an NYU scholarship anyway. In 1969, shortly before he

---

* "You know who my inspiration was, for becoming a comic book writer?" Gerry Conway asked in *Comics Interview* #13. "Jim Shooter—because Jim Shooter is only a year and a half older than I am, and I saw his name mentioned in a Superman story that he'd written in the mid-Sixties, and it said, 'Thirteen-year-old Jim Shooter wrote this story,' and I thought, 'Jesus Christ, I'm thirteen years old and I could write as well as this!'"

was due to fly to New York, he had a falling-out with Weisinger. So he decided to cold-call his inspiration, Stan Lee, from a pay phone at the airport. Amazingly, he talked his way into a job interview, and then an offer. But the only thing available was a full-time assistant position. Marvel's environment was shockingly different from the jacket-and-tie, insurance-company vibe of DC. It seemed like it might be . . . fun.

He gave up the scholarship.

Shooter, flat broke, checked into a local YMCA after his first day on the job and then slept on the floor of Marvel receptionist Allyn Brodsky. He sat in on story conferences. Morrie Kuramoto taught him how to paste corrections onto art pages. Sol Brodsky gave him samples of art-work by Kirby and Gene Colan so he could try his hand at inking, and Lee asked him to submit plot pitches, but nothing came of it. After four years of being a wunderkind, he was suddenly a ghost. An impoverished ghost. "I literally did not eat for two weeks, I had no money. When I got my first paycheck, and I saw how many taxes came out, and I saw the prices for rent on apartments . . . I couldn't survive. I couldn't do this."

Shooter, shell-shocked, gave up and went back to Pittsburgh.

He tried to get a job in advertising, and eventually scraped together some freelance work, but no one wanted to hire a high school graduate. By the time a couple of *Legion of Superheroes* fans tracked him down for an interview in 1974, the twenty-one-year-old former boy wonder, the one-time local celebrity who'd practiced signing his name with a Superman-style S, had spent a year managing a Kentucky Fried Chicken.

When Marvel assistant Duffy Vohland heard about this, he called Shooter, and—representing himself as an editor—convinced him to travel to the offices to discuss a return to comics.

To Shooter, Marvel's newer and bigger offices looked even more crowded and shabby than the 1969 space had. "There was a huge papier-mâché figure of Thor, donated by some fans, suspended on wires from the ceiling in the production area. There were piles of stuff everywhere—old comics, envelopes, trash, books. Two people were sword fighting with yardsticks in the hall." The dozens of employees, he thought to himself, were "young, strange looking, and dressed for playing Frisbee in the park." Vohland pointed out the sleeping bags that transient employees used to sleep under their desks.

Shooter, flummoxed by the chaos and unfamiliar with the new Marvel characters, darted over to DC—Weisinger had retired—and began writing *Legion of Superheroes* again, for another year, from Pittsburgh. But eventually, once again, the DC style began to chafe, and he started thinking about leaving comics behind. Then, in December 1975, Marv Wolfman called him. Would he like to come into the Marvel offices to talk about a staff job?

Wolfman was nowhere to be found when Shooter flew into town the next morning, but the desks that surrounded the editor in chief's door were buzzing with energy. Near the secretary's desk, Claremont's girlfriend was sitting on his lap. Assistant editors—Roger Stern, Roger Slifer, Scott Edelman—ran around frantically. One of them shoved nineteen pages of art from the latest *Captain Marvel* into Shooter's hands, so he sat down and worked while he waited for his job interview to begin.

At noon, Wolfman breezed in. "Marv comes right through the big room, goes into his room, closes the door. And then he opens the door, Len comes in, and Marv says, 'We're going to lunch.'" The editorial assistants went out for coffee.

After lunch, Wolfman explained the job, which was to be "pre-proofreader." Too many plots, he said, were going straight from the writer to the artist, without editorial supervision, and no one was seeing mistakes until they were drawn and lettered in ink. "That's why these guys are so busy," said Wolfman. "So much stuff comes in like that. Instead of doing it at the end, you should do it when it's still in pencil. Just re-read the plots." Wolfman had found a secret weapon to combat the inefficient workflow.

This secret weapon even had a nickname: "Trouble Shooter."

From California, Jim Starlin and Steve Englehart were, quite literally, destroying and re-creating galaxies. As Kirby had done with Ragnarok in *Thor* and as Steranko had done with the Prism of Miracles in "Nick Fury," the respective Armageddons in *Warlock* and *Doctor*

Strange—unleashed simultaneously, at the end of the year—left lingering trauma. Adam Warlock had defeated his corrupted future self, the Magus, only by allowing the universe to end and start anew; he remained haunted by the memory of "this explosive reshuffling of time." Simultaneously, Doctor Strange had battled his old foe Mordo for the fate of the world, and lost. The world was brought back, of course—but Strange alone carried the heavy knowledge that everything was a recreation, a living replica of what had died.

Much like, some readers were beginning to say, Marvel Comics. "The notion," said Gerry Conway, "was that you had a cycle, and every three years you replaced your readership. Once boys hit puberty they would stop reading comics, and you'd be picking up the next group of ten-year-olds. So the goal was to write material appropriate for that age group."

If you couldn't have anything but the illusion of change, the most you could hope for was to reset the buttons for the new crop of ten-year-olds.

The big news at the beginning of 1976 was *Howard the Duck* #1. Gerber's weird creation—and the promise of sophisticated humor, and the popularity of artist Frank Brunner—inspired a wild gold rush among comic-collectible dealers, who hurried to newsstands and bought up every copy of the issue—sometimes before it even hit the racks. Rumors circulated that Marvel had conspired to keep the issue from the hands of fans, or that a computer error caused half the press run to be shipped to Canada, where unsold copies had been promptly destroyed.

"I said, 'What's with this duck? He's just another Walt Disney character. It won't work,'" Marvel circulation director Ed Shukin told the *New Yorker*. "So that's why we only printed 275,000. At the time, I hadn't actually read a copy of *Howard*. That was a mistake. I underestimated that duck."

Speculators did not. Within weeks, the comic was selling for nearly ten times the cover price—if you could find someone to sell it to you at all. It wasn't uncommon for comic-shop owners—of which there were now a few hundred throughout the country—to keep piles in the storeroom, unsold, as they watched prices soar. Pretty soon, *Howard the Duck* was the first Marvel comic to make mainstream headlines since Spider-Man had gone up against the Comics Code. Howard's image was emblazoned on the front cover of the *Village Voice* ("The Last Angry Duck Stands Up For America") while Gerber humored the press. ("There's a sensual quality to him," Gerber told *Playboy*. "If you stood Howard next to Superman, you could tell instantly which would be more interesting to jump into bed with.") It wasn't long before Marvel announced that Howard the Duck would be running for president in the 1976 election.

Gerber's *Man-Thing* had carried healthy doses of social satire, but *Howard the Duck* really seemed to loosen something inside the writer. He had a lot to get off his chest about American materialism, about the cheap violence in martial arts movies, about groupthink, about Sun Myung Moon and the Unification Church. The agitation rubbed off on his work in *The Defenders*, too—the alien Nebulon tried to conquer earth not with cosmic blasts, but by posing as a Werner Erhard–like leader of self-improvement seminars, in which attendees were given clown masks and told to declare themselves "Bozos." Another issue depicted protesters outside a screening of *Waste*, a stand-in for the real-life 1976 surprise hit *Snuff*.

Marv Wolfman greatly respected Gerber's work, and he'd been an early champion of *Howard the Duck*. But he found the darker stories— including one that Stan Lee called "one of the best written comics I've ever been jealous of"—to be "gruesome" and "revolting." Increasingly, the tone of the comics was a point of contention for Wolfman, who'd even dusted off Nova, a character he'd created as a teenager, in hopes of getting back to the kid-friendly spirit of the early 1960s Marvels. The inclination was not contagious.

"I was working at that particular time with very highly tempered people," Wolfman said. "It was very difficult—maybe a stronger editor could do it—to tell Steve Englehart to do something, or Steve Gerber, or Don, or . . . 90% of the staff that was there was very emotionally high-strung people."

Don McGregor, no longer on staff—and thus no longer able to push his own comics through unhindered—had become evangelistic about creative freedom, the battle lines of which, for him, often involved issues of race (despite editorial queasiness, he'd pushed through mainstream comics' first interracial kiss) and issues of verbiage. Englehart had once poked fun at McGregor's self-serious and long-winded prose in an issue of *The Avengers*, in which Black Panther declines membership to the group in a monologue that pushes at the boundaries of the panel:

> "Thor, the fine fool's gold of stark velvet morning seems to light the mottled tapestry of desire and disaster that comprises the legend of life for my people and myself in this hidden, half-slumbering nation-state we proudly proclaim Wakanda—but the amber eyes of reason widen as mauve shadows of regret creep across all the outside worldscape, and scream the bleeding need for Panther's presence at this time."

"('Nay')," an impatient Thor thinks to himself, in a thought balloon.

Around the same time, Wolfman himself had written a borderline-vicious one-page parody of McGregor, "the Harmony Factor Syndrome Beneath Wakanda"—in the Marvel fan-club magazine *FOOM*, of all places. But he'd also made a promise to McGregor that he was now regretting.

"Don and I used to be friends until I became his boss," Wolfman said. "I was basically told at one point to fire him and didn't because I had promised him when I was black-and-white editor he'd always have all the work he needed. Much to my chagrin, he would never do anything to fix up the books. As much as I pleaded and begged and everything else, because the books were *dying*."

McGregor's *Jungle Action* #20 hit the newsstands in mid-December; it included a monologue about standing up for ideals that continued on for seventeen panels. Kevin Trublood, the character who delivered the speech, was a reporter who'd been told to not bother with his story about the Klan; he was an obvious stand-in for McGregor himself, with closely held beliefs ("I *believe* in the fairy tales . . . the *myths* I was taught in school") and his own troubles with editorial resistance: "I *am* getting carried away!" Trublood shouted. "Because my character was questioned when I said I was going to do that story—that I was going to expose it . . . I realized I was afraid to write that story. My friends, my relatives, my coworkers. They made me afraid to write that story. And *they* were afraid."*

McGregor—going through a messy divorce, a custody battle, and health scares—refused to yield on the stories in which he was investing so much energy. "The pressure was on to bring in the Avengers," he said, "but it was important for a black hero not to have to have white heroes come in to save the day."

Wolfman couldn't take it. "When a writer is specifically told—maybe 40 times—by two separate editors before me and three later as well, that his stuff is not selling, you've got to make changes, and the writer refuses to make the changes, there is something wrong, because again, you're not working for yourself totally. You have to be able to compromise as long as you're being paid by someone else." This refusal to accede to employers' wishes, Wolfman thought, was becoming an epidemic within the industry.

But this was just one of many problems. Wolfman was mentally and physically exhausted, feeling like he couldn't delegate his workload. "The assistants were all new, so you really couldn't give them a lot of heavy work to do; you couldn't ask them to edit the stuff, and no one person can edit 53 books." All he could really do, he decided, was "occasionally goose the people in the right direction. I had a secretary who had a list of people—just to call. The only way I knew that I'd be able to make sure I spoke to everybody that worked at Marvel was to have a secretary have mandatory phone calls and it was on the chart. Once a month I managed to speak to everybody." He was arguing with Production Manager John Verpoorten about deadlines; he was fighting with Cadence about ill-considered cost-cutting efforts (Marvel's parent company wanted, for instance, to print comics with single-color covers); he was going through a separation with his wife. He was publicly predicting that the already barely surviving comic industry

---

* A week later, *Howard the Duck* #2 featured a character named Arthur Winslow, a lovesick "author and collector of old movie stills" with outdated, idealized codes of romance and heroism. As he's transformed into the "Space Turnip," he cries, "I stand *apart*, because I dare to believe in the power of what one man can do—the Lone Ranger, the Green Hornet, James Bond—the *heroes*, the stuff of legends!"

would face a bigger slump before things turned around—in fact, he and Len Wein were already looking at writing screenplays as a possible exit strategy. "It was a job that was just impossible," Wolfman said. "I think it's what finally killed everybody that's been in the job."

Verpoorten asked Roy Thomas how he felt about coming back to his old job, now that Landau was gone. Thomas's marriage had completely fallen apart, and he was restless. Maybe it would be better this time. He met with Galton, worked out his salary with Sol Brodsky, and held one-on-one meetings with editorial and production staffers.

"I'm kind of second in command," Jim Shooter told him, "and I completely understand if you need someone else to be your right-hand man."

No, no, Thomas shrugged—you'll do. "And then," said Shooter, "he gave me a nice chunky list of people he was going to fire."

Don McGregor wondered if he was going to be one of those people—he'd been told that he was going to be taken off *Power Man*, and to be prepared that Thomas was "totally against" his writing. When he met with Thomas, though, he was assured that wasn't the case. In fact, Thomas told McGregor, he'd be getting even more work—it was just that Wolfman wanted to do *Power Man*. "It was like being caught in some political intrigue," McGregor said. "Who can you trust? These are people I've known for years; somebody's not telling the truth."

While McGregor tried to solve the mystery, Thomas scheduled a vacation in Los Angeles, a last breath of freedom before returning to the daily grind. The news of his return began leaking to the fanzine press.

Wolfman waited eagerly.

The drama wasn't confined to the office walls. *Howard the Duck* artist Frank Brunner was tired of having to follow fully scripted stories by Gerber—and tired of Marvel's refusal to raise his page rate. He left the book, and through a small mail-order company began selling poster prints of a mobster duck, titled "Scarface Duck." It looked a lot like Howard . . . but then, hadn't Howard looked a lot like Donald anyway? "I was filling a void left by slow-moving Marvel," Brunner reasoned, "which did not immediately see the potential of the fan market—or of the duck."

The print sold quickly. Gerber wasn't pleased. He told Brunner he wanted some of the profits from his co-creation.

"Which part of the print," Brunner asked Gerber, "did you write or draw? What part of the deal did you arrange?" Then he got together with Mike Friedrich, and hatched plans for Star*Reach to cash in on Howard Fever by publishing the adventures of another identically rendered character he called "The Duckateer." The comic was called *Quack!*

Mary Skrenes, meanwhile, had gone to a New York comic store and presold enough orders for HOWARD FOR PRESIDENT buttons to cover production costs for an entire run. Although she and Gerber were unable to convince Marvel to pull the trigger on marketing *Howard* merchandise, they did manage to get a license to sell the buttons themselves. "We didn't have to pay a fee," said Skrenes, "because they didn't believe it would work."*

No longer speaking with Brunner, they recruited celebrated horror-comics artist Berni Wrightson to draw the button, which they advertised for one dollar plus a quarter shipping. From the Mad Genius offices, Jim Salicrup, Mary Skrenes, and David Anthony Kraft stuffed envelopes while *Mary Hartman, Mary Hartman* played on the television. The orders kept rolling in.

"Why are you taking the job again?" Gerry Conway asked his old friend Roy Thomas—and while Thomas was on the West Coast, that question kept ringing in his ears. It turned out that he really liked being in California. He liked it so much, in fact, that he rented an apartment at a singles complex in Toluca Lake and soon informed Lee that he was not going to return after all. But, he said, he had a solution: Conway, who'd been so unceremoniously passed over in 1974 and departed for DC, should be the new editor in chief.

"Gerry swooped in the day before he took over," said Jim Shooter, "and there was terror and weeping and wailing and gnashing of teeth. There

---

* According to a contract signed March 12, 1976, Marvel was paid a 5 percent royalty fee on each button.

was panic everywhere." Conway didn't like what he saw at 575 Madison. "A handful of writers had what amounted to their own fiefdoms. They ran their five or six titles as if they were editors themselves. So you ended up with this informal and dysfunctional setup with no lines of authority. There were a lot of egos running rampant, because no one was telling anyone what to do.

"Len and Marv's primary interest was in being creators, not bosses. When your basic group was Roy and me and Marv and Len as primary writers, and Englehart and Gerber, you have no problems. But once the company started expanding to forty or fifty titles, you had to bring in other people who needed more guidance, and they weren't getting it. So when I came back, it was chaos. They were missing shipping deadlines all over the place, penalized by the printers, almost to the point of losing the profit margin. And nobody was responsible."

Conway was ready to shake things up, to root out the freelancers who were not making deadline. He immediately called the writers he anticipated having trouble with, including Steve Englehart, Wein, and Wolfman, and laid down the rules. Don McGregor, no longer protected by Wolfman's promise, was immediately removed from the Black Panther strip in *Jungle Action*. Conway insisted that the decision was purely financial, that poor sales had combined with blown deadlines (and subsequent late fees charged by the printer) to create a money-losing endeavor. "Maybe the Panther would have done equally well with a minuscule print-run and no color," Conway said, "but that's not the kind of book we were publishing, and Don just couldn't sell the kind of book the Panther was." So *Jungle Action* was canceled and the Black Panther was given his own title, with Jack Kirby assigned as writer and artist.*

But Shooter was himself clashing with writers whose scripts he was proofreading—many of whom had been given free rein for years. To his

---

* "Gerry was going to make the trains run on time," said Shooter. "But he seemed to be especially hard on LenMarv and their people. I was like, 'If you pull these books away from Len, and you have all these fill-ins for his books and then we use them right away, because you say he's not catching up enough, we are going to lose him. He's going to quit.' And he closed the door, and he said, 'Of *course*, he's going to quit. What do you think I'm doing this for? The bastard screwed me, and *I want rid of him.*'"

mind, the line was 5 percent magnificence, 95 percent trash. He thought Gerber, McGregor, and Englehart's stories were indulgent. "I tried to read the 'good' stuff," he said, "and it was complicated and convoluted and didn't make any sense and wasn't written in English."

He told Tony Isabella to rewrite the climax to a two-year *Ghost Rider* story line, in which the hero was saved by Jesus Christ, on the grounds that it would be seen as religious propaganda. When Shooter and Englehart had a blowup over a plot inconsistency on finished pages, Englehart mailed circled copies of the original script, pointing out that he'd had it right all along. Conway and Shooter both apologized to Englehart, but the environment had turned inescapably toxic.

"It was a cesspool of politics and personality issues," said Conway. "I was not ready for it—just twenty-three years old, and thrust into this morass that had built up in the previous year and a half of chaos."

Conway spelled out the protocol in a staff-wide memo dated March 12: "There's been a problem in the past with communications between the writers and the editorial staff. It should be understood that all the assistant editors are surrogates for the editor, and that my authority is delegated to them on a day to day basis . . . assume that their decisions are my decisions."

That was it, then. Shooter's word was final.

To much of the staff, Conway was an outsider, a DC guy who'd come barreling back into their clubhouse and tried to make up new rules. They stuck together, in their weird way. When a young writer was removed from his book, a member of the production team came to Conway and insisted the writer not be fired.

"What are you talking about?" Conway demanded. "Why not?"

"Because he's a member of our coven!"

The writer was not given his job back, and Conway's relationship with the production department was never the same.

Meanwhile, Conway's secretary—inherited from Wolfman—refused to do anything but answer fan mail. Conway told her to change her ways or she'd be gone. Then he received a visit from one of his top writers, who happened to be dating the secretary.

"Gee," the writer said in measured tones, "my girlfriend's really unhappy. I really hope you can keep her . . ."

She stayed.

Steve Englehart's latest idea for *Doctor Strange* was appropriately zany: Strange and his lover/apprentice Clea would be whisked back in time to explore "The Occult History of America," an adventure that would put them in contact with notable Freemasons like Francis Bacon, George Washington, and Thomas Jefferson. Clea and Benjamin Franklin would have a torrid affair—cuckolding Strange—as they sailed from England to bear witness to the occult-influenced drafting of the Declaration of Independence. Finally, they'd return to the present, where the evil sorcerer Stygro was vampirically feeding off the energy of American patriotism. "It seemed like the thing to do for the bicentennial," Englehart said.

But he only made it through two issues. When he missed a deadline on an issue of *The Avengers*, Conway called to remove him from an assignment, and he snapped. "I found myself in a real sort of schizophrenic thing," Englehart said, "sitting there sort of watching myself saying, 'well, then fuck you, I quit.' And part of me was thinking, 'Do you realize what you're doing?'"

Englehart wrote the last eight pages of the delinquent comic in five minutes. "I just said, 'I'm going to get this out of here,' and wrote just silly shit. It wasn't a real *Avengers* comic book, it was just dialogue for the sake of dialogue." When the *Avengers* pages arrived at the Marvel offices, the last panel read, "Dear bullpen: stick it in your ear.—Steve."

After half a decade at Marvel, Englehart began writing for DC Comics; his Marvel titles were divvied up between Conway, Wolfman, and Claremont. All three titles suffered from Englehart's loss.

Then Jim Starlin called, upset about art corrections on an issue of *Warlock*, and demanded the opportunity to make changes. Conway refused, on the grounds that the corrections would incur late penalties. Starlin, too, quit.

Starlin, Englehart, and Alan Weiss got on the phone together and called Stan Lee from California, insisting that he do something about

Conway. It shouldn't have come as too great a surprise to the writers who'd taken such a stance against conformity that Lee would back his editor.

But Conway was exhausted. "It was like the worst high school dysfunctional mishegoss," Conway said. "Artists were unhappy, and I had this angry editorial staff. Every decision was fraught. I was nauseous all the time. I couldn't see my way out of it short of firing everybody. At one point I was ready to do it. 'Let's get rid of this entire staff and start over.'"

Instead, he turned in his own resignation. He'd been in the position for less than a month. "It hadn't occurred to me," Conway later said, "it would be as horrific as it was."

8

AMID A FLAT MARKET AND AN EXODUS OF TALENT, ARCHIE GOODWIN, editor of Marvel's black-and-white magazines, was drafted to be the fourth editor in chief since Roy Thomas had left twenty months before. Thirty-eight years old, Goodwin was experienced, respected, and beloved by nearly everyone in the industry. Unfortunately, he didn't really want the job—he'd been perfectly happy working on the magazines—and only accepted it, he said later, because he was afraid to turn down a promotion.

"Archie was never great in an executive position," recalled one of his assistants. "He loved to write more than anything, and he loved to edit books, but he did not like doing the business part. Everybody who got that job thought that meant they could do the comics they wanted. They didn't understand it also involved advertising space, printing bills, and keeping the businessmen who owned the company happy. You had to answer questions about personnel."

And managing the personnel was an increasing challenge. In one of his first tasks in the new position, Goodwin helped Stan Lee negotiate Gerry Conway's outgoing freelance arrangement. Conway would now write and edit a substantial number of comics from home: the pointedly wholesome new projects *Peter Parker, The Spectacular Spider-Man* and *Ms. Marvel*, plus *The Avengers* and *Captain Marvel* (both vacated by an angry Steve Englehart), *Ghost Rider* (vacated by an angry Tony Isabella), *Iron Man* (vacated by Goodwin), and *The Defenders*.*

---

*To his credit, Conway managed to inject some Gerberian weirdness into the eventually brand-diluting *Peter Parker*: in the first issue, real-life New York City mayor Abe Beame blackmailed J. Jonah Jameson into paying the ransom money that South American terrorist the Tarantula was demanding for American hostages.

Gerber, removed from *The Defenders* specifically so that Conway could meet his quota, was angry, too; an item in a fanzine even leaked the news that he was leaving *Howard the Duck*. But he resolved his differences with Marvel—greased by the offer of a writer-editor title of his own—and for *Marvel Treasury Edition* #12 wrote a final adventure for the Defenders, in which they teamed with Howard. Gerber supplied those who were paying attention with plenty of chewy subtext: the story featured a team of second-rate ne'er-do-wells ("we're too derivative—too stereotypical—even to make names for ourselves as supervillains!") whose greatest motivation was, in a nod to the perpetually starstruck Stan Lee, to be "on the cover of next month's issue of *Celebrity*."

With Starlin and Englehart and McGregor gone, Steve Gerber was the last renegade standing. "I think in most cases," a stung McGregor told an interviewer, "they've weeded out all the mavericks." Maybe that's why Stan Lee went to Gerber when a rock manager named Bill Aucoin approached Marvel about producing a comic book starring the band Kiss.

Kiss frontman Gene Simmons was a lifelong comics fan. He'd known Marv Wolfman through fanzine circles, and based part of his onstage costume on Jack Kirby's Black Bolt. With a spectacular live act that included pyrotechnics and simulated blood-spitting and fire-breathing, Kiss had finally climbed the album charts after three years of struggling. Now they wanted to be comic-book stars.*

Gerber didn't know their music, but after attending a concert with a nonplussed, ear-holding Lee, he agreed to chronicle their adventures. It was a rocky road. At one early meeting, Aucoin's VP went ballistic when he saw that Kiss were being depicted not as superheroes but as mere musicians. "What the fuck is this?" he shouted as he ripped the pages in half. "If you're gonna be doing a story, they're not musicians, they're superheroes!"

As negotiations dragged on over the following months, Gerber found

---

* They weren't alone in this. Marvel had spoken with Elton John's manager about doing a Captain Fantastic comic book, and David Bowie's wife, Angela, had licensed the rights for Black Widow—she even went so far as to do a photo shoot of her dressed up in costume, with actor Ben Carruthers as Daredevil. Kiss had expressed interest as early as March 1976.

himself allied with Kiss management in the pursuit of a higher-quality product than the usual floppy newsprint pamphlet. They demanded that Marvel publish the story in a 1.50 magazine format with hand-separated color; Gerber pushed to use metallic ink for the cover logo, and for Marvel to exchange advertising with rock magazines like *Rolling Stone*. He involved himself in the design, the typography, the paper stock, the photo selection. As he saw it, high-quality color comic magazines were a way out of the industry free fall—getting Marvel out of the advertising ghetto of Sea Monkeys and X-Ray Spex and You Too Can Draw Timmy the Turtle, appealing to real Madison Avenue advertisers like respectable periodicals did. To draw in Kiss fans not familiar with the Marvel line, he wrote an ad for the inside front cover that shouted, "Welcome to the Marvel Universe!" It was, he proudly pointed out afterward, "the first bit of sophisticated ad copy for itself that the company has ever put before the public."

Stan Lee was also interested in ads. At the end of March, he shot a thirty-second television commercial for the Personna Double II twin-blade razor ("Here at Marvel, I've got Spider-Man and all these characters and super villains like Dr. Doom to worry about . . . I can't waste time worrying about things like shaving!"). Pleased with the results, he dashed off a letter to Marvel's licensing agent. "I wonder if the basic idea mightn't be expanded for some other sponsor who might have a big enough budget to really get the most mileage out of it," Lee wrote. "Additionally, I could mention the ads in our 'Bullpen Bulletins' pages, which are printed in more than 75 million Marvel Comics annually. Needless to say, I'd be happy to personally promote the product any way I could. . . . Considering the vast influence and appeal Marvel and I seem to have with today's so-called 'youth market,' it seems a shame not to be harnessing this tremendous asset in areas other than the sale of comic books alone."

Lee's editorial input by now largely consisted of last-minute second-guessing, in which he would grab a pile of makereadies and sit down with Archie Goodwin. With more than a decade of editorial experience, Goodwin had little use for a tedious page-by-page review of which word balloons had crooked pointers. "You know," Goodwin finally said, "Jim Shooter is actually the guy who does the hands-on editing. You should talk to him." (Shooter, the perpetual second in command, had briefly quit after Goodwin was named as Conway's successor, but retracted the resignation before it took effect.)

Goodwin found the other aspects of the job no more rewarding. Conversations with the executives upstairs were fruitless. In one meeting, the businessmen wondered how to hang on to Marvel's freelance writers and artists, more and more of whom had been migrating to DC (even Conway had bolted to the competition, only six months into his freelance arrangement). Goodwin suggested profit sharing, health insurance, and the return of artwork. After a three-hour conference about this, the response was not encouraging.

"Why are we talking about giving benefits and royalties to these people?" one of the executives asked Goodwin. "These aren't employees on the books—they're people we hire for *piecework*. They have no loyalty to us." Goodwin, furious, threw up his hands. After continued conference talks between editorial and Cadence, the most that Marvel could offer its freelancers was royalty payments for reprinted stories—a practice that DC had already instituted, months earlier.

Cadence wasn't about to sink more money than it had into keeping freelancers happy. After a letter from Sheldon Feinberg to stockholders cited cover-price increases and lower rates of returned product—but conspicuously omitted mention of newsstand sales—Galton shut down the company's men's magazines. The increasingly *Playboy*-like publications had been in Galton's sights the moment he arrived on the job—"I'm not a pornographer," he said—but the threat of unionization from the other magazines was the final nail in the coffin. *Celebrity* shut down. *Stag* and *Male* were sold off to Chip Goodman. After half a century, Magazine Management was nothing but a name.

Marvel's handling of the Kiss negotiations was another distressing signal. Skrenes remembered Gerber returning home one evening, devastated by the corporate attitude toward the band's trademarks. "Kiss just looked like wild and crazy superheroes to them. So Marvel was going to do its own book of characters like the Kiss guys. Like, 'We have the trademark on weird-looking guys, and these guys are stealing the idea by painting their faces. We'll just do it ourselves.' It made no sense."

Gerber, ashamed of Marvel, informed Kiss of the scheme; the band threatened the publisher with a lawsuit unless the book proceeded as planned—with Gerber on board. By the time the matter was settled, Gerber had negotiated for himself something unheard-of at Marvel, something not even Jack Kirby—nor Stan Lee—had managed: a royalty.

Gerber, of course, had gotten none of the residuals or merchandising action on *Howard the Duck*. "I'm the most famous duck writer in the world, and I'm going broke," Gerber told a magazine interviewer, who pointed out that anyone who'd invested in twenty copies of *Howard #1* made more than the four hundred dollars that Gerber ("who lives in Manhattan's unglamourous Hell's Kitchen and sublets a shabbily furnished office in a dreary midtown building") had been paid to write it.

A royalty was more than just a symbolic victory for Gerber, but the thrill was gone. He couldn't believe that Marvel would be so stupid as to try to duplicate Kiss, and squander the advantage of the publicity of one of the most popular acts in the country. Even worse was the disillusionment he now felt toward Lee, his boss and hero. "I don't know if Stan knew about this, or was forced into it," said Skrenes. "But I knew Steve's life was never going to be the same."

While Gerber finished the Kiss project, Lee and the band flew in a DC9 to Buffalo, where they got a police escort to a printing plant. Lee smiled as they mixed samples of their blood into the ink supply and cameras flashed. (Bill Aucoin later claimed that the blood mistakenly ended up in an issue of *Sports Illustrated*.)

Gerber was simultaneously at work on a syndicated *Howard the Duck* newspaper strip, and trying to keep up with deadlines on the monthly *Howard* book, and a *Howard* annual, and packing up his Hell's Kitchen apartment and preparing a move to Skrenes's hometown of Las Vegas. It proved to be more than he could handle. *Howard the Duck #16*, conceived in desperation as he drove cross-country, was seventeen pages of Howard illustrations by various artists, set to thousands of words of text by Gerber about the difficulty of his deadlines. There were imaginary conversations between Gerber and Howard, a downbeat short story about domesticity (followed by a negative self-critique of the story), and a scenario in which "outraged Marvelites" forced Howard and Gerber into a whirring machine that produced jars of "Gerber Strained Brains"; pictures of production manager and deadline taskmaster John Verpoorten lurked on various pages. At the conclusion was a typed letter of comment on the issue: "What I did not like was your self-conscious self-effacement throughout the story," the third paragraph began. "Okay, so maybe you'll never grow up to be another Tom Robbins or Thomas Pynchon . . . your material may always consist more of invective than inventiveness. . . . Come on, Gerber! Get with it!"

The letter was signed, "Steve Gerber."

Before leaving New York for Los Angeles, Roy Thomas had been approached by a marketing consultant who'd tried, and failed, to convince Stan Lee that Marvel should adapt an upcoming science-fiction film that was in production in Algeria. After looking at pre-production sketches, Thomas agreed to appeal to Lee.

Ed Shukin, the circulation director, was skeptical. It was a cast of mostly unknowns, and the deal called for a six-issue adaptation; the third issue would be on stands before the movie even opened. It was, he thought, an unnecessary risk at a time when Marvel's sales were in free fall. But there was one recent shift in the company's strategy that worked in Thomas's favor: what seemed to most interest Lee and Jim Galton lately was shoring up copyrights and brand names (hence the creations of Spider-Woman and Ms. Marvel) and creating relationships with Hollywood. In the span of months, Marvel licensed the rights for Hanna-Barbera cartoons, science-fiction films (*Logan's Run*; *2001*), *Godzilla*, Edgar Rice Burroughs characters (*Tarzan* and *John Carter, Warlord of Mars*), and even a real-life costumed stuntman from Montreal (*The Human Fly*). Maybe they could take a chance on this, too. After all, Thomas had been right about Conan the Barbarian.

Thomas won his argument, and Marvel prepared its adaptation of *Star Wars*.

Meanwhile, titles with original characters, like *Iron Fist*, *The Inhumans*, *Black Goliath*, and *Omega the Unknown*, were canceled. Gerber and Skrenes had planned ahead the next two years of *Omega the Unknown*, in which the extraterrestrial hero experienced various human weaknesses—addictions to alcohol, gambling, and women—and which would reveal his link to James-Michael Starling. The final issue before cancellation brought Omega to Las Vegas and ended with the announcement that the story would be continued in an issue of *The Defenders*. It never happened. "They said they wanted new ideas," Skrenes recalled. "But when you gave them something new they said, 'but what is it *like?*'"

Jack Kirby—who recognized similarities between his *Fourth World* creations (Mark Moonrider, Darkseid, and the Source) and elements of *Star Wars* (Luke Skywalker, Darth Vader, and the Force)—also had ideas to spare. The contract he'd signed with Marvel called for him to essentially package entire comic books independently, choosing who would ink his work, and getting no interference from the New York office. "Once Jack came in," said Gerry Conway, "the attitude Stan had was, 'If Jack wants to be his own boss, that's what he's going to be. Just leave him to himself.' So that was Jack's own corner."

Kirby's *The Eternals* was another variation on the ancient-aliens-visited-earth themes that had also informed his creations of the Kree in *Fantastic Four* and the New Gods for DC. But Marvel was more interested in Kirby building on his old ideas, and there was editorial pressure for Kirby to include references to S.H.I.E.L.D., and the Thing and the Hulk. "We felt, or maybe Stan felt, it should have been connecting more with other books," Archie Goodwin said of Kirby's *Captain America*. "We wanted Jack to use some of the villains that were current in other books so the kids reading this book would read *Avengers*, and the kids reading *Avengers* would read this book. . . . I guess we figured it could only help sales. But Jack said he didn't want to do it." Kirby roundly ignored the story lines that directly preceded his own; he made almost no reference, in fact, to anything that had happened in Marvel's history.

The hermetic distance that Kirby tried to keep from the rest of the Marvel Universe caused some problems. In *Captain America*, assistant editor Roger Stern had to rewrite a Kirby reference to a flying saucer being "the first alien space craft ever to visit the Earth," a description that would discount scores of Marvel adventures and not a few of the characters. Rumors circulated that the *Captain America* letters pages, which were edited in the New York office, had been intentionally tilted toward negative feedback—some of it fabricated by members of the staff.*

Steve Lemberg, the music-biz entrepreneur who'd secured exclusive television and movie rights for the Marvel characters, never got further than the Carnegie Hall show and the Spider-Man rock record. Out in California, Motown's Berry Gordy took an interest in Lemberg's plans and set up several meetings with movie studios, but there was one problem that everyone kept stumbling over: budgets. "They did not have the technology to make the film we wanted to make," Lemberg said. "It would have cost a fortune."

Cadence Industries' legal team eventually managed to extricate Marvel from Lemberg's open-ended options. "There are still companies . . . which have rights of first refusal," read one strategic memo, "but we won't let that delay us any longer." Marvel sold Steve Krantz the rights to film live-action Spider-Man and Hulk movies, and a former Hollywood executive named Dan Goodman bought the rights for television in 1976. As the low-budget pilot was prepared for CBS with independent producer Chuck Fries, Lee found that his input was not encouraged. "I was supposedly the consultant," he said, "but they really didn't listen to me very much."

Shortly afterward, Frank Price, the new head of Universal television, asked his son about the green monster on his sweatshirt, and decided that the Incredible Hulk would make good television. For $12,500, he secured the live-action television rights to twelve Marvel characters of his choice; as both Dan Goodman and Chuck Fries had done, Price took his pitch to

---

* "I grew up loving Stan and Jack's comics," one of the people who oversaw those letters columns insisted, years later. "But it was hard going to find any positive letters. I confess I even made some up to try to balance the negative. Mostly, any positive feedback came from kids younger than the general Marvel reader's level of maturity. So I resorted to padding the positive—not the other way around."

CBS, preparing life-sized cardboard cutouts of the characters—including Doctor Strange, Captain America, the Human Torch, Ms. Marvel, and the Sub-Mariner—and arranging them around the network's conference room. CBS agreed to finance two-hour pilots of eight of them, and in a matter of months *The Incredible Hulk* joined *Spider-Man* in production. For the first time in a decade, Marvel would be transmitted into American living rooms. Hopefully, the children in those living rooms would then buy some comic books.

Just in time, lifelines were being thrown to Marvel. The phenomenal success of the *Star Wars* movie translated into a sales bonanza for the tie-in comics, which went into multiple printings and pulled the company out of its immediate financial straits. On the heels of that triumph, the Kiss special sold more than half a million copies—unprecedented for a $1.50 comic publication. "For a while," Gerber said, "they had one drawer for Kiss mail, and another drawer for all the fan mail on all the other Marvel books."

There was also a lot of mail for *The X-Men*, for the first time in years. Claremont and Cockrum had carved out a corner of the Marvel Universe that was perfect for the blockbuster age, filled with plane, boat, and rocket ship crashes, and gleaming high-tech space odysseys that fell into place just as *Star Wars* fever started. But *The X-Men* had something else that played against the spectacle: intimacy. In their two years of collaboration, Claremont and Cockrum had already carefully defined their characters with familiar catchphrases, nicknames, and sound effects that would eventually turn into something like secret passwords for fans: "Mein Gott," "fastball special," "bub," "muties," "Elf," "Bamf," "Snikt!" Although the members of the X-Men were hardheaded individualists with diverse backgrounds, many of them flummoxed by American culture, they slowly came together as a surrogate family for one another. If Gerber's Defenders were, as he'd said, an encounter group, Claremont and Cockrum's X-Men were the members of a halfway house, where everyone tried to figure out how to live in close quarters without letting their emotional baggage get in the way.

It seemed that every issue brought major changes in the X-Men: death, departure, reunions, new costumes. But the biggest transformation was that of Jean Grey, aka Marvel Girl, who under Lee and Thomas had been a girly goof, the weak link of the team. "I don't want to say anything bad against Stan," Cockrum said, "but when he was creating the characters of the early '6os, all the girl characters he created were simps—the house-wife heroes . . . they were there to be looked at and rescued, mostly."

And so Claremont and Cockrum proceeded to turn Marvel Girl into Phoenix, the most powerful female superhero in comics. After Jean Grey was believed dead in a plane crash, she reemerged with more power than she knew what to do with.* She had tapped into "the phoenix-force . . . a manifestation of a primal force of the universe which derives from the psyches of all living beings in the universe, and which therefore has lim-itless power." Pretty soon she'd be blasting foes twelve miles away and opening portals into other worlds.

Claremont began drawing on his own interest in the occult and religion† when an insane space emperor attempted to destroy the uni-verse with something called the M'Kraan Crystal,‡ Phoenix partook in cosmic kabbalah tree-of-life rituals to defeat him. The X-Men was now the closest thing Marvel Comics had to the glorious mind-fryings of En-glehart's Doctor Strange or Starlin's Warlock, only a year in the past but worlds away from the new, kid-friendly Marvel of Nova and Godzilla and Dynomutt.

Cockrum loved working on the book—and especially on the swash-buckling Nightcrawler, whom he considered an alter ego of sorts—but once he joined the Marvel staff as a cover designer, even the bimonthly pace of The X-Men was a struggle to maintain. When Marvel decided that the title was selling well enough to go on a monthly schedule,

---

* "My power—it's hitting me like a drug," Phoenix marveled in X-Men #105. "I've never felt such . . . ecstasy! God in heaven, what have I become?"

† In early 1977, Claremont married Bonnie Wilford, a Gardnerian Wiccan; according to one friend, they were "quite active in the New York City demimonde."

‡ Claremont, who'd spent time on a kibbutz in college, was liberal with his use of geresh.

Claremont's friend John Byrne began licking his chops: "I made it known at Marvel," he said, "that men would die if Cockrum ever left it and it didn't come to me."

Jim Shooter had seen how well Byrne worked with Claremont and pushed them together on the Spider-Man-plus-a-monthly-guest comic *Marvel Team-Up*. When *Iron Fist* was canceled and combined with *Power Man* (the new name for black badass Luke Cage) in the black-and-white-buddies book *Power Man and Iron Fist*, Byrne and Claremont took over the art on that as well.

The speedy Byrne added *The Champions* and a few issues of *The Avengers* to his workload (*Marvel Team-Up* and *Power Man*) while he circled around an irritated Cockrum, who'd gotten wind of his intentions. "John was the heir apparent to that book and he was panting to take it over," Cockrum said. "But every time he came to the Marvel offices, he pissed everybody off. I stayed on a little longer just to aggravate him." Even after he left the book, Cockrum continued drawing *X-Men* covers, just to annoy Byrne.

After introducing the Shi'ar Imperial Army and the Starjammers—he later estimated drawing more than fifty individual characters in his final issue—Cockrum finally left in the middle of 1977, exhausted and behind deadline. John Byrne was happy to step in.

As the writer and editor of *Amazing Spider-Man*, *Incredible Hulk*, *Fantastic Four*, and *Thor*, four of Marvel's biggest titles, Len Wein should have felt on top of the world. But he was quibbling with John Verpoorten, going into a rage over such minor details as, say, which letterers were being hired. He was challenging Chris Claremont and Tony Isabella on the way they used characters borrowed from his titles. "I had become obsessively involved with the books," Wein recalled. "I was watching my books with such a hawk-like eye that I had no sense of perspective on this stuff anymore." He arranged to write *Detective Comics* for DC. It wasn't expressly forbidden in his contract; still, when Archie Goodwin and Stan Lee found out, they told him he'd have to write *Detective* under a pseudonym. DC begrudgingly agreed. But after a long weekend of thought, Wein decided "it was a lot simpler to make a clean break of it, and start all over, than to sit there working for both companies and have nobody like me. My emotional make-up is just fragile enough that I couldn't cope with that for very long. So I came back to Marvel the following day and told Archie that I was going to leave."

Stan Lee didn't take the news well. He told Wein that he would never again work for Marvel.

If Kiss could sell, thought David Anthony Kraft, why not the Beatles? "Everyone was for it," Kraft said, "except for Jim Galton, who had to approve it, because it was such a high-profile, expensive project, and he just didn't get that the Beatles were *the Beatles*."

Lee called Kraft into a meeting in Galton's office and instructed him to make the pitch. "I had long hair and I wore a black leather motorcycle jacket," Kraft recalled, "and my knees hung out of my jeans. Even though there were three of us in that meeting, Galton would say to Stan, 'Weren't the Beatles sort of like the Monkees?' and Stan would say to me, 'Dave, explain that.' And I'd respond, and then Stan would respond, and then Galton would respond to what I said *to Stan* without ever making eye contact or addressing me."

Kraft stopped by Lee's office afterward and announced that he was going to give himself a makeover to see if he could penetrate Galton's corporate filters. By Monday, he declared, he'd be wearing a three-piece suit and a new haircut. With characteristic enthusiasm, Lee cheerily told Kraft where to shop: Saks, Barneys, Bloomingdale's. "Lo and behold, when I had meetings following that, I just had meetings with Galton, not even Stan, and he could see and hear me, and everything. It made such a sensation. I remember Marie Severin following me around the office, effusive: 'If only more people would do this . . .'"

Jim Shooter, who as associate editor regularly met with Lee to review makereadies, also started dressing up. Gone were short-sleeve shirts with T-shirts showing from underneath, replaced by long sleeves and ties. Although Lee appreciated the wardrobe upgrade, his relationship with Shooter was rocky at first, owing to the problems he kept finding in the flood of comic product.

"The fourth or fifth time around," Shooter said, "we're still seeing the same kinds of problems, and now he's starting to think I'm a moron, and explaining it to me in one syllable words. *Don't. Let. Them. Do. This.* I'm like, 'Stan, there's just so much I can do. I'm doing everything I can.' And I'm trying not to throw Archie under the bus—because he won't fire these people."

When Shooter was drafted to provide plots to Lee for the *Spider-Man* newspaper strip, Lee patiently explained the process—"You see, every day, there's a daily strip . . ."—as though Shooter were a child. When the first batch of plots was turned in, though, Lee was impressed.

"These are good."

"Thank you."

There was an awkward pause.

"How come the *comics* are not so good?"

"Jim Shooter wanted that job desperately, desperately, desperately," said Jo Duffy, Goodwin's assistant. "He was Archie's right-hand man but he really wanted to be Archie. In a sense his entire tenure working for Archie was him auditioning for the job. I don't think Archie would have left had it not been so apparent that somebody who wanted it much more was standing right next to him saying, 'If he leaves, me, pick me, please, please, me me me me me?' So I think Archie felt more harassed than supported. Everybody's perception was 'Jim wants that job.'"

"I never brought up Archie at all," Shooter said. "Stan starts realizing that Archie won't take the reins and fire people; he knows that Archie is not an administrative guy. So he starts concocting this idea that maybe I should be editor in chief. And maybe we can move Archie to some other thing. So, he came up with this idea that Archie would do some special projects and he tried to think of something that would sound prestigious, and a contract forever. No one wanted to get rid of Archie."

On a bus ride back from Pittsburgh with a friend, Shooter held forth on how the editorial division might be restructured, with multiple editors, each responsible for specific titles, reporting to the editor in chief. It was how DC Comics had done it for decades, so why shouldn't it work for Marvel? And the autonomous writer-editor title—held by Roy Thomas,

Marv Wolfman, Steve Gerber, and Jack Kirby—that would have to be done away with. It was time for someone to consolidate control. No prima donnas allowed.

Even from Los Angeles, Roy Thomas had sensed that Goodwin wouldn't be long for the job. Thomas knew that Shooter was probably next in line, and that Shooter had the writer-editor positions in his crosshairs. So he wrote a letter to Stan Lee expressing his alarm at the idea of Shooter as editor in chief. "Among other things," Thomas later recalled, "I said that Jim wanted total power, and that I could not and would not live with such a situation, and that I felt he had ambition enough to dance on all our graves."

When Archie Goodwin got wind of Lee's plans to replace him with Shooter, he was pissed. Lee took Shooter out to lunch at a Chinese restaurant and broke the news that Goodwin had resigned. "His read was that I had stabbed him in the back," Shooter said. "Even though he was going to get a raise and title, he just basically told me to go to hell." Goodwin began working out a writer-editor contract for three books a month.

Lee planned to announce Jim Shooter as the new editor in chief the week before Christmas. But on Monday, December 19, 1977, Marvel receptionist Mary McPherran, accompanied by the building superintendent, entered the duplex apartment of John Verpoorten. He had died in his recliner, up in the loft bedroom, after leaving work sick on the previous Friday. His cat cowered in the corner. "He always made me swear if he didn't show up for work that I would find out what happened to him," McPherran said. "He was afraid of dying in his apartment." The barrel-chested Viking of a man who intimidated delinquent creators and editors concealed his softness—they didn't know that every vacation he took was to Disneyland, or that he collected reels of old animated films. And most of them didn't know that he was running a complicated, stressful, and selfless scam of "pre-vouchering," through which struggling artists were floated paychecks before assignments were turned in. "This was his deep dark secret," McPherran said. "I think that's what killed him." Verpoorten was thirty-seven years old.

"I helped clean out his office," Danny Crespi said, years later. "And I took his cigarette lighter just to have something of his. I don't smoke anymore, but I still carry that lighter in my pocket. Someone also gave me his Mickey Mouse cufflinks. They're too big for me but I keep 'em anyway. I still keep his picture around my office."

With the news of Verpoorten's death, Lee decided it would be better to wait until after the holidays to announce Shooter's promotion. But that Friday, at the Christmas party at the bar downstairs from the office, he threw a wrench into his own plan. "Stan and Joan had been to another Christmas party," Shooter said, "and I guess they had a glass of wine or something. And Stan just blurted it out: 'Hey everybody! Jim is going to be the new editor in chief.' Archie and his wife are sitting there shooting daggers at me with their eyes. You could have heard a pin drop. No applause. The only two people who came up to me were Danny Crespi and [inker] John Tartaglione. But everybody else was silent."

The next morning, Shooter's home telephone rang at seven o'clock. "I pick it up," he recalled, "and it's Marv Wolfman's voice. He doesn't say hello.

"He says, 'What are you going to do?'"

PART III

Trouble Shooter

(9)

*Stan wants me to run Marvel Comics, and he's disappointed when
I don't. He doesn't want to be hassled. The way he sees it, for the
most part, I deal with them and he deals with me.*
                                        —Jim Shooter, February 16, 1978

*Everything that has been done to us in the past years has been
from the attitude, "Here, my boy, have a lollipop." It's been a parent dealing with an unruly child. We're not children! We're people!
We're creators! It's about time we stood up and made them take
notice of that fact.*   —Chris Claremont, May 7, 1978

THE COMMERCIAL VICTORIES OF THE *STAR WARS* AND KISS TIE-INS HAD, UNFOR-
tunately, been anomalies. *Howard the Duck*'s popularity had dropped
markedly after the first several issues. The added exposure from the CBS
Spider-Man and *Hulk* television shows had boosted the popularity of
those titles—sales of the *Hulk* comic rose 35 percent—but the line as
a whole was still anemic. Record-breaking blizzards in the northeastern
United States had punishing effects on shipping and sales of all newsstand periodicals. And then there was the chaos of the Marvel offices
themselves. In January 1978, Jim Shooter's first month as editor in chief,
Marvel was scheduled to ship forty-five comics; only twenty-six were de-
livered on time, and some of the titles ran as much as four months late.
Trying to stop the bleeding was John Verpoorten's former assistant, Lenny
Grow, who was suddenly pushed into the role of production manager.
With John Romita swamped with *Spider-Man* newspaper strip deadlines,
Brodsky gave Marie Severin the title of art director. Shooter, meanwhile,

barely had time to glance at the comics Marvel was printing—he was busy overhauling the structure of the expanding editorial division.

He hired a young and motley bunch. Two editors shared stewardship of the color comics: former associate editor Roger Stern, who had extensive knowledge of the Marvel characters, and Bob Hall, an artist who'd been a protégé of John Buscema and who also moonlighted as a playwright. The magazine line was edited by Rick Marschall, a former newspaper syndicate editor and comic-strip historian; his assistant, Ralph Macchio, was another prolific letter writer who'd been a vocal Don McGregor fan. In February, Shooter hired an assistant of his own. Mark Gruenwald, who resembled Bill Murray and had a sense of humor to match, was a comic-book obsessive on the level of Roy Thomas, and impressed Shooter with his publication of *The Omniverse*, a scholarly zine that chin-scratchingly parsed the minutiae of fictional superhero worlds. Gruenwald would serve as liaison between Marvel and the writer-editors—while they lasted.

Steve Gerber, the last to sign a writer-editor contract, and falling behind on deadlines once again, was the first to go. In February, he was relieved of his duties as the writer of the *Howard the Duck* newspaper strip. Gerber's lawyer informed Marvel that this was a violation of his contract, and that he was considering legal action regarding the ownership of the Howard the Duck character; shortly thereafter Marvel terminated Gerber's contract altogether. Asked by the *Comics Journal* if chronic lateness was the reason for the company's decision, Shooter replied, "I would just say that we found it advantageous to get out of the contract we were in." Gerber maintained that he and Gene Colan were not getting advance payments on time.

Stewardship of Howard was split up: Marv Wolfman took over the newspaper strip, and Bill Mantlo took over the comic book. When the strip was canceled later in the year, Gerber complained publicly about the "downright horrible" quality of Wolfman's work. "Once I was gone," he told the *Village Voice*, "Howard was lobotomized, devoid of substance, and turned into a simple-minded parody. So, they're putting him out of his misery."

An ending to Gerber and Skrenes's *Omega the Unknown* saga, repeatedly promised in letters columns and repeatedly rescheduled, was
finally written without its creators' input. "It just got to the point where
we couldn't work with Shooter anymore," Skrenes said. "He was screwing
with us and punishing us and trying to have somebody else write it, like
they always did with *Howard*." Omega was killed off in an issue of *The
Defenders*. Gerber and Skrenes swore to each other that they'd take their
original plans for the character's ending to their graves. "I'd heard for
years," Skrenes said of Shooter, "'Mort Weisinger gave this guy a nervous
breakdown.' And they make him an editor, and it's like, he didn't get the
memo that we get to do what we want with the book."

Jack Kirby's contract was up for renewal in April 1978. At a convention
in West Virginia, Stan Lee announced that Kirby had signed a long-term
contract as an artist only; he said Kirby's scripting was "imaginative but
undisciplined," but Lee was confident that the artwork would return to
form once Kirby was paired with other writers.*

But there was no new contract. Kirby's tour of duty was, in fact, coming to an end. His latest return had been a major disappointment, to him
and to Marvel. None of his books had sold as well as hoped, the reaction
from readers was less than enthusiastic, and even his supposed autonomy
had been undermined. "The editorial staff up at Marvel had no respect
for what he was doing," said Jim Starlin. "All these editors had things on
their walls making fun of Jack's books. They'd cut out things saying 'Stu-
pidest Comic of the Year.' . . . [T]his entire editorial office was just littered
with stuff disparaging the guy who founded the company these guys were
working for. He created all the characters these guys were editing."

Tensions were now worse than they'd ever been in the sixties. Kirby reportedly received hate mail on Marvel letterhead, and crank phone calls
from the office. When Roy Thomas persuaded him to draw an issue of
the imaginary-tale series *What If?* (it was a self-reflective story called

---

* Lee also characterized Kirby's work on their just-completed Silver Surfer graphic
novel, two years in the making, as "better than recent stuff, but not his best."

"What if . . . The Fantastic Four were the Marvel Bullpen?" starring Lee, Kirby, Thomas, and Flo Steinberg), Kirby refused to allow Thomas to script it, and replaced the Thomas character with a Sol Brodsky one. Once the pages arrived at Marvel, an editor went through and changed all of Kirby's references to "Stanley" to "Stan" and corrected all the grammar in the dialogue—except for that of the Jack Kirby character.

"I didn't really get a shot," Kirby later said of his 1970s work at Marvel, pointing to professional jealousy. "A guy will create a book, another will fill his book up with knock letters—he's off in five months, or three months, and the other guy's got his shot. . . . I see it as a serpent's nest. And in a serpent's nest, nothing can survive. Eventually all the snakes kill each other. Eventually they'll also kill whatever generated them."

In the end, Kirby's exit plan from the frustrations and limitations of the comic-book industry was the same that Stan Lee's had been: Hollywood. Kirby was invited by Hanna-Barbera to produce storyboards for NBC's new *Fantastic Four* cartoon—for which both Lee and Thomas were writing. Kirby still wasn't calling the shots—because the Human Torch had already been optioned by Universal, Kirby had to create a cute robot named H.E.R.B.I.E. to be the Fantastic Four's fourth member— but the pay was better, and the treatment was more respectful.

Jack Kirby would never work for Marvel Comics again.

In the spring of 1978, Marvel's lawyers, faced with new copyright laws going into effect, decided that the company needed proof that its publications were being produced as work-for-hire. Previously, a legally questionable "contract" had been rubber-stamped on the backs of paychecks—if you signed the check, you signed the contract. But now Jim Shooter began handing out single-spaced one-page contracts that granted Marvel "forever all rights of any kind and nature in and to the work." When freelancers read the contract, they flipped. Then they tried to organize.

DON'T SIGN THIS
CONTRACT!!
YOU WILL BE SIGNING
YOUR LIFE AWAY!!

COMICS CONTRACT MEETING
SUNDAY, MAY 7, 9 E. 48TH STREET
THIRD FLOOR 4:00 PM

Neal Adams was by now the de facto leader in the battle for creators' rights—he'd recently made headlines for insisting that DC Comics compensate *Superman* creators Jerry Siegel and Joe Shuster. Now he led the discussion at the first Comics Creators Guild. The demands he advocated were radical: that work sold to comic companies would entail North American rights only, that artwork remain the property of the talent, that all disputes be determined by arbitration, and—the kicker—that the scale of artists' pay be tripled.

But it was a difficult time to build consensus among comics professionals. Steve Englehart, Frank Brunner, and Steve Gerber, unsurprisingly, were among those who were ready to take up arms. Others, like Roy Thomas and Mark Gruenwald, worried that Adams's success removed him from the economic realities of the average freelancer; some felt that his strategy favored pencilers over writers, inkers, and other professionals. Many feared that the industry was on the brink of collapse. "I think with things being tight this way, when the industry's hurting this way, this is not the time to push for the Guild," said Ross Andru.

Bill Mantlo wanted to go further. "A guild isn't strong enough," he told the *Comics Journal*. "We need a union." But an attempt to unionize had been the last straw at Magazine Management before Galton pulled the plug. The fear in the hearts of those who'd spent their lives working for Marvel Comics, who'd seen their livelihoods ebb and flow with the fluctuating market, was summed up by Gene Colan: "They've treated me pretty decently and I don't want to go off on a limb. It's a little risky at this point and I'm not going to make any waves."

"If we really want to take John Byrne and consider him as a phenomenon, it starts with the *X-Men*," John Byrne once told an interviewer. He was unsettled, he said, by all the attention, the hooting and hollering his name caused at convention panels while his heroes received only polite smatterings of applause. But Claremont and Byrne's *X-Men* was undeniably something special, the most perfect blend of angst and exaltation Marvel had seen since Lee and Ditko's Spider-Man. The visual facility wasn't just the work of Byrne, but the regular team that began coalescing: the smooth delineations of inker Terry Austin, the high-contrast hues chosen by colorist Glynis Wein, and the neatly uniform Art Deco characters of letterer Tom Orzechowski all contributed to a streamlined reading experience that contrasted with the often-murky visuals that had crept into superhero comics. In a sense, the look of the *X-Men* was a return to the "Pop Art Productions" of Marvel's heyday.

Claremont and Byrne's skilled pacing (and their rare ability to regularly meet deadlines) allowed them to freight some of the same Big Ideas that had distinguished Starlin and Englehart's work—meditations on corruption, mortality, mysticism, and totalitarianism—into page-turning potboilers, a smoother-edged synthesis of the cult favorites that had come before. They juggled more subplots than even Lee and Kirby's *Fantastic Four*, and snuck in plenty of personal drama, for which Byrne's glamorous characters—cheekbones, full lips, dimples, and almond-shaped eyes—were perfect vehicles.

It was also the soapiest saga ever put forth by the House of Ideas, filled with agonized romances, self-confidence crises, lectures on morality, psychic scars, and worrying. In the first story that Claremont and Byrne plotted together, Jean Grey and the Beast were separated from the rest of the X-Men, each group believing the other killed. Jean flew to Scotland to clear her head; halfway across the world, Cyclops sat by a pond and thought, "Jean and Hank *died*. . . . *How* am I going to tell the *professor*? It'll break his *heart*. I'm *surprised* it hasn't broken *mine*. Surprised . . . and a little *scared*." Joined by Storm, he continues, "I *mourned* for Hank, but—for Jean there's *nothing* there. After the *shuttle flight*, nothing had changed between us, yet *everything* had. She wasn't the girl I'd *loved* anymore."

There was drama behind the scenes as well. When editor Roger Stern visited Byrne in Calgary, Alberta, with a makeready of the issue in hand, Byrne blew a gasket over the way Claremont rendered Cyclops's monologue. "I was tempted to throw it off my balcony," he said. "We were sitting on my balcony reading it and I was yelling and screaming and the neighbors were coming out and going, 'What's going on down there?'" He began writing margin notes in blue pen, so that if Claremont changed something, Byrne could take the pages and prove he'd intended something else.

Byrne complained, loudly, about what he called "Chris-shticks," and Claremont certainly had trademark tics—rampant italicization for emphasis in dialogue, confident women, psychic bonds, and characters who always took vacations in the United Kingdom. There were also the endlessly reflective thought balloons and somber monologues. "Chris' idea of a perfect issue of the *X-Men*," Byrne once said, "would be 22 pages of them walking around in the Village or at Scott's apartment or something like that, where they sit around, out of costume, in jeans and t-shirts, and just talk." Claremont, for his part, said that all he cared about was the emotional relationships. "To me," he told an interviewer, "the fights are bullshit." But at a time when so many superhero comics were devoid of personality, it was easy to cut some slack to someone who was investing so heavily in human interaction.*

Jean Grey's powerful reincarnation as Phoenix was at the flashpoint of many disagreements, and Byrne labored to eliminate her from the book, preferring instead to showcase Wolverine, his favorite. But although the writer and artist seemed to often be working at cross-purposes, by the time their collaboration reached the printed page, it was a mesmerizing, unified vision of sci-fi extravagance and human-scale tear-jerking. Sales climbed.

David Anthony Kraft, who'd followed Gerber's lead and begun to negotiate a royalty for the *Beatles* comic, soon heard from Sol Brodsky. Even with his VP title, Brodsky couldn't shake the burden of being the hatchet man, bearing bad news that Stan Lee couldn't—or wouldn't—deliver.

"They've decided they're not going to pay royalties on the Beatles book," he told Kraft. Then he shut the office door. "I'll deny this conversation," Brodsky said, "but between you and me, you'd be a fool to let it go."

---

* Byrne was not the only artist to note Claremont's involvement in psychological nuances of characters in those days. "He used to call and give me the plot on the phone and he would talk and talk and talk and talk!" recalled *Ms. Marvel* artist Jim Mooney. "I used to think, My God, does he *need* to take this long?"

Kraft visited Lee. "If this was a Marvel character and you did this," he told his boss, "I'd be kind of stuck, wouldn't I? But you don't own the Beatles, and you don't own me, so I'll just take this project to another publisher." He walked back to the office he shared with Shooter, and began making phone calls—to *Rolling Stone*, to *Circus*—before Lee shouted for him to come back.

Lee expressed sympathy. After all, he said, he himself had created so many of Marvel's properties with no royalties to show for it. He sent Kraft up to meet with Galton. "How about you and Galton fight it out?" he said.

"It was a Friday afternoon," Kraft remembered, "and Galton wanted to leave early and go golfing or whatever his weekend plans were. The crux of it was, he had contracts with the top creators, and their contracts said that their rates would automatically adjust upward to the best deal that was going. And his concern was if he paid me royalties, he'd have to start paying royalties to everyone at Marvel Comics." But if Kraft and artist George Perez did business as an incorporated entity, a royalty deal wouldn't transgress the other creators' contracts. Kraft took the name that Gerber was no longer using, Mad Genius Studios, and via this loophole got his royalty deal.

Marvel, however, wasn't about to make the same arrangement for its wholly owned *The Defenders*, which Kraft was also writing (and, rock-and-roll fan that he was, filling with constant references to Rush and Blue Oyster Cult). When it finally came time to sign the work-for-hire agreement, Kraft promptly quit *The Defenders*.

In the current climate, such courage was getting harder and harder to come by. On June 22, DC Comics, which had recently undertaken an ambitious but ill-fated expansion campaign, announced staff layoffs—and the cancellation of 40 percent of its line. The next day, Jim Shooter recalled, there was a line at the door of the Marvel offices, and he spent the entire day signing work-for-hire agreements for the resigned masses. Soon afterward he hired Al Milgrom and Larry Hama, both of whom had been editing for DC, to join Marvel's growing staff of editors. DC's art director even began sending younger talent over to Shooter. There weren't a lot of new guys lining up for the dying industry, just the most driven and most in love with the art form, hungry for assignments and happily taking direction. Shooter put twenty-one-year-old Vermonter Frank Miller on a *Spectacular Spider-Man* story, and twenty-year-old Pennsylvanian Bill Sienkiewicz on stories about Moon Knight, a sort of ersatz Batman, that ran in the back of the *Hulk* magazine.

Many of the most provocative and vital writers and artists of the previous generations, chased away by the industry's paternalistic and/or just plain unfair policies, were off to other pursuits: animating Saturday morning cartoons, writing novels and screenplays, illustrating for ad agencies, producing lithographs for the nerd-collector market. It seemed like the mass exoduses that marked the 1950s might be just around the corner. A year or two earlier, when a teenage fan approached Marv Wolfman at a comic convention and asked for career advice, the candid response was startling: "Confidentially, everyone in the business is looking to get out, so my suggestion to you is . . . do something else," Wolfman told him. "In five years there aren't going to be any comics."

Those who remained in the field would have to make a go of it within the strictures of the system, waiving royalties and reining in their more esoteric flights of fancy. Jim Shooter's own stories for *The Avengers*, illustrated by George Perez, might have doubled as a manifesto of what he saw as the ideal commercial Marvel comic book: banter-heavy dialogue and small medium-shot panels that showcased the colorful costumes, all adding up to a staccato rhythm of adventure and whimsy.

It wasn't all cold formula: sneaking into Shooter's stories, almost helplessly, was a recurring motif of persecuted deities. Most notable was a yearlong *Avengers* story about "Michael," a golf-shirt-and-short-shorts-wearing preppy in Forest Hills, Queens. Shooter revealed that Michael was actually the reincarnation of Korvac, a minor villain from Steve Gerber's *Defenders* (a kind of techno-centaur, Korvac's legs were replaced by a mainframe computer) who had transformed himself into an enlightened God. His blond suburbanite form gave way to a glowing, oversized, purple and yellow astral projection.

Korvac entered the pantheon of Marvel's most powerful, and trippy, characters, like Kirby's Watcher and Ditko's Eternity, both of whom appeared in cameos and took notice of his actions, as if to ratify his very importance. "His position was unique," the captions in *Avengers* #175 confided to the reader. "He would be free to make subtle alterations in the fabric of reality, eventually taking control—and correcting the chaos, healing the injustice that civilization had heaped upon a battered universe."

But the suspicious Avengers attacked Korvac, tragically preventing him from eradicating the world's cruelties. "I was in the unique position to alter that, to bring all of existence under my sane and benevolent rule," he told the super-team. "I am a God! And I was going to be your savior!" Where others saw megalomania, Jim Shooter saw a beleaguered hero who only wanted to bring order to the galaxy.

By the end of the 1970s, Stan Lee was making over $150,000 as Marvel's publisher, had signed a lucrative contract with Harper & Row for an autobiography, and was pulling in additional income through speaking engagements and television consultation. A *People* magazine article noted his self-described workaholism, and his expensive tastes: "On his wrist hangs a heavy link silver bracelet. His feet are contained in thoroughbred Guccis. Piercing green-gray eyes are hidden behind prescription shades, but their hip image is offset by a conservative Paul Stuart herringbone jacket and tan slacks."

His wide smile now framed by a silvered mustache and sideburns, Stan Lee's well-practiced anecdotes were an increasingly regular sight on television talk shows and in newspapers, where he never missed a chance to profess that his chosen medium was worthy of attention and respect. "Comic books are like the last weapon left against encroaching televisionitis, which is making non-readers out of a whole generation," Lee told one university audience. "Most kids, if not for comics, wouldn't read anything at all." But in fact, he wanted nothing more than to change Marvel's Hollywood fortunes, to get out of publishing, to get his vision of Marvel on television.

Partnered with DePatie-Freleng, the animation studio that created the *Pink Panther* cartoons, Marvel began developing more Saturday morning shows, starring Spider-Woman and the Silver Surfer; Hanna-Barbera spun off a member of the Fantastic Four for the unfortunate *Fred and Barney Meet the Thing*. But when it came time to package a cartoon based on the current X-Men lineup, nearly the entire team was unfamiliar to Lee ("I didn't know we had any Russian superheroes," he told one interviewer) and he had to summon Jim Shooter for help.

"Sol Brodsky got pictures of all the X-Men, old and new," said Shooter, "and they were sitting on the couches in Stan's office, but they didn't have any names on them. And he had a list on paper with the names and powers, but there were no names on the pictures. So he called me in, and he said, 'Okay, look. I know the old X-Men. Now who are these guys?'"

"I should have gotten out of this business twenty years ago," Lee told *Circus* magazine in 1978. "I would have liked to make movies, to be a director or a screenwriter, to have a job like Norm Lear or Freddie Silverman. I'd like to be doing what I'm doing here, but in a bigger arena."

The CBS president who'd purchased rights for Marvel characters had been fired before any shows had aired; the CEO who fired him said he didn't want "CBS turning into a cartoon network." Although the *Hulk* show garnered respectable ratings, plans for other properties began drying up. After *Man from Atlantis* bombed, a *Sub-Mariner* series was deemed too similar and scrapped. A *Human Torch* show was abandoned because CBS feared it would lead children to set themselves on fire. A *Doctor Strange* pilot aired opposite *Roots*, and bombed. When indifferent producers ignored Lee's notes on the *Spider-Man* show, he publicly complained about the writing.

Lee and Galton, worried that the days of the comics industry were numbered, wanted an escape hatch. They convinced Cadence to investigate the purchase of a small studio, only to then be told it would be too costly. Finally, after Warner Bros.' *Superman* movie became a runaway hit, Lee was sent out to California to work out a permanent partnership with DePatie-Freleng. He stayed in Los Angeles for most of 1979 and fantasized about settling there permanently. While he was there, he shopped around his *Silver Surfer* treatment—based on the book he'd done with Kirby. It was optioned by producer Lee Kramer, with Kramer's girlfriend, Olivia Newton-John, attached; a budget was set at $25 million.

Marvel began taking out a series of full-page ads in *Variety*, attempting to pimp their characters to the highest bidder . . . or any bidder, really.

One featured a head shot of Daredevil: "Daredevil is but one of over 100 exciting Marvel Characters ready right now to star in your next motion picture or television production," it read. "All Marvel Characters have their own identity—their own *personal* story—and the potential for outrageous stardom." Nothing happened.

Back in New York, Galton and Shooter discussed the launch of *Epic*, a science-fiction comic magazine in the vein of the popular European publication *Heavy Metal*. It would continue the trend of high-quality color printing begun with *Kiss*, and even better, there would be royalties for the creators. If they couldn't turn around the downward spiral of sales of regular thirty-five-cent comics, maybe they could succeed with higher-profit upscale magazines aimed at readers with disposable incomes and pretensions of sophistication.

The idea of producing a range of higher-quality product for the fan market had been kicking around for a while. "With a new approach to distribution," Archie Goodwin had mused three years earlier, "you could think in terms of new formats for comics and start tailoring them for particular audiences instead of producing for the wider mass sales. You could possibly have comics that are right for the bookstores." Even as overall sales of new comics had slumped, the fan/collector market had grown—Marvel's nonreturnable sales had increased twentyfold in just five years—and others had figured out how to benefit. Phil Seuling, the former high school teacher who was buying directly from Marvel and DC at a 60 percent discount, had made a small fortune over the past few years; he was now supplying to more than three hundred comic stores, which were popping up at lightning speed. Other dealers had followed his lead of purchasing directly from publishers at a low rate, but no one managed to snag terms quite so favorable. So in November 1978, one such distributor filed a lawsuit against Seuling's Sea Gate Distribution, as well as Marvel, DC, and other publishers, alleging they'd formed a monopolistic distribution operation.

While lawyers moved toward settlements in that case, a Denver comic-store owner named Chuck Rozanski wrote a pointed letter to Marvel.

The company was missing a great business opportunity, Rozanski said, by refusing to offer other sellers the same deal they'd given Seuling, whose demands of advance payment from store owners was discouraging bulk orders. Rozanski pointed out that industry-wide comic sales had dropped more than 50 percent over the past twenty years, that erratic newsstand distribution was costing the industry readers, and that comic-store retailers should be the publishers' closest allies. He sent copies of the letters to three hundred of his peers.

Rozanski's timing was perfect. He was invited to New York to meet with Galton, Shooter, and circulation director Ed Shukin, who considered his suggestions about setting up a credit line for direct purchasing, cooperative advertising, and better information about upcoming product. Shukin placed an ad for a direct-sales manager who would attend all the major conventions, and who possessed the "ability to structure, instruct, and assist in the opening and operation of new shops." That summer, Shukin, Shooter, and COO Barry Kaplan flew out to the San Diego Comic-Con, where they met with about fifty retailers. Within months, Marvel announced that a number of "classy" projects with slick paper and cardboard covers were in the works; in time, they'd be called "graphic novels."

Shooter's impact, which not only had expanded the editorial staff but siphoned power from the Bullpen, was undeniable. "With the other editors-in-chief," he said, "it often seemed like they were sort of an appendix, a necessary evil. The company was really being run by John Verpoorten . . . technically, Verpoorten reported to the Editor-in-Chief, but he was, in fact, the man who was getting the stuff out."

Those days were over. Shooter fired the production manager. He stripped Marie Severin of her art director title, and shuffled her over to Sol Brodsky's Special Projects division.

Shortly afterward, Dave Cockrum, on staff as a cover designer, sent an excoriating letter to Stan Lee. When the Avengers' faithful butler, Jarvis, resigned from his post in an issue of *Iron Man*, editor Jim Salicrup took Cockrum's letter, changed the names, and inserted it into the comic:

To: Anthony Stark

This is to notify you that I am tendering my resignation from my position. This resignation is to take effect immediately.

I am leaving because this is no longer the team-spirited "one big happy family" I once loved working for. Over the past year or so I have watched The Avengers' morale disintegrate to the point that, rather than being a team or a family, it is now a large collection of unhappy individuals simmering in their own personal stew of repressed anger, resentment and frustration. I have seen a lot of my friends silently enduring unfair, malicious or vindictive treatment.

My personal grievances are relatively slight by comparison to some, but I don't intend to silently endure. I've watched the Avengers be disbanded, uprooted and shuffled around. I've become firmly convinced that this was done with the idea of "showing the hired help who's Boss."

I don't intend to wait around to see what's next.

Sincerely,
Jarvis

cc: The Avengers

No one would mistake Marvel for one big happy family now. Shooter replaced Rick Marschall, the editor of Marvel's magazine line, with Lynne Graeme, who'd never worked in comics, and directed her to oversee the text features in *Tomb of Dracula*, on which Marv Wolfman had previously enjoyed autonomy. "I don't want to continue working with chimpanzees," Wolfman declared, and stormed off to DC, where his best friend, Len Wein, had recently been hired as an editor. A dispute between Shooter and Gene Colan over rejected *Howard the Duck* pages nearly ended in Colan's departure after fourteen years at Marvel, until Lee stepped in and smoothed things over. One Marvel staffer suffered a recurring dream in which he pushed Shooter from an airplane hatch.

Meanwhile, throughout the line, the creative assignments began to resemble a laconic game of Whac-A-Mole, with each substitution having little effect on the acceptably bland quality that had defined many of the series throughout the 1970s. Bill Mantlo's *Fantastic Four* and David

Michelinie's *Amazing Spider-Man* differed little from Wolfman's work-manlike renditions; Mantlo's *Incredible Hulk* was as aimless as Roger Stern's had been; every issue of *Captain America* allowed different writers and artists to showcase nothing much at all. There was nothing new, of course, about a legion of journeymen filling page after page with standard-formula fight scenes and talky expositions, and, in fact, the bottom level had been brought up slightly. The difference was that, through all the strife with personnel, the high points had been noticeably attenuated.

By October 1979, morale at Marvel was low enough to attract the attention of *The New York Times*, which quoted anonymous staffers grousing about middling-quality comics and a focus on licensing toys and Slurpee cups and bath towels. Even Roy Thomas, the last remaining writer-editor, sounded off. "There is a feeling among most of the people I know," he said, "that Marvel has become more callous and inhuman." Stan Lee, who was spending most of his time in Los Angeles, had to call a meeting to reassure the staff that Marvel's focus was still on publishing comic books. "I have the sense that he wants to be like Walt Disney," said one writer of Lee. "Comics are sort of beneath him."

Shooter called the story "garbage" and denied that merchandising deals were overshadowing the comics. The direct-sales market, in fact, was already looking like a bright future; in 1979 the roughly 750 comic stores may have accounted for only 6 percent of Marvel's gross sales, but those $3.5 million in sales had grown from $300,000 in 1974, and from $1.5 million in 1976. Even as newsstand sales continued dropping—and only 20–40 percent of issues shipped to distributors ended up in the hands of customers—nonreturnable sales to comic stores meant a far greater profit margin.

Marvel hired a full-time publicist for the first time, brought its licensing operations in-house, under Galton, and poured more energy into merchandising deals. All they needed to do now was to get people to buy their product. "The old Marvel needed comic books to sell so they would turn a profit," wrote industry columnist Joe Brancatelli. "The envisioned new Marvel needs comic books to sell to ensure the profit potential of the characters portrayed within. Which means that the new Marvel and the old Marvel share one massive problem: how do you sell comic books?"

The staff continued to reshape. When Shooter hired Denny O'Neil back from DC to replace Wolfman, O'Neil noted how much things had changed. "Fourteen years ago," he told an interviewer, "it was a three-person office. Stan Lee, Flo Steinberg, and Roy Thomas were it. You had a lot of day-to-day, minute-to-minute contact with what was going on. It was a small enough operation. Now there's four or five editors, a magazine department, Epic, merchandising . . ." Roger Stern left his post to write freelance, and began a memorable run on *Captain America* with John Byrne; Jim Salicrup was promoted to replace him.* A few months later, Shooter hired Louise "Weezie" Jones, a beloved editor at Warren Magazines. The editor-to-writer ratio was growing.

Corporate synergy drove the publishing decisions. In comic stores, Marvel's most popular title was the first issue of *Rom*, based on a Parker Brothers toy; among the many titles that outsold *Captain America* were *The Micronauts*, based on a line of Japanese toys; *Shogun Warriors*, based on Mattel toys; and adaptations of *Star Wars* and *Battlestar Galactica*.

When Stan Lee became worried that Universal was going to try to create a female Hulk character for its television show, which it would then own the rights to, he hurriedly wrote a preemptive solution. In the first issue of *Savage She-Hulk*, Bruce Banner visited his heretofore-unmentioned criminal-defense-attorney cousin, Jennifer Walters, in Los Angeles. When Walters was shot by gangsters, Banner gave her a life-saving transfusion of his Gamma-ray-tainted blood, and she became big and green when angered. Presto: copyright secured. "It was done under duress," said David Anthony Kraft, who took over the writing of the series. "It was like, 'We need to create a character called the She-Hulk,

---

* *The X-Men* was one of the titles on which Salicrup succeeded Stern, which meant that Chris Claremont began to occasionally get his way, and Shooter had to field complaints from Byrne. Salicrup: "Even though Chris was the guy who'd come into the office more, Roger, I guess, was very close friends with John Byrne. It got to be kind of awkward in editing situations. If the two were quibbling over something, probably John had an unfair advantage in that one of his best friends was the editor. When I took over, I tried to be fair to both of them."

and we need to get it out in the next thirty seconds.' If you look at that first issue that Stan did, there's really nothing to it: Bruce Banner gives a blood transfusion to his cousin, she growls and runs around, and that's basically it. I grew up on Marvel Comics, and remembered Stan making fun of how DC had endless iterations of the characters: Super-Monkey, Super-Horse and Streaky the Super-Cat and on and on. We were all pulling our hair out and wailing and bemoaning the day that Marvel had to create a She-Hulk."

Ms. Marvel had also been conceived as a trademark strategy (and an empty gesture toward feminism), but Chris Claremont had transformed her into a carefully shaded character by dwelling on her relationships with her parents and the challenges of her career. "We're trying to appeal to a female audience, trying to make her a hip, happening, 70s woman striking out on her own," Claremont recalled. "We say to the artist, ' . . . and we need her to look sexy.' Well, his interpretation of sexy was derived from the '40s, so what we got was a continuous series of crotch shots." Claremont lobbied to get his old *X-Men* partner Dave Cockrum on the title, and they went through several dozen costume redesigns, trying to get it just right. No one had invested so much energy into a female superhero before, and, as Cockrum observed, no one else much cared. "When I brought in the one that was ultimately approved, Stan said, 'why didn't you bring me this one first? This is what I'm after . . . tits and ass.'" It wasn't what the readers were after, though. Just as Claremont found his rhythm, *Ms. Marvel* was cancelled abruptly, without resolution, after the twenty-third issue.

Meanwhile, plans were in the works to reteam with Kiss's label, Casablanca Records, for an ambitious cross-pollination experiment: Marvel would create a comic for the adventures of a new character called the Disco Queen; Casablanca would produce a record by a singer who would take on that persona. And Casablanca's new film division would produce a Disco Queen motion picture.*

---

* For a time, according to writer Steven Grant, there was talk of Donna Summer going on the road as the Disco Queen—performing one set as herself, and another in character. A lawsuit between Summer and Casablanca, however, quickly ended that possibility.

Since John Romita's son, John Jr., frequented disco clubs, he was given the task of designing the character, which was renamed Disco Dazzler. "They said, 'let's do a character that's a nightclub girl and a dancer and a disco queen,'" said Romita Jr., "and all I thought of was Grace Jones, a very statuesque, international-looking model with short hair." Blue makeup—in a mask pattern not unlike that sported by members of Kiss—was added to her face.

A committee of employees—including Stan Lee, Jim Shooter, and Cadence attorney Alice Donenfeld—all contributed ideas to the character, and the record label gave plenty of notes in return. "At one point Casablanca decided they wanted her to talk 'funky black,'" said Tom DeFalco, a former Archie Comics writer, who was assigned to script the first issue of *Dazzler*. By the time Bo Derek expressed interest in playing the character onscreen, Romita Jr.'s long-legged black roller-skater had transformed into a white girl named Alison with aspirations of pop stardom. Her super-power was to transform sonic energy into powerful blasts of light, which not only made for an impressive stage show but stopped criminals as well.

Even as the project was getting off the ground, though, disco was fading. In the summer of 1979, nearly a hundred thousand people had shown up for Comiskey Park's Disco Demolition Night in Chicago. Casablanca, plagued with financial troubles, soon pulled out of *Dazzler*; there were multiple rewrites, and five cancellations and reschedulings, as Marvel scrambled to find new corporate partners to make the *Dazzler* film. "I swore that I would not believe that it was going to be published until I saw it on the newsstands," DeFalco said. Although it would be another year before the first issue of *Dazzler* saw print, the character was quickly rolled out as a high-profile guest star in *The X-Men* and *The Amazing Spider-Man*.

Marvel creators bristled at the rampant shilling. As soon as the *Fantastic Four* cartoon went off the air, Bill Mantlo and John Byrne gleefully used the comic book to explode the NBC-sanctioned character of H.E.R.B.I.E. the Robot, much as Gerry Conway and Ross Andru had once demolished the Spider-Mobile. As a triumph of creative purity over bottom-line concerns, though, it was a pyrrhic victory. Elsewhere in that very same issue, Johnny Storm sauntered into the Studio Infinity discotheque and ran into a special guest star: the Dazzler.

Not every Marvel comic was an advertisement for something else. One of Shooter's first creative shake-ups had been to hire DC exiles Bob Layton and David Michelinie to write *Iron Man*. They added depth to Tony Stark's personal life, playing up the caddishness and self-loathing that might go along with being a heavy-drinking, disco-dancing captain of industry and international playboy. Between whiskey sours and amaretto-and-scotches, their Iron Man flew around listening to Poco on his headphones and breaking promises to pretty ladies. *Iron Man's* new penciler, John Romita Jr., was only twenty-one years old when he got the assignment, but already possessed a storytelling style as brisk as John Byrne's. Layton inked the comic himself, paying special attention to the gleam of metal and the shine of the wine bottles and chrome furniture; he scanned *GQ* and *Playboy* and electronics magazines to nail the consumerist details, updating Marvel superheroes for the age of *American Gigolo*.

Daredevil also found its niche, after years of neglect. Veteran artist Frank Robbins had been set to take over the title, but when he retired to Mexico at the last moment, assistant editor Jo Duffy advocated for Frank Miller, whose interest in film noir and ballet made for a dark, elegant crime saga. Before long, Miller was giving plot input to writer Roger McKenzie, and planning a next step as a writer.

The jewel in Marvel's crown, though, was *The Uncanny X-Men*. At conventions, fans bestowed their praise; at comic stores, they spent their dollars. The title's indisputable star attraction was the beer-guzzling, cigar-smoking Wolverine, whose gruff loner persona offered a romantic archetype onto which introverted readers could project their own solitary existences. Behind the scenes, Claremont and Byrne hashed out the kind of intricate character origins that might be employed by a dedicated method actor: Wolverine was old enough to have fought beside Captain America in World War II, they decided, and his father was Sabretooth, a villain who'd appeared once in *Iron Fist*. But instead of disclosing these details, they slowly parsed out clues to the excruciated and enraptured audience that reveled in the mystery: *Why does Wolverine speak fluent Japanese? Is "Logan" his first name or his last name?**

Not since Lee and Kirby's *Fantastic Four* had a single title contained so many interconnected characters, so many mini-mythologies. Over long months Claremont and Byrne teased their readership with revelations that Professor X had wandered through Egypt after the Korean War; that the interplanetary pirate named Corsair was actually Cyclops's long-lost father. In one issue, Byrne rolled out a whole team of super-powered Canadians at once, so colorful and varied they seemed instantly ready for their own title. The group, named Alpha Flight, was a clue to some kind of Canadian government experiment that had given Wolverine his claws . . . but for the specific circumstances, well, the readers would have to stay tuned.

The X-Men's most rewardingly labyrinthine adventure involved the return of Jean Grey. Still wandering around Scotland, believing the X-Men dead, Grey fell under the spell of Jason Wyndgarde—a mustachioed dandy in Victorian dress who was actually Mastermind, an old Lee and Kirby villain, in disguise. With the help of psychic villainess Emma Frost, Wyndgarde burrowed deep into Grey's mind; soon she was fantasizing that she was an eighteenth-century aristocrat, married to Wyndgarde, and a member of a kinky, evil secret society called the Hellfire Club.†

When Jean Grey reunited with the X-Men, Wyndgarde followed her back to the States, where he tapped into her darkest desires, and where Frost, headmistress of her own school for mutants, raced against Xavier to recruit two potential students. The first was Kitty Pryde, who could turn her body intangible and "phase" through solid objects. (It turned out that a

---

* Wolverine had a lot in common with the characters of Clint Eastwood, from the shadowy origins of *A Fistful of Dollars'* Man with No Name to the tough-justice tactics of *Dirty Harry's* Inspector Callahan. In 2011, when director James Mangold and actor Hugh Jackman made plans for a Wolverine film, the model they reached for was Eastwood's *The Outlaw Josey Wales*.

† Based on a real-life English secret society given to weeklong orgies in the bowels of a desecrated church, the Hellfire Club had earlier been fictionalized on a 1966 episode of the British television show *The Avengers*, in which Emma Peel went undercover with a spiked dog collar, corset, and whip. It was from this leather-intensive vision that the Claremont and Byrne edition took its visual cues.

plucky, Jewish, ballet-studying thirteen-year-old math whiz with Leif Garrett and Mickey Mouse posters was just the ingredient *The X-Men* needed to snag the hearts of young readers, who began writing letters asking how they could be her boyfriend.) The other mutant was the Dazzler, in her first appearance, and it was a testament to Claremont and Byrne's skills that they managed to turn a mandated cross-promotion to their advantage by tying the seediness of the overripe disco scene to the hedonism of the Hellfire Club. In a downtown Manhattan club, Cyclops watched in horror as Jean locked lips with Wyndgarde under gleaming mirror balls.

Grey went on to assume the persona of the Black Queen of the Hellfire Club's Inner Circle. Decked out in bondage gear, she helped to capture the X-Men before finally breaking Wyndgarde's spell. But all this naughty indulgence of her repressed desires had permanently corrupted her, and her personality submerged within the darkened power of the Phoenix force. She exacted a furious revenge on Wyndgarde: "You came to me when I was vulnerable," she seethed as she attacked him. "You filled the emotional void within me. You made me trust you—perhaps even love you—and all the while, you were using me!" And then she drove him insane with what was essentially a bad trip—expanding his mind beyond his capability, until he was a vegetable. It was the darkest behavior ever seen in a Marvel comic, and it wasn't over yet.

Stan Lee finally got the go-ahead to move out to California, and began shopping for homes in Los Angeles. Since Cadence was paying the relocation costs, Lee called Sheldon Feinberg at his office in West Caldwell, New Jersey, to give him the good news.

"I found Moe's house—I want to buy it!"

The price was more than Feinberg had in mind. "Moe?" Feinberg asked. "Who's Moe?"

"You know, Moe! From the Three Stooges!"

Roy Thomas was also out in L.A. submitting scripts for ABC's *Plastic Man* cartoon and *Three's Complany*, but things with Marvel weren't so sunny. He'd prepared to re-sign his writer-editor contract that spring, but he was in for a surprise. "I can't and won't" guarantee writer-editor status, Shooter wrote in a letter.

I'm willing to go along with your doing your own line-ups, cover designs, cover copy, etc., and pay you for these things. I'm willing to give you editor credit or co-editor credit on the books that you do editorial work on, and in general, see to it that you are left alone. However, I want all work to pass through the office at each stage, and all assignments made from the office. I want the vouchering and records-keeping handled entirely at the office, and I want a regular staff editor to traffic and have ultimate responsibility for every book we publish.

Thomas would later complain that he'd been strung along for months, and that this was the first he'd heard that he wouldn't be able to extend the contract as an editor. A terse phone call ended with Thomas telling Shooter, "I guess we have nothing more to say to each other," and he called DC Comics to begin talks about a defection. An April 10 letter informed Galton of his resignation. "I was willing to accept his authority as editor-in-chief," Thomas wrote of Shooter, "but could see little to be gained by knuckling under to the rest of the mostly uninspired and uninspiring lot he has hired as editors the past year or so." A distressed call from Lee (who told Thomas that Marvel was fixing the contract) followed, and then another conversational standoff with Shooter, and then a call from Galton. Lee would be in town the following week, Galton told him—please come, as a personal favor.*

On Tuesday, April 22, Thomas, Shooter, Galton, and Lee had a heated meeting, in which Thomas was again told that there would be no contract guaranteeing him control of his titles, nor could there be a provision to do any work on the side for DC, an arrangement that DC was willing to accept. Thomas could sign the contract he'd been mailed—take it or leave it. "It's been a nice 15 years," Thomas told Lee, then walked out of the office and picked up his waiting girlfriend. "I feel very dirty," he said to her. "Let's get the fuck out of here." He went directly to the DC offices, where

---

* Lee, anxiously trying to sell his New York apartment so that he could move to Los Angeles, was at the time finalizing his own contract negotiations with Marvel, after entertaining offers from other parties.

he delivered a signed contract. He'd probably create characters at DC, he told interviewers. Unlike Marvel, they offered royalties.

"These fifteen years have been a ball," Thomas wrote in a farewell note to readers, to be published in his final issue of *Conan the Barbarian*. Shooter refused to run the note. "It drove the final nail into the coffin," Thomas said, "to the illusion that Marvel was anything more than just a company like any other."

While Lee was shopping for a new home, and Thomas and Shooter were exchanging frustrated phone calls, the makereadies for *X-Men* #135 arrived at the offices. Jean Grey was now calling herself Dark Phoenix. The green of her costume was now dark crimson; the pupils of her heavily shadowed eyes were now blank. She raced out to space, hungry for energy to feed the force within. One panel in particular leaped out at Shooter: Jean Grey snuffing a distant galaxy's sun, annihilating the population of a nearby planet. (A few pages later, for good measure, she murdered the crew of a ship in Princess Lilandra's Shi'ar fleet.) Right there, amid ads for Hostess Fruit Pies, Bubble Yum, and Daisy BB Rifles, one of Stan Lee and Jack Kirby's superheroes had committed an act of genocide.*

Shooter asked *X-Men* editor Jim Salicrup to see what was in the works for upcoming issues. In the pages of #136, ready to ship, Dark Phoenix returned to earth, and fought the X-Men, until Jean Grey returned to her senses—just in time for Lilandra and the Shi'ar to summon them so that Grey would stand trial for her crimes. In #137, Xavier demanded a "duel of honor," and the X-Men battled the Shi'ar's Imperial Guard on the moon. The X-Men lost, and Jean Grey was given a kind of partial lobotomy, preventing her from accessing the Phoenix force ever again. Depowered and slightly meek, she returned to earth with the rest of the X-Men.

The X-Men #137 was a double-sized issue, one of Marvel's first big-splash publications since its decision to focus on the hard-core fans in the direct market, where advance orders had already reached a tremendous

---

* "It was the quest for the cosmic orgasm," said Claremont. "Her feeding on the star, was an act of love, of self-love, of masturbation probably."

one hundred thousand. But the story's resolution, Shooter told Salicrup, wasn't good enough. "Having a character destroy an inhabited world with billions of people, wipe out a starship and then—well, you know, having the powers removed and being let go on Earth . . . it seems to me that that's the same as capturing Hitler alive at the end of World War II, taking the German army away from him and letting him go to live on Long Island."

Jean Grey had to pay for her crimes, insisted Shooter. She had to die.*

Claremont had spent the last four years building up to a resolution of the Phoenix saga. All thirty-five pages of #137 had already been drawn. Now he and Byrne had to redo it within a matter of days. It was the first time, Shooter said, that he had handed down an edict that interfered with someone's story.

It wouldn't be the last. As soon as he signed off on X-Men #137, Shooter rolled up his sleeves and tinkered with another heavily promoted, double-sized comic: Avengers #200, in which Carol Danvers, Ms. Marvel, gave birth. In the original plot, Danvers was impregnated by the Supreme Intelligence, a blubbery, Wizard of Oz–like organic computer that led the Kree race. Shooter rejected this plot not for its general ickiness but because it was, amazingly, too similar to another comic that Marvel had recently published. A last-minute marathon plotting session between Shooter, writer David Michelinie, and artist George Perez yielded a story that revealed the baby's father to be a stranded time-traveler named Marcus, who'd plucked Danvers from our time-stream and brought her to him. "I was able to implant my essence within you," Marcus recounted creepily, "causing a condition that resembled pregnancy." She was transported back to earth and gave birth to a child that grew at an accelerated rate of several years per day—eventually becoming . . . Marcus himself. When the Avengers, presuming Marcus a threat, forced him back to limbo, he scolded them for their folly. "I could have lived among you, using my knowledge of time and history to better the human race." (As with Shooter's Korvac story, the moral here seemed to be: *trust power*.) At

---

* According to Claremont, at first "Shooter wanted Jean punished. He wanted her to suffer. His idea was she go to prison, that she be tortured horribly, that she be drawn and quartered, whipped, chained . . ."

the story's end, Ms. Marvel volunteered to follow Marcus, thus sacrificing her life on earth to become the lover of her own son.

The political implications did not go unnoticed. The fanzine *LoC* published an essay titled "The Rape of Ms. Marvel," zeroing in on a line of dialogue in which Marcus admitted using the "subtle boost" of an electronic device to seduce Danvers. Chris Claremont, who had invested two years of toil and tears and screaming with editors to transform Ms. Marvel into a respectable character, only to see her cosmically roofied and whisked away to a literal limbo, was aghast.

So was Perez. While the issue was being completed, Marv Wolfman approached the frustrated *Avengers* artist and asked if he'd be interested in joining him on a relaunch of DC's kid-sidekick group *The Teen Titans*. Perez immediately left *The Avengers*, and the two ex-Marvel creators began developing what would soon be DC's best-selling comic.

X-MEN #137 HIT THE STANDS ON JUNE 17, 1980. A LEGION OF DEDICATED READ-ers, unwilling to wait for the issues to arrive at newsstands, flocked to comic stores, returned to their homes, and tore through the pages until suddenly it was over, and they were trembling. Jean Grey's personality flickered in and out like a weak radio signal in the final moments, as the now-dark Phoenix force continued to overwhelm her. "I'm scared, Scott," she cried to Cyclops, just before stepping into the path of an ancient Kree weapon. "I'm hanging on by my fingernails. I can feel the Phoenix within me, taking over. Part of me . . . *welcomes* it." And then, suddenly, Cyclops kneeled and wept before a smoking crater.

Fandom was agog. "The flawed tragic lead whose actions bring about his or her own doom has been fused with the helpless, innocent female victim of the tragic course of events. It is as if Lady Macbeth and Desdemona were the same person," wrote Peter Sanderson in a review for *Comics Fandom*. An unprecedented number of distraught letters poured into 575 Madison. *"The X-Men* used to be my favorite mag, but after this hideous issue I seriously doubt if I will ever touch another issue again!"

Claremont acknowledged that Shooter's mandates had improved the story, even if he felt that the long-term result—Jean Grey's death—was the wrong one. "Unfortunately," he said diplomatically, "you come to a situation where different attitudes and different books reflect the different moral and philosophical attitudes of the different writers and artists." Many fans blamed him anyway, and called him a murderer. He received multiple death threats. But comic shop cash registers rang up *The X-Men* more than twice as much as any other comic that month. Shooter asked Jim Starlin if he'd like to kill Captain Marvel.

Stan Lee's mind was on other things. That Thursday, the *Hollywood Reporter* announced the formation of Marvel Productions, which was planning "twenty developmental presentations for Saturday morning cartoons, prime time specials and pilots."* The DePatie-Freleng studio, Marvel's intended partner, had dissolved, but David DePatie and Lee Gunther were named president and vice president of Marvel Productions, and took over projects abandoned by the old studio. Lee, who had finally relinquished his New York apartment for a luxury condominium in Beverly Hills, was named creative director of the new company. He also retained his publisher title at Marvel Comics, but for the first time in forty years, the comics weren't his responsibility.

Steve Gerber noted the announcement. He'd been working on Saturday morning cartoons for Ruby-Spears Productions in Los Angeles, swallowing the bitter pill of being asked to work up a presentation for a series based on Marvel characters that would team heroes like Black Panther, Thor, Machine Man, the Scarlet Witch, Ms. Marvel, and Doctor Strange with canine companions. To Gerber's relief, the series was not picked up,† and he soon made public his feelings about the man who'd once been his hero. "Stan was responsible for a massive infusion of creativity into the industry twenty years ago," he wrote in a letter to the *Comics Journal*, "but he is also the man who, under the protective umbrella of Marvel company policy, has robbed Jack Kirby, Steve Ditko, and others of the credit due *them* as creators for those same twenty years."

In August, Gerber filed a copyright infringement suit against Cadence Industries, Marvel Productions, and Selluloid Productions (which produced a *Howard the Duck* radio show starring Jim Belushi). The suit asked for more than a million dollars in damages for Marvel's pursuits

---

* Later, Lee would joke, "We figured if people are going to ruin our characters, we could probably do it as well as anybody else." According to a May 2, 1980, letter from Jim Galton to David DePatie, the development budget for the remainder of the year was only $100,000.

† When Joe Ruby brought Gerber along to a pitch meeting with producer Fred Silverman, Gerber waxed enthusiastically about how Captain America's throwback patriotism made him a "man out of time." Silverman stared at the writer. "You know, we're not doing Ibsen here."

of "derivative media work" without Gerber's permission or compensation. Central to Gerber's claim was the fact that he'd created the character before the institution of work-for-hire contracts—and, indeed, before the 1976 copyright law went into effect.

As Marvel's lawyers prepared a response, Gerber worked on *Thundarr the Barbarian*, a Saturday morning cartoon he'd created for Ruby-Spears. Among the other prospective shows that *Thundarr* beat for its time slot on ABC that fall were *Spider-Man* and *Daredevil*, making Gerber's success especially sweet. And *Thundarr the Barbarian* had another connection to the Marvel of old: it featured characters designed by Jack Kirby, now gainfully employed in the animation industry.

While Gerber celebrated, he also began promoting a paperback comic he'd written for Eclipse Comics, which offered royalties and copyright retention and had become the de facto home of Marvel expatriates like Don McGregor and Steve Englehart. Gerber conceived *Stewart the Rat* partly as a riposte to both Marvel and Disney, who had earlier forced Howard the Duck's appearance to be altered so that he looked less like Donald Duck. "For me it was almost like revenge against both companies," he said. "Fine, if you're not going to let me do this duck, I'll do a mouse and we'll see how you feel about that!"

Stewart the Rat was only one in a flood of exciting new projects that summer, and publishers courted the hard-core fans at conventions across the country, as star writers and artists flew in and out of Chicago, Los Angeles, Houston, and New York. The convention circuit stroked many an ego—"I've got fans in the sense of people whose brains fall out when they hear my name," John Byrne said—but it was still, largely, a musky and nebbishy subculture. The rock stars of the comic world did not have rock-star groupies. Being a "fan favorite" meant "you get to hang out with a lot of pimply little kids with loads of money to spend on original art," complained Bill Mantlo, whose *Micronauts* had developed a following. Chris Claremont was slightly more generous about the situation. "Rarely will you find among fans, comic or SF, a magnificent physical specimen of humanity," he observed. "Because if you're that good mentally or physically, you don't need the fantasy—the reality's good enough. It's people who need the fantasy who indulge in it, and people who need the fantasy are usually lacking something. They're usually a bit too smart, or they're not Raquel Welch or Dolly Parton—any of the clone varieties of cuties you see on TV."

There was plenty to discuss on panels and at autograph-signing booths, with or without cuties. Fans were flocking to *The New Teen Titans*. It was deemed "DC's *X-Men*" for the way that it, too, dusted off adolescent characters from the 1960s, paired them with new members from faraway lands, and mined the cultural conflicts for melodrama—but it was also an undeniably well-done comic, and the first threat in a while to Marvel's hype monopoly. For the three hundredth issue of *Thor*, Mark Gruenwald and Ralph Macchio stepped in to tie up the saga that Roy Thomas had left unfinished. The first issue of Doug Moench and Bill Sienkiewicz's *Moon Knight* was off the presses in early August, a slick throwback to both the Shadow and to Neal Adams's early 1970s *Batman* comics. There were announcements about a series of oversized paperbacks called Marvel Graphic Novels: sixty-four-page albums on high-quality paper, to be sold for five or six dollars at comic stores and, hopefully, regular bookstores like B. Dalton and Waldenbooks. Oh, and the comic that Marvel had promised to sell exclusively to direct-sales retailers was finally going to come out: the world would see *Dazzler* #1 after all.

Mobbed by fans with one question on their minds—*is Jean Grey really gone for good?*—John Byrne walked through throngs with a shirt that read SHE'S DEAD AND SHE'S GOING TO STAY DEAD. The next issue, *X-Men* #138, filled with Cyclops's tormented memories of Jean, was to hopeless-romantic Marvelites what the last five minutes of *Annie Hall* were to Woody Allen fans. It sold even more copies than its predecessor. As if that weren't enough, Byrne had, with Roger Stern, made *Captain America* popular again, taking the hero back to his Nazi-fighting roots, and imbuing his alter ego Steve Rogers with something resembling a personality.

But another Marvel artist was coming up quickly, a rival for the fans' attentions. Frank Miller's expressionistic work on *Daredevil* had made the title a reader favorite for the first time in its fifteen-year history. Miller began to sit near Byrne at convention panels and whisper menacingly, "I'm right behind you, John."

————

Frank Miller had moved to Soho in 1977, a tall country boy enchanted with New York City. When he wasn't scraping together rent money with ad agency jobs and carpentry work, he hung out in the lobbies of DC and Marvel, pestering editors, or asking advice from artists at Neal Adams's Continuity studio. "Neal in particular took a great deal of time with me, and was very generous," Miller said, "even though at the end of every meeting he was telling me I should go back to Vermont."

Instead, Miller landed a gig on *Daredevil*, working with writer Roger McKenzie, and put his interests in film noir and elaborate cityscapes to use. *Daredevil* was the closest thing Marvel had to a private eye and it gave Miller a venue with which to celebrate his love affair with New York. Unlike nearly every popular artist since Adams, Miller favored expressionism over realism; he took inspiration from the cartooning of Will Eisner and EC artists like Harvey Kurtzman and Bernie Krigstein. His pages were filled with elevated trains, water towers, glass skyscrapers, and dive bars, all shoved into thin, claustrophobic rectangles.

Miller took storytelling advice from Jim Shooter; they'd get drinks and talk about Matt Murdock's character and motivations. When Denny O'Neil took over the editorial reins of *Daredevil*, he, too, took Miller under his wing. "He was one of the best students I ever had," O'Neil said. "We would play volleyball on Sunday afternoons, and when everybody would walk to Nathan's for hot dogs afterward, he'd ask me questions about my work. He became like a second son." They shared meals two or three times a week, picking apart stories and discussing their craft. O'Neil hired Miller to draw an *Amazing Spider-Man* annual, and together they plotted a story in which Spider-Man, looking for Doctor Strange, found himself at a punk-rock show at the Bowery club C.B.G.B. It was a perfect introduction to Frank Miller's aesthetic: while the rest of Marvel's heroes were still lingering at stale discos, Miller ripped it up and started again, with a stripped-down vocabulary and a throwback to the grit, violence, and threat of the early 1950s.

Meanwhile, *Daredevil* had evolved, in O'Neil's words, "from a weak-tea *Spider-Man* to a shooting star." Miller started contributing more to the plots, and when he and McKenzie began to disagree on the comic's direction, the editor didn't hesitate to let Miller take charge. "I decided it was probably the art more than writing that was getting attention," O'Neil said. "So I chose Frank."

"Everybody liked Frank's artwork on *Daredevil*," said Jo Duffy, "but when he was working with Roger, I don't think anybody realized they were seeing a phenomenon. People didn't go, 'Oh, my gosh, he's come down from the mountain—we're saved!' until he'd been writing for two months."

Miller worked up a tale about a character he called Indigo. She was Matt Murdock's long-lost college girlfriend, the daughter of a Greek diplomat. She'd left Murdock—and the United States—when her father was assassinated; her innocence gone, she'd trained to become a high-paid mercenary. Now she was back, and Matt Murdock, as Daredevil, had to stop the woman he'd loved. Indigo was based largely on an old femme fatale from Will Eisner's *Spirit*, the international spy Sand Saref, but Miller's emerging fascination with Japanese martial arts—Indigo wielded a pair of *sai*, which resembled mini pitchforks—instantly gave the story a new, visually striking, twist. Then he decided to play up the mythic potential of the story by changing Indigo's name to Elektra. *Daredevil* #168—the debut of *Frank Miller, auteur*—was an instant hit. The whole industry finally sat up and took notice of the young Vermonter.

Calling all the shots on a comic seemed like a pretty good arrangement to John Byrne, too. At the San Diego Comic-Con in early August, when Shooter told him that Doug Moench was leaving *The Fantastic Four*, he volunteered to be the new writer; a few weeks later, upset again with the way Claremont had written a page of *The X-Men*, he decided he'd had enough of sharing control—enough fighting with Claremont about Cyclops's personality, or whether Wolverine should keep his mask, or whether Magneto's villainy allowed for nobility. He called *X-Men* editor Louise Jones one Saturday and quit on the spot. Then he called Jim Shooter and said he wanted to draw, as well as write, *The Fantastic Four*. And—why not?—he'd ink his own pencils, too.

Oddly, there had never been two writer-artists at one time at Marvel, despite the fact that most of the company's greatest works tended to be the ones where the artist had story input. Although some critics suggested that the divisions of labor at Marvel and DC had been an insidious attempt to decentralize creative control, the truth was that Marvel was thrilled to have, in Miller and Byrne, two multitasking superstars trying to one-up each other. "This rivalry was very much encouraged by Jim Shooter, because he wanted good comics," Miller said. It didn't exactly hurt the bottom line, either, especially in the fan-driven direct market, which by the fall was representing 30 percent of Marvel's sales.

Claremont and Byrne eked out one last high note in *The X-Men* before dissolving their collaboration: for the two-part "Days of Future Past," they borrowed plot devices from old episodes of *Dr. Who* and *The Outer Limits* to share a glimpse of the future Marvel Universe as a dark dystopia in which mutants are hunted down and murdered by the giant robot Sentinels. A forty-something Kitty Pryde—or Kate, as she calls herself—travels back in time from this nightmarish 2013, and explains to the present-day X-Men that the murder of Senator Robert Kelly, an advocate for a piece of legislation called the Mutant Control Act, will trigger the widespread mutant hysteria that leads down the dark path of her future world. She enlists the present-day X-Men to prevent the Brotherhood of Evil Mutants from assassinating Kelly. With these stories, the idea of a widespread "Mutant Scare" truly took hold, and the civil rights metaphors that had been hinted at since the beginning of *The X-Men* would be increasingly apparent.

But that would be left to Claremont and Dave Cockrum, who returned to *The X-Men* immediately after Byrne departed. It was all fine with Marvel, and with retailers: they'd sell more copies of *Fantastic Four*, thanks to Byrne, and they'd keep selling *The X-Men*. No one was going to give up reading it now.

The direct market was transforming the entire industry. Advance orders for the direct-only *Dazzler* #1 were at 250,000 in the fall; by the time it was published in December, more than 400,000 copies of what had once seemed a guaranteed failure were being carted from delivery trucks. And this was without the benefit of any newsstand sales.* DC quickly started

* For comparison, *The Savage She-Hulk* #1, which had been considered a smash one year earlier, sold a *total* of 250,000 copies between the newsstand *and* the direct market.

its own direct-sales department, and some distributors even began publishing their own comics now that there was an entire distribution network that could efficiently handle small press runs.

Marvel's top brass finally realized that if the company wanted to attract, or even maintain, talent, it would have to offer better terms. Shooter and Friedrich began with the contracts for the upcoming graphic novels. They'd tried to figure out how royalties were paid to authors in the "real" world, acquiring and sifting through sample contracts from Simon & Schuster and Grosset & Dunlap, soliciting consultation from Neal Adams and Jim Starlin, but when it came time to work out details with Cadence's legal team, they reached an impasse. With Stan Lee trying to package cartoons on the West Coast, visiting New York maybe once a month, and Jim Shooter overseeing a growing number of experimental comic formats, help was needed. Jim Galton hired Michael Hobson, a former William Morris agent who'd spent the 1970s at Scholastic, to serve as the vice president of publishing. Balding, bespectacled, and mustachioed, Hobson looked like the Monopoly Man come to life. He also knew what he was doing. "They really hadn't had a publisher," said Hobson. "Stan was 'publisher,' but he wasn't a business person, thank goodness. Comic-book people were absolutely unaware as to what their business was like as compared to the book business." Hobson moved into Stan Lee's now-empty office at 575—unlike Galton, ensconced on the eleventh floor, he would mingle with editorial—and began the long process of what he called "calming the beasts." It would be another year before a satisfactory contract was drafted. Starlin walked away from the royalty negotiations more than once, but Shooter kept wooing him back. Eventually, Starlin agreed to kill Captain Marvel, the character he'd made his name with, for the first Marvel Graphic Novel—on the condition that he could do another graphic novel featuring Dreadstar, a character he owned.

In the meantime, Shooter kept leaving his mark on Marvel Comics. Concerned about accessibility for new readers, he instituted a rule against stories that stretched for more than two issues. (When *Captain America* editor Jim Salicrup tried to enforce the rule, Roger Stern and John Byrne quit the book in protest.) He hired Tom DeFalco, the former Archie Comics editor who'd spearheaded *Dazzler*, to edit all three Spider-Man titles

("Spider-Man's a teenager," Shooter told him. "It's just like doing the Archie books, except with superheroes"). Shooter personally took over the editing on *Dazzler*, and even drew two issues of *Peter Parker, The Spectacular Spider-Man* to serve as an example of what he was looking for (which was, often, a grid of six or nine uniformly sized panels of eye-level, medium-size shots that sacrificed dynamism for absolute clarity). He began writing *The Avengers*, and then came to loggerheads with its artist, Gene Colan, who'd been drawing for Marvel continuously since 1965, over disagreements on Colan's artwork, which was the antithesis of the Shooter grid. Colan, naturally, went to DC, where he soon began drawing *Batman*. All of this intrigue was gleefully reported by an increasing number of comics-related magazines that fed industry gossip to fans.

Intending to return the *Fantastic Four* to the mood and style of Lee and Kirby's first twenty issues, John Byrne was confident enough in his powers that he led off with the returns of the villains Diablo—seldom seen since 1964, and bad-mouthed even by co-creator Stan Lee—and the majestic-but-ridiculous Ego, the Living Planet. Then he worked up to Dr. Doom, the Inhumans, and Galactus. He revived the inclusion of pinups and broke his issues down into chapters, just like Lee and Kirby had. Reed Richards, Sue Storm, Johnny Storm, and Ben Grimm started to feel like a kind of family again, like they hadn't in years. Byrne removed the superhero bulk from their bodies, giving their costumes a baggy appearance. But the little ways in which Byrne tweaked the mythology (relocating the Inhumans from the Andes to the moon, for instance, or planning to kill Franklin Richards, the young son of Mister Fantastic and the Invisible Girl) didn't sit well with past writers, like Len Wein and Marv Wolfman, who openly criticized Byrne.*

And the new *Fantastic Four* riled Jack Kirby as well, for a different reason. The title celebrated its twentieth anniversary with the triple-sized #236, which Shooter had directed Byrne to write as a grand adventure, as if it were *Fantastic Four: The Movie*. Stan Lee had his own idea to

---

* One positive, and permanent, change that Byrne would make would be to change the name of the Invisible Girl—who'd been a mother since 1968—to the Invisible Woman.

make the issue extra special: He'd rework some Kirby storyboards from DePatie-Freleng's *Fantastic Four* cartoon series—which had itself been adapted from FF #5—into a fourteen-page backup story.

But the repurposing was done without Kirby's permission or remuneration. "Some friend of John Byrne's called," he recounted, "and asked if I would do something for the 20th anniversary issue. I said no. So they took the roughs I did for DePatie and put six inkers on it. I didn't know anything about it until the goddamn thing was published."*

His lawyer knew, though, and told Marvel not to use Kirby's name in conjunction with the project. When the issue was published, the cover blared AN ALL-NEW FF BLOCKBUSTER BY STAN (THE MAN) AND JACK (KING) KIRBY! The illustration showed the Fantastic Four surrounded by three dozen colorful Marvel characters—and Stan Lee. Between Lee and the Silver Surfer was a white space, where Byrne's depiction of Jack Kirby had been removed.

Steve Gerber, Kirby's colleague at Ruby-Spears, approached the veteran artist and explained that he was having his own legal troubles with Marvel. After talking about the various injustices propagated by their former employer, Gerber told Kirby about a new project he was working on to raise money for the Howard the Duck lawsuit. It was called *Destroyer Duck*. Nervously, he asked Kirby if he'd be willing to draw the comic—for no pay. Kirby rubbed his chin for a minute. Then he smiled, very slightly.

"Yeah," he said, "sounds like fun."

---

* There were, in fact, *ten* inkers.

11

WHEN FRANK MILLER TOOK OVER *DAREDEVIL,* HE TOLD INTERVIEWERS THAT HIS interpretation was going to be more lighthearted than Roger McKenzie's had been. But as the femme fatale Elektra became a recurring character, that vision was bound to change. "Her presence led the whole series down a very dark path," Miller said years later. "Because I was a kid in my twenties, and making up a sexy killer woman, it was bound to get pretty grim." Miller had also been mugged—twice—since starting the series, which further added to the title's grittiness. "I never stopped loving the city. But having a knife in your face can really change your day. The experience filled me with anger, and that translated right into my comics."* *Daredevil* became heavily concerned, and filled, with violence. After Miller read about a woman who was going into movie theaters and shoving ice picks into the necks of the patrons seated in front of her, Elektra carried out an assassination in similar style. "I like to play into very daily fears," he said. "Why else do stories on subways?"

The body count was high in *Daredevil*, with a scuzzy New York City at the flashpoint of two inherently bloody genres. There was a mob story, precipitated by the return of the old *Spider-Man* villain the Kingpin— suddenly a scary presence for the first time—and there was a ninja story, prompted by Elektra's emergence. Miller had spent long hours watching martial arts films in boisterous Times Square theaters, an experience he compared to "attending a revival meeting." He synthesized his fascination with ninja lore into comics that would add further fuel to the burgeoning

---

* "After I got mugged," he told the magazine *Amazing Heroes*, "I was really eager to see criminals shot on sight."

craze of Japanese martial arts. The kung-fu movies of the early '70s had already given exposure to *nunchaku*—two sticks connected by a chain—and just before Elektra's debut, the Eric Van Lustbader novel *The Ninja* and the Chuck Norris movie *The Octagon* were surprise hits. But Miller, as much as anyone, was responsible for adding *shuriken* (throwing stars) and *sai* to the contraband wish lists of junior high school kids everywhere.

Miller quickly discovered one of the benefits of taking control of an under-the-radar title with minimal merchandising tie-ins: he could get away with a lot. By the time sales were approaching those of *The X-Men*, no one—not even *Daredevil*'s vocally pacifist editor, Denny O'Neil—was going to pull him back now. And so Daredevil wondered if he should let the murderous Bullseye die on subway tracks; he went from dive bar to dive bar, Popeye Doyleing the unlucky bottom-feeders of the underworld; he tracked down a rapist at an S&M club and beat on leather-outfitted bondage fans. He teamed up with reformed supervillain the Gladiator, only to find that the Gladiator's loss of a killer instinct was a detriment. On the other hand, there was always the sense that Daredevil—"probably the most Christian of heroes," to Miller's mind—operated out of a sense of compassion for victims, and that Matt Murdock believed in the goodness of the legal system. If the comic's stance on vigilantism was confusing, *Daredevil*'s dastardly supporting cast allowed Miller to have it both ways by making Daredevil's barrage of kicks and punches look reasonable in comparison. The psychotic Bullseye and the poor-little-rich-girl Elektra were both unrepentant assassins; the Kingpin was an elegant, bald, 450-pound mobster who wore ascots and plotted crimes from a skyscraper. Even the antihero Punisher, who'd been popping up in various comics for years, showed up to provide contrast to *Daredevil*'s relatively innocuous beatdowns.

Miller played Matt Murdock's law partner, Foggy Nelson, for klutzy comic relief, and portrayed Murdock's girlfriend, Heather Glenn, as a slightly unhinged party girl. If there was a moral center of the comic, it was Ben Urich, a coffee-guzzling, chain-smoking beat reporter for the *Daily Bugle* who'd learned that Matt Murdock was Daredevil—but who decided he'd rather have a guardian for his city than a Pulitzer for his mantel. Urich was frail, potbellied, and wore big, square glasses that gave him a Larry King quality; a scene in which he lovingly leaned over his frumpy wife and tickled her, ready for making love, may have been the most jarringly human in Marvel's history.

But it was Elektra who gripped *Daredevil*'s readers. Miller had used Lisa Lyon, a professional bodybuilder and Robert Mapplethorpe muse, as a model for Elektra; like her inspiration, Elektra blended athleticism and sex in a way that young men couldn't resist. Miller knew how popular Elektra was—and how catastrophic it would be for his audience if something happened to her.

"When I told Denny that Elektra was going to get killed," Miller said, "he was like, 'Oh, I don't know how Jim is going to feel about that. She's more popular than Daredevil now.' And I went down to Jim's office—he was working on some papers—and I said, 'I have a story, and I need to kill Elektra.' And he sort of sunk his face in his hands and said, 'Tell me the story, Frank.' And I told him what I had in mind, and he said, 'That's great. Do it.'"

When the 1981 San Diego Comic-Con kicked off in the last week of July, Miller had just put the finishing touches on an issue that devoted four pages to nearly wordless fighting between Elektra and Bullseye on Sixth Avenue. Their confrontation ended when he impaled her with her own weapon; she crawled to Matt Murdock and died in his arms.

With no idea what was in store, the blissfully unaware audience at the Comic-Con instead celebrated Elektra's triumph in the latest, all-ninja-battle issue of *Daredevil*, obsessed over the marital strife of Yellowjacket and the Wasp in *The Avengers*, and pored over Magneto's return in the new double-sized issue of *The X-Men*. The shocking revelation that the X-Men's silver-haired archenemy had been a child prisoner at Auschwitz ramped up the title's long-present themes of bigotry and persecution and pointed to the direction that *The X-Men* would take for the decades to come, in which discrimination toward mutant characters was put explicitly in the contexts of racism and homophobia. In the Marvel Universe, "Mutie" became a regularly uttered epithet, bigotry bloomed, and the X-Men became increasingly paranoid about their place in the world.

By and large, the *X-Men* stories in the year since the "Dark Phoenix

Saga" had paled in comparison to what had come before. The old hands who weren't writing *The X-Men* were all too happy to point out that its sales had surpassed its aesthetic achievement, and that it benefited from a lack of other exciting options. If *The X-Men* had been published in the mid–1970s, Steve Englehart insisted in interviews, it wouldn't have been such a phenomenon. "In the country of the blind, the one-eyed man is king," sniffed Roy Thomas. It was a dedicated kingdom, though: according to Diana Schutz, a manager at the now-closed Comics & Comix store in Berkeley, California, "People were buying case lots of *X-Men*. Two, three hundred copies. Some people were buying two lots, for investment purposes." Appearances by Man-Thing, Spider-Woman, Dazzler, and Doctor Doom reestablished the X-Men's ties with the rest of the Marvel Universe, but there was also the nagging feeling that those crossovers were just meant to jump-start sales of less popular characters. Or maybe something was just being held back. Dave Cockrum created an amphibious heroine named Silkie, and then retracted the character when he couldn't negotiate to retain partial ownership. He had a whole group of new heroes, he said—but they'd remain his now.

At the weekend's end, on the way back to Los Angeles from San Diego, Miller and Claremont were stuck in traffic for two hours. A conversation about Wolverine—a character about whom Miller had previously expressed disinterest—shifted into talk about their mutual appreciation of samurai movies and manga. By the time they'd reached their destination, they'd begun plotting a story for a four-issue *Wolverine* series.

Shortly after Claremont got back to New York, he learned that someone else wanted to use idle *X-Men* characters. Tom DeFalco, noticing that the multiple Spider-Man titles had sustained strong sales, had pitched Shooter on a sort of West Coast X-Men comic, which would include original members like Angel, Iceman, and Beast. Claremont and Louise Jones headed it off at the pass. "I wanted to handle it. I didn't want anybody else poaching," Claremont said. "[We] basically said, 'Screw that, we'll do our own X-title.'" It would return the focus to Lee and Kirby's vision of a school for young mutants. They said, only half-jokingly, that it would be called *The X-Babies*.

Now Claremont was operating a virtual X-Men franchise: in addition to the *Wolverine* and *X-Babies* projects, there were two graphic novels in the works, and a one-issue *X-Men/Teen Titans* joint venture between Marvel and DC, to be drawn by Louise Jones's husband, Walter Simonson. There was one corner of the X-universe he wouldn't be handling, though: Jim Shooter was pressuring John Byrne to launch a series starring the Canadian super-team Alpha Flight.

By the time *Spider-Man and His Amazing Friends* hit Saturday morning TV in the fall, it seemed like it was going to be leading a parade of shows and movies. *Thor* had joined *Silver Surfer* in development at Universal Pictures; *Ghost Rider* and *Man-Wolf* were optioned by Dino De Laurentiis, *Daredevil* and *Howard the Duck* by Selluloid Productions. A *Fantastic Four* film was in talks, as were *Black Widow* and *X-Men* television series. Now that *Urban Cowboy* had replaced *Saturday Night Fever* as the zeitgeist soundtrack of choice, Marvel Productions was trying to sell Hollywood on a country singer named "Denim Blue." There was a *Spider-Man* musical in the works, and a *Captain America* musical, in which a paunchy, balding, middle-aged man was transformed by the "Spirit of Liberty" into Captain America. Galton didn't mind the changes. "We poke fun at ourselves all the time," he reasoned.

Captain America's co-creator, Jack Kirby, was doing some poking himself. As he finished work on *Destroyer Duck*, the comic that would raise money for Steve Gerber's legal battle with Marvel, he gave an interview in which the full extent of his vitriol toward the industry came to light. He dismissed Marvel's and DC's comics as "ads for toys," characterized work-for-hire as "everything that comes out of you, they own," and gave his surprising account of the early 1960s Marvel Comics: "I wrote them all."

"I never wrote the credits. Let's put it that way, all right?" he said. "I would never call myself 'Jolly Jack.' I would never say the books were written by Lee. I did a mess of things. The only book I didn't work on was *Spider-Man*, which was my creation. The Hulk was my creation."

For many in the comics community, it was a fiercely worded affirmation of what they'd heard murmurs of for years—that Stan Lee had hogged the credit, and that Jack Kirby had been hung out to dry. But creating

Spider-Man? Even Kirby's staunchest supporters were perplexed. Had he been bottling up so much anger that he was exploding beyond reason?

Destroyer Duck fed off Kirby's anger, and Gerber's. It told the story of Duke, a war veteran whose drinking buddy (an unnamed but thinly disguised Howard the Duck) disappears, only to return on his doorstep years later, bloody and dying. He'd been transported "into another space-time continuum . . . where ducks can't talk . . . and pink primates call all the shots . . . I was broke, starving . . . I signed on with this company . . . Entertainment Concepts, Ltd! Division of GodCorp . . . that world's biggest corporation . . . they said they'd make me a star . . . exploit my curiosity value . . . but all they did was humiliate me." Duke travels to the faraway world, and exacts revenge on GodCorp, whose motto is "GRAB IT ALL OWN IT ALL DRAIN IT ALL." It wasn't hard to see that God-Corp was a stand-in.

When Stan Lee was asked about the controversy over creator ownership, he pointed to his own contributions. "I've created a number of characters for Marvel that have been successful, but when I created them, I knew they were the property of the company. That was the understanding; that had always been the procedure. For me to suddenly start saying, 'Wait a minute, I wrote that, I'm going to sue,' to my way of thinking, that would be dishonest. I had the right to leave at any time and if I felt I was so good I could create characters and make a fortune, I had every right to do it. And I think any artist or writer who doesn't want to work for us doesn't have to sign the contract, he's perfectly welcome to, with no hard feelings." He offered his own disclaimer. "I'm probably the quintessential, ultimate company man," he said. "I think it is very hard for me to separate my own feelings from those of the company."

John Byrne went a step further, in an infamous editorial published in the same magazine as Jack Kirby's interview: "I have, of late, taken on the mantle of a 'company man,' and in many ways I am deserving of the title. Even proud. I am a cog in the machine which is Marvel Comics, and I rejoice in that." He even criticized Jerry Siegel and Joe Shuster for suing DC over *Superman.* "I'm all in favor of campaigning for changing the rules, but let's live within the rules while they're around." Gerber and Kirby promptly paid tribute in the second issue of *Destroyer Duck:*

the character of Booster Cogburn—as in "Cog-Byrne"—had a removable spine and declared, "I'm a company man . . . I'm not paid to have opinions."

While Marvel was making deals with Hollywood, though, DC had beaten them to the punch by introducing a royalty plan for comic creators: after 100,000 copies of a title were sold, DC's policy stated, 4 percent of profits would be split between artist and writer. Marvel scrambled to match the terms, rolling out a similar announcement in the final days of 1981. The company was careful to avoid the word *royalty*; as internal communication between its lawyers stated, "most definitions of that word contain language which indicated that it is a payment to an 'owner' or 'author' for use of *his* work. Indeed, the derivation of the word is that of royal status or the privilege of a monarch or sovereign." Thus, in future company correspondence, such monies were always referred to as "incentives."

Still, with *The X-Men* selling over 300,000 copies a month, several other titles selling over 200,000, and almost everything else selling over the 100,000 mark, champagne spilled at typewriters and drawing boards. Marvel had to renege on a few raises it had just given to the most successful writers and artists, but the creators didn't mind. They'd hit paydirt.

Meanwhile, Elektra's demise, in *Daredevil* #181, provoked fulminations and death threats from fans—Miller, scared for his life, marched into an FBI office with a selection of mail from angry readers—and, just as Phoenix's death had, record-breaking sales. The issue was on newsstands just as the new incentives policy kicked in. Two weeks later, Marvel's first graphic novel—Starlin's *The Death of Captain Marvel*—was finally published; ten times more expensive than a regular monthly comic, it quickly sold out of three printings, and Jim Starlin made a tidy sum and bought himself a new Camaro Z28. (Marvel would hold on to its trademark, though—there were already plans to bring back a new character named Captain Marvel.) Shortly after that, Chris Claremont was asked about the *Wolverine* series. "It's me and Frank Miller and [inker] Josef Rubinstein," he said, "and we're going to make lots of money."

But Miller held out for more. He met with Jenette Kahn, DC's publisher, and talked about a futuristic-samurai series he wanted to do, called

Ronin. After lengthy negotiations, DC offered him a vastly increased royalty, his name above the title, and ownership of his characters. By the time Shooter found out about the deal, it was a fait accompli. The defection was nothing personal, Miller said, just smart business. "I learned from my mentor Neal Adams to play one publisher against another to get a better deal. These are things I could have gotten out of Marvel, but I wanted it to be a fresh start. And also by taking my name to another publisher, that was a critical statement—saying that I could bring my audience with me. And to me, that was very important." He'd already begun leaving more and more of the artwork on *Daredevil* for inker Klaus Janson to finish; now he receded further from the process, and just provided rough layouts. He'd keep writing *Daredevil*, for now, and he'd draw *Wolverine*. Then he would be gone.

For those who delighted in *Daredevil's* filthy cityscapes and hard-boiled rhythms, a sort of ersatz Miller style began to develop in the least likely of places: *Peter Parker, the Spectacular Spider-Man.* Bill Mantlo and Ed Hannigan's introduction of the morally ambiguous duo Cloak and Dagger was serendipitously timed: two weeks before Elektra's death, an issue of *Peter Parker* told the story of a pair of teenage runaways—a white female and a black male—who'd been the sole survivors of synthetic-drug experiments by the mob. Now they sought revenge on the drug trade. Dagger threw knives of light that caused shock to the victims' systems; Cloak enshrouded victims in a sort of black-hole darkness that left them disoriented and shivering. Often, the results of these attacks were fatal.

Mantlo and Hannigan, excited by Miller's work, began injecting the secondary Spider-Man title with dark alleys, silhouettes, and organized-crime plotlines. Hannigan's cover art borrowed, even more explicitly than Miller had, from the inventive designs of Will Eisner's *Spirit.* The title logo was incorporated into the action—part of a neon Times Square logo, or part of a word balloon, or slashed by razors, or swirling into underwater illegibility. They were the kind of innovations that grabbed attention from the other comics on the rack (the kind of experiments, in fact, that had been rejected when Neal Adams tried them fifteen years earlier).

"I think they're the best two characters so far this decade," Mantlo boldly claimed of Cloak and Dagger. If you discounted Miller's Elektra, he might have been right; there wasn't a lot of competition. Marvel was not exactly the House of New Ideas. Roy Thomas had been saying it all along: why give creations away?

But Frank Miller's deal with DC had made waves. At Marvel's monthly press conference in May, Jim Shooter announced that a newly formed division of the company, called Epic Comics, would allow for artists and writers to retain not just a percentage of the sales, but also ownership of their creations. Jim Starlin, who hadn't drawn a regular series since *Warlock*, was the first to sign up; Steve Englehart, who hadn't worked for Marvel since he quit *The Avengers* six years earlier, soon followed.

(12)

AT THE END OF APRIL 1982, MARVEL COMICS MOVED THIRTY BLOCKS DOWN-town to new, bigger offices at 387 Park Avenue South. For the first time since the mid–1950s, it was no longer part of the Madison Avenue world. "Stan had this thing—'God damn it, we're publishers! We'll stay on Madison Avenue as long as I live and breathe,'" said longtime secretary Mary McPherran. "Then he got lured to California, and he didn't care where we were."

Marvel's expansion had brought in an entire wave of younger staffers, few of whom had much concern for prestigious locales. Many of them fell under the spell of Mark Gruenwald, recently promoted from assistant editor to editor and seemingly determined to will the mythical old Marvel Bullpen—a fantasy realm of practical jokes, crazy nicknames, manic creativity, and cheerful labor—into reality. The single, skinny-tied twenty-somethings who swarmed around Gruenwald had more varied backgrounds than the fans-turned-pros that preceded them: Al Milgrom's assistant Annie Nocenti had tended bar and worked on children's books; Gruenwald's assistant Mike Carlin had studied cartooning but also toiled in a rug factory. Eliot Brown, a typesetter and stat machine operator whom Gruenwald had befriended, had worked on an elephant farm. Energetic and mischievous, they quickly broke in Marvel's new space; posters and sketches covered the windows and the walls of every office. Even the sales department radiated youthful vigor: Carol Kalish, a twenty-seven-year-old former comic-store manager, replaced Mike Friedrich as the liaison between three thousand stores and the number-one comic-book company in the world.

Marvel employees' social lives were entwined with their work lives like they hadn't been in years, maybe more than they ever had, although the move downtown further insulated Marvel from DC—the intercompany softball games and volleyball matches faded away. Instead the staff shared dinners and movies, or drinks at the Abbey Tavern on Third Avenue. When summer came around—and with it, half-day Fridays—they'd pile into cars and head to Ralph Macchio's parents' pool in the New Jersey suburbs. After Tom DeFalco suggested an all-comedy issue of *What If?*, the whole staff jumped into the act, and used the centerfold spread to celebrate their glorious workplace, just like Stan Lee had done, back when they were first learning to read.

But the cartoonish self-portraits and profiles adorning that centerfold weren't just of the younger employees: production manager Danny Crespi and letters-column paste-up specialist Morrie Kuramoto were there, too, smiling at readers. Crespi and Kuramoto were near constants in the offices, quietly plugging away after all these decades, and bantering like lovable characters on a sitcom. Kuramoto played the quiet codger, dropping cigarette ash on everything, losing pages of artwork in the giant stacks that surrounded his desk at all times. The desk was covered with scraps of paper and thick masses of dried-up rubber cement. He was a bundle of contradictions, eating homemade health-food concoctions even as he chain-smoked. "He would squeeze your fingernails, and see when the blood came back," remembered Ann Nocenti, "and then he would feel the top of your head and tell you to eat a carrot." Few who worked with Kuramoto knew the tragedies of his past: following the bombing of Pearl Harbor, he'd been kicked out of the U.S. Army because of his Japanese ancestry; when his family was sent to an internment camp, he'd moved to New York City and enrolled in the Art Students League. Now he celebrated Pearl Harbor Day in perverse fashion, wearing a leather pilot's cap and aiming paper airplanes at passersby from his drawing board. He would render beautiful watercolors on his lunch break, then crumple them and throw them in the trash. "I'll be in my office," he'd say, as he took the *Daily Racing Form* to the men's room; he'd use his winnings to take his coworkers on tours of sushi restaurants.

Crespi, a former letterer, was short, round, and jolly—the women at Marvel would rub his belly, for good luck, or snap his red suspenders, for kicks—and wore reading glasses that he often forgot were on top of his head. He was a joker, and a gravelly-voiced storyteller who maintained a forest of houseplants in his workspace. He'd been back at Marvel since 1972, when he called Morrie to ask if there was any work for him. "I didn't give a damn about the money," he said. "I just wanted to belong here."

"It was like *Butch Cassidy and the Sundance Kid*," recalled one member of the Bullpen. "They would always be yanking each other's chain and cursing each other out. Morrie would go into Danny's office to eat lunch and make a huge mess on his desk, and Danny would come back from lunch and curse him out. They had no problem exchanging ethnic slurs. It just brought them closer." Kuramoto and Crespi even argued, like an old married couple, about how often to water the plants they kept on the windowsill.

George Roussos, sixty-six, oversaw the coloring of covers, and John "Pop" Tartaglione, sixty-one, handled art corrections. Shuttling in and out were old-time freelancers who'd been Marvel presences for decades: among them were Frank Giacoia, Mike Esposito, Joe Rosen, Joe Sinnott, legendary for his inking work on Kirby's *Fantastic Four*, and Vince Colletta, legendary (and controversial) for his inking work on whoever had missed a deadline. Colletta's rush jobs were notorious among artists, but a godsend to frazzled editors, and so he never lacked for work. To pick up pages for inking, Colletta would arrive with white hair groomed, impeccably dressed in overcoat, with young women on each arm. Or sometimes he'd have Crespi meet him on the street corner, where he'd pull up in the back of a limo—again, with beauties by his side—and roll down the window.

Jack Abel, who'd drawn for Atlas Comics in the 1950s and inked for Marvel in the 1960s and '70s, had suffered a stroke in 1980 that paralyzed his right hand; Jim Shooter gave him a job as an assistant editor until he'd recovered well enough to ink.

Nobody waited in line to meet those guys at comic conventions, or interviewed them in fanzines. But even as Marvel Comics started to gleam a little more brightly, as new-wave T-shirts and Walkmans and Ray-Bans began to fill the hallways, they were the link to the past.

———

As an outrageously chummy sense of community returned to the letters pages and editorial notes, there was also a return to the idea that reading Marvel Comics was more than a casual undertaking, an assumption that an *X-Men* fan was also conversant in *Iron Man* lore. With Marvel's comic sales rising 20 percent in just the last year, and a direct market that catered to hard-core collectors—gambles could be taken on smaller print runs and higher-priced items—why not package and sell inside jokes and minutiae to dedicated readers? There were reprints, more expensive and on higher-quality paper, of fan favorites that hadn't sold well the first time: *Giant-Size X-Men #1*; Jim Starlin's *Warlock*; Englehart and Brunner's *Doctor Strange*. *Marvel Fanfare* printed unused inventory; *The Official Marvel No-Prize Book* highlighted the biggest goof-ups in the company's history. Although *Crazy*, Marvel's decade-old *Mad* rip-off, was discontinued, its trash-talking mascot got crossover exposure with *Obnoxio the Clown vs. the X-Men*. The cosmology of the Marvel Universe itself became a selling point. As they had in the mid–1960s, covers became crowded with heroes, as many as would fit, flying and punching and dancing and mugging, their primary-colored costumes liable to hypnotize young children and aging obsessives. Twenty-one heroes crowded onto the cover of *What If #34*, and three dozen onto the cover of *Marvel Super Hero Contest of Champions*, Marvel's first miniseries. In the back pages of *Contest of Champions* was "a complete list of every single super hero alive today," along with powers, secret identities, and first published appearance. For the *Fantastic Four Roast* one-shot, cartoonist Fred Hembeck drew doodly versions of more than sixty popular characters exchanging Catskills-style zingers. And Carol Kalish and her assistant, Peter David, began putting together *Marvel Age*, a coming-attractions-and-behind-the-scenes comic that picked up where *FOOM* had left off. It was, in many ways, a return to 1965.

Some, frustrated with Marvel's lack of exciting new characters, were unimpressed. "They've taken wholly upon themselves the traditional function of fanzines: the cataloguing and discussion of their own work," read a letter in the often prickly *Comics Journal*. "How soon 'til we see a comic entitled *Marvel Letters Pages* devoted exclusively to fan raves? All they'd need then would be *Mighty Marvel Amateur Fan Art* and the *'Nuff*

Said newsletter." Perhaps someone at Marvel saw this, and panicked: plans for a publication entitled *Strange Fan Letters*, already in the works, were quickly scrapped.

But cynicism was not at the heart of these endeavors, at least not at the ground level. *The Official Handbook of the Marvel Universe* was not only the culmination of all this geekery; it was the point at which the staff's dedication became astonishingly evident. An initial twelve issues of encyclopedic entries for hundreds of characters—something like player's stats on the backs of baseball cards—were followed by two issues of "dead and inactive" characters, and another of "weapons, hardware, and paraphernalia." *OHOTMU* was an enormous undertaking, requiring more labor than anything Marvel had attempted before, and although the entire staff felt the burden, the project was spearheaded by a core suicide squad: Mark Gruenwald, who'd become the caretaker of narrative continuity within the Marvel Universe; his assistant, Mike Carlin; Eliot Brown, who was skilled at drafting architectural plans for, say, the Avengers Mansion; and Jack Morelli, a member of the production team. They dragged pillows and sleeping bags out at night, stole couch cushions from the reception area, endured wintertime all-nighters by the heat of the Xerox machine, and secretly commandeered Marvel president Jim Galton's private office shower. The intensity of the project ramped up as it went; eventually they'd be cramming more than 50,000 words of text into each issue.

Such intense dedication couldn't have happened without Gruenwald. At any other company, he might have been the HR department's worst nightmare; at Marvel he was revered, a source of inspiration. After hitting a tough deadline, he might order that the next day be spent writing songs about coworkers, or holding paddleball contests (each paddle personalized with a caricature of its owner), or drawing, or redecorating offices. Smitten by a local newscaster, Gruenwald offered a dollar for every Michele Marsh subway poster that employees could procure; he ended up with about eighty of them, and covered every square inch of his office, lining even the insides of drawers. When he'd had enough of that, he removed the posters, and declared that all walls and desks in his office be cleared completely—even the phones went into the drawers. The only excess furniture was a small school desk at which his young daughter could sit when she visited him after school.

After work on the *Handbook* was finished, Gruenwald started a public-access cable comedy show, *Cheap Laffs*, with Carlin and Brown. "We dressed up in costumes," said Ann Nocenti, who appeared in several episodes. "Mark was the director: 'Dress like a vampire. Now look vampy.' It was like Ed Wood on acid."

There were pranks, too. Many of them were directed at Jack Abel, who briefly shared an office with Gruenwald and Carlin, and whose unflappability (he might respond with a calm "Hey") only managed to send the pranksters into further conniptions. When Gruenwald placed leftover ham from a sandwich in Abel's cabinet, it was weeks before Abel noticed. Opening the drawer to find a brush, his measured response was, "Hey. Someone left a ham sandwich in my desk . . . without the sandwich." Another time, Abel—in the habit of taking catnaps—awakened in total darkness, encased in a fortress that Gruenwald and Carlin had constructed from couches, desks, and other nearby furniture. From inside this ad hoc room came a measured, muffled voice. "Hey. Who turned out the lights?"

"Even while it was happening," Carlin said, years later, "I knew this was going to be 'the good old days.' It was going to be what everyone was talking about for the rest of their lives."

Stan Lee, far away in California, was as dedicated as ever to getting Marvel Comics onto the big screen, and Jim Galton, one floor above the editorial offices, was still pursuing all possible licensing partnerships. But the old, cautious refrain of only giving the illusion of change seemed to fade away. "There are writers and artists who think that Shooter will stop them if they try to do something different," John Byrne opined. "The problem is that we've had Marv and Roy and Len who were bozos, and who you did have to sneak good stories by in order to get something done and people think Shooter's going to do the same."*

---

* Byrne retracted the statement after threat of legal action from Roy Thomas.

It was quite clear, actually, that Jim Shooter was interested in shaking things up. Nova—a character that Marv Wolfman had created for a fanzine, a decade before donating him to the Marvel Universe—lost his powers in the pages of *ROM*. J. M. DeMatteis—a former *Rolling Stone* writer and DC freelancer who'd gotten his break at Marvel when Roy Thomas left *Conan*—engineered the death of Nighthawk in *The Defenders*. In an *Amazing Spider-Man* annual, Roger Stern introduced the new Captain Marvel: a black woman named Monica Rambeau, a lieutenant in New Orleans's Harbor Police Department. Of course, the new Captain Marvel's CV—feminist security guard turned cosmic warrior—wasn't too different from that of the former Ms. Marvel, Carol Danvers, and a week later, in *X-Men* #164, Claremont and Cockrum gave Danvers new powers and a new superhero name. Out in deep space with the X-Men, and offered membership with the team, Danvers hesitantly declined, preferring to explore the universe. "Returning with you means rejecting my heart's desire—but fulfilling that desire means leaving everyone, everything I love. Earth was Carol Danvers' home . . . but I fear it has no place for—Binary."* Presumably, Claremont was happy to send her away from the meddling hands of other writers and editors. (Giving her an overblown farewell monologue was just a Claremontian bonus.)

Denny O'Neil, now writing *Iron Man*, began plans to replace the man within the armor: Tony Stark, fallen off the wagon and sleeping in the gutter, would step aside as his black pal James "Rhodey" Rhodes became the new Iron Man.

Mark Gruenwald offered *Spider-Woman* to Ann Nocenti, who'd written only one short story for Marvel. "No female character has been written regularly by a female writer before," he told her. "You'll bring a whole new perspective to comics." The only catch was, by the way, that Nocenti would have to kill the character. "I think he had probably asked everybody else to do it—and everyone said no, because it's a creepy thing to kill a hero. But I didn't know better. I thought, 'Okay, it's just like a cardboard cutout; it's a girl in a spider suit on a Slurpee cup. So I did four

---

*This speech could well have been written for Dave Cockrum, who finally left behind, for good, his most successful creations. He began work on *The Futurians* graphic novel, which Marvel would publish but the ownership of which he would retain.

issues, and killed her, and then got torrents of email from sad, horrified kids. I didn't quite understand the intense bonds that kids have for these characters. They're *alive*, you know? That was a real introduction to the whole Marvel universe."

Allegedly, the idea behind Shooter's proposed "Big Bang" was this: the Marvel Universe had become much too complicated, the histories of the characters too long and involved for the creation of accessible new stories. Years later, Tom DeFalco remembered the pitch. "'There'll be something in the sky that will indicate things are changing. And then there will be the Big Bang, and then we're gonna come out with new versions of pre-existing characters.'

"We said, 'Why would you do this?'

"Shooter said, 'A lot of the stuff we're producing today really isn't of the high quality we want it to be.'

"We said, 'Yeah, but we're gonna be using the same people! It's not like we can do a big bang for our creative staff.' At that point we had twenty years of continuity, so we'd start fresh—but in four or five years it would be just as complicated anyway. You'd have to be constantly rebooting everything. Why bother?"

Doug Moench heard it this way: "Donald Blake would be killed, but someone else would find the walking stick and become the new Thor. So instead of Thor being a doctor, now Thor would be a plumber or whatever. Steve Rogers would die, but an investment banker would become the new Captain America. I said, 'This is crazy! We can't do this!' And Shooter insisted that it was going to be done. Peter Parker would be killed, and someone else would get bitten by another spider, and so on. I kept ignoring it; Shooter kept pushing it. It got to the point where the editors were calling me, assistant editors, including Ralph Macchio and Mark Gruenwald. But all of them were afraid of Shooter. They'd seen me in the Marvel offices having epic battles, in which I would just bellow at the guy. I was, I guess, the only one who fought back against him. Everybody else felt cowed and didn't want to risk getting fired or whatever. I just didn't give a shit and I hated the guy so much."

———

In August 1982, Moench was writing *Thor*, *Moon Knight*, and *Shang-Chi, Master of Kung Fu*. *Thor* was mediocre—he'd later grumble that Gruenwald hadn't allowed him to handle it the way he wanted to—but *Moon Knight* and *Master of Kung Fu* were exceptional. After years with a reputation as a Neal Adams clone, *Moon Knight* artist Bill Sienkiewicz had hit his stride, seemingly every issue displaying a wider range of influences and styles: Ralph Steadman was in there, and Bob Peak, and Gustav Klimt. Editor Denny O'Neil kept trying to bring *Moon Knight* closer to *Batman* territory, but Moench and Sienkiewicz kept delivering delicious psychodrama. *Master of Kung Fu* was also reaching new heights. Over the past decade writing the title, Moench had fruitful collaborations with artists Paul Gulacy and Mike Zeck, each of them helping him nudge the title from chop-socky hokum to sleek espionage adventure, each providing exciting page designs in the tradition of Steranko and Starlin. But the third time was the charm. Moench found his dream partner in Gene Day.

Renowned for his unconventional page layouts and for his punishing work habits ("He works eight hours," reported inker Joe Rubinstein, "never leaves the table, has his brother there to bring him coffee, eats, gets back to work for eight hours"), Day was by all accounts a wholly dedicated Marvel employee who held no grudges about work-for-hire terms. He and Moench threw themselves fully into their work on *Master of Kung Fu*, resulting in the title's artistic ascendancy.

Unfortunately, *Master of Kung Fu* wasn't selling terrifically. It was still making a profit—just about everything Marvel published was, now—but it was on the lower rungs, and Shooter felt that it had fallen into a rut. He was unhappy with Day's atypical approach to visual storytelling and regularly ordered pages redrawn. Soon, even the committed Day couldn't hack it anymore. In what he called "one of the most traumatic experiences in my life," he quit the title. Shooter phoned Moench and said that sales had been piddling for a long time, and that he wanted "drastic, sweeping changes" to the title.

The Comics Buyer's Guide ran an interview with Moench, explaining why he'd quit Marvel Comics after eight years of continuous service. Jim Shooter, he said, had told him to kill the cast of *Thor*—Thor's alter ego Don Blake, and all the inhabitants of Asgard. That didn't sound like a good idea, Moench said in the interview, but that wasn't the deal-breaker. Shooter had also offered him a number of ways to handle *Master of Kung Fu*. Fu Manchu, the villain, would be removed. So would the hero. "I could kill off Shang-Chi, or replace him with a ninja, or turn him into a villain like Fu Manchu, and perhaps have a ninja hero try to bring him to justice. . . . Jim also suggested that I kill off the entire supporting cast. . . . I have spent years with these characters. I love them. I told Jim I couldn't kill them. He told me I could go ahead and try to give the book a new direction without killing them, but he said, 'I doubt it will work.'" By the end of the phone call, Moench's eight years of service to Marvel Comics had come to an end. When Bill Sienkiewicz got the news, he decided it was time for him to leave *Moon Knight*, too.

Marvel addressed the controversy surrounding the "Big Bang" proposal at a September press conference. According to Moench, Shooter got up in front of a group of reporters and dismissed his claim as "an allegation by a disgruntled former employee." But the twist of the knife, Moench said, was that "sitting right next to him were Ralph Macchio and Mark Gruenwald and all the other editors—and not one of them said a peep. They'd been calling me, begging me: 'You've got to stop him from doing this!' They let Jim Shooter lie, and call me a liar in the process."

Although articles reported that freelancers as well as editorial staff members had confirmed, off the record, the existence of a "Bang List" that included low-selling titles like *Master of Kung Fu*, *Thor*, and the *Defenders*, the official Marvel response remained adamant and definite. "I never told anyone to kill anyone," said Shooter. "Not Tony Stark, not Don Blake, not anyone else." Mark Gruenwald, reached for comment by *Comics Feature*, promised that Iron Man, Thor, and Captain America were safe. "None of them or their supporting characters are going to die," he said. "It's not true. I can firmly say that Shooter never said to kill the characters. He said to be creative, do things that people won't expect. Doug Moench and Jim Shooter always had creative differences."

Everyone passed the buck. "Jim had an idea that he wanted to make some changes in some of the books with *Kung-Fu* and *Spider-Woman* being the first two," *Comics Scene* quoted Ralph Macchio as saying. "Jim wanted to make changes and as the editor it was my job to carry them through." Shooter, meanwhile, emphasized that Macchio's displeasure with the comics' direction had opened the discussion. He also slightly revised his claim about never telling Moench to kill characters. "When I was talking about 'wholesale slaughter,'" he said, "I was having trouble making myself clear to Doug. I said, 'I'm trying to tell you there are no limits. . . . Get rid of them, keep them all . . . I don't care, just do something different.'"

While the back-and-forth played out in the press, Moench began working, like so many before him, for DC Comics. "The only thing that stopped this thing from happening," Moench said later, "was when Stan Lee read this stuff. And Stan put the brakes on it. To this day, a lot of people still think I'm crazy and made the whole thing up."*

Chris Claremont understood Moench's struggle. "He had been writing *Master of Kung Fu* for eight or nine years, and had come to view the characters as very real people—as *friends*. And he was being asked to do something to them that would have disoriented the whole concept of the book and the characters. It would have destroyed them for him. It would have destroyed these people within whom Doug had invested, I think, time, effort, friendship, and caring. He couldn't do it. He couldn't step back and be this emotionless god; he was part of the book, rather than being apart from it."

Maybe turning Captain America into an investment banker really was, as Shooter told one interviewer, "a rhetorical example." And anyway, according to Tom DeFalco, the idea had been abandoned by the time the fanzines got wind of it. But all the elements of the controversy—the idea that someone would even *consider* sabotaging Marvel's sacred characters; the reminder that tension still existed behind the curtain of the creative process; the obvious fact that someone was lying—provided something for every armchair prognosticator, every self-appointed expert, every fan, to channel into outrage. And the situation was about to get worse.

On the morning of September 22, Gene Day died of a heart attack at

---

* In 2011, Jim Shooter offered an alternate scenario. "My guess is that someone, probably Macchio, took idle office chatter about the idea I'd proposed and twisted it around to bait Doug so they could watch the ensuing fun," he wrote on his website.

age thirty-one, only a few months after leaving *Master of Kung Fu* under duress. His death may have been caused by any of a number of factors. "Gene was a creature of bizarre working habit," Doug Moench wrote in a eulogy. "A gonzo session of 42 hours at the board, then collapse, then up for another 28 hours and collapse again. Lopsided cycles. Cigarettes and coffee every waking moment. A bad back from the artist's perpetual hunch. No exercise." Still, stories began to circulate about a trip Day had taken to New York City, to do emergency last-minute work finishing a story for Marvel, about how Day had no choice but to spend the night in the unheated offices overnight, about how *that's what had really killed him.* So what if the stories were filled with half-truths and exaggerations? Marvel Comics was starting to look like the bad guy—the Evil Empire—to more and more people. As the employees got more defensive, they started looking even worse. Tom DeFalco appeared at a press conference and said, "Gene Day left *Master of Kung Fu,* in which his incentives were about twenty bucks a month, and went over to *Star Wars,* in which his incentives were about $1,400 a month. If that's persecution, I hope to hell I get on Jim Shooter's hate list."

Shortly after Day's death, the Canadian fanzine *Orion* published an interview that painted him as a model employee. "I'm a big Marvel supporter," Day had beamed. "My home is the house that Marvel built. It's their money that gives me all the pleasures in life that I have now." One could interpret his words in either of two ways: to cast him as a martyr, or to let Marvel off the hook.

In the weeks following Moench's departure, Marvel announced that assistant editor Ralph Macchio had been promoted to editor, and that *Spider-Woman, Ghost Rider,* and *Master of Kung-Fu* were being canceled. The characters themselves were canceled, too. Spider-Woman died. Johnny Blaze exorcised the Ghost Rider demon. Jim Shooter asked Starlin, who'd already killed Warlock and Captain Marvel, if he'd be interested in doing another bit of housecleaning: How about killing Shang-Chi? This time, Starlin passed.

$$\textcircled{13}$$

OUT IN SHERMAN OAKS, CALIFORNIA, STAN LEE PRESIDED IN MARVEL PRODUC-
tions' ranch-style building on Van Nuys Boulevard, taking meetings at a
glass-top table that occupied the sunny courtyard just outside his dark-
paneled, high-ceilinged, leather-filled office. Things were cooking. The
Academy Award–winning writer Stirling Silliphant had completed a draft
of a live-action *Daredevil* pilot for ABC. There was talk of getting Tom
Selleck for a *Doctor Strange* movie; Carl Weathers, fresh off the success
of *Rocky III*, was eyeing a *Power Man* film; and disaster-movie mogul
Irwin Allen wanted to put *The Human Torch* in theaters. Although CBS
Theatrical Films had placed *Fantastic Four* in turnaround, now Roger
Corman was taking out an option for a *Spider-Man* movie, and the Canadian animation company Nelvana had obtained the rights for a live-
action film of *The X Men*.

Lee had a lot to feel good about, then, when he visited New York in January 1983. The editorial staff was at the peak of its yuk-yuk, hand-buzzer
giddiness. They'd been shooting photos of each other in superhero costumes for some of the covers—several staff members appeared on the
cover of the last issue of *Spider-Woman*—and now they were putting
together a comic that consisted wholly of photos of intra-office hijinks,
and they wanted to include Stan the Man. Lee, the original ringmaster,
jumped at the chance to pose for the centerfold. "I got Stan to agree to
do it naked," said Ann Nocenti. "We photographed him with a comic
book covering his private parts, and then I got a call from his assistant or
something in L.A., who said, 'Stan's wild. He should not have been naked
for your centerfold. Please don't.' But he was going for it. He got to rip

his clothes off and lay down on the couch." (A Hulk costume was later superimposed over Lee's body in postproduction.)

But if one thing was sure to puncture Lee's good mood, it was what Jack Kirby was saying about Marvel—and Lee personally—in the new issue of Will Eisner's *Spirit* magazine. The previous July, Kirby had taken a break from Comic-Con engagements to sit in a San Diego hotel lobby and give an unsparing interview to Eisner; now the bomb he'd set was going off. Of Marvel's rejuvenation after the 1957 layoffs, he said, "I came back the afternoon they were going to close up. Stan Lee was already the editor there and things were in a bad way. I remember telling him not to close because I had some ideas. . . . I felt I had to regenerate things. I began to build a new line of superheroes."

Kirby gathered steam. It wasn't Lee and Kirby who came up with the ideas for superheroes—it was Kirby alone, fighting against Goodman's resistance. "Stan Lee was not writing. I was doing the writing," he insisted. "Stan Lee wouldn't let me fill the balloons. Stan Lee wouldn't let me put in the dialogue. But I wrote the entire story under the panels." Again, he took credit for creating Spider-Man.

Kirby's relationship with Lee and Marvel corroded further. Lee insisted that he himself came up with the notion of doing a character called Spider-Man, but that Kirby's rendition wasn't up to snuff. "I don't know whether this is the case or not, but maybe when Ditko did the story, he used the costume that Jack created. I don't remember. I guess Ditko and Jack are the only two guys who know that. If Ditko is still around, I'd appreciate it if you would ask him . . . but in no way, shape, manner or means did Jack Kirby create Spider-Man. I don't even know how he can dare to say that. It is the one strip that we did that he had virtually nothing to do with at all, except for a few pages that we never used."*

As for the notion that Kirby had been responsible for Marvel's early 1960s foray into superheroes? "Well, I think that Jack has taken leave of his senses. . . . Jack was at home drawing these monster stories, until the day I called him and said: 'Let's do the *Fantastic Four.*'" Lee also took

---

* In 1977, Lee wrote a five-page article about the creation of Spider-Man that made no mention of Jack Kirby's involvement; Steve Ditko's name appeared only once. *Quest* magazine ran Lee's article in its July issue, with the title "How I Invented Spider-Man."

credit for providing the initial sparks for the Hulk and Thor. "I said, 'I want to do a god. Let's do the god of thunder—Thor. Nobody has ever done Norse mythology before. . . .' So, if that doesn't give me the right to say I created it, I don't know what does."*

For fans, the bad blood between Kirby and Marvel was impossible to ignore, and thrown into stark relief by the generous (or, at the very least, publicity-savvy) overtures of DC Comics, which, by the time the rift was news, had given Kirby more work. Jenette Kahn and Paul Levitz took Jack and Roz out to dinner in Los Angeles, and gave them news that Kenner—the manufacturer of the *Star Wars* line of action figures—was going to do a series of figures based on DC Comics characters. If Kirby wanted to draw up designs for his New Gods characters, DC would give him the same royalty that was now being given to creators—even though Kirby had signed away his rights on the New Gods years ago. Furthermore, the publisher wanted to reprint his 1970s New Gods stories in a deluxe series, on nice paper. Would Kirby like to finally have a chance to conclude the saga?

Kenner's deal to produce action figures of Superman, Batman, Wonder Woman, and others instigated its panicked competitor Mattel—which had bid, and lost, on the DC characters—to hammer out a similar deal with Marvel, thus preventing Kenner from having a superhero monopoly. Mattel's "He-Man and the Masters of the Universe" toys were already a tremendous success, however, so the company didn't want to pour too much money or effort into a similar product. All Mattel required of Marvel was that a big-event comic be launched to coincide with the toy line—and that the comic carry the title of *Secret Wars*, which, according to its market research, were two words that made kids go wild.

So Jim Shooter had the assignment of coming up with ideas for a series that would include the slew of heroes that Mattel had licensed: Spider-Man, the Hulk, the Fantastic Four, the X-Men, the Avengers, plus more

---

* Whether or not Lee realized it, Thor had, in fact, been depicted in DC's *Tales of the Unexpected* #16, back in 1957. In "The Magic Hammer," a man who found Thor's hammer gained the ability to control thunderstorms. The artist was Jack Kirby.

than a dozen villains. It was serendipitous, the perfect wide-scale project on which to hang an idea that he'd been kicking around for a while—a multi-character adventure called *Cosmic Champions*—and an opportunity for Shooter to finally try out some more changes to characters. The previous summer, he'd paid $220 for an unsolicited story idea from a Chicago fan; now he would put that idea—in which Spider-Man gets a new, black, high-tech costume—into action.

Marvel had been ramping up the interconnectedness of its characters in the last few years, realizing that the shared fictional world was a big part of the draw. Now they'd all be thrown together in one giant battle. "In essence," Shooter would say, "I was fulfilling the destiny of the Marvel Universe from its inception."

One could argue that *Cosmic Champions* was, more specifically, fulfilling the destiny of Marvel Comics Group, a division of Cadence Industries Corporation. For more than a year, investor Mario Gabelli had been aggressively buying stock in Cadence, a move that caused no small alarm in the hearts of its directors. In August 1983, Sheldon Feinberg and six long-term Cadence executives—including Marvel president Jim Galton and Marvel VP of business affairs Joe Calamari—took the company private, as Cadence Management, Inc., to avoid a takeover. But having taken out short-term debt to buy back a substantial number of open shares of stock, CMI was suddenly looking for a dramatic increase in profits. It was at this time that the name of *Cosmic Champions* was changed to *Marvel Super Heroes Secret Wars*, and rushed into production, accompanied by a flood of in-house ads.

"*Secret Wars* was the first of the many, many event comics that didn't have star creators behind it, but threw all the characters in one pot," said Diana Schutz, at the time a manager for the Comics & Comix store in Berkeley. "We read Marvel in the '60s because of both the characters and the guys who created them. They never would have had that pull without Stan and Jack, or Stan and Steve, behind them. As we got into the '70s, that equation began to weigh more heavily on the side of the creators, and that spawned the independent companies and the direct market—driven by the creators, not the characters, and not the companies that published those specific characters. By the mid-'80s and the advent of *Secret Wars*, it seems to me Marvel was trying to redress that balance and pull things back in favor of the characters, not the creators."

It was true that the *Secret Wars* creative team—it would be personally written by Jim Shooter, and illustrated by Mike Zeck and John Beatty— was not a superstar lineup. Zeck and Beatty's work on *Captain America* had been popular, but they lacked the hard-core following that John Byrne or Frank Miller had—a following that would guarantee sales. The truth was, Marvel was running low on King Midas writers and artists who could, on name alone, get customers to line up for any old comic. Byrne, once regularly penciling three titles or more, was tied up as both writer and artist on *Fantastic Four* and now *Alpha Flight*, the debut is- sue of which sold terrifically and put a record-breaking thirty thousand dollars in his pocket. Byrne was also writing—but not illustrating—*The Thing*, but that wasn't exactly setting the world on fire, and it quickly became clear that it wasn't his typewriter that moved copies. Miller had gradually ceded duties on *Daredevil* to Klaus Janson, and then finally de- parted Marvel altogether, as he focused entirely on *Ronin* for DC. (After a few months, an overwhelmed Janson departed, too.)

Jim Starlin and Steve Englehart, turning out work for Archie Good- win and Jo Duffy at Marvel's Epic subsidiary, had been joined by Don McGregor and—once the Howard the Duck lawsuit was finally settled out of court—Steve Gerber. Even Doug Moench, not on speaking terms with Shooter, and Paul Gulacy, who'd walked away from Marvel long ago, signed up for Epic. But none of those titles, hermetically sealed from the narrative of the Marvel Universe, approached the commercial successes of the mainstream superhero titles. Marvel simply wasn't turning out su- perstar creators anymore.

And then, in mid–1983, Walter Simonson took over *Thor*, which was on the verge of cancellation. Simonson was a respected and well-liked ten- year veteran of the comics industry—he was married to Louise Jones, and shared studio space with Frank Miller. But despite his wildly imaginative page designs, he'd remained more of an "artist's artist," never exactly a star. Mark Gruenwald gave Simonson carte blanche, although he also handed him a list of possible directions in which to take the book, suggestions very similar to the ones Doug Moench claimed to have been given, including one in which Thor died and a new hero wielded the hammer.

In Simonson's interpretation, it was a horse-headed alien warrior with the unlikely name of Beta Ray Bill who took possession of Thor's weapon. The cover to *Thor* #337 featured the horrifying sight of Beta Ray Bill in full Thor regalia, smashing Mjolnir through the logo, coming toward the reader. Inside, Simonson's exploding stars, giant spaceships, and carefully researched Norse architecture conveyed more exuberance than anyone had brought to *Thor* since Kirby. It sold out in days, a surprise that made dealers scramble like they hadn't since *Howard the Duck* #1. What Frank Miller had done for *Daredevil*, Simonson had done for *Thor*, instantly.

It was, in a way, a vindication of Shooter's plan to push for drastic changes on stagnant titles. Shang-Chi had been retired, and Tony Stark and Don Blake had been replaced by a new Iron Man and a new Thor. There was a new Captain Marvel, too, and Ghost Rider and Spider-Woman were dead. In the pages of *Doctor Strange*, Roger Stern put a stake through Marvel's Dracula, which Marv Wolfman and Gene Colan had developed for the better part of a decade. And nobody seemed to mind any of it.

Shooter could even laugh about it now. He asked cartoonist Fred Hembeck if he'd like to do a follow-up to his gag-a-minute *Fantastic Four Roast*, and when Hembeck wondered if Shooter had anything particular in mind, he said, "Why don't you do something about this Big Bang controversy that's been going on? Maybe you can make something funny about that?" Hembeck began work on *Jim Shooter Destroys the Marvel Universe*.

There was a time, not long before, when Marvel was so in need of capital that it would have bent over backward to work out a big-event character crossover with DC Comics—especially if it was drawn by George Perez, whose star had risen impressively since leaving Marvel and embarking on *The New Teen Titans*. But throughout 1983, the two companies engaged in a sniping match about a *Justice League of America/Avengers* team-up, a conflict that stretched over numerous editorial pages and spilled into

fan-magazine interviews and convention panels. The crux of the disagreement was the speed at which Jim Shooter exercised his right of approval
over the plot of the proposed series; eventually, Marvel just walked away.

Now, it could afford to. Marvel's sales on newsstands, quite miraculously, had stopped falling. But the real success story was at comic
shops, where tremendous growth was taking place. Direct-market sales
increased 46 percent in 1982, then another 32 percent in 1983. A rash of
miniseries not only provided a constant stream of "collectible" number-
one issues, but also served as a convenient way to test the market waters
for a regular series. Now in the works were miniseries starring Hawkeye,
Cloak and Dagger, Black Panther, Falcon, and a second Avengers team,
made up of all the characters who couldn't fit into the main one (eventually it was decided to set them up in Los Angeles, naturally, and call them
the West Coast Avengers). Also in the planning stages were miniseries
starring Machine Man and the Eternals, neither of which had been given
much respect when Jack Kirby created them. Of course, the real cash
cows were all those X-Men spin-offs that would fly on and off the shelves:
X-Men and Micronauts; *Illyana and Storm*; *Beauty and the Beast* (which
costarred the Dazzler, in a remarkable testimony to Marvel's stubborn-
ness, and former X-Man the Beast); *Kitty Pryde and Wolverine*. The Beast
joined the lineup of *The Defenders*, which now also included two other
former X-Men, the Angel and Iceman.

Carol Kalish, not yet thirty years old, had a lot to do with Marvel's sales
success. She'd lobbied for various policies that benefited retailers—an
advertising co-op program, a comics rack program, and a cash register
program—realizing that the publisher's continued growth depended on
their health. She distributed copies of Jay Conrad Levinson's *Guerrilla
Marketing* to shop owners, and persuaded Marvel to accept returns on
last-minute fill-in issues. She pushed for distribution in Waldenbooks and
B. Dalton, too.

She loved selling as much as she loved comics, and the retailers loved
her. Regarded by many as the smartest person in the comics industry,
she dressed the part of the Young Urban Professional and regularly com-
municated in well-polished corporatespeak, but she could also talk the

language of a hard-core comics fan—she *was* a hard-core comics fan. "Carol would come visit shops, take people out to dinner, ask what was selling, what fans wanted to see," said Diana Schutz. "And after dinner, the Marvel plastic would pay for dinner, and when somebody would say, 'Are you sure? Can you pay for this whole table?' Carol *always* had the rationale that the money she spent on taking retailers out to dinner was another nail in the coffin of some book she despised, like *Dazzler*. That was one of the ones she was eager to get rid of."

Kalish, hyperarticulate and strong-willed, earned the fierce loyalty of her boss, Ed Shukin, and her assistant, Peter David. But she was not so beloved elsewhere in the Marvel offices. "There was a good deal of hostility and suspicion," David said of the relationship between the editorial and sales departments. "Editorial did not understand what the need for sales was at all. They were afraid that sales would become the tail wagging the dog. They didn't want their stories to be sales driven, they wanted to be purely creatively driven."

Shooter was given to repeating what Stan Lee had told him, after he'd called in a panic to ask about the rumors that Marvel was killing off its characters. "If the comics are good, sales will take care of themselves." It was not a philosophy the sales and marketing staff was fond of.

Peter David—a former journalist who'd been unsuccessfully pitching *Moon Knight* ideas to Denny O'Neil—found himself at the center of one particularly public clash between editorial and marketing. David, charged with regularly distributing preview pages of upcoming material at events, was given photocopies of future *Alpha Flight* pages. The problem was that Marvel had been hyping that one Alpha Flight member would die in the still-upcoming issue #12, and the photocopies, from issue #13, included a dream sequence in which that dead hero rose from the grave. When Byrne saw the spoiler-heavy photocopies, he found where David was stationed and screamed at him, before knocking over furniture and storming out. (A quarter century later, the two men were still debating the specifics of the story on online message boards.)

The truth was, though, that Shooter's goals and Kalish's goals were overlapping quite nicely, and nothing demonstrated their lockstep better than *Secret Wars*, which finally came out in January 1984. Mattel wasn't much help—their toys were lagging months behind, and they weren't going to put much marketing muscle into them anyway. But Shooter's "Bullpen Bulletins" column and the articles in *Marvel Age* hammered it through the minds of readers and retailers alike: *this is going to change everything about these characters, and you are going to buy it.*

The plot for *Secret Wars* was simple: an otherworldly, ethereal force known as the Beyonder transports a few dozen superheroes and super-villains to a planet called Battleworld, where they are told to fight it out. "I am from beyond!" shouts the cosmic voice. "Slay your enemies and all that you desire shall be yours!" One could argue that the fight-filled *Secret Wars* went against everything that made Marvel Comics special—although there were the usual squabbles and misunderstandings between the good guys, there was a minimum of moral shading, other than a few pages where Mister Fantastic flirted with (and decided against) pacifism.* In recent *X-Men* story lines, Chris Claremont had taken great pains to transform Magneto into a compelling, possibly noble Auschwitz survivor who'd made peace with the X-Men; in *Secret Wars*, he was again reduced to a violent ideologue who would slay all who stood in the way of his dream of peace. The bad guys were all either thugs or megalomaniacs, with one exception.

The Molecule Man was clearly the character that most fascinated Shooter. A throwaway Lee and Kirby villain from the early days of the *Fantastic Four*, the Molecule Man had been just another nebbish named Owen Reece when an accident at an atomic plant gave him the power to rearrange physical matter. He'd been dusted off a few times by Steve Gerber and Len Wein in the 1970s, but it was Shooter who had played up the revenge-of-the-nerd angle in a couple of *Avengers* issues, and made Owen Reece a strangely sympathetic sociopath. "When I got my power," Reece explained, "I wanted to get even with the whole world 'cause I've been picked on all my life—but I couldn't figure out a way to do it . . .

---

* In the pages of *Fantastic Four*, John Byrne's "Trial of Reed Richards" had made the point that Galactus was a crucial part of the universe, and neither good nor evil. Now, in *Secret Wars* #9, Reed Richards concluded, "I'm still not certain that, in the cosmic scheme of things, what we're doing is right—but I realized just how badly I want to see my baby born, Cap! I want that more than anything! And I'm going to fight for it!"

till now!" At the end of that story, Reece had agreed to go see a therapist. Now, in *Secret Wars*, Shooter had Reece preaching enlightenment to the criminal goons around him, who grew only angrier when they realized he could incinerate them at will.

But the Molecule Man's story was abandoned without resolution, in favor of explosions and speeches about never giving up. It would be Mister Fantastic's words that would echo most strongly in the minds of readers. "Why would a being so far removed from us and so powerful as the Beyonder bring us across the universe for a stupid, simplistic 'good-versus-evil' gladiatorial contest? Is he a mad god? A cosmic idiot? . . . There must be more to this . . . but what possible purpose could there be?" It was better not to think too hard. As Shooter would later say, the comic was simply a way to "teach the kids how to play with the toys."

Secret Wars never transcended its awkward mix of exposition and cliché. Characters constantly restated their motivations. To please Mattel, there were three new female characters introduced, but one was just a new Spider-Woman, and the other two were in the statuesque female-wrestler mode. The dynamism in Mike Zeck's artwork began to slip away as Shooter continually ordered pages redrawn, insisting on more establishing shots, and more eye-level long shots. They fell behind schedule, and Bob Layton stepped in for a few issues; upon his return Zeck's contribution was limited to workmanlike renderings of Shooter's stick-figure layouts, the natural visual analog of the straight-ahead storytelling rules he espoused. When the final issue was completed at last, the emotionally strained Zeck received from Shooter a bottle of Dom Perignon, with an attached card that read, "The War Is Over." Zeck opened it and downed the entire bottle immediately.

In the end, there were signs that remnants of Shooter's Big Bang plans had worked their way into the series: *Secret Wars* #11 ended with the "bolt from the blue" that was mentioned in those earlier meetings, and the cover copy of #12, the final issue, read "After the Big Bang!" But apart from a few new costumes, and a new Spider-Woman, nothing much had really changed in the Marvel Universe. Which, maybe, was what the fans wanted all along.

———

The first signs of *Secret Wars'* commercial prospects came a month into 1984, with a tie-in issue of *Amazing Spider-Man*. Tom DeFalco and artist Ron Frenz had taken over the title just as *Secret Wars* was solidifying, and one of their welcome presents was an issue that Roger Stern had already plotted, in which Spider-Man's new, black costume would first appear. Because the word around the office was that this new-costume stunt would be a disaster, DeFalco stepped in to write other Spider-Man titles while regular writers backed away, wanting nothing to do with it, especially after news of the costume leaked. "We got a ton of mail saying what a bad idea it was," DeFalco remembered. "To the point where Shooter came to me and said, 'What issue does Spider-Man get his black costume?' And I said, '252,' and he said, 'Get rid of it by 253. Sales are going to plummet; everybody hates it.' I had a long discussion with him and convinced him we had to keep it for at least eight issues. He wasn't gonna get it in *Secret Wars* until issue 8. I said, 'We have to *introduce* it before we get rid of it.'"

DeFalco and Shooter needn't have worried—when Mattel heard about the new Spider-Man costume, they were thrilled. Now they could sell two versions of the toy. "The day we're sending the issue out," DeFalco said, "Shooter comes in and says, 'Oh, by the way, keep the black costume.'"

On February 1, the day after *Amazing Spider-Man* #252 hit stands, Eliot Brown and Tom DeFalco arrived in California for a signing tour of comic stores. It turned out that *Spider-Man* #252 was an instant record-breaker, even more of a surprise than Walt Simonson's first issue of *Thor* had been. By the time they arrived at the first shop, there was nothing left for DeFalco to sign—the store was already out of stock. Meanwhile, at a signing in Canada, Ron Frenz saw the issue going for fifty dollars. "The Fire Marshal shut it down because too many people had shown up," he said. "It was like *Soylent Green*. . . . The crowd was pushing the table back and back, because it was huge and it didn't have any direction, so the table kept migrating on me. It was like Beatles time, and nobody was expecting it."

A week later, DeFalco flew to the Atlanta Comics Festival, where Jim Shooter, basking in the glow of *Secret Wars* #1, laughed sportingly as some of his most trusted friends and employees—including John Byrne, Mark Gruenwald, Mike Carlin, and Tom DeFalco—provided a comics version of a celebrity roast. When they returned to New York, things looked like they were only going to get better: in an astonishing turn of events, Bill Sarnoff at Warner Publishing, DC's parent company, had called Shooter to say that although DC's superheroes were making a killing in licensing, the comics were losing money. Sarnoff asked if Marvel would be interested in licensing and publishing seven of DC's titles. Marvel began negotiating for the rights to *Superman, Batman, Wonder Woman, Green Lantern, New Teen Titans, The Legion of Superheroes,* and *Justice League of America.* Shooter projected that Marvel's acquisition would result in an additional 39 million copies sold over the first two years, at a pretax profit of $3.5 million. It wasn't just a lucrative opportunity that was falling into Marvel's lap; the removal of its chief competitor would be the "elimination of an irritation," as Shooter put it in one memo.

But the timing was off. One week later, on February 28, First Comics filed a suit against Marvel and World Color Printing—the press that serviced nearly the entire industry—for "anti-trust and anti-competitive activities." The suit claimed not only that Marvel was getting preferential pricing from World Color, but also that the publisher was intentionally flooding the market with product, in an attempt to drown its fledgling competitors. Marvel wasn't about to cut down on the barrage of new titles, but the company quickly decided that taking over the reins of the major properties of the DC universe might not be wise at this point.

Shooter was disappointed, but it wasn't a devastating loss. Marvel, he figured, could always create a new universe of its own.

$$\textcircled{14}$$

NOTING THAT THE TWENTIETH ANNIVERSARY OF FANTASTIC FOUR #1—AND thus, of the Marvel Universe—was approaching, Jim Galton gathered executives and VPs to talk about what kinds of special publishing events might be scheduled. Shooter's first idea had familiar elements. "I proposed that we do a Big Bang—that is, bring the Marvel Universe to an end, with every single title concluding, forever, in dramatic fashion," he later told an interviewer. At this point, he said, the titles and characters would all be relaunched, and royalties would be paid to the creators of the classic heroes, like Kirby and Ditko, for whom there'd been no systemic incentives a quarter century ago. "We could just include them from that point on in the standard creator participation programs that I'd installed, as each of the characters they had created long ago were re-introduced." When this idea was shot down, Shooter suggested a new, separate fictional universe that would have no relation to the current Marvel one. He got the green light, and a $120,000 budget, to launch a series of titles in two years, for the 1986 anniversary.

In the meantime, now that *Secret Wars* was up and running, Jim Shooter already had an entire universe to fix. He seemed a little less than pleased with how other writers were handling their titles. "I think Shooter felt some of the characters were no longer being portrayed properly," said Tom DeFalco. "Y'know: their *essence*. He wanted to use this as an opportunity to show us how it should be done."

"It sold through the roof," John Byrne said of *Secret Wars*. "Better than anything up to that point. Shooter had to justify it in his mind. He had to convince himself it hadn't sold just because it had every super-hero in the world in it. It sold because it was brilliant." Now even Byrne was getting the graded makereadies that Doug Moench had complained about. "It was wonderful being in school again. 'C-minus. See me.' And he would add notes that said, 'See *Secret Wars* for how to do this right.' . . . I don't think so. I don't think I'd see *Secret Wars* for how to do anything but possibly fold it."

There was a full-court press to promote the series in other Marvel titles, as evidenced by a darkly funny memo that was posted in the Bullpen:

Date: April 27, 1984
From: Jim Shooter
To: The Editors
Subject: Secret Wars

Since I don't have a lettercol to hype Secret Wars *(and myself) I'd appreciate some help. How about, in your lettercols for the rest of the year, mentioning how marvelous a job I'm doing, and how being the E.I.C., and therefore the ultimate authority on all the characters and like unto the Very God of the Marvel Universe, my work is absolutely perfect. Definitive, even. That seems to be the only gripe we're getting—that the characters are not exactly* ~~as dull and boring~~ *the same as they appear in their regular titles. If you guys would talk up the wonderful job I'm doing we could* ~~trick the little fucks~~ *make it clearer to the charming readers that, despite my stylistic differences from the other writers, we're writing the same characters.* ~~Only I write them better.~~ *Let's legitimize the hell out of it, okay?*

When the memo leaked to the *Comics Journal*, a Marvel spokesman confimed its veracity, but then assistant editor Eliot Brown suddenly stepped forward and accepted responsibility for staging a hoax. Shooter refused to comment. Regardless of its true author, the memo captured a sentiment that Marvel employees recognized: nobody understood the characters like Shooter did. As *Captain America* moved toward its three hundredth issue, Shooter started reworking dialogue at the last minute. The writer, J. M. DeMatteis, was in the midst of a yearlong story, building to a climax in which the Red Skull, Captain America's archenemy of nearly half a century, was killed. An exhausted Captain America would hurl his shield into the East River, walk away, and try to find a meaningful life as Steve Rogers. "My idea," said DeMatteis, "was that Captain America's gonna just say, 'You know what? I've tried punching people and dropping buildings on their heads for forty years, and there has to be another way.' He was ultimately going to become a global peace activist which was going to create all kinds of problems for him—the government would turn against him, all the Marvel heroes would turn against him, and the only allies to support him would be Doctor Doom and the Sub-Mariner. I had recast the Bucky of the 1950s as Nomad; he was basically going to freak out about all this and, in the end, assassinate Captain America." Black Crow, a Native American character that DeMatteis had created, would now be the new Captain America.

DeMatteis's plan was, in a way, a politically radicalized echo of those old Big Bang rumors in which Steve Rogers would die and a new Captain America would take his place. But while DeMatteis and his artist plugged away on upcoming issues, Jim Shooter took a look at Steve Rogers throwing away his shield in the final pages of #300 and insisted that there was simply no way this could happen—Captain America, he said, would never act like this. Shooter cut the double-sized issue in half and rewrote it himself. Steve Rogers would never have his crisis of faith, and Black Crow would never become Captain America. DeMatteis, disgusted, quit the title he'd been writing for three years.

After *Secret Wars* came out, Marvel's editors, writers, and artists started to wonder if only Jim Shooter knew what Jim Shooter wanted. Of course, Shooter wasn't the only one to have proprietary instincts about Marvel-owned characters—Stan Lee had for years been territorial about the usage of Silver Surfer. And as the leader of the editorial department, it was well within Shooter's rights—it was his duty, really—to act as the custodian of the characters.

And Shooter was still open to the persuasions of his editors, still willing to take chances. The new artist on *The New Mutants*, Bill Sienkiewicz, had been making huge strides on *Moon Knight* before he and Moench left; now, more than a year later, his work was like nothing ever seen in superhero comics. His very first page depicted a bear's head that morphed into a crossword puzzle that morphed into a blanket; on the following pages, it looked like he'd dropped his brush, dripping India ink everywhere. To exploit Sienkiewicz's outside-the-box experimentation, Chris Claremont and editor Ann Nocenti fed him the idea for a hyperactive, bionic, shape-shifting character. And then there were the near abstractions of the painted cover, the first in a series that would push the boundaries of Marvel's visual style. "I let him do the craziest covers he could think of," said Nocenti, "because it was about trying to explode out of old-school Marvel into something more modern." Sienkiewicz began working with other media, something few artists since Jack Kirby had done: "I went to Radio Shack and bought circuit boards and transistors and soldered all these transistors into a pattern and painted them, slapped them on with modeling paste and ran wire and tape and painted this whole biocircuitry collage."

Letters of praise and letters of horror poured in. One, written in crayon to Shooter, simply read, "GET RID OF HIM JIMMY BEFORE HE RUINS EVERYTHING." But readers were buying it compulsively—trying to figure out if they hated it or loved it, but buying it just the same. For a while, at least, Shooter allowed Sienkiewicz a free hand.

"That was the thing about Jim," Nocenti said. "He was kind of old-fashioned, but he could see to the future if you battled hard enough."

Of course, embracing the new meant ditching the old. To make way for Bill Sienkiewicz, Sal Buscema—whose unwaveringly straightforward style had offset the absurdity of Steve Gerber's *The Defenders* and Steve Englehart's *Captain America*—had been taken off *New Mutants*. "I knew you couldn't have an old-fashioned artist on something geared to bring in new readers," said Nocenti. "Probably the hardest call I ever made at Marvel was to Sal Buscema, to say, bluntly—too bluntly—'I am taking you off this book.' He asked why, and I said, 'You're old fashioned. This needs to be new.' And he was really mad, then upset. Then he turned around, and in the next issue of *The Incredible Hulk* . . . it was fucking magnificent. It was like Sal saying, 'You want to see what I can do?' He just pulled all the guns out." Not everyone, though, had a *Hulk* gig on which they could prove themselves.

Shooter had a reputation for keeping the old hands, the guys who'd been around the industry for decades, busy with work—not just Vinnie Colletta, but Don Perlin, Mike Esposito, and Frank Springer. But stories began to circulate of some veterans being put out to pasture. While inker Chic Stone recuperated from a heart attack, he received a dispatch from Shooter that shut the door on future work. "The letter was basically two sentences long," Stone remembered, "and it said something to the effect of, 'Dear Chic, Your services are no longer needed by Marvel Comics. If anything comes up I'll let you know.'"

When Jim Mooney's contract expired, he sent a letter of inquiry to Shooter. "I got a very short note," Mooney recalled. "'Retire.' I'm paraphrasing that a little bit. It wasn't quite that abbreviated, but it was damn close."

Don Heck, the original Iron Man artist, had been kicked around plenty in recent years, already feeling underappreciated before Harlan Ellison and Gary Groth had a laugh about him as "the world's worst artist" in a *Comics Journal* interview. More recently, after Jim Shooter accepted DC's suggestion to hire Heck to replace George Perez on *JLA/Avengers*, Perez suggested that bluffing was afoot. "Shooter," he said, "knows full well that Heck will never sell the book."

Jack Kirby wasn't looking for new work from Marvel, but he was still looking to get his *old* work back, as he had since the 1970s, when Marvel had started returning new art pages in exchange for the signing of a release statement. (At that time, he said, he'd "pleaded and cajoled" for some recent pages, "but when I told them I wanted the 60s stuff back, they said they were too valuable.") In 1983, as the company went through its stockpiles of original art, and finally began returning older pages to artists, there was an additional release form that acknowledged its status as work-for-hire. But the warehouse was a mess, Kirby was told, and the inventory list had been lost. The salt in the wound was that pages were regularly turning up for sale at comic conventions.

Kirby told the *Comics Journal* that no one at Marvel would listen to his problem, and he did so in uncharacteristically angry language. "They don't give a shit," he said. "I feel adamant; I feel like I've contributed a lot when people really needed me, and there's a hell of a lot of ingratitude. It smells like garbage."

Kirby watched as vintage artwork was returned to Steve Ditko, Dick Ayers, and Don Heck, among others. Word got out that several pages had been stolen from the Marvel offices, while other pages sat on the rusty, collapsing shelves of a warehouse. And then, in August 1984, Kirby was sent a list of artwork that Marvel had recovered—only 88 of the 8,000 pages he'd sent them throughout the 1960s. Accompanying the list was a four-page form that no other artist had been asked to sign. He wouldn't be allowed to sell the artwork; he couldn't make copies of the artwork; he couldn't publicly exhibit the artwork; he'd let Marvel access the artwork whenever it wished; and if Marvel wanted to modify the artwork, it was free to do so.

Kirby refused to sign. His words got tougher. "I wouldn't cooperate with the Nazis, and I won't cooperate with them," he said. "If I allow them to do this to me, I'm allowing them to do it to other people." As the stalemate continued, Marvel would claim that the Kirbys, through their lawyers, were threatening to sue for the rights to characters Jack had created. "We've never tried to get the copyrights back from Marvel," Roz Kirby told Shooter at a heated panel convention in 1985. "It's you people who keep bringing it up."

By that time, though, the Kirbys' lawyer had, in fact, broached the subject of copyright claims for Spider-Man, the Hulk, and the Fantastic Four—after a *Variety* ad announcing Cannon Films' planned *Captain America* film credited the character not to Joe Simon and Jack Kirby, but to Stan Lee. Things deteriorated, and they got more personal. "I saved Marvel's ass," Kirby told an interviewer, and compared Lee to Sammy Glick, the backstabbing main character of Budd Schulberg's *What Makes Sammy Run?* When asked if he would ever consider working with Lee, he was adamant. "No. No. It'll never happen. No more than I would work with the SS. Stan Lee is what he is. . . . He has his own dreams and he has his own way of getting them. I have my own dreams but I get them my own way. We're two different people. I feel that he's in direct opposition to me. There's no way I could reach the SS. I tried to reach them. I used to talk with them and say, 'Hey, fellas, you don't believe in all this horseshit.' And they said, 'Oh, yes, we do.' They were profound beliefs. They became indoctrinated. And Stan Lee's the same way. He's indoctrinated one way and he's gonna live that way. He's gonna benefit from it in some ways and I think he'll lose in others. But he doesn't have to believe me."

Apparently, Lee didn't. After refuting Kirby's versions of the creations of the Fantastic Four, Thor, the Hulk, and Spider-Man ("All of them came from my basement," Kirby had said), Lee grew exasperated. "I don't know much of what Jack is talking about these days," he said. "I just feel I'm listening to the mouthings of a very bitter man who I feel quite sorry for. I don't know what the problem is, really."

Twenty years after the Merry Marvel Marching Society record testi- fied to the familial joy of the Bullpen, everything had fallen apart. Sol Brodsky had died in June 1984; Lee sent a eulogy from Los Angeles, but didn't attend the funeral. On a Thursday night in March 1985, riding the subway home from the Marvel offices, Morrie Kuramoto died of a heart attack. Danny Crespi—Kuramoto's closest friend and constant bantering partner—died two months later, at fifty-nine. He'd kept his leukemia a secret, continuing to come into the Bullpen every day without telling anyone.

Almost immediately after the last issue of *Secret Wars* had shipped, Carol Kalish addressed a gathering of comic-book store owners. "Let's be honest," she said. "*Secret Wars* was crap, right?" (The retailers agreed wholeheartedly.) "But did it sell?" The room cheered.

"Well, get ready for *Secret Wars*, series two!"

Upon the publication of the first *Secret Wars* series, Shooter told report- ers that he didn't want to write a sequel—if there ended up being one, he said, he'd rather get Tom DeFalco to do it. For whatever reason, though, Shooter decided to keep it for himself after all, and DeFalco, who'd ed- ited the first series, did not return. Bob Budiansky drew the short straw and was assigned as *Secret Wars II*'s editor. "The traditional thing to do if you inherited a book that Jim Shooter was writing," explained Budiansky, "was to fire him immediately. And that was okay, he understood. He was a nightmare to work with on deadlines. His work came in really late, and created all sorts of havoc. By being so late, it demanded that the Bullpen stop everything to cut out every word balloon and paste them down on the board with rubber cement. So it would mess up everybody's schedule because books with minor corrections would be pushed aside while everything ground to a halt to do *Secret Wars*."

Sal Buscema, a reliable workhorse, drew the first issue, but after the pages came back, Shooter hired Al Milgrom to redraw it from scratch. Despite urging from other editors, Budiansky refused to replace Shooter with another writer. "I figured Jim would inevitably get involved at the tail end of the process since it was his baby," he said. "He'd review the book after it was all penciled and inked and lettered, and want massive changes and then it would be even worse if he wasn't the writer."

The plot of *Secret Wars II* was a kind of inverse of its predecessor: the Beyonder, the ethereal force from the first series that had imported all those heroes to Battleworld, now came to earth, took human form, and yearned to understand what made people tick.

The problem was that *Secret Wars II* took the big-event strategy of its predecessor and multiplied it exponentially, so the action spilled into almost every regular title the company produced. More than thirty issues of other Marvel comics—from *Daredevil* to *Doctor Strange* to *Micronauts* to *Rom*—had a Nabisco-like triangle marking them as a crossover, and although Shooter *wasn't* the writer on those, he took a special interest in each of them.

No one questioned Shooter's instincts for storytelling craft. But his repeated iterations of rules had started to grate: there was the harping on the necessity of establishing shots, the pointing to Jack Kirby panels for instruction, and the citing of "Little Miss Muffett" as a story that contained the crucial elements of conflict and resolution.

Roger Stern, the writer of *Doctor Strange*, called Peter Gillis, a fellow freelancer, and told him he was running out of ideas for the book. Would Gillis like to take over? When Gillis happily accepted, Stern told him there was just one catch—he'd start writing it with the *Secret Wars*

II tie-in. "Every crossover got redone about three times because Jim just didn't like it," Gillis said later. "And that was no exception."

After Denny O'Neil was asked to integrate the Beyonder into an issue of *Daredevil*, editor Ralph Macchio relayed to him that Shooter didn't feel he understood the character. "I kept the Beyonder offstage as much as possible," O'Neil said. "That so offended Jim that he took the royalties away from me." Shooter rewrote the issue himself, and, according to O'Neil, "Our relationship deteriorated pretty quickly."*

"There was a lot of criticism of the content," added Howard Mackie, who was Mark Gruenwald's assistant at the time. "And the requests for rewriting became more and more. There were times things were completely written, and you were told, *you're not getting it*. There was an issue of the *Avengers* that Roger Stern had written, with the Beyonder. A whole bunch of it had to be redrawn, because there was a costume change on the Beyonder that no one had been told about."

"Shooter was bouncing a lot of the tie-ins," said Mike Carlin. "He'd read the stories and say, 'This doesn't match what I was going to do'—but he hadn't *done* it yet, so it was hard for anybody to imagine."

That the Beyonder spent most of *Secret Wars II* outfitted in shoulder pads, turned-up collars, jumpsuits, and Jheri curls was an early indicator that Jim Shooter had some quibbles with United States culture in 1985. For all the gripes that the series was another cynical cash-in, it possessed moments of truly biting satire, often aimed at mindless consumerism: the geeky Molecule Man returned, but instead of using his staggering powers, he chose to sit on a couch with his unitard-wearing girlfriend Volcana; the two would call each other "baby-kins" and "snookums" while taking in *Hogan's Heroes* and *Laverne and Shirley* marathons. Meanwhile, the stranger-in-a-strange-land Beyonder fell in with a bad crowd of mobsters and hookers, and took joyrides in a Cuisinart-equipped Lamborghini.

---

* In *Power Man & Iron Fist* #121, Jim Owsley provided the most unique version of the Beyonder: arriving in a black neighborhood, he sports mirrored shades, an outrageous Afro, and black skin. "Slide me a piece o' the porgie on the down fry side," he tells the waitress. "Greens 'em beans, 'em walking Johnny to the rocks. Cool?"

Ironically, the character strongly resembled Steve Gerber and Mary Skrenes's poor-selling 1970s hero Omega the Unknown: a powerful, fish-out-of-water naïf corrupted by junk culture and vice.*

The series petered out into an endless shaggy-dog tale, in which the Beyonder repeatedly destroyed and restored people and places, his own fulfillment always just out of reach. Despite appearances by the most cosmic of Marvel's entities—Starlin's In-Betweener, Ditko's Eternity, Kirby's Galactus and the Watcher—the story was grounded by odd, simplistic characterizations, and chirpy expositional dialogue that seemed to cater to small children even as it included references to prostitution. Worse, the superheroes—the characters Jim Shooter was so protective of—were by turns boorish and pious. "Aw, who cares? He's someone else's problem now!" shrugged Spider-Man, as the Beyonder escaped in an elevator, echoing the hubris that allowed Peter Parker's Uncle Ben to be murdered years before. Had Spider-Man really learned nothing about being a hero?

If you wanted to find out, you'd have to read a lot of comic books. In ten years, the price of a single issue had tripled to seventy-five cents, which meant that the nine parts of Secret Wars II, plus the flood of its tie-in cross-overs, added up to more than thirty dollars of allowance money. In fact, Marvel in 1985 was in the business of breaking piggy banks—suddenly, it seemed, no series stood alone. In the midst of the Secret Wars II run, John Byrne gave up on writing Alpha Flight and decided to switch jobs with Hulk writer Bill Mantlo; they engineered a crossover between those titles, so you were obliged to read both or neither. Claremont's X-Men and New Mutants titles became increasingly intertwined, even as the steady stream of spin-off miniseries continued. Spider-Man was now a franchise in itself, as Web of Spider-Man joined Amazing Spider-Man and Spectacular Spider-Man, and each of their stories figured into one another, too.

Specialty comic-book stores now accounted for as much of Marvel's

---

*The Beyonder wasn't easy to like. Just as the cosmic seducer named Marcus had caused all that trouble for Ms. Marvel in Shooter's Avengers Annual #10, the Beyonder used his otherworldly powers to woo the Dazzler in Secret Wars II. Presto: a bearskin rug, a hansom cab, a Paris café. Thankfully, though, the Beyonder realized the vileness of his gambit before impregnating the Dazzler.

sales as newsstands. The company's audience was growing more dedicated, and flush with disposable income, and older. Were you in or out?

The ideal Marvel Comics fan bought all these crossovers, and bought
the maybe-they'll-be-collectible number-one issues, and didn't necessarily have much in common with the dope-smoking chin-scratchers
who'd rallied behind Jim Starlin's *Warlock* and Steve Englehart's *Doctor
Strange* and Steve Gerber's *Howard the Duck*. In *Secret Wars II*, Shooter
had reserved his harshest measures for a character named Stewart
Cadwell, a former comic-book writer, who hurled brickbats at trash
culture even as he profited from it by writing for animated television.
"I'm sick of the violence, the mediocrity, the idiocy—Reaganomics, for
Pete's sake," shouted the angry liberal Cadwell, who subsisted on Mc-
Donald's and cigarettes. When the Beyonder offered him super powers,
Cadwell used them to lash out—but after he destroyed the NBC studio that employed him, the X-Men and Avengers quickly defeated him,
reducing him to a simpering fool. Not coincidentally, Stewart Cadwell
looked exactly like Steve Gerber.

Gerber had, in fact, recently quit animation, and worked on a Wonder Woman pitch for DC Comics. When he and Frank Miller, who was
working on a Batman miniseries, heard about each other's projects, they
got together and pitched a Superman project. Talks fell apart, though,
after DC wouldn't give them 20 percent of a new Supergirl they created for the project. Gerber then shopped around a series he'd created
with Val Mayerik called *Void Indigo*. The independent publishers passed,
DC showed interest but wouldn't agree to let Gerber and Mayerik retain
copyright, and Gerber found himself talking to Archie Goodwin at Marvel's creator-owned Epic Comics line. Gerber took some heat from the
comics press for returning to Marvel—the target of several issues of *Destroyer Duck*—but what could he do? They had promotional muscle, and
they were interested. Two issues of *Void Indigo* were published before,
amid controversy surrounding its violence, it was canceled.

Shortly afterward, Marvel made plans to revive the *Howard the Duck*
comic series in order to capitalize on a big-budget movie adaptation that

George Lucas was producing. In accordance with the terms of his settlement with Marvel, Gerber was offered the chance to write it. In April
1985, shortly after reading himself satirized in *Secret Wars II*, Gerber
turned in a script of what was to be the first issue of the new *Howard*.
It was a parody of multi-issue, multi-character crossovers, called "Howard the Duck's Secret Crisis." But after Jim Shooter requested editorial
changes to the script, the plans fell apart.* Gerber went off to work as a
creative consultant on a *Howard the Duck* movie.

Meanwhile, Jim Starlin, who'd been happily chugging along on *Dreadstar* for Epic for a few years, began having trouble getting paychecks on
time. "I'm of the opinion at this point, though people up at Marvel deny
it, that Marvel is less than enthusiastic about continuing creator-owned
characters and wouldn't be sad to see them all go," he said. Proving that
Marvel had indeed allowed him to retain all rights to *Dreadstar*, he took
his property and departed for the independent First Comics.

Steve Englehart fared better in his reunion with Marvel. Like Gerber,
he'd come to miss the benefits of working for an established company,
and was ready to return to the land of work-for-hire, which now offered
the added lure of incentives. "I got tired of writing stories and not having them come out," he explained. "It's something that you always could
and can count on at the two majors, that they'll publish the stuff." Returning to Marvel, Englehart immediately wove together a story about
Wonder Man, Black Talon, and the Grim Reaper—the very story he'd
been working on in the *Avengers*, nearly a decade earlier, when he'd told
off Gerry Conway. But the story had turned into melodrama now, more
ponderous even than Claremont's *X-Men*. It wound through double-sized,

---

* The first plot that Gerber submitted explained away Bill Mantlo's late 1970s *Howard
the Duck* stories as a hallucination. When Shooter raised the concern that Mantlo
might be offended, Gerber next devised a story in which the events of the Mantlo
issues had simply been black-and-white movies created by an alien "techno-artist"
named Chirreep. (Mantlo, no stranger to metafictional games, had himself originated
the techno-artist plot device in a 1982 issue of *The Incredible Hulk* to invalidate earlier
stories by Doug Moench, then in the process of leaving Marvel for DC.) Finally, when
Shooter requested multiple changes to this script, Gerber demanded that he once
again be allowed to edit himself on *Howard the Duck*. Marvel refused, and Gerber
withdrew his script.

higher-priced issues of *West Coast Avengers* and *The Vision and Scarlet Witch*, one more multivolume narrative event.

Frank Miller had returned to working for Marvel, too, even as he used his celebrity to speak, at every turn, against the company's treatment of Jack Kirby. Fed up with New York City—"one Bernhard Goetz is enough," he explained—Miller had taken off for downtown Los Angeles, holing up in an industrial space loft, across the street from a dive bar where one had to step over hypodermic needles. In addition to a gritty, futuristic reimagining of Batman, he began working on two dark, ambitious graphic novels for Marvel: one about the late Elektra, which he was illustrating himself, and one about Daredevil, on which he was collaborating with Bill Sienkiewicz.* That collaboration would lead, in turn, to the nine-issue *Elektra: Assassin* series for Epic, fully painted by Sienkiewicz.

But these were all in the future. Miller's move to California had cost more than he expected, and he was in debt, with all his committed projects many months from completion. Sitting in his bathtub, broke, three thousand miles from New York, he had an idea. "I thought, what if this happened to Matt Murdock? What if he lost everything?" Shortly afterward, Ralph Macchio called, telling him that Denny O'Neil, no longer getting along with Shooter, had left *Daredevil*. Miller told him his idea, and it was settled: he'd write *Daredevil* once again.

Chris Claremont was a decade into his *X-Men* tenure—not even Stan Lee had stayed on a title for ten years—and had seen artists come and go, but each departure and arrival had noticeable effects on his writing. After Dave Cockrum left to work on *The Futurians*—characters he would finally retain rights to, even if they'd never catch on—Paul Smith, a former animation artist, gave the *X-Men* an uncluttered, airy look that brought out Claremont's warmer, more playful side.† And so even as

---

* The *Daredevil: Love & War* graphic novel had begun as a two-issue fill-in for the regular *Daredevil* comic but was rejected as inappropriate for the monthly series.

† Cockrum had tried to work in this mode: "Kitty's Fairy Tale," in issue #153, had imagined Wolverine as a beer-guzzling Tasmanian Devil and Nightcrawler as a fuzzy-elf doll. Cockrum bristled when Claremont was credited for the issue's change of pace.

Claremont began shaking up the characters (Storm lost her powers, gave herself a Mohawk, and started to dress in leather; Cyclops quit; Wolverine was engaged and then jilted), Smith's sleek work made the soap-opera moments more palatable.

Once John Romita Jr. replaced Smith, though, the darker elements of *X-Men* gradually came to the fore. Lectures and debates between characters began to spill over pages. Kitty Pryde traveled to Japan and returned as a ninja assassin. Rachel Summers—the daughter of an alternate-timeline Scott Summers and Jean Grey—appeared from a dystopian future, an escaped slave burdened with a spiked collar and psychological problems. The fear and loathing that bombarded mutants became a central theme; the X-Men's old archenemies, the Brotherhood of Evil Mutants, became the National Security Council–sanctioned Freedom Force, charged with bringing renegade mutants into government custody. In one issue, Professor X was even the victim of a hate crime, attacked and left for dead by a group of college students. (When he woke up in the care of the subway-dwelling Morlocks, he found that he'd been dressed in bondage gear.)*

If *X-Men* was noticeably bleaker than ever before, it only proved that Chris Claremont, more than any other writer, had managed to retain control of the way his characters were portrayed, had refused to tailor his comics for an audience of eight-year-olds. If there was a mandate for a new mutant-related spin-off, the notoriously proprietary Claremont would take a deep breath, look at his schedule, and figure out a way to do it himself.

By the spring of 1985, though, Chris Claremont finally had to face the cracks in his kingdom. Artists Bob Layton and Jackson Guice, noticing that original X-Men members Angel, Iceman, and Beast were languishing in the low-selling *New Defenders*, and that Claremont had married

---

* According to Jim Shooter, Claremont had wanted to dress Professor X in "transvestite gear" for the story. "He had this thing for bondage and fetish," said Annie Nocenti. "He was always finding excuses to give the White Queen some kind of . . . the only thing with Chris was saying 'That's going too far.' He wanted to run a story line where Xavier wanted to wear women's clothes and I said, 'No fucking way.' There are certain things you do not do to heroes, if you want them to keep being heroes."

off Cyclops and sent him to Alaska, had suggested to Jim Shooter that the original team be reunited. Since Jean Grey was no longer alive, they'd need a different woman to balance things out—how about Dazzler, whose own title was about to be canceled? Together, in *X-Factor*, the five heroes would pose as freelance mutant-hunters—kind of a spin on *Ghostbusters*—with the aim of secretly aiding those very mutants.

And then John Byrne heard about the plan, and remembered an idea a fan had pitched to his old friend Roger Stern at a convention two years ago: a way to bring back Jean Grey. She had become Phoenix when the X-Men had crash-landed a space shuttle near Long Island; what if the woman who'd emerged from Jamaica Bay all those years ago—who'd been possessed by Mastermind, who'd committed cosmic genocide, who'd been incinerated on the moon—had not, in fact, been Jean Grey? What if the "Phoenix Force" had taken her shape, while Grey remained alive, in a kind of cocoon? What if somebody found that cocoon?

"It would really be a cheat to the readers to bring her back," Byrne had told an interviewer in the wake of Jean Grey's death, but now he'd changed his mind. He and Roger Stern passed the idea to Shooter, and plans for this new title, *X-Factor*, were adjusted. Byrne and Stern would lay the groundwork of Jean Grey's return in issues of *Fantastic Four* and *The Avengers*, respectively. Another tie-in event.

X-Men editor Ann Nocenti broke the news to Claremont on a Friday night, during a restaurant plotting session with artist Barry Smith. Claremont, in high dudgeon, raced for a pay phone, only to realize he couldn't remember Shooter's direct line. Nocenti refused to give him the number, though, and when he considered going back to the office to confront his editor in chief, she told him to sit down, order another drink, and relax. "If I had actually gone to see Shooter on Friday night," Claremont recalled, "I would have quit." *X-Factor* mangled Claremont's ride-into-the-sunset plans for Scott Summers and Madelyne Pryor, his Jean Grey–lookalike bride—instead, Summers deserted his wife and infant son to be with Jean Grey. Claremont would spend the entire weekend coming up with counterproposals for Monday, but Shooter would shoot them all down. The marketing potential far outweighed Claremont's artistic concerns. "By then," he said, "it had become too commercial, and the desire to make a buck had become paramount." Around the office, people began referring to *X-Factor* as *Chris-busters*.

Commerciality, though, had its rewards. Claremont spent May 1985 with Romita Jr. and Nocenti, doing a promotional tour through France, England, Spain, and Holland, conducting research for *X-Men* #200, which would be set in Paris and The Hague. They signed comics at events, but mostly enjoyed the fruits of expense accounts—visiting fancy restaurants, strip clubs, and museums.

And Claremont wrote at a furious clip. He'd come up with such a complicated narrative that a scorecard had to be printed on the "Bullpen Bulletins" page. "How to Read the X-Men and the New Mutants" directed fans in which order they should consume *New Mutants* #34, *X-Men* #199, *X-Men/Alpha-Flight Team-Up* #1 and #2, *New Mutants Special* #1, *X-Men Annual* #9, *X-Men* #200, and *New Mutants* #35. Since they didn't necessarily hit stands in that chronology, the complicated reading assignment was one more trying scavenger hunt in the Year of the Crossover. Claremont's best-selling corner of the Marvel Universe, stretching as fast as Marvel executives could read a balance sheet, had grown almost as complicated as *Secret Wars II*.

After returning to the States, Claremont took a look at how Byrne was handling the backstory of Jean Grey in *Fantastic Four* and petitioned Shooter for a chance to rewrite Byrne's two-page flashback sequence, which *X-Factor* penciler Jackson Guice then drew in his best faux John Byrne style. This was Shooter's chance to appease his star writer, still stinging from the way Jean Grey's return had been commanded, and even John Byrne didn't have enough clout to stop it.

The revocation bothered Byrne, a lot, especially since the plot had already been green-lighted by Shooter. If he couldn't call the shots in *Fantastic Four*, if Claremont was still making last-minute changes on a title he wasn't even writing, Byrne thought, perhaps it was time to reconsider his contract as an exclusive Marvel writer.

The relationship between Byrne and Shooter became increasingly tense. Recalled John Romita, "Shooter would come in and ask me, 'Do we want to take John Byrne off *Fantastic Four*'? I was very diplomatic with him; I wouldn't say 'You're crazy' or anything like that. I would just tell him 'Fantastic Four is selling very well, why would we change artists?' And then he would leave him on there. But if it wasn't the way he wanted things done, he would start to run it down and make changes." By the fall, word had leaked out: John Byrne, the most popular artist in the industry, was going over to DC to relaunch Superman. He planned to continue on Incredible Hulk and Fantastic Four for Marvel, too, but the story on everyone's lips was that the most eagerly awaited superhero comics of 1986 were John Byrne's Superman and Frank Miller's Batman, iconic DC characters as interpreted by once-loyal Marvel superstars.

Shooter was also making a lot of demands on Bob Layton and Jackson Guice, the creative team on X-Factor. They drew seven covers for the first issue, each rejected by Jim Shooter, until finally Walt Simonson came in to pinch hit. Then, in September 1985, two weeks before the shipping date, Layton and Guice were told to redo the entire contents of the double-sized issue, or else Shooter would find someone who could. Unfortunately for them, Hurricane Gloria was headed for New York City. They holed up in a Manhattan hotel room, working day and night even as the rest of the city shut down. As the hotel staff evacuated, a concierge placed a roll of masking tape in Guice's hands, asked him to tape up the windows of his room, and wished him luck.

Forty-five years earlier, Bill Everett, Carl Burgos, and a handful of other writers and artists had holed up at Everett's apartment for several days, setting up on tables, on floors, even in the bathtub, leaving only for food and liquor, so that they could deliver a huge, blowout Human Torch and Sub-Mariner battle issue. But where that sixty-four-page monster had been delivered in a spirit of celebration, X-Factor #1 felt more like a detention assignment.

Despite the hurricane, they made the deadline, but weeks later more problems arose. Shooter proved impossible to please. "We gave him the second issue," said X-Factor editor Mike Carlin, "and he wanted us to redo that one from scratch. I said, 'You know what, I'm not quitting Marvel, but I'm quitting this book. You should edit this yourself. You're the only one that knows what you want to have happen here.' And he goes, 'Alright, alright,' and he gave it to Bob Harras to do after that, and for the next six months, I edited books, but I was given things like Chuck Norris comics. I think by quitting *X-Factor* I got on his radar pretty heavily." A few months after Carlin's departure, Layton also left *X-Factor*, and Guice followed shortly afterward.

There were tensions elsewhere, too. John Byrne surprised Denny O'Neil, his *Incredible Hulk* editor, by submitting an issue consisting entirely of twenty-two full-page illustrations; O'Neil rejected it. Byrne, believing that it was Shooter's doing, contacted Jim Galton and protested. ("Who the hell is John Byrne?" an annoyed Galton asked Shooter, annoyed to be contacted by the company's number-one artist.)

Soon after that, O'Neil and Shooter's own conflicts came to a head, and O'Neil, the longest-tenured Marvel editor, requested a meeting with publisher Mike Hobson. "When Shooter heard about that meeting," said Bob Budiansky, "he dismissed Denny from staff."

Byrne, the self-described "company man" who was once regularly turning out three comics a month, was now only doing *Fantastic Four*— edited by Carlin, who had remained on the title even as he was saddled with assignments on low-prestige licensed comics like *Thundercats* and *He-Man*. Carlin now found himself unfortunately positioned between Byrne and Shooter, whose relationship had deteriorated since DC's *Superman* announcement. Byrne had felt that Claremont's rewriting of the Jean Grey flashback had been a way for Shooter to punish him for taking the *Superman* job. For months, according to Byrne, Shooter "continued to snipe at the *FF*, so I ultimately left the book just to spare Mike Carlin the constant barrage of nitpicks." With that final tie severed, Byrne's defection was complete. (Within months, Shooter would fire Mike Carlin. Carlin called up Denny O'Neil, now working at DC, and got a job as an assistant editor on John Byrne's *Superman*.)

And then, just as news about Byrne's departure got out, Frank Miller left *Daredevil* once again, along with artist David Mazzucchelli. They'd continue collaborating . . . at DC, for another *Batman* project.

In the course of a year, as Marvel watched its founding fathers Jack Kirby and Stan Lee feud in public, as John Byrne, Frank Miller, and Jim Starlin—the company's three most valued writer-artists—abruptly ceased work on projects, and as two editors stormed out of the building and over to the competition, morale hit an all-time low.

Jim Shooter, meanwhile, was busy creating something new.

The New Universe was the twenty-fifth anniversary launch that Shooter had proposed a few years back, and for which he'd been allotted $120,000. But now, as Sheldon Feinberg started shopping Marvel, the higher-ups repeatedly cut the start-up budget: first halved, then quartered, and finally eliminated altogether. By November 1985, Shooter had conscripted a motley crew of staffers and rookies to begin work on eight titles under the New Universe umbrella, the details of which were closely guarded. "The world outside your window" was the unofficial motto. These stories were to be about a world just like ours, in which the sudden ability to fly would truly carry a sense of wonder. Shooter himself called it "the Shooter-verse."

Eliot Brown was offered the job of editing half the line. Almost immediately, though, he ran into trouble getting the writers and artists to make deadlines. John Romita Jr. was unhappy that he'd left *X-Men* to work on the Jim Shooter–penned *Star Brand*; Archie Goodwin, who'd always been notoriously slow anyway, was busy tending to the Epic line; even the usually prompt Tom DeFalco fell behind. It was, said Brown, "a clusterfuck."

Brown wasn't the only one having difficulties. "[Shooter] started pulling creative teams together and forcing certain people on books that the editors might not have liked," said Bob Budiansky, who edited the New Universe's *Psi-Force*, a series about a team of paranormals. "A lot of the editorial decisions weren't met with agreement by the editors. Mark Texeira did a beautiful cover and Jim was upset because a character's shoelaces weren't clear. It wasn't like the cover was a close-up of the shoe; it was a full-figure shot. And he got very focused on that, to the point where he wanted the cover re-drawn. We fixed it, but it became emblematic of the things that were going on."

The first New Universe titles went on sale in July 1986 and sold an average of 150,000 copies, disappointing retailers across the country. By that time, Eliot Brown, too, had been fired from Marvel.

———

Stan Lee didn't know much about the New Universe. In fact, he didn't keep up with the Old Universe, the one he'd helped create. That summer, when Lee appeared on a panel with Jim Shooter at the Chicago Comic-Con, he was surprised to learn that, two years earlier, Mary Jane Watson had discovered Peter Parker's secret identity. An audience member asked if Peter Parker and Mary Jane would get married. Lee turned to Shooter and asked if he would allow it.

The crowd went wild.

Afterward, Lee and Shooter began to take the idea seriously. Circulation of the *Spider-Man* daily comic strip was down lately; a big event like this might give it a boost. They agreed to coordinate the wedding to occur simultaneously in the comic book and the newspaper strip. John Romita voiced his concern—he still remembered, after more than thirty years, how quickly *Li'l Abner* went downhill after Abner married Daisy Mae. Romita was ignored.

For the rest of the comics industry, 1986 was the annus mirabilis, the point at which the rest of the world started to afford the medium a little respect. Frank Miller's *Batman: The Dark Knight Returns* led the parade in the spring, with splashy *Rolling Stone* and *Spin* articles that mentioned the artist's recent return to *Daredevil*—but in passing, almost dismissively. How could Daredevil hope to compete with Batman in name recognition? And this new Batman had the novelties of jarring violence and a heavy-stock paper that screamed "art." The Miller profiles suggested a few other acceptably hip titles worth investigation, including Alan Moore's *Swamp Thing* (also DC) and Howard Chaykin's *American Flagg* (which Epic had tried, and failed, to acquire)—but nothing by Marvel. That summer, as the New Universe titles sat on shelves, John Byrne sat down with Jane Pauley on the *Today* show to promote *Superman*.

Amid celebration of its twenty-fifth anniversary, and intent on finding someone to buy the company, Marvel Comics attempted to control spin. As Viacom and Western Publishing sniffed around, Marvel VP Mike Hobson released a public statement on the matter of Kirby's artwork controversy, which blamed the holdups on "a series of letters from Mr. Kirby's attorneys during the past four years asserting claims of copyright ownership," and asserted that Kirby had demanded "credit as sole creator of certain of Marvel's characters, including Spider-Man, the Fantastic Four and the Hulk." On July 24, the television news program *20/20* provided a fifteen-minute overview of the House of Ideas, including interviews with Stan Lee and Jim Shooter.* Praising Lee as the creator of the Fantastic Four, Spider-Man, the Hulk, the Silver Surfer, Thor, and Doctor Strange, the program made no mention of Steve Ditko or Jack Kirby.

Frank Miller continued to speak out for Kirby at every opportunity, as did many of the 150 industry professionals—including Steve Englehart, Steve Gerber, Don Heck, Doug Moench, Bill Sienkiewicz, Roy Thomas, Marv Wolfman, Superman co-creator Jerry Siegel, and future *Simpsons* creator Matt Groening—who'd signed a petition for the unconditional return of the artwork. After Jim Starlin arranged a brief, impromptu meeting between the Kirbys and Shooter at the San Diego Comic-Con, there were whispers that a settlement was on the horizon, but that hope dwindled quickly. Although much of the comics audience was outraged, there was little mainstream media coverage of Kirby's plight. "The fact that 30,000 fans were pissed off didn't mean anything," said Tom DeFalco. "Nobody wants bad p.r., but the only people aware of the press were the comic book people. The rest of the company was not really paying attention to it. The lawyers weren't really running up to the president saying, 'We're doing this, we're doing that.' In the fishbowl it meant something, outside of the fishbowl . . . I don't think most people were aware of it."

There was another, more public failing for Marvel to deal with. The same August weekend that Shooter met with the Kirbys, Universal Pictures released its adaptation of *Howard the Duck*. "If the movie is as good as the trailers we'll be in business," Steve Gerber told an interviewer. "I'm keeping my fingers crossed." But despite its $37 million budget—plus an additional $8 million spent on promotion—it bombed miserably, and received a critical drubbing that embarrassed everyone involved. Within

---

* In an awkward bit of B-roll footage, Jim Shooter first appears pacing the Bullpen, then towering above one frantic artist, asking, "Are we going to be done today?"

weeks, there were rumors that Universal executives Frank Price and Sidney Sheinberg had exchanged blows in their offices, each blaming the other for the $45 million failure.

Stan Lee, who'd waited for two decades to see a big-budget Marvel adaptation conquer Hollywood, would have to keep waiting. The prospects of the front-runners—*Spider-Man* and *Captain America*, each in development with Cannon Pictures—were dim. The first draft of the *Spider-Man* screenplay had been, perplexingly, about a man who turns into a tarantula; Galton himself had deemed the *Captain America* script, cowritten by *Death Wish* director Michael Winner, "bloody awful." And although Marvel didn't know it at the time, Cannon itself was headed for trouble with the Securities and Exchange Commission.

Finally, in November 1986, word reached Marvel that the company had been sold. "I had a little office with a desk that had a broken leg that was kind of propped up," said Tom DeFalco. "And I'm proofreading a comic, and this guy comes in, and he starts criticizing the desk and the office décor and everything, and I'm thinking he's an interior designer. I look up at him and I say, 'Listen, I don't know who you are, but I've really got to get this book out to the printer.' And he stands up with this big 'Hi, I'm Bob Rehme! I'm president of New World!'"

Marvel's new owner, New World Pictures, was Hollywood, through and through: in 1983, Harry Sloan and Larry Kuppin had purchased Roger Corman's mean-and-lean production company and film distributor, and aggressively expanded it into a multimedia concern via loans and advances, buying their way onto television (they had shows on every major network), setting up a syndication division, and releasing thirty feature films a year. Sloan and Kuppin were lawyers who doubled as savvy entertainment-industry insiders, hardball players who'd helped to pioneer the concept of lead actors walking off the set to hold out for better pay. At New World they brought in the smiley and smooth Robert Rehme, the former head of marketing and distribution at Universal. Sloan, Kuppin, and Rehme were excited about the synergistic opportunities that Marvel presented; Sloane, in particular, was fond of saying that he wanted to be a "mini-Disney."

Stan Lee was excited about the Hollywood connection, too, and he shared it with his readers. "The young, hip, fun-loving guys who run New World dig Marvel Comics as much as you do! That's why they bought us! They want to make some real dynamite movies and TV shows based on all your favorite characters. . . . I don't wanna sound like I'm trying to snow you, so I'll just mention two of their latest smashes—the movie *Soul Man* and the TV series *Sledge Hammer*. 'Nuff said?" For Lee, the appeal was that Marvel would not merely license but also self-produce, and that he'd have some creative control once again.

But once again, he would learn, Marvel's fate lay in the hands of people who knew nothing about comic books. Out in Los Angeles, as soon as the sale was made, Rehme had summoned his vice president of marketing and proudly told him, "We just bought Superman."

The vice president was perplexed. Warner Bros. was selling DC Comics?

"No, no, no—we bought Marvel!" said Rehme.

"No, Bob," the vice president corrected him. "We bought Spider-Man."

Rehme raced out of his office. "Holy shit," he said. "We gotta stop this. Cannon has the Spider-Man movie!"

Jim Shooter, too, was optimistic about the sale, and he saw the change in management as his chance to get out from underneath Galton, with whom he was increasingly in conflict. "When New World came," said one editor, "Shooter right away wanted to talk to Bob Rehme, hang out with Bob Rehme, and kind of make his play." Immediately he began strategizing about how to cut back production levels, which he saw as a strain on the editorial department. "We were doing like fifty titles a month," said John Romita. "The main titles would suffer, because we were spending so much time and effort on comics that were second-rate. Every time comic companies expanded to too many titles, they generally cut their own throats. Shooter and I agreed, 'When we first get together with New World, we've got to tell them we want to cut down to 24 or 25 books, and do the best job we can.' They sent two representatives," Romita said. "One was a lawyer, one was a producer. Shooter told them, 'We'd like to cut back on the amount of titles—we're treading water, and the best books are not getting the talent and attention they deserve.' The guy listened calmly, and after Shooter finished his presentation, they said, 'We hate to disappoint you, but our plan is quite different. We're going to add ten titles to the schedule.' And the air went out of the room. Shooter and I looked at each other like we wanted to commit suicide. Not only were they going to create ten titles, they wanted to create the names and the premises for the ten titles. That was the beginning of the end for Shooter; it was probably the most traumatic period of my life. They sent in logos that looked like they were done by amateurs. They sent in characters that looked like they were out of some junior high school kid's sketchbook."

Shooter put on a good face, and he and Romita tried to make a go of it. But the writers and artists despised the mandated titles, despised the costume designs that New World told them to follow, and Romita's own attempts to make improvements were met with refusal. "It was a nightmare," he said. "They were so out of touch, and so lacking in taste."

Nonetheless, when it came time for Shooter to write a state-of-the-company memo to Rehme, it wasn't New World that he blamed. Instead, he described in scathing detail his opinion of Marvel's executives, and insisting that he be put in charge of New York operations. Before sending it off, he read the memo aloud to a room of editors. Two of the editors, sensing that Shooter was on the verge of making an enormous mistake, locked eyes, sprung out of their chairs, and yelled in unison, "Don't mail that letter!" The rest of the room quickly crowded around Shooter and convinced him not to act rashly. He relented.*

A few weeks later, Tom DeFalco was headed to the West Coast to meet about movie adaptation for New World's *House II: Second Story.* "Jim says to me, 'You're going to New World? I have to go out for a management meeting, why don't we fly out together?' We go out, have dinner. The next morning we're driving into New World, and Jim turns to me and says, 'Oh by the way, I did send that letter. And you and I have a meeting with Bob Rehme this morning.' Just as he said that, we hit the hump of the New World parking garage. I turned to him and said, 'What?' He explained to me that he was crashing the management meeting, and going

---

* Later, in interviews, Shooter would state that the executives were cashing out the pension fund and trying to retroactively eliminate the royalties, and that he'd screamed threats of a class action lawsuit in the hallway outside Galton's office.

there to explain to Rehme and give an ultimatum that basically unless they put him in charge of the company, everyone was going to quit. I said, 'Everybody's gonna quit? How many people know about this?' He said, 'You and me.'

"We got out of the car, went up the elevator, and into the reception room, he goes, 'Jim Shooter and Tom DeFalco to see Bob Rehme.' I turned to the receptionist and said, 'No. Jim Shooter to see Bob Rehme. Tom DeFalco to see publicity.' We were separated, I never heard from him or saw him again until we were both back in New York."

Shooter and DeFalco had their own disagreements. DeFalco had begun challenging some of Shooter's calls for redrawing and recoloring various comics, not realizing that the arguments were carrying out to the Bullpen for all to hear, or that editors were gathering in the office next to Shooter's and listening through the heating system. Then DeFalco would lose the argument, and have to go out and play the role of hatchet man.

"It was like there was this thundercloud hovering over the office," according to editor Carl Potts. "And you knew lightning was going to strike. You didn't know when, but you knew somebody was gonna get fried." Rewriting increased to unprecedented levels. "The watershed moment," said Ann Nocenti, "was when Shooter said every single comic had to have a 'can't-must' moment: *I am not a thief . . . I don't want to steal. But I must steal because my grandmother is starving.* Every comic had to have that in the first three pages. Literally, a panel where the superhero had to say, 'I can't steal—but I must, for my grandmother.' Or, 'I can't kill Mephisto—but I must, because he has my soul.' He was sending comics back to the Bullpen to have the 'can't-must' panel squeezed in, in the middle of the page."

"We would put together the book and it would have to be signed off on by the editor in chief before it could go to print," said Terry Kavanagh, Nocenti's assistant editor. "And then he'd come in with his comments. They could be criticisms or compliments. In some cases he'd say fix this, in some cases he'd say make sure not to repeat this. That graduated, not all that slowly, to him coming in and yelling about things not being right, and being angry. And then, him coming in and yelling, 'This isn't right, do it better,' and then eventually, him coming in and yelling, 'This isn't right and you knew it wasn't right, and you did it anyway.' And then finally, 'This isn't right and you knew it wasn't right, and you did it on purpose just to drive me crazy, just like all the other editors.' And he would do this very loudly; he got very close to her face and was very red in the face and I would've been scared if I were her."

"He liked to say he'd put together the best comics editorial team ever," said Potts. "Then he shifted to, everybody was clueless. What flipped that switch?"

By the end of 1986, Stan Lee's plan to marry Spider-Man had gotten New World's interest. Plans stormed ahead on promoting it as a live event the following summer. But Sal Buscema had a blowup with Shooter after the editor in chief sent detailed instructions on how to draw the special issue—including references on how to draw human anatomy—and quit. When a less established freelancer was offered the gig, he took it—because he'd heard that Shooter was going to blackball the next person who refused him.

At the end of March, a group of freelancers and editors decided to demonstrate an organized complaint. Walter Simonson, Louise Simonson, and Michael Higgins knocked on office doors, gathering editors—"like villagers with torches," in the words of one staff member—and made their way toward Jim Shooter's office.

When he heard voices stirring in the hallway, Tom DeFalco, tired of all the arguments and ready to leave comics for good, was sitting at his desk, on the phone, negotiating salary and moving costs for a job on the West Coast. He tried to settle the crowd that had amassed in the hallway.

Standing by Shooter's secretary's desk, he put his foot up to block people from streaming between the desk and the office wall. Walter Simonson stormed past, while others went behind DeFalco, around the desk. They stopped at Shooter's door. It was shut. "At one point," DeFalco recalled, "Mike Hobson showed up and said, 'What's going on?' Everybody said, 'We want to confront Shooter.' 'You guys want to talk to Shooter? Okay, let's go.' And everybody went in."

"We need to talk to you," Simonson said, opening Shooter's door.

"I'm in the middle of a meeting with Mark and Ralph," Shooter told him.

Everyone barreled in anyway, as Mark Gruenwald and Ralph Macchio, whose meeting had already been a tense one, began slouching downward in their chairs, so far down that their heads were invisible. DeFalco stood behind Shooter, ready to go down with his captain.

Bodies packed into the office. Assistants crowded around the door, or gathered in the office next door, listening through the heating duct as editors took their turns confronting their boss with complaints. Hobson looked on, amused, as Shooter turned red, and challenged the accusations.

"I felt at any moment Jim might just eat me," said one staffer. "I said, 'Oh God, he might just start gnawing on my bones.' Even though, I have to stress, he'd never even raised his voice to me."

On Saturday, April 4, John Byrne hosted a party at his house in Connecticut, attended by several Marvel staffers and freelancers. In the backyard, a suit was stuffed with unsold issues of New Universe titles, a picture of Shooter's face was affixed on the head, and the editor in chief of Marvel Comics was burned in effigy. "In retrospect," says one of the staffers who was there, "it's a little macabre, a little offensive, probably overkill. But it seemed that everybody needed it at that time. It was becoming increasingly oppressive. We all knew how to do our jobs well; we all knew how to do comic books. We were putting together the best comic books we could. But now, every stage of the way, when you'd be talking to writers about how to tell the story and you'd say, okay, we know 'this is the right way to tell the story,' now we had to look and see 'What are the things that Jim might go insane over?' It was really an unnecessary step to making comic books. And probably in some cases didn't serve the stories and made for weaker stories and issues. Because our sole focus should've been getting the best comic books out. Instead it became getting out the best comic books that we could get past Jim. And in some sense we were probably able to rationalize that it really was our moral obligation—because we all took ourselves a little too seriously—that in order to make the best comics for our fans, Jim had to be out of the equation."

"He had helped build Marvel into a powerful juggernaut," said Tom DeFalco, "and then decided that he didn't like the way it worked anymore, and that it needed to be completely rebuilt instantly. And you know, juggernauts don't get rebuilt instantly."

The New World owners liked Shooter and couldn't figure out why he wasn't happier, but they only knew how to deal with temperamental actors and film directors. Couldn't they just send him a fruit basket, or offer him a more important-sounding title? But when a videotape of the effigy made its way to California, just before Shooter's contract negotiations were about to begin, it was clear to New World that the commander had lost control of the soldiers.

On April 15, Bob Layton and David Michelinie came into the Marvel offices to meet with Mark Gruenwald and Shooter about redesigns for an Iron Man costume. When they brought the pages into Shooter's office, Shooter calmly told them his changes wouldn't matter. He'd just gotten the news that he would no longer be the editor in chief.

Gruenwald stopped by Macchio's office, mimed a knife across the throat, then put a finger to his lips, signaling to be quiet. But word traveled fast, with CompuServe messages relayed quickly to Chris Claremont and Walt Simonson. "Ding-dong," one of the messages read: "the witch is dead."

PART IV

Boom and Bust

(15)

WHEN JIM GALTON AND MIKE HOBSON HAD TAKEN TOM DEFALCO OUT TO lunch to tell him they wanted him to replace Jim Shooter as editor in chief, he'd balked. "You guys are crazy," DeFalco told them. "Find a way to make up with Shooter." Unbeknownst to them, DeFalco was still hoping for another week or two to finish negotiating that job on the West Coast. "I always assumed that as the number-two guy, when they decided to lop off his head, mine would go too," he said, years later. "It never once occurred to me that they would keep me." News that DeFalco was being promoted reached his prospective employers on the West Coast, and they withdrew the job offer, sure that they wouldn't be able to match the new salary.

Now that he was at Marvel to stay, DeFalco's first task was to try to restore a sense of order in an office that had divided between the pro-Shooter and anti-Shooter factions. In an angry and profane open letter to the editorial staff, veteran freelancer Vince Colletta painted the former editor in chief as an unappreciated martyr. "He gave you a title, respectability, power and even a credit card that you used and abused. He made you the highest payed Editors in the history of the business. He protected you against all that would tamper with your rights, your power and your pocketbook. . . . The roof over your head, the clothes on your back, the car you drive and the trinkets you buy for your blind wives and girlfriends you owe to the Pittsburgh kid."

A boom-voiced Noo Yawka, DeFalco might have seemed an unusual choice to calm the waters. But he was well liked, and the Marvel troops considered him as one of them. Slowly, the hijinks and pranks returned to the offices: One assistant's desk drawers were lined with plastic and filled with water and goldfish. Hundred-dollar bills were cast on nearly invisible fishing lines down ten stories to tempt passersby on East Twenty-Seventh Street.

DeFalco also managed to skirt one of the greatest thorns that had stuck in Shooter's side: the controversy over the nonreturn of Jack Kirby's artwork. Jim Galton had been confident of Marvel's legal standing, thanks to agreements Kirby had signed in 1966 and 1972, and had seen no reason to kowtow to popular opinion on the matter. "Galton's attitude was, 'Why is anybody wasting any time with this? If Kirby's gonna try to sue, let him try to sue!'" said DeFalco. Only weeks after Shooter departed, though, Marvel changed course, after Galton told the lawyers to put an end to the holdout. Within weeks, the list of eighty-eight pieces of artwork that had been dangled before Kirby grew to an inventory of more than two thousand pages—only a fraction of what he'd drawn, but a sizable, and lucrative, stash nonetheless. The long ordeal had come to a close, just like that, with a simple command.

Shortly afterward, on the occasion of his seventieth birthday, Jack Kirby was a telephone guest on the New York radio station WBAI. After the interviewer asked about working as part of the apparently fervent and joyous "Merry Marvel Marching Society" era Bullpen, Kirby responded flatly: "I didn't consider it merry. In those days, it was a professional-type thing, you turned in your ideas and you got your wages and you took them home. It was a very simple affair. It's nothing that could be dramatized, or glorified, or glamorized in any way. . . . I created the situation, and I analyzed them, I did them panel by panel, and I did everything but put the words in the balloons." But, Jack, said the interviewer, what about those legendary story conferences with you and Stan, livening up the office? "It wasn't like that at all," he said. "It may have been like that after I shut the door and went home."

And then the radio host introduced a surprise call-in guest: Stan Lee. "I want to wish Jack a happy birthday!" the familiar voice sounded over the airwaves. "This is a hell of a coincidence, I'm in New York, and I was tuning in the radio and there I hear him, talking about Marvel, and I said I might as well call him and not let this occasion go by without saying, many happy returns, Jack!"

Kirby jumped right in: "Well, Stanley, I want to thank you for calling, and I hope you're in good health and I hope you stay in good health."

Lee praised Kirby's artwork. "Nobody could convey emotion and drama the way you did."

"Well, thank you for helping me keep that style, and helping me to evolve all that," Kirby said. "I was never sorry for it, Stanley. It was a great experience for me." And then, after five years of not speaking, Kirby told Lee that he respected him.

After ten more minutes of reminiscences and niceties, Stan slipped in an "I'll say this: every word of dialogue in those scripts was mine." Uncomfortable laughter from the studio. "Every story."

KIRBY: I can tell you that I wrote a few lines myself above every panel.

LEE: They weren't printed in the book! Jack isn't wrong by his own lights, because, answer me truthfully—

KIRBY: I wasn't allowed to write—

LEE:—Did you ever read one of the stories after it was finished? I don't think you did! I don't think you ever read one of my stories. I think you were always busy drawing the next one. You never read the book when it was finished. . . .

KIRBY:—my own dialogue, Stanley. And I think that's the way people are. Whatever was written, it was the action I was interested in.

LEE: I know, and look, Jack, nobody has more respect for you than I do, and you know that, but I don't think you ever felt that the dialogue was very important. And I think you felt, anybody can put the dialogue together, it's what I'm drawing that matters. And maybe you're right, I don't agree with it, but maybe you're right.

KIRBY: I'm only trying to say, I think that the human being is very important. If one man is writing and drawing and doing a strip, it should come from an individual. I believe you should have the opportunity to do the entire thing yourself.

When asked to make closing statements, Lee went first: "Jack has made a tremendous mark on American culture, if not on world culture, and I think he should be incredibly proud and pleased with himself, and I want to wish him all the best, him and his wife Roz, and his family, and I hope that ten years from now, I'll be in some town somewhere listening to a tribute to his eightieth birthday, and I hope I'll have an opportunity to call at that time and wish him well then, too. Jack, I love ya."

"Well, the same here, Stan," said Kirby. "But, uh . . . uh . . . yeah. Thank you very much, Stan."

Dead air, for a moment.

"Warren, are you there?" Kirby asked the cohost. "Uh . . . you can understand now, what it was really like back then."

Tom DeFalco, flailing at first, had urged Mark Gruenwald to accept the editor in chief position instead, but Gruenwald begged off. So Gruenwald was appointed as DeFalco's executive editor, and the two of them sat down and made a five-year plan for Marvel's expansion: just as there had been a whole line of X-Men titles, soon there would be an expanded line of Avengers titles, and Spider-Man titles, and so on. If someone thought four Spider-Man titles was too many, DeFalco had a quick answer: *Not for someone who really likes Spider-Man, it's not.* Now, every time a new super-team was introduced, its individual members would spin off into their own solo titles.

Gruenwald would be left to sort out the ways that all the stories wove together. In the 1970s, before he'd even worked at Marvel, Gruenwald obsessively catalogued the continuity of Marvel's story lines in pseudo-academic self-published journals. Now he kept lists and charts on his walls to manage the traffic of the overarching Marvel Universe narrative. "If you wanted a Spider-Man villain, you had to check with the Spider-Man office," DeFalco said. "They were supposed to pull out a chart on the next bunch of issues and say, 'We have no plans for Electro.' Or, 'We have a plan for him in our May issue, and he's allergic to hamburgers. If you're going to have him come out in your April issue, you should at least show a sensitivity to hamburgers.'"

DeFalco was not immediately given a vice president title, which Jim Shooter had held, and which would limit the amount of clout he'd have in any disagreements about publishing strategy. But DeFalco was happy to expand anyway; he'd never had much use for precious worries about brand dilution. He was a throw-it-at-the-wall-and-see-what-sticks kind of guy, determined to push the limits of both the marketplace and the creative staff. "Retailers will always tell you you're publishing too much; wholesalers will tell you there's no room on the racks, you can't publish anything more," he said. "You've got to force everybody to do the work."

Editors were put on a royalty plan, which helped to ease their pain—and helped to encourage commercial thinking. Three-part stories, continued between the three different Spider-Man titles, began to crop up, with the intention of testing the market limits. Yet another X-Men title was needed, so Chris Claremont pitched the idea of moving Nightcrawler and Kitty Pryde to England, where they would become part of a new team called Excalibur. Multi-title crossovers, which had popped up here and there since *Secret Wars II*, would soon begin to take place every several months.*

There was one notable instance of belt-tightening—in the spring of 1987, the mediocre-selling New Universe, Shooter's one year-old baby, was unceremoniously cut in half. One of the surviving four titles was Jim Shooter's *Star Brand*; editor Howard Mackie called John Byrne and asked him if he'd want to take it over. It was an inspired choice: only months earlier, in an issue of DC Comics' *Legends*, Byrne had drawn a remarkably Shooter-like character named Sunspot. "From this day forward," Sunspot declared, "I will show you all how power is meant to be used! I will remake this sorry world in my own image!" Then, just in case anyone missed the reference to Shooter, the character boasted,

* "Originally we weren't going to do a big crossover the following year," said Louise Simonson, "but 'Mutant Massacre' sold so well that Shooter told us to do another. That became 'Fall of the Mutants' and the next year was 'Inferno.' I think a lot of people wanted a play in that one."

"I wield the ultimate power—the power to create a New Universe!"* before shooting himself in the foot.

Star Brand was one of the company's lowest-selling books, but Byrne agreed to return to Marvel for the chance to put his own stamp on Shooter's most autobiographical creation. Immediately, he conceived a story line in which the Shooter stand-in character, Ken Connell, destroyed the city of Pittsburgh—Shooter's hometown.

Other exiled freelancers made their returns to the company. Editor Mike Higgins, a Deadhead who'd been a fan of Marvel's 1970s head trips, reached out to as many Shooter enemies as he could—including Steve Gerber, Doug Moench, and Gene Colan—and offered them work on a new title called *Marvel Weekly*. By late 1987, everyone from Marv Wolfman to Paul Gulacy to Don McGregor to Don Heck was getting the first calls they'd had from Marvel in years. The idea was that each issue would feature a rotation of four serials that revived cult characters like Man-Thing and Shang-Chi. They'd be staggered so that if one character's story line concluded in an issue, the other three would end with cliffhangers—so that at no time would a reader feel a sense of closure.

By the time the first issue was published—almost a year later—the title had changed to *Marvel Comics Presents*, the publication schedule had been scaled back to every other week, and Higgins had left the company. The front covers featured not Shang-Chi or Man-Thing but Wolverine, whose ever-growing popularity guaranteed brisk sales.

By now, Marvel determined to introduce a regular *Wolverine* solo title as well. Chris Claremont had just launched *Excalibur* when he was informed of the plans. He complained to DeFalco about the integrity of the character, and about the threat of dilution, but the editor in chief would have none of it. Wolverine was his own franchise now, one that had become too big to contain. The series would happen with or without Claremont. After twelve years, the idea of someone else determining the character's fate was unthinkable, so once again Claremont rolled up his sleeves and got to work.

---

* This issue, *Legends #5*, was scripted by another Marvel expatriate, Len Wein.

"New World didn't want to be in the comic book business," said one for-mer employee, "but you couldn't throw the baby out with the bathwater." What the company really hoped to do was capitalize on the multiple-platform potential of intellectual property. A luncheon was held at the '21' Club to promote the idea of a Spider-Man cartoon; plans began for a $300,000 Spider-Man Macy's Thanksgiving Day Parade float; and the media was alerted that Spider-Man and Mary Jane Watson would be married in a ceremony at Shea Stadium, just before the world-champion New York Mets took the field.*

Officiating at home plate on that Saturday night was Stan Lee, pleased to be at the center of a sellout crowd of 55,000, for an event that was covered by *Good Morning America* and *Entertainment Tonight*. Lee was thrilled that New World was exploiting the Marvel characters in ways that Cadence never had.

After New World tried, and failed, to purchase the Spider-Man film rights from Cannon, the company shifted to a strategy of producing sixty-five half-hours of X-Men animation, which could be sold as first run or syndication, and then exploited through licensing and merchan-dising. For New World, the Marvel characters provided an opportunity to expand in ways never possible with low-budget horror movies like *Hellraiser*. "Marvel represented a beachhead into that younger market that Clive Barker didn't have," said Rusty Citron, then the vice president of marketing. "You're not going to put Pinhead onto Saturday morning television."

Plans commenced for a Marvel retail venture at shopping centers across the country, developed in consultation with the team behind Canada's colossal West Edmonton Mall, and modeled after the recently launched Disney Store: every muraled store space would include back rooms for birthday parties; merchandise was on wheels, to create "different spatial

---

* In the 1980s, Marvel couldn't help but brush up against New York City's cocaine culture. By sheer chance, the Spider-Man wedding at Shea ended up on the night of Dwight Gooden's return from rehab; a reception afterward was held at the recently opened but already infamous Tunnel club, which had weeks earlier been the site of filming for the *Bright Lights, Big City* adaptation.

representations" for various products and characters; a comic book rack would sell every Marvel title.

But the ambition and aggression of the company—which changed its name from New World Pictures to the more sweeping New World Entertainment—soon hit the limits of reality. Its film revenues were down, and money was tied up in television production just as the syndication market was collapsing. New World sought synergy within the marketplace of children's entertainment, but bids to take over Kenner and Mattel were both unsuccessful. After six months of planning, the New World board voted down the $1 million budget necessary to move ahead with the Marvel Store project.

New World continued its attempts to develop films based on Marvel characters, although the company's understanding of the properties was haphazard at best. A flood of scripts that had been developed at other studios and died—*Doctor Strange* by Bob Gale, *The X-Men* by Roy Thomas and Gerry Conway—were optimistically resubmitted to New World, but the executives who'd confused Spider-Man and Superman still weren't sure what they were looking at. "They tended to look down on the titles, gravitating toward projects that made fun of the medium," said William Rabkin, a former comic-store clerk who was evaluating scripts for the company. Rabkin boldly fired off a note to his boss. ("You've just bought Alaska. You need to dig below the surface and find out what's there.") Within days, New World's head of production asked him to make a list of B- and C-level Marvel properties that could be fast-tracked and made on the cheap in South America.* Boaz Yakin, a twenty-one-year-old NYU graduate, called up New World personally, set up a meeting with a New World executive, and pitched a movie about the Punisher, who had by now emerged in the action-movie 1980s as a fan favorite. "He didn't know what the fuck the Punisher was," Yakin said, even though the character

---

* As reward for his effort, Rabkin was allowed to submit his own script for the character of his choosing. He wrote a Mexico-set western starring Blade, the vampire hunter who was part of the supporting cast of Marv Wolfman and Gene Colan's *Tomb of Dracula*, and who'd since faded into obscurity. Although there were meetings with Richard Roundtree to star, the project never got off the ground.

was by now the star of two ongoing comic titles. Nonetheless, Yakin's script, written in ten days, zoomed into production.

Lee continued pitching characters he'd co-created a quarter-century earlier. "Stan Lee loved Ant-Man beyond all reason, and nobody ever gave a damn," said Rabkin. "He was always on about Ant-Man; he wanted an Ant-Man script in the worst way. I had been arguing against Ant-Man because, let's face it, he can shrink down, go through a keyhole, and look at secret papers in a desk drawer and that's it. It's pretty boring. But we're sitting around the table, and Stan is pitching Ant-Man, and Bob Rehme, who ran all New World, comes in. Bob was this energetic wild guy. He never actually opened a door; he would just *vroop!* through it like the Tasmanian Devil. He comes into the room, and says, 'Marvel meeting! What's going on?'"

Lee said, "We were just talking about Ant-Man!"

"What's that?"

"He can shrink down like . . . this!"

Rehme thought for a minute. Disney was about to make *Teenie Weenies*. If New World rushed *Ant-Man* into production, no one would ever know who had the idea first.

"That's brilliant!" Rehme said.

Vroop! He was out of the room, and *Ant-Man* went into development. *Teenie Weenies* was eventually released as *Honey, I Shrunk the Kids*.

Although Lee had a pleasant working relationship with Rehme, it was clearer than ever that he wasn't going to be able to call the shots when it came to movies. Even Jim Galton, in his reserved, old-publishing-world manner, could never engage with the Hollywood aggression of Sloane, Kuppin, and Rehme. That fell to Joe "the Squid" Calamari, a longtime Cadence executive who'd been hired out of law school by Sheldon Feinberg and who had now become very interested in seeing movie deals happen. To those at New World, Calamari's ambition and aggression made him the lead voice at Marvel.

Stan Lee, now in his mid-sixties, had behind him twenty years of dreaming of seeing his creations on the big screen, still to no avail. "Stan's not in the loop, because he's not a player; he's not a partner," said one

New World executive. "He wasn't a vote. But he was like a pit bull. He just didn't want to walk away."

Lee would outlast them all, though—New World was in trouble. "In retrospect," said Mike Hobson, years later, "it was shocking that Marvel had sold themselves to such a fly-by-night outfit as New World." The studio's movies were bombing at the box office, its stock was plummeting, and, on top of that, in the aftermath of the market crash of 1987, its Wall Street investments had tanked. The company retained the junk-bond kingpin Drexel Burnham Lambert to help it restructure its staggering debt, and put on a brave face as it rebuffed purchase offers for Marvel Comics, its only profitable holding. But by the summer of 1988, the writing was on the wall. In July, as cameras in Australia were about to roll on *The Punisher*, New World put Marvel Comics on sale.

The winning bidder was Revlon chairman Ronald O. Perelman, who had set up Compact Video, a former division of Technicolor, as a shell corporation.* Wall Street had wondered for months what major brand name would be swallowed by the nebulous void of Compact, which had sat quietly since the spring like an open trunk, or an empty casket. The $82.5 million paid for Marvel was, for Sloan and Kuppin, a nice return on its $46 million investment of only two years before. For Wall Street, it was a shock. Ron Perelman, the man who'd bid more than $4 billion for Gillette, was now turning his attention to . . . comic books?

One magazine article outlined the Perelman strategy like this: "find an undervalued company, buy it with junk bond financing, sell the inessential product lines to recoup most of the purchase price, and return the core to profitability." It was, in a way, just the steroidal 1980s version of the Perfect Film or Cadence model. But Marvel, Perelman knew, had a potential to be a "mini-Disney in terms of intellectual property," ripe for exploitation and profit.

Perelman himself was like some kind of Frankensteinian amalgam of

---

* Perelman edged out a competing bid of $81 million from a group of investors led by former Allman Brothers manager Steve Massarsky and, to the surprise of many, Jim Shooter. Soon afterward, Massarsky and Shooter would form their own comic publisher, Valiant/Voyager.

past Marvel owners, sometimes to an eerie extent. Martin Goodman met his wealthy wife-to-be on a cruise ship; so had Perelman. Martin Ackerman had an East Side headquarters that he dubbed "The Townhouse"; so had Perelman. Sheldon Feinberg had made his name as CFO at Revlon; twenty years later, Perelman gained fame for his hostile takeover of Revlon. Like all the others, Perelman was a short, Jewish, cigar-chomping mogul. The difference was that Perelman *owned* a cigar company, only one of many holdings in his personal $300 million portfolio. His pockets were deep enough that, once he'd picked Marvel from the bones of New World, he would return months later and buy New World, too.

Because he was the head of Revlon, the Marvel staff quickly dubbed Perelman "the lipstick guy." When he first visited the Marvel offices, he was escorted around to different departments by a blond, masked staff member dressed as Spider-Woman. During the tour, he asked one editor to see some of the highest-selling comics that were being worked on. "I pulled out some beautiful pages of *Uncanny X-Men* by Barry Smith," the editor said. "He couldn't even look at them. I knew: *This guy does not like comics.*"

Stan Lee's own initial impressions of Perelman and his firm, the Andrews Group, were undoubtedly boosted by a meeting with Perelman's number two, Bill Bevins. Bevins was all business—a well-groomed, impeccably dressed workaholic who'd met Perelman at the Predator's Ball junk-bond conferences hosted by Michael Milken of Drexel Burnham Lambert. "We exchanged pleasantries for a few minutes," Lee recalled, "and then, unexpectedly, he asked what my annual income was at Marvel. After I told him, he looked at me thoughtfully for a minute or two and then, in the calmest, most matter-of-fact way, he told me that henceforth I'd be earning approximately triple that amount."

Marvel's publishing business was booming, and expanding ever more rapidly; not only were new titles continually popping up, but the bestselling *The Uncanny X-Men* and *Amazing Spider-Man* had each moved to a twice-a-month summer schedule. DeFalco and Gruenwald began looking back into Marvel's past for new-series fodder; the economics of the direct market, they reasoned, would allow room for titles that appealed to a dedicated, if smaller, audience. They'd initiate the returns of 1970s-vintage characters like Guardians of the Galaxy, Ghost Rider, Deathlok, and Nova—the last of which was reintroduced as a member of *New Warriors*, a market-research-generated comic about teenage superheroes.

Incentive checks were growing for writers, artists, and now editors, many of whom were enjoying a renewed sense of power now that Shooter had departed. There were still, occasionally, conflicts over control of characters: Steve Englehart was fired from *West Coast Avengers* (for refusing to include Iron Man in the title); months later, he was fired from the *Fantastic Four* (for refusing to include Mr. Fantastic and the Invisible Girl) and *Silver Surfer*. Englehart claimed that DeFalco was instituting a "plan to end innovation across the line." DeFalco said he was just backing his editors.

DeFalco had seen firsthand what happened to morale when the editorial staff was divested of responsibility. But his management style was about more than just taking their side in an argument; he felt that the editors needed to be accountable caretakers, protecting the legacy of the grand narrative and keeping the company's best interests in mind.

Because Marvel still had the characters that everyone clamored to write and draw, and the royalties that everyone wanted to enjoy, there was no shortage of big-name talents to keep the wheels in motion. After Englehart's departure, Walter Simonson took over *Fantastic Four*, John Byrne took over *West Coast Avengers*, and Jim Starlin took over *Silver Surfer*—until they, too, each had problems, at which point the rotation would begin again. When Byrne said he would quit *She-Hulk* unless DeFalco removed an editor he didn't like, DeFalco repeated his mantra: *I back my editors*. Byrne was fired from the book, and *She-Hulk* was given to Steve Gerber. Byrne didn't go far, though—he began work on *Namor*, a new series that cast the Sub-Mariner as a venture capitalist.

Less than a decade earlier, it had seemed as though publishers like Pacific and Eclipse were going to pull all the big names away from Marvel and DC. But the smaller companies had fallen on hard times, especially after market gluts in 1986 and 1987. Comic-store owners, faced with a flood of product, played it safe and stocked shelves with perennial bestsellers from Marvel and DC. For all the qualms that Starlin, Gerber, and even Steve Ditko had voiced over the years, it seemed that it was only at "the Big Two" that there would always be work.

Although Marvel's Epic imprint had yielded some interesting projects, it had failed to launch any breakout characters, and its original mission of providing a venue for creator-owned concepts had been diluted over the years. After the more "mature" content of Miller and Sienkiewicz's *Elektra: Assassin* found a home there, Epic had begun to serve a second role, that of a high-production-value vanity press for previously existing, Marvel-owned characters. Because *Elektra: Assassin* and *Havok & Wolverine* were, by far, the most successful of Epic's releases, an effort was made to create an interconnected line of superhero comics within Epic. Although Archie Goodwin, Epic's editor, conceived of the characters, Marvel would retain all copyrights. By the middle of 1989, Goodwin saw the writing on the wall for Epic, and he departed for DC Comics.

Jim Starlin's *Dreadstar*, Steve Englehart's *Coyote*, Steve Gerber's *Void Indigo*, Doug Moench and Paul Gulacy's *Six from Sirius*—none of these properties had lasted at Epic, and the rabble-rousers behind them now had families to worry about. Frank Miller was still making noise, snubbing Marvel and DC for the independent start-up Dark Horse, but he was a special case—still soaring from *Batman: The Dark Knight Returns*, still possessing the juice to sell comics on his name alone, and nearly a decade younger than the rest. This generation had pushed for changes in the industry, and they'd made a difference. But someone else would have to come along to take the torch.

$$\left(16\right)$$

FOR YEARS, THERE HAD BEEN A DEARTH OF POPULAR NEW ARTISTS MAKING their names at Marvel Comics. The biggest names of the 1980s—John Byrne, Frank Miller, Bill Sienkiewicz, Walter Simonson—had all been with the company since the previous decade. The exception to this trend was the self-taught Art Adams, who after high school had washed dishes at a pizza parlor and spent all his spare time drawing submissions for Marvel. Five years later, when Marvel finally showcased his heavily detailed work—in the 1985 miniseries *Longshot*—he was an instant hit with fans. The title character had a fashion style that leaped out from the parade of standard primary-color capes—a mullet haircut, leather jacket, bandolier, and a side pouch—and an otherworldly origin that showcased Adams's talent for strange alien creatures. But his extensive cross-hatching took time, and Adams never took on a regular monthly assignment—instead, he became a perpetual guest-star artist, a surprise flash of excitement on the comic racks.

Still, Adams had an immediate impact on his aspiring peers, the young men who'd been weaned on Claremont and Byrne's *X-Men* and Frank Miller's *Daredevil* and who'd seen the visual style of Marvel Comics settle into staid functionality. In the last days of the Jim Shooter reign, there emerged a clutch of young artists who determinedly rendered every strand of hair, every stretch of clothing, every tooth in their characters' mouths. If there was a scene with a brick wall destroyed, you could bet that every single brick would be delineated.

The inker on Adams's *Longshot* was a Filipino art school dropout named Whilce Portacio. Portacio was great at rendering details but needed improvement when it came to anatomy and perspective, so editor

Carl Potts had him work over Adams's pencils, hoping he could learn a thing or two along the way. In the meantime, Potts fed Portacio books like *The Five C's of Cinematography* and kept him busy with work inking *Alpha Flight*. Shortly afterward, when Potts hired Jim Lee, an excessively polite, South Korean Ivy Leaguer, to draw *Alpha Flight*, the two artists meshed artistically and personally. Now Lee, too, got a copy of the cinematography book, and Potts drilled him on storytelling fundamentals, much like Denny O'Neil had with Frank Miller a decade earlier. Then Lee moved to San Diego and into a studio with Portacio. Their lives and careers were now entwined for good.

After a while, Portacio figured out a way to campaign for his own penciling job. After inking Lee's *Alpha Flight* pages, he'd draw his own pictures of the Punisher on the backs before sending them back to Marvel. Potts hired Portacio to pencil *The Punisher* just as the movie adaptation went into pre-production. When a second title starring the character was launched—*Punisher War Journal*—it went to Jim Lee.

Within a year, *Uncanny X-Men* editor Bob Harras—always on the lookout for the latest, hottest artists—asked Portacio if he'd like to fill in for a few issues of Marvel's number-one title. When Portacio passed, the job went to Jim Lee, and his popularity went through the stratosphere. Before long, Lee was made the regular *X-Men* artist.

While Lee and Portacio were first impressing Potts on *Alpha Flight*, Todd McFarlane, a cocky and foulmouthed Canadian jock, was making a splash on *The Incredible Hulk*. Back in 1980, in the summer of Dark Phoenix and Elektra, McFarlane was on a baseball college scholarship, soon to be recruited by a Seattle Mariners scout. But he'd attended the San Diego Comic-Con, and stood mesmerized as he watched Jack Kirby graciously speaking to the fans who swarmed around him. If he didn't make the majors, he told himself, he'd be a comic book artist. Sure enough, when an ankle injury dashed his big-league hopes, McFarlane began spending more and more time practicing at the drawing table, and reading with interest about Kirby's and Gerber's struggles, and the soapbox speeches of Neal Adams and Frank Miller, in the pages of the *Comics Journal*. Racking up rejection letters, the self-taught McFarlane finally got his breakthrough assignment just before graduation: a backup story in Steve Englehart's *Coyote*. He landed the *Hulk* assignment at the end of 1986; a year later, his editor was bringing pages around to other offices at Marvel, explaining that McFarlane was growing restless, and looking for new challenges. The thin-lined, detail-fetishizing samples spoke for themselves. He was hired as the new artist on *The Amazing Spider-Man*.

McFarlane and writer David Michelinie reintroduced Spider-Man's thirty-year-old rogues' gallery—Sandman, the Prowler, Mysterio, the Lizard—but it was a new villain that sealed the success of this freakier, darker version of *Amazing Spider-Man*. Spider-Man's discarded black costume was revealed to be a sentient alien being; when it took as its host body a disgruntled former journalist named Eddie Brock, it called itself Venom. McFarlane gave the bloodthirsty Venom a hulking figure and an enormous grin of razor-sharp teeth. Now that *Spider-Man* had fierce iconography to match Wolverine's claws and the Punisher's arsenal, the title began putting up the kind of numbers it hadn't seen for twenty years, and climbed the sales charts toward *The X-Men*'s number-one spot.

By the summer of 1988, the majority of Marvel's most popular artists—including Art Adams, Portacio, Lee, McFarlane, and *X-Men* penciler Marc Silvestri—were once again under the age of thirty. As Marvel editors began to loosen the Draconian storytelling rules that Shooter had imposed, this new wave of artists began to embrace the visual language of postnarrative music videos, moving away from establishing shots and two-shots and toward frantic nonlinearity. And, in the wake of Adams's success, there was detail, always detail, in the faces and machinery and architecture. The pages started to blacken with it.

In these artists there was also a restlessness, or at least a lack of docility, that hadn't been seen since the days when Jim Starlin turned down John Romita on *The Fantastic Four*. Maybe it was youth; maybe it was the fact that none of them was close to Marvel's New York headquarters, that none of them had moved to the city and paid their dues on-site. Or maybe it was just that they'd seen what had happened to Kirby and Ditko, and vowed not to let it happen to them. McFarlane pestered other artists about starting a union, a notion that had hardly been considered by anyone since the 1978 guild plans fell apart. If Marvel could screw Jack Kirby and Steve Ditko, McFarlane thought, they could screw anybody.

McFarlane felt a particular debt to Steve Ditko. He restored the original underarm webbing to Spider-Man's costume, accentuated the black borders around the eyes, and contorted the hero's body into odd poses, just like Ditko had done. But McFarlane went further: the webbing that shot from Spider-Man's hands now looked like intricate rope (or spaghetti, as Tom DeFalco said); the whites of the eyes doubled in size; the contortions no longer exactly obeyed anatomical rules. McFarlane said he wanted to bring out the character's spiderlike qualities; the editorial department got nervous. Pages were brought to the Bullpen, to John Romita himself, so that Peter Parker could be made to look like himself. "That's all you want me to change?" Romita would ask, looking down at the distortion of the character that hardly resembled the near-official interpretation he'd forged in 1966. McFarlane's Peter Parker looked like a bodybuilder, and his Mary Jane like a Playmate. Before long, McFarlane's version was the house style, and the artists on *Spectacular Spider-Man* and *Web of Spider-Man* were told to conform to this new vision.

But McFarlane still had to draw whatever the writer told him to draw, and in 1989, after a second summer in which *Amazing* ramped up to a punishing every-other-week schedule, he'd had enough. He told his editor, Jim Salicrup, that he wanted off the title, that he wanted a project on which he could call all the shots. McFarlane expected that he'd quickly be given a low-selling comic on which to learn the craft of writing. To his surprise, Salicrup asked him if he wanted his very own Spider-Man title. "It wouldn't have been my choice to bring in a fourth Spider-Man book," McFarlane said, "but I wasn't fool enough to say no to it."

It was a sweet deal: in a break with Marvel policy, McFarlane wouldn't even have to worry about keeping continuity straight with the other Spider-Man titles. If the company's other writers had any hard feelings about the special treatment afforded the hot artist, they were hardly comforted by what he said in interviews. He only read the sports page, couldn't remember the last book that he read. "Uh . . . I don't really consider myself a writer, so I don't pay attention to writing. Now I'm sure the people at Marvel won't be too impressed with that statement, but by the time they read it, it'll be too late." He was going into the project, he said, assuming "that it's going to be a piece of shit."*

What made Todd McFarlane stand out was that he really didn't seem to need Marvel Comics. He'd already sunk his earnings into starting a sports card company and opening a comic shop in Washington; he sorted through cases of hockey cards while he coasted through phone interviews. The candor of his answers was either unbearably crass or refreshingly unpretentious, depending on your perspective. "As long as I get Spider-Man in the right pose, and I've got a cool shot of him coming at you in the splash page, it's not that important what's behind him," he told one journalist used to long-winded discussions about craft. "If I can fill up the space with stuff that kind of sort of, looks right—or at least fill it with linework—the kids figure there's more detail put in than there really is."

With extra time on his hands in the months before he made the leap to writing the new *Spider-Man* title, McFarlane pitched in and inked a few *New Mutants* covers over the pencils of Marvel's latest discovery, a twenty-one-year-old Anaheim, California, native named Rob Liefeld. Liefeld's father was a Baptist minister; his grandfather had been a Baptist minister; all that young Liefeld had ever wanted to do was draw Star Wars characters, ride his bike to the comic shop, and hide his stacks of *X-Men* from his mother. Although he'd quickly gotten work doing pinups and covers at DC Comics, his narrative instincts were shakier than McFarlane's. But he was hardly timid: one editor was surprised to receive an entire story drawn sideways. Bob Harras liked the audacity, though, and after giving him fill-in assignments on *X-Factor* and *Uncanny X-Men*, he told Liefeld he wanted a new look for *New Mutants*, and a new character to replace Professor X as the leader of the team. Liefeld shot off pages and pages of costume designs and brand-new characters: *Bob—some future friends and/or foes for the Muties! If ya don't like 'em, trash 'em! 's okay with me—but if you're interested—give me a call!* One of the characters

---

* In marked contrast to Byrne's comment about getting out of the trenches, McFarlane said, "Right now, I still feel good about monthly comic books, and I want to stick to the trenches. Maybe in a few years I'll get bored; I'll go for the golden ring then."

was submitted to be the new leader: a half-cyborg "man of mystery" with a glowing "cybernetic eye." His name, the notes said, should be either Cybrid or Cable.

When Harras and writer Louise Simonson suggested other names, Liefeld took a page from the playbook of his new friend McFarlane, and stood his ground. "Bob said, 'Let's call him Quentin,'" Liefeld recalled. "I said, 'Yucch!' I had already put 'Cable' down as his name on the sketches. Then, in Louise's plot, after being told his name was Cable, he was called Commander X throughout. I said, 'If this guy is called Commander X, I want nothing to do with it.' That seemed ridiculous to me." Harras gave Liefeld his way.

The issue of *New Mutants* that introduced Cable—he wielded a giant gun; the New Mutants were depicted in crosshairs—was an instant hit, and marked a sudden turnaround for the title's sales. But it was the beginning of the end for Simonson, who suddenly felt expendable. As Liefeld's illustrations of muscles and artillery became more outrageous, as backgrounds disappeared and reappeared, as he discarded 180-degree rules, the readership only grew. Liefeld "would do square windows on the outside of the building, but round ones when you cut inside the building," complained Simonson. "It took me about six months to figure out that Rob really wasn't interested in the stories at all. He just wanted to do what he wanted to do, which was cool drawings of people posing in their costumes that would then sell for lots of money." And management, she felt, was uninterested in addressing her complaints. "The books were suddenly being used to make Marvel a lot of money in the short term, with no concern for the long run or the characters," she said. "Immediate cash appeared to be what Marvel was bought for—to be milked and milked and milked. I think that at that point anyone who looked like they could produce lots of instant cash for Marvel was likened to a god, and Rob Liefeld looked like he could do just that."

While Simonson struggled with Liefeld and Harras, Marvel threw itself into promotional planning for Todd McFarlane's *Spider-Man #1*. Eager to please the comic shops, Carol Kalish pushed for a special edition of the issue to be sold exclusively to the direct market, one that would include silver ink on a black background. In all other respects but the cover, the comic would be exactly the same.

Meanwhile, the director of Marvel's newsstand sales noticed that *Sail* magazine's highest-selling issue was the one that came sealed in a plastic bag with its annual calendar. It wasn't just the added value of the calendar—the poly bag made it stand out on the racks. Maybe that strategy could help *Spider-Man* on the newsstands, too.

"The direct-market retailers freaked," said Kurt Busiek, who worked in Carol Kalish's department. "'You're gonna put out a bag for the newsstand, and we can't have the bag?'" The release of *Spider-Man* #1 had become a multiplication problem.

McFarlane's comic itself was nothing special—twenty-two pages of a bare-bones plot in which Spider-Man battled a few criminals and visited with Mary Jane, while the Lizard bloodily dispatched three thugs and an innocent bystander, all of it delivered with overwrought narration and constant sound effects. But more than a million copies of the issue—a silver-ink edition, a regular-ink edition, and bagged versions of each—were sold at comic shops in late June 1990. One Los Angeles store rented footlights to welcome flocks of news media (and hundreds of customers) to its Midnight Madness sale. Before the issue even reached newsstands (800,000 unbagged copies; 125,000 bagged copies), Marvel already had a record-breaker on its hands. Collectors tried to figure out if they should remove the bag or not, then realized they'd better buy two if they wanted to read one.

Retailers wanted more. "They wanted to be able to sell everything," said Busiek, "even if it was a stupid thing, like, oh, *this one's in a bag*." A gold-ink reprint edition was produced, and then, in an attempt to reward shop owners, Marvel produced a complimentary "platinum" version— their version of the record industry's presentation of platinum records— which would be mailed out to each retailer. After various cover formats were experimented with, the platinum edition ultimately had to be printed on a heavier card stock to properly retain its special combination of inks. Estimated as an $8,000 promotion, it wound up costing more than $35,000. At first it seemed like a disaster—not just the cost, but the ways in which it failed to please retailers, who started begging for *just one more copy* of the instant collectible.

Marvel, meanwhile, had just opened a gateway to its future. The manufacturing department's five months of experiments on the platinum edition had yielded various prototypes—foil stamp covers, embossed covers—that would be perfected and utilized on future titles in the months to come, and not just in limited editions, but for print runs of hundreds of thousands. Was it just Todd McFarlane that sold *Spider-Man* #1, or was it the covers? An issue of *The Incredible Hulk* was quickly produced with Day-Glo inks; sales spiked an astonishing 300 percent, and the issue was quickly reprinted. A shiny, metallic *Silver Surfer* cover and a glow-in-the-dark *Ghost Rider* cover followed, to equal success.

In retrospect, some would view this moment as the opening of a Pandora's box. "I was taking advantage of the desires of the market and fueling speculator greed," the sales director who'd developed the platinum edition *Spider-Man* wrote contritely, years later. "There's nothing intrinsically wrong with creating product to fill demand; but taking advantage of the condition of a consumer base is akin to date rape, as far as I'm now concerned."

Since Ron Perelman's purchase of the company, new faces had gradually been showing up in the Marvel offices: corporate delegates focused on maximizing profit while maintaining a distance from the creative process. But Perelman and his right-hand man, Bill Bevins, couldn't help but take notice of the publishing division's recent triumphs, and soon that distance disappeared as executives began keeping a closer eye on their investment. The Andrews Group prepared to take Marvel Comics public. Vice presidents and consultants populated the halls more and more, and in October 1990, when Jim Galton—the quiet, reserved head of Marvel since 1975—retired at the age of sixty-five, Perelman had already groomed a successor.

Terry Stewart came from a mergers-and-acquisitions background, but another way in which he differed from Galton served to make him more palatable to suspicious comic cognoscenti: he was a fan. "Beneath this cloak of smokestack America that I wear beats the heart of a collector," he told *Fortune* magazine, shortly before he was appointed president of Marvel. In the context of the Perelman regime, Stewart easily played the role of rock-and-roll rebel, wearing black T-shirts under his sport jackets.

Stewart had told the press that he would focus on getting movies made, and appointed longtime Cadence suit Joe Calamari as chief executive of Marvel Productions. The studio had, in fact, been noticeably quiet since New World had sold it to Perelman. President Margaret Loesch, growing restless under the new management, had only been let out of her contract after Fox's Barry Diller convinced Perelman at a cocktail party that the sooner she started at Fox, the sooner she could work to bring *The X-Men* to television. Now Calamari would benefit from Loesch's cooperation at Fox, but he would also be stuck trying to sort out the continuing legal tangles of the Spider-Man film rights.

There were other changes: Barry Kaplan, Marvel's longtime CFO, was shuffled to the side. Kaplan had already discovered a difference in philosophies between old-guard Marvel and the Andrews Group. "I had these arguments with Perelman's people, because they believed in full absorption accounting. I'd say, 'Well, great, *Captain America* is losing money. Should I discontinue *Captain America*?' Their attitude was, 'Yeah! If you publish something else, it may make money!' But it's not like lipstick, where you come up with another color. You can't just come up with another character. In the meantime, while you're not publishing *Captain America*, you have writers, pencilers, inkers, and colorists who may not have enough work."

In the sales department, Carol Kalish found herself reporting to a newly appointed executive with monogrammed shirts and zero interest in comic books, a calculated buffer between her and upper management. She bristled at the direction of the company's latest sales strategies, which favored aggression over long-term success. Marvel giddily noted that a 33 percent hike in cover prices had not significantly reduced sales, and started planning another price increase. As the chief liaison between Marvel and comics retailers, Kalish was a crucial player — in 1990, comic stores accounted for 73 percent of Marvel's sales—but following the other October management changes, she was quickly promoted out of the department and into a new position, vice president of new product development, where she would be less of an impediment. Lou Bank, a twenty-five-year-old from the sales department, took her place. "I think it was a lot easier to strip-mine a company underneath a naïve 25-year-old than it would have been underneath someone like Carol," Bank said years later. "And I was much easier to manipulate."

Shortly after the reshuffling, as executives crunched sales numbers and strategized Marvel's public offering, Tom DeFalco submitted his budget for the following year. The response from upstairs was that 1990 was terrific, and now they needed to top it. DeFalco met with his editors. "How the hell," he asked, "are we gonna do better than that?"

DeFalco went to editor Bob Harras and told him it was time to expand the *X-Men* line. "I thought it was the worst idea on the face of the Earth," said Harras. "I remember thinking, 'How much more can we expand this thing? We have four X-books already: *Uncanny X-Men*, *Wolverine*, *New Mutants* and *X-Factor*.' I thought that if we went to five, we were going to kill the golden goose." Nonetheless, Harras and Claremont worked to differentiate the new title—simply called *X-Men*—from *Uncanny X-Men*. They'd merge the original 1960s lineup, now appearing in the pages of *X-Factor*, with the current cast of *Uncanny X-Men*, and then redistribute them into two rosters. *Uncanny* would feature the Gold Team; *X-Men* would feature the Blue Team. *X-Factor*, meanwhile, would feature a group of peripheral younger mutant characters who'd been introduced over the last few years.

If that wasn't confusing enough, there was now the matter of *New Mutants*. As Louise Simonson reached the end of her rope, Liefeld had campaigned for a new writer—Fabian Nicieza, who also worked as Marvel's advertising manager. When he was still a teenager, Liefeld had acquired Nicieza's phone number, and called him up to compliment his script on the New Universe title *Psi-Force*. "I'm going to make it as an artist in the industry real soon," Liefeld told Nicieza, and suggested they might work together in the future. Now, three years later, that time had come. "Rob had a million ideas, and no filter, and no maturity to know how to best present those ideas," Nicieza said. "So he started to flood ideas to the point where, I guess it was starting to choke Louise's ability to create the book. He wanted it to be muscle and power—and she wanted it to be about a group of kids growing up. And those two things are hard to reconcile."

Louise Simonson finally quit, after ten years at Marvel. "She got fucked out of a job by Rob," said Chris Claremont, but Simonson herself laid most of the blame at Harras's feet. "He would change plots, and blame it on the artist. He would change dialogue, and then say, 'I'm sorry, but I tried to call you and you weren't home' or 'I'll be sure and tell you the next time.' He would change some of the dialogue, but not other parts, so the things people said wouldn't make sense. It was his way of letting you know he was wishing you'd go away."

With Simonson gone, Liefeld had told Nicieza and Director of Marketing Sven Larsen that he wanted *New Mutants* to relaunch under a new title, and the three of them began campaigning DeFalco for the change—perfect timing, since DeFalco needed a second big book for 1991. Canceling a Top 10–selling comic and relaunching it under a new name went against everything Marvel knew about brand strategy, and some worried that yet another number-one X-issue would look like a cash grab, but Liefeld was insistent. How long could you go on calling something *"New"* *Mutants*? "I guarantee you we will sell more," he promised, and DeFalco finally went along with the plan. *X-Force #1* went on the schedule, to be published two months before *X-Men #1*. The summer of 1991 would be the summer of X.

INTERVIEWER, 1988: What would you do if Chris Claremont walked in and said he was off "The X-Men"?

BOB HARRAS: That is almost an unrealistic question. I can't even contemplate Chris doing that. I think if he did I'd have a nervous breakdown. (*Laughter.*)

With the franchise-wide changes, Harras now had an opportunity to solve a problem that had been nagging at him: Claremont's stories about aliens and magic just weren't pleasing him; they didn't seem like the kind of tales that *The Uncanny X-Men* did best. In the five years since the return of Jean Grey had ruined Claremont's happy ending for Cyclops, the book had gone through radical changes: Dazzler and Longshot had joined; the X-Men had been presumed killed in battle and spent time in Australia, where they depended on a mute Aborigine to teleport them from adventure to adventure; Nightcrawler and Kitty Pryde, its most playful and bighearted members, had left. Professor X and Magneto, the opposing poles of the title's philosophical quandaries, were nowhere to be found. "Times have changed since Charles Xavier founded this school and created the X-Men," Storm declared in one issue. "Changed even since he brought in myself and my companions to be the team's second generation. Now there is a third, and we must answer, my friends—are we fit caretakers any longer, for Xavier's school and his dream? Or has the time come to turn that role over to others . . . ?"

Some wondered if Chris Claremont was asking those questions of himself. *The Uncanny X-Men* was still, of course, the number-one-selling title in the entire industry, but retailers—who were, by and large, aging fans themselves—had complained to Marvel's sales representatives about the dangling plot lines, wondering when Claremont was going to get back on track. With constant whisperings in his ear, Harras made his move.

He'd held brainstorming sessions while out to dinner with Rob Liefeld, Whilce Portacio, and Jim Lee, and found that they were on the same page as to the direction that should be taken. "It just happened that Bob hated anything that Chris said," recalled Portacio, "and anything that we said, fifty percent of the time, was a match-up with what Bob was thinking." Portacio and Lee would now plot the X-Men stories together, with Chris Claremont writing the dialogue over their artwork—Portacio on *Uncanny X-Men*, and Lee on *X-Men*. After shepherding the characters from throwaway sales gimmick to international stardom over the course of sixteen years, Claremont's role would be reduced to typing dialogue fit to order. Aghast, he tried to get control of just *one* of the two titles, much like how Byrne had been handed *Fantastic Four* when he'd come to loggerheads with Claremont a decade earlier. No dice. "It wasn't even a case of 'Jim will handle *X-Men*, you can take *Uncanny*,'" Claremont said. "No one on the editorial side wanted to talk about it, it was just a take it or leave it situation."

Claremont tried to go along with the plan but found that even his limited role was compromised by blown art deadlines. "Jim was not a consistent producer," he said. "I'd get seven pages; a week or two would go by, and I'd get fourteen pages. There were cases where I'd get the pages and I'd have to script them and send them to the printer a day later. It was a panic."

Portacio, meanwhile, wanted to make a splash by killing off older characters in *Uncanny*. Claremont complained vociferously to Harras while he tried to juggle the interlocking plots of three titles. "At the same time we're arguing back and forth," said Claremont, "I'm trying to do this four-issue run on *X-Factor* tidying up all the loose ends left over from Weezie, asking her 'Is it okay if I do this?' She said, '*I don't care.*' At that point I was just like, *fuck.*" As they approached the big launch of *X-Men*, Claremont said, the battle with Harras became "an outright knock-down drag-out fight." Harras wanted to bring Professor X back into the stories; Claremont wanted to kill Wolverine and complete Magneto's transformation from villain to hero.

At Marvel, some felt that Claremont had put Harras into a difficult position, that he'd overstayed his welcome on the titles. "Chris wasn't prepared for the level of imposition that was going to be placed on those titles," said Nicieza. "He wasn't ready for the budgetary needs that those titles were going to demand from him—the expectation of multiple crossovers, the expectation of story events that were not going to be what he wanted to do or how he wanted to do it. It was going to be a different book than the book he created." Claremont and Harras began communicating exclusively via fax machine so that there would be a paper trail of the increasingly tense exchanges. Claremont appealed to DeFalco and delivered ultimatums to Terry Stewart.

After Claremont's wife reminded him that they had a mortgage to pay, he negotiated to write the first three issues of the new *X-Men;* this would be, in effect, his severance pay. He gave up on his last issue of *Uncanny* after eleven pages. No one—not Stan Lee, not Jack Kirby—had stayed on a title as long as Claremont had.

There was no good-bye in the letters column, no announcement to the press. Almost overnight, Claremont was without illusions about corporate loyalty. When an interviewer expressed surprise at the seemingly sudden end of the sixteen-year tenure, Claremont reminded him that comics were exempt from the rules of "straight" publishing, in which genre-fiction authors owned their franchises. "What you have is a corporate disagreement between an employee and his supervisor. And in that light, the course of action becomes as clear as it is inevitable: the corporation instinctively supports its supervisors." If Marvel had survived Kirby's departure, why would it think Chris Claremont was necessary? Claremont couldn't even draw.

Walter Simonson, who'd been writing and drawing *The Fantastic Four* while his wife was being brushed aside from *New Mutants*, followed Claremont out the door. Years later, he characterized the company's behavior as "abrupt, rude, and disrespectful," and railed against the mothballing of veteran creators. "The atmosphere at Marvel was becoming less enjoyable," he said, "the scope for good creative work more limited."

Without missing a beat, Bob Harras called up Claremont's onetime partner and longtime rival, John Byrne, and asked if he'd like to write *The X-Men*. Although Byrne had been slow to embrace the independent-publisher model, he had just begun work on his own creator-owned title for Dark Horse Comics—with the winking title of *Next Men*—over which he would have complete control. But Byrne had been surprised by the low sales on his Sub-Mariner relaunch, *Namor*, and had no guarantee that *Next Men* would provide a cash flow. So he had more than just storytelling at stake when he took the job of scripting both X-Men books—in fact, he had the same thing on his mind that Claremont had upon leaving: "The X-Men," Byrne volunteered to an interviewer, "are going to pay my mortgage."

But within a few months, Byrne, like Claremont, was faced with impossible turnaround times, forced to dialogue from last-minute faxes of Lee and Portacio's artwork. The pages were arriving piecemeal, three at a time, and every time another fax came through, the plot would take an unexpected turn, so that Byrne would have to rewrite the previous pages.

He found his breaking point when Harras called and asked him to script an entire issue overnight. Byrne refused. "Something's gotta be done about this," he told Harras. "This is insane."

"We'll take care of it," Harras assured him, then hung up the phone and hurried over to Nicieza's office. "John's not scripting this issue," Harras said. "Can you do it for me?"

"When do you need it by?"

"Tomorrow."

"There's no way."

At that very moment, Scott Lobdell, a struggling stand-up comic who was always hustling for freelance writing gigs, walked by Nicieza's office door. Nicieza, smiling, pointed his finger, and Harras looked up.

Harras hung his head and let out a resigned sigh.

Lobdell finished the issue overnight. Two weeks later, Byrne heard from a friend who'd seen Lobdell at a party. Lobdell had been given the regular *X-Men* writing assignment. "Years later," Byrne said, "I was told you should always be careful when Bob says, 'We'll take care of it.'"

Rob Liefeld, meanwhile, weighed his options. He and Nicieza had already begun introducing flashy, violent new characters into *New Mutants*—Deadpool, Domino, Shatterstar, Feral—the future members of *X-Force*. As he prepared for the launch, he wrote a letter to director Spike Lee, who had put out a call for people doing "extraordinary things" in their Levi's 501 jeans. Liefeld, with his boyish good looks and bottomless enthusiasm, was chosen from a pool of 700,000 entries to appear on a national commercial. He and *X-Force* were going to be on television.

Liefeld also thought back to a standing offer he'd had from a black-and-white comics publisher called Malibu Comics, to do his own independent comic. Testing the waters, he placed an ad in the *Comics Buyers Guide* for an upcoming title, to be called *The Executioners*. It was a team of "rebel mutants from the future come to destroy their past"—a plot familiar to X-Men readers. One character in the ad, Cross, looked a lot like Cable, the leader of X-Force; others resembled Feral and Domino. Harras called Liefeld at six thirty one morning and asked what he thought he was doing. Marvel would sue if Liefeld didn't drop the plans.* *The Executioners* was put on the back burner.

But Liefeld had an itch now, and he began talking it over with some

---

* In September 1991, Marvel would also send a cease-and-desist letter to Voyager Communications, where Jim Shooter was now editor in chief, for a new comic Voyager had advertised. "Your title *X-O Manowar* is confusingly similar to X-Men," the letter read, "and suggests and mimics the titles of Marvel's 'X-prefixed' series of properties."

of his friends. Back in 1985, when he was just starting out, he'd created another team of superheroes, called Youngblood. Maybe it was time for them to see the light of day—and not at Marvel.

Todd McFarlane never liked the idea of editors, and when the hands-on Danny Fingeroth replaced the laissez-faire Jim Salicrup as his boss on *Spider-Man*, McFarlane absolutely hated it. "You sell a million, I'll listen to you," he told Fingeroth. "If I can turn in 22 blank pages and the kids buy a million copies, who cares how comic books have been done for the past 50 years? I don't care that there used to be words or pictures—if the kids are buying a million copies, then they're happy, I'm happy and you're selling comic books."

McFarlane, who'd always resisted authority, bristled at plenty now: not receiving a Spider-Man T-shirt that Marvel had sent out as a pro motion, not getting invited to editorial summits that determined future plans for the comics, not getting to use the villains he wanted to use. He'd filled *Spider-Man* with stories about drug addiction, police corruption, and child molestation, but in the end it was a drawing of a sword in a villain's eye that brought him to loggerheads with Fingeroth and Tom DeFalco, who assured McFarlane that the Comics Code wouldn't allow the depiction.

McFarlane quit, and didn't even bother to line up more work. "There's no reason for me to take over a monthly title when I could do a special project that would give me creative freedom, better reproduction, a bigger PR push," McFarlane had told a brand-new comics magazine called *Wizard*, just before he took his exit. "Probably what you'll see me do if and when I leave *Spider-Man* is special projects for a couple of years and then—if I do go back to monthly comics—I'll self-publish. If I'm going to work day in and day out, I'll do it for myself." He'd talked about creating a series of hockey cards, and getting out of comics altogether, but now McFarlane started thinking about this idea that Rob Liefeld had, of publishing creator-owned titles through Malibu Comics. What if they could get a few other big names to join them—what kind of message would that send to Marvel and DC?

———

In the past two years of expansion, Marvel's sales had grown more than 30 percent, and its net income more than quadrupled. The company was now squeezing out profits everywhere it could, with editor-generated series like Tom DeFalco's *Darkhawk* (which, according to Marvel, combined the "gritty realism" of Ghost Rider with the "urban vigilante tactics" of Punisher), and Bob Budiansky's *Sleepwalker*. In March 1991, it made its first foray into the world of 1–900 telephone number rackets, with a "Help Me Save Mary Jane" touch-tone interactive audio trivia game that cost $2.70 for two minutes and earned the company about $20,000 in the first five days. But the real windfall was yet to come. Eight days after spinning the news of Claremont's departure—he'd be taking a "sabbatical," a Marvel rep said—Nicieza and Liefeld's *X-Force* #1 went on sale. Its nearly four million copies was the new record-holder, leaving Todd McFarlane's *Spider-Man* #1 in the dust. Double-sized and priced at $1.50, each issue was poly-bagged with one of five trading cards, unavailable elsewhere. Once-casual collectors tried their hands at investment purchases, stocking up by the hundreds. Skeptics wondered who would buy all these down the road—after all, there were only a few hundred thousand comic readers in the world. "It's got that '90s feel," Bob Harras told a reporter, and perhaps the straight-faced, ass-kicking, drill-sergeant barking, and heavy artillery of the one-eyed Cable did reflect some kind of zeitgeist, or at least a trend that had carried through Wolverine and the Punisher and the first *Batman* movie. Liefeld's California smile appeared with increasing regularity in newspapers, in magazines, and on late-night television shows. It was rumored that his tax bill that year was more than most comic-industry salaries.

The timing of Marvel's July 16 public offering couldn't have been better. A week earlier, following the $54 million opening of *Terminator 2: Judgment Day*, James Cameron had spoken to *Variety* about his plans to tackle a Spider-Man movie, legitimizing the idea that Marvel could finally transcend four-color newsprint. Seeing the possibility of high returns were Wall Street number crunchers and hordes of collectors alike, and stock went from $16½ to $18 on the first day, trading at a volume of 2.3 million shares as a man hired to dress as Spider-Man walked the floor of the New York Stock Exchange. Most of the money raised would not go back into Marvel, however—it would be split between MacAndrews & Forbes, a holding company wholly owned by Perelman, and Perelman himself, who enjoyed a $10 million dividend.

Of course, as *USA Today* noted the following day, "revenue growth depends on Marvel producing a blockbuster issue every year," and the company wasn't taking any chances. On August 16, the first of four $1.50 editions of Chris Claremont and Jim Lee's *X-Men* #1 hit stands. Every week a different cover was shipped to stores, building up to a fifth version, a $3.95 bonanza with a foldout of the previous four covers. When the smoke cleared, nearly 8 million copies had been sold—roughly seventeen copies for every regular comic book reader.*

Retailers were split on the wisdom of such bonanzas—for some, it seemed like money in the bank; others worried about getting stuck with inventory. But other Marvel initiatives were unanimously troubling: serial-numbered, sealed blister packs of comics, aimed at the collector market ("You are on the ground floor of one of the major collectibles of the 90s") were sold to Wal-Mart at a cost lower than what the direct market paid. A line in the Marvel prospectus that mentioned plans for a Marvel retail chain also had shop owners squawking. Where was the company's loyalty to those who had been selling its products through the tough times?

In September, Carol Kalish, who'd been a crucial component of Marvel's success in the direct market, died at the age of thirty-six after suffering a coronary embolism on the way to work. Her death sent shockwaves through the industry. "Comic-store owners saw her as one of them," said Sven Larsen, who had worked under her as a distributor liaison. "She'd come from the fan background, and she was sort of Champion of the Geeks, as far as they were concerned." The affection and trust that the retail community felt for Kalish would not easily be replaced.

Differences of philosophy began to fracture Marvel's sales department. While Kalish's successor, Lou Bank, wanted to branch out into nonsuperhero genres, Sven Larsen wanted to get the most out of the

---

* Many of these copies, of course, never reached retail customers, but remained in boxes as investments.

company's existing franchises. Larsen, who had been spending more and more time developing special covers, wrote a lengthy memo to Terry Stewart warning that Marvel had to work harder on brand property strategy, to better leverage big-event releases. Up until now, Larsen argued, sales and marketing had been entirely driven by content. There were dozens of different formats for paperback books; why not for comic books? Larsen proposed that Marvel begin a marketing department, which he would head.

Stewart agreed, got Larsen a marketing budget, and brought in a marketing superstar named Richard T. Rogers as a consultant. Rogers could boast of masterminding the introductions of red- and green-colored M&Ms and king-size bags of candies—getting customers excited about buying the same old thing in a new package, and getting them to buy in bulk. Now he would do the same thing for Marvel Comics.

As Marvel's stock climbed to forty dollars a share, Stan Lee hit the publicity trail from coast to coast. On Larry King's radio show, in the pages of the *Chicago Tribune*, on cable news programs, he tirelessly promoted a coffee-table history of Marvel Comics and gushed excitedly about the prospective James Cameron *Spider-Man* movie. Occasionally he'd be asked about the current line of comics. "We've been accused of being too commercial, you know, trying to make too many editions for the collectors and so forth," he told the *Washington Times*. "But there's a self-leveling effect: When we start doing it too much, they're going to stop buying them. The readers seem to want these things, and they buy them in great numbers." When the reporter asked if Marvel was pushing whatever the market would bear, Lee's carefree exterior cracked for a moment. "It's a negative way to word it, and I didn't word it that way," he said, showing annoyance before he settled on a better way to phrase it. "It's giving the public what they want."

Lee had never been one to publicly question Marvel's publishing strategies, even when it directly affected him; now that he was in Los Angeles, detached from the comic business, he had even less incentive to rock the boat. Privately, though, he'd grown ever more tired of seeing Marvel's Hollywood projects derailed by forces out of his control. At

Cannes that year, the Perelman-owned New World had announced plans for a *Punisher* sequel and a *She-Hulk* movie starring Brigitte Nielsen; a two-hour *Power Pack* pilot, based on the Louise Simonson series, was filmed. But New World was withering, and in October Perelman sold most of the company's operations to Sony. *The Punisher 2* and *She-Hulk* were never filmed; and *Power Pack* went unsold. So Lee had quietly begun a film-producing venture with a former New World executive and an agent for cartoonists. Their first project was *Comic Book Greats*, a series of videotapes in which Lee interviewed legends and rising stars. Profiled alongside Will Eisner and Bob Kane would be some of Marvel's hottest commodities, including Jim Lee, Todd McFarlane, Whilce Portacio, and Rob Liefeld.

McFarlane and Liefeld were the first guests. But to Lee's surprise, by the time McFarlane showed up at the Burbank studio with his wife and newborn daughter, the superstar artist had turned in his last issue of *Spider-Man*. He and Lee didn't talk about this during the episode—nor was any comment made about the McFarlane artwork on the wall behind them, a drawing of a new character called Spawn.

When Liefeld visited the studio, he showed off some new characters, too— in fact, he drew them for Stan Lee while the cameras rolled. One was named Diehard. Liefeld didn't mention that Diehard was going to be a member of Youngblood, the super-team that he was planning on publishing with Malibu. The other, Cross, was the astonishingly Cable-like creation that he'd advertised in *Comics Buyers Guide* as a member of the Executioners.

"Have you ever drawn him before, or are you making him up now?" Lee asked.

"This is the world premiere."

"Really? So I'm in at the beginning of a new superhero called Cross . . . obviously, if our lawyers are tuning in, you and I are creating this together, so we both share the copyright," joked Lee.

Liefeld smiled. "Have your lawyer call mine."

After Marvel nixed the idea of *The Executioners*, Liefeld and McFarlane bonded through their determination to stand up against Marvel. Liefeld in particular felt threatened by all the foil-embossed covers, and thought that Marvel was trying to use gimmicks to take the spotlight away from the artists. He started whispering in the ear of Jim Valentino, who was penciling *Guardians of the Galaxy* for Marvel, and Erik Larsen, who'd replaced McFarlane as the artist on *Amazing Spider-Man*—and who also had an ax to grind with Marvel. Larsen's proposal for a new *Nova* title had been trashed when DeFalco decided to put the character in *New Warriors*; now Larsen was also frustrated with the *Amazing* scripts he was being asked to draw. He wrote a bilious letter—he asked his name to be withheld from publication—to the widely read *Comics Buyers Guide*: "More artists writing won't spell the end of good comics, just as it didn't when Jack Kirby and Steve Ditko started doing all their own scripting. What it may mean is that fewer mediocre writers will find themselves with work or decent artists to work with—but then the repetitious, re-hashed, reworked hackwork of these tired writers is likely to drag this industry down, anyway." If McFarlane and Liefeld were going to jump ship, Larsen would join them.

McFarlane had taken Liefeld's curiosity about alternate options and transformed it into something like a military strategy. He began calling for a mass exodus, one that would hit Marvel where it hurt. "Quitting one at a time doesn't work," he insisted. "Neal Adams and Jack Kirby quit one at a time, and they replaced those guys, but if Neal, Jack, Gil Kane, John Buscema, Jim Starlin, and Don Heck had all quit at the exact same time and started their own company, they probably would have been some-what successful."

But they still had to collect another superstar, he figured, someone that Marvel would never expect to leave the comfortable confines of work-for-hire. He and Liefeld began to work on Jim Lee from both sides. "Marvel Comics felt they could lose me and Rob, because we were uncontrol-lable," said McFarlane. "Here's an idiot and an asshole. But Jim was the company man. They felt they would have won the war if they lost us and kept Jim. Jim ended up being the cornerstone piece."

Lee had reasons to hesitate. He was getting along fine with Bob Harras, still enjoying working on the *X-Men*, and his wife was pregnant with their first child. But he wasn't as thrilled about all the money he wasn't getting from T-shirts and posters, and when he was asked by Marvel to fly to New York for Sotheby's first auction of comic-book art—which would include the complete pages of *X-Men* #1 and *X-Force* #1—he was surprised to be told that his wife's airfare would not be covered by the company. "That's the wrong thing to say to a guy like Jim," McFarlane said. "Jim does his homework. He knows he's probably brought in 22 million dollars in the last three months. . . . They can't even spring for a $200 plane ticket? When they started saying that kind of stuff, that's when they pushed the wrong buttons."

On December 17, the day before the Sotheby's auction, Liefeld, Lee, and McFarlane—and McFarlane's wife and baby daughter—headed over from their hotel to get drinks near Central Park with representatives of Malibu Comics. Then they walked over to Marvel, where McFarlane had scheduled a meeting with Terry Stewart. To McFarlane the Malibu exodus was a fait accompli; he just thought that they should explain themselves in dramatic fashion. As the baby cried, the three artists failed somewhat in their efforts to put up a united front.

One of them threw out the idea of 75 percent character ownership; when Terry Stewart offered them control of the Epic line, they scoffed. According to Liefeld, Stewart said, "There'll always be somebody to pick the cotton."

Tom DeFalco, who wandered into the meeting in progress, remembered it differently, as something that devolved into a round-robin demand for better hotel accommodations at conventions, and free meals, and expenses paid for wives and girlfriends: "Terry basically said to them, 'You know, guys, we can keep discussing and discussing, but even you guys don't agree what you want. Why don't you get together, figure out what you want, and present it to us?'"

After they left the Marvel offices, they walked over to Central Park South and had dinner with the Malibu Comics folks. We're through with Marvel, McFarlane said. Let's talk about terms.

The next day, McFarlane, Lee, and Liefeld headed over to the auction on the Upper East Side. Lee sat next to *Wolverine* artist Marc Silvestri—who'd been bumped from *Uncanny X-Men* in favor of Lee—and watched as Liefeld's original artwork from *X-Force* #1 sold for $39,000. Then Lee's *X-Men* #1 pages sold for $40,000.* By the end of the night, Jim Lee had convinced Silvestri to leave Marvel, too.

No announcement was made immediately, and in interviews Liefeld paid lip service to the idea that he would remain on *X-Force* while working for Malibu. Lee and Silvestri agreed to stay on *X-Men* and *Wolverine* for a few more issues. But it was only a matter of time before they realized that the relationship with Marvel was unsustainable.

"We were angry at them," said Fabian Nicieza, who was getting last-minute stick-figure *X-Force* layouts from Liefeld. "Even those of us who understood why they were doing it. Rob thought I was mad at him for leaving. I wasn't mad at him for leaving—I was mad at him for wanting to have his cake and eat it too. He was putting me out because he was also working on *Youngblood* or whatever the hell he was working on."

"Jim and a couple of the other guys still thought they could work at both companies," McFarlane said. "Just so they didn't burn any bridges. Rob and I? Not only did we burn 'em, we friggin' torched 'em and poured on the gas. You know why? We figured we'd build another bridge."

---

* Steve Ditko's artwork from the 1965 *Amazing Spider-Man* issue that featured the first appearance of Gwen Stacy netted only $20,000.

BARRON'S WAS THE FIRST TO RUN WITH THE STORY THAT SEVERAL MAJOR
Marvel artists were planning to defect, in a two-page article that warned
investors that a bursting bubble was imminent. After reporter Douglas
Kass noted that most of the publisher's IPO proceeds had been redirected
into other Perelman properties (rather than paying back company debt),
he pointed out that Marvel "pushed through another price hike in January and increasingly resorts to gimmickry to break down consumer resistance," and then twisted the knife: "The brash kid willing to take artistic
and literary risks has grown too big, fat and timid. Marvel's continued
focus on violent themes and stereotyped heroes is wearing thin with con-
sumers, who increasingly are turning to upstart competitors." Perhaps
most alarming was the intimation that collectible comics were some kind
of Ponzi scheme. "Visiting a dozen specialty comic book stores," Kass
wrote, "I saw boxes upon boxes filled with unsold copies of the highly
promoted premiere issues of *X-Men* and *X-Force*—titles that were introduced nearly six months ago."

On February 17, 1992, the day the article ran, Marvel's stock dropped
more than eleven dollars a share. The *Los Angeles Times*, CNN, and *USA
Today* all chimed in about Liefeld, Lee, McFarlane, and the other renegade artists who were standing up to big business. In response, Marvel
president Terry Stewart made a statement that "the importance of the
creative people is still secondary to the (comic book) characters," a stance
that hardly discouraged Marvel's new image as a corporate overlord.

Two days later, Malibu Graphics and the eight Marvel émigrés announced that the artists were forming their own imprint, to be called
Image Comics. Although Malibu would be the publisher of record, each

artist would own his intellectual property and have editorial control of his work. The press release emphasized that Lee, Liefeld, and McFarlane had been the men most responsible for Marvel's recent record-breaking sellers, and played up the idea of Image as a refuge for creators who wanted to retain creative and economic rights. By the time Image's maiden title, *Youngblood*, was published, its advance orders had nearly reached the one million mark. Todd McFarlane designed T-shirts to promote Image's second release, *Spawn*, which would showcase the character he'd already slyly previewed in his *Comic Book Greats* interview with Stan Lee. Somehow they were managing to be the hot new thing and the underdog all at once. For the first time in its history, the media was painting Marvel as a Goliath and not a David.

When Chris Claremont—cut loose from his beloved X-Men, on the outs with Marvel—had heard that Jim Lee and Whilce Portacio had departed the company, he noted with wistful irony that he might have outlasted them if he'd just played along for a few more months. Bob Harras had given the artists the keys to the kingdom, only to see the artists fling them into the sea. "That was the 'be careful what you wish for' side effect," Claremont said. "Bob should have thought a step or two ahead, or I should have thought a step or two ahead, or . . . *somebody* should have thought." But now Claremont saw an opportunity—he fired off a proposal for a series called *The Huntsman*, and got Whilce Portacio to agree to draw it. It would be an Image title. Claremont's name started turning up in the company's press releases.

At the Marvel offices, the talent exodus left scars. Fabian Nicieza and Scott Lobdell scrambled with Bob Harras to come up with the annual summer crossover for the X-titles, now that the Image guys had left them holding the bag. "In my opinion," said Nicieza, "they were waiting as long as they possibly could in order to sabotage the production of those books. The longer they waited under the assumption that they'd still be drawing those issues, the harder it was going to be to get quality artists to draw it, the harder it was going to be to write it. They were hurting, for no reason, the people they'd worked with for the last several years, who'd helped them get to that level. To this day, I think that was a little bit of hypocrisy and mean-spiritedness."

Still, any office debate about the long-term damage to Marvel was strongly discouraged. "No independent comic artist has ever sold numbers that could do anything to us," DeFalco insisted to staffers in meetings. "It's not gonna happen!" he'd shout back at them if they protested.

With pressure to beat 1991's astronomical sales figures, DeFalco and the editorial staff focused on its big launches: "Big Guns" was a campaign to publicize new titles like *Silver Sable*, *Nomad*, and *Punisher: War Zone*, each of them starring characters who were, literally, armed with "big guns." Since *Ghost Rider* had been a breakout hit, it was used to jumpstart a series of new horror-themed titles under the banner "Midnight Sons." A discarded Stan Lee/John Byrne project about Marvel characters in the year 2099 was retooled into an entire new line of comics: futuristic versions of Spider-Man, the Punisher, and Doctor Doom provided plenty of collectible product.

And then there were the special covers, developed and instituted by Sven Larsen and consultant Richard Rogers. "When I was told Sven [Larsen] would be starting a marketing division, I didn't even know what the hell that meant," said Director of Sales Lou Bank. "What the hell is he gonna do? We're the guys who place the ads, we're the guys who put together the catalog. It turned out what he was gonna do was do those covers with Rogers."

For every enhanced cover, a meeting was called to determine special pricing. It wasn't just the cost being added, of course, but extra profit margin as well. Add in markups between distributors and retailers, and the ten-cent addition of foil on the cover translated to an extra dollar on the cover price. This, however, wasn't a problem for Marvel—price increases had been a part of the plan all along, a promise to the stockholders.

With a constant increase in the amount of product, as well as price hikes, Marvel managed to top itself, quarter after quarter. Sales in 1992 would nearly double 1991's $115 million. But the company would never beat the single-issue numbers on *X-Men #1*, or *X-Force #1*, or even *Spider-Man #1*. "When we got the orders in on *Silver Sable*," said Lou Bank, "and they came in at only half a million units, Tom DeFalco said to me, 'That's it, that's the beginning of the end!' I thought, 'Goddamn, half a million units!' At that point we were canceling titles that came in below 125,000, but it wasn't so long before that we'd *never* seen a comic sell half a million. How could Tom say this? It didn't sell the million you wanted, but . . . *half a million units*! But he was sure right. That was the beginning of the end."

"It was like cocaine culture without the drug use," said editor Tom Brevoort. "Everyone was getting more and more hopped up on this explosion of sales. You'd launch a book, and editors would be lamenting the fact that, 'Oh it only sold half a million copies.' Five years later, they'd be thanking their lucky stars."

To some, the monetary incentives offered to editors clouded judgment. "You had editors who tried to gerrymander hits in order to get themselves a great deal of money," said Jo Duffy, who'd left her staff job to work as a freelance writer. "Suddenly the editors seized control. It used to be if the writer and editor weren't getting along, change editors. Now it became: *change writers*." The empowerment of the editorial staff, begun as a morale-building necessity in the wake of Jim Shooter's stormy departure, now resulted—in extreme examples—in instructions to writers and artists on how to appeal to the lowest common denominator. "If the Punisher appears in a panel with another character," Jim Starlin was told, "that character should be killed within the next few pages by either the Punisher or someone else. If the Punisher appears with any object, it should be destroyed in an explosion as soon as possible."

"Everyone decided, 'Hey, we get royalties on this, so let's put Wolverine and Spider-Man and the Punisher in every one of the books, and dilute the product,'" said editor Mike Rockwitz. "I was working on that piece of shit *Secret Defenders*. Tom DeFalco came to me one day and said, 'Let's do a super-book that has Doctor Strange and Wolverine in it.' I'm like, 'Okay . . .' None of those things made any sense, but on the first book, I made seven grand in royalties. It was just absurd."

Still, many had reservations about the ways in which commercial concerns were starting to overwhelm the contents of the comics. Some editors complained that the sales, marketing, and publicity teams only worked to sell the books that were already selling, that the response about underperforming titles was, *Sure we can help you push this book. Just put Wolverine or Ghost Rider in it.*

To many in the editorial department, the face of the enemy was Richard Rogers, the marketing executive who was calling more and more of the shots and itching to crank up production at every turn, as though comic books were as infinitely reproducible and conveyer-belt-ready as the candy bars he'd worked with before he came to Marvel.

"It's hard for people who haven't come up through the comic book industry to understand just how hard it is to get a comic book out," said Sven Larsen, who struggled to mediate between Rogers and Harras. "It's very easy to turn around and say, 'Why don't we take this 32-page book and make it 96 pages?' All these right-brain thinkers on the editorial side were like, 'Let's let this happen organically. Why do we need to make all this money? We were doing just fine before you came along.'"

Peter David, writing *X-Factor*, threw up his hands after a number of his story ideas were put on hold to accommodate crossover events. "The editors are as trapped in this 'Crossover Uber Alles' mentality as anyone else," David wrote. "The stockholders expect massive profits from the X-books, and crossovers remain the only way to give them what they want . . . right now, there are quite a few people in very difficult situations. Some of those situations are of their own making. Others are imposed from other directions. There's a great deal of stress going on there with a lot of folks caught in a lot of vises. It may be that, sooner or later, it all blows apart."

When Terry Stewart and Richard Rogers decided that Spider-Man's thirtieth anniversary was the perfect opportunity for 3-D hologram covers and more crossovers and double-sized issues, editor Danny Fingeroth voiced resistance, worrying about workload and compromises in quality. Larsen stepped in. "I think one of the things that helped convince Danny was explaining that it would make a lot of money for the people who'd been loyal freelancers. That brought Danny a lot more on board with the program."

Not everyone was convinced. "Right after the Spider-Man 30th anniversary went on the schedule," said Lou Bank, "a memo came out of Sven's office, detailing the anniversaries of all the other characters, one after the other. That, I believe, is when editorial let out a collective growl. It was year after year of anniversary after anniversary."

Bank's concerns weren't rooted in some naïve idealism about artistic purity; he worried about Marvel's long-term business interests. Field representatives had gone out to nearly forty different stores, collecting sell-through numbers—the number of copies that retailers actually sold to readers, as opposed to the larger number of copies that distributors sold to retailers—for a dozen different comics over a three-issue period. The findings were stunning.

"Every time we did one of these stupid-ass covers that caused us to increase the price by 33 percent—say issue #475—we would have a 20-percent drop-off from 474 to 476. The numbers would spike for #475, but we'd actually lose readers from #474 to #476. It was consistent with every single example."

Of course, none of this would have an impact on Marvel's quarterly goals. Marvel's bottom-line reports, which only reflected distributor-level numbers, would continue to show sales and profits going up, even as the readership began to cool and the retailers, who couldn't return unsold copies, absorbed the costs. "In the meantime," said Bank, "we were killing the stores that were feeding us."

Bank sent a memo to Terry Stewart, citing the research, and warning of the possible dangers in continuing the enhanced-cover strategy. Presumably the sentiment was passed up the chain of command, to Bill Bevins uptown at the Townhouse, and maybe even to Ron Perelman. Whatever the reaction from above, says Bank, "Terry continued to behave in a way that was detrimental to the long-term future of the company."

Beyond the publishing concerns, Marvel was expanding in other ways. Toy Biz, the company that had partnered with DC on a line of massively successful toys in the wake of the *Batman* movie and then introduced a popular series of X-Men action figures, followed with X-Force figures. With former Marvel Productions head Margaret Loesch now running the Fox Kids network, an X-Men animated series finally had a television-industry advocate—and plenty of input from Toy Biz's Avi Arad—and was scheduled for the fall. And, in what would be the first in a series of costly acquisitions, Bevins pulled the trigger on a $265 million purchase for Fleer, one of the largest manufacturers of sports cards. It was through this maneuver that Marvel doubled its 1991 sales—and racked up nearly $240 million in debt. "Marvel has a growing involvement in the entertainment trading card business since 1990 with the introduction of Marvel Universe trading cards," Bevins said in a statement. "The acquisition of Fleer enables us to rapidly increase our presence in the $1.2 billion market for sports and entertainment cards." The Marvel Comics staff, however, was nervous. The card market was already showing signs of collapse, thanks to fervent speculation and a flood of special collector-edition cards. Could this happen to comic books, too?*

In June 1992, Martin Goodman died, after a long illness. The founder of Marvel Comics, who'd retired to Florida in 1975 after the failure of Atlas Comics, was eighty-two years old. A single-paragraph notice ran in the company's official hype magazine, *Marvel Age*—under an eight-paragraph obituary of EC Comics publisher William Gaines. "Nobody talks about Martin Goodman," Irwin Linker, an art director at Magazine Management, said years later. "It's like he never lived, and he's the guy who started the whole thing. It's like he never existed."

Even in Florida, Goodman was fond of swinging by newsstands and seeing what was selling, keeping an eye on the world in which he'd been such an integral force. But by the middle of 1992, the $600 million comics industry was almost unrecognizable from the days before the direct market. In fact, it was a vastly different world than it had been even one year earlier, before Marvel's public offering and the formation of Image. There were eight thousand comic-book stores in the United States, double the number of only five years earlier; many of them were baseball card shops that had converted to comic sales to fill the void left by the floundering card market. The required reading for every fanboy was a slick magazine called *Wizard*, which featured a fifty-page price guide in each issue, along with investment tips, a list of number-one issues, and rankings of artist popularity. Todd McFarlane's *Spawn* arrived in May, with computerized coloring and slick paper, and sold 1.7 million copies, outselling

---

* The previous December, a front-page headline in *Baseball Weekly* had asked "Is Card Collecting Going Up in Smoke?"

Rob Liefeld's *Youngblood* and setting a new record for an independently produced comic book. At the Chicago Comi-Con, tens of thousands of fans lined up in a parking lot tent rented by Image, where Liefeld—who had, by then, made the front page of the *Los Angeles Times*—participated in a marathon twenty-four-hour signing session. "We're like the fucking Beatles," he said to one of his Image partners. At San Diego that year, as Todd McFarlane appeared on a panel called "Do Artists Need Writers?," a nervous DC Comics—which had briefly moved into third place for the first time in memory—announced plans to do a crossover with Image.

Not everyone was sold on the industry's new phenom. John Byrne and Peter David devoted numerous editorial columns to their problems with Image's product and attitudes, while the *Comics Journal*'s Gary Groth was apoplectic that Todd McFarlane and his friends had become the new poster boys for artistic autonomy. "The founding creators have managed to dumb down and vulgarize an idiom not known for its application of intelligence or sensitivity," Groth wrote, "and have consistently displayed an arrogant contempt for the medium and an unbridled ignorance of its history, coupled with a moral obtuseness rivaled only by the corporations to whom they owe their success."

But Image's comics sold, and Marvel's comics sold. "Everyone had expense accounts," remembered Tom Brevoort. "Christmas parties became decadent affairs—the hotel in Grand Central Station, big ice sculptures of Spider-Man, crazy DJs in a control room like Professor X. It was an insane spectacle of excess."

Jim Lee framed the formation of Image as a kind of karmic imperative. "We have to take our shot now," he told an interviewer, "as opposed to 15 years from now when we're bitter, older men." Even as Marvel's quarterly reports boasted of continued growth, much of its talent was departing for greener pastures. In an unprecedented deal, DC signed a group of black comic creators—many of whom had worked for Marvel—to produce, off-site, a number of new series for the publisher, under the name Milestone; two of the principals had met while working on Marvel's *Deathlok*—and raised their start-up capital with the checks they earned on that title.

Meanwhile, Jim Shooter, who with Marvel alumni Bob Layton and Barry Windsor-Smith had carefully built a success with the slowly growing Valiant Comics, accepted an award for Independent Publisher of the Year in June. (Shooter would be removed from the company by the end of the month, after a power struggle with his cofounders; he'd soon dust himself off and begin yet another comic-book start-up, called Defiant.)

There were, for the first time in memory, a great number of viable alternatives to Marvel and DC, but the financial risks involved in creator-owned properties remained.

John Byrne's *Next Men* #1 had gone into a second printing by the time that McFarlane, Lee, and Liefeld left Marvel, but the buzz was short-lived: John Byrne doing projects outside of Marvel was no longer big news. He'd already taken his big shot, at the peak of his popularity, with the *Superman* relaunch. "I had my turn," Byrne admitted. "I was exactly where Todd and Jim and the other Image guys are ten years ago, when there were no royalties and no creator ownership. When I was number-one dog, I didn't make a billion dollars. Todd happened to happen when he did make a billion dollars."

Chris Claremont's proposed Image project with Whilce Portacio never saw fruition. When Portacio put *The Huntsman* on the back burner, Claremont cast about for a collaborator, but found that creator-owned projects didn't work so well if one couldn't draw—if one had to hire an artist to execute the vision. The rest of the Image team could subsidize their start-up costs with trading cards and licensing deals, but what was he going to do, sell T-shirts with script pages on them? Instead he poured his energies into sci-fi novels, a comics adaptation of a licensed property—*Predator vs. Alien*—for Dark Horse, and taking shots at his former employer. "There's nothing to differentiate, on a individual basis, one Marvel book from another," he complained. "It all blurs together into one giant, amorphous, primal shout." Noting that the "short-term staccato bursts" of the event-driven story lines were designed to satisfy quarterly financial reports, he lamented what had become of the X-Men. "I look at that and I think, this is my entire working life, up until two years ago, and it's taken them 18 months to gut it like a fish, to trash the characters, to kill off a tremendous amount of the context and cast, and to turn it into, to me, a parody of what it was."

Other disgruntled Marvel creators began working for Malibu, which, fearful of putting all its eggs in the Image basket, was putting together plans for a shared universe—an "Ultraverse"—of its own characters. At a Scottsdale, Arizona, resort hotel, seven creators—including Steve Gerber and Steve Englehart—brainstormed in conference rooms, by tennis courts, and next to the swimming pool. They wouldn't own the characters they created for Malibu, but they'd get a bigger share of profits than they would from Marvel. Even more important, they could follow their imaginations to the limit, creating comics about, say, a superhero who needed alcohol to manifest his powers, or a corrupt cop who was reincarnated as a sentient mass of sewage. Gerber and Englehart had grown frustrated with the thirty years of backstory baggage involved in writing Marvel characters, with having to ask editors for permission every time they wrote a line of dialogue. Walking around the complex at the end of the weekend, Gerber turned to Englehart. "This is what Marvel used to be like."

The most notable assortment of former Marvelites, however, was gathered at Topps Comics. The leader of the sputtering sports card industry had hired Todd McFarlane's former *Spider-Man* editor, Jim Salicrup, to help it move into the comic-book racket. Salicrup promptly flew out to California and cut a deal with Jack Kirby to purchase leftover animation concepts from the 1980s. It was exactly what Kirby had wanted to do twenty years earlier—get paid for being an idea man, and let others do the follow-up work. Salicrup turned around and hired a murderer's row of onetime Marvel faithfuls: Steve Ditko, Dick Ayers, Don Heck, John Severin, Roy Thomas, Gerry Conway, and Gary Friedrich. It was Stan Lee's All-Star Team, circa 1958–65, with a few latter-day ringers thrown in. Only now, when the comics came out, they were poly-bagged with trading cards.

18

"PAYING CREATORS A RESPECTABLE WAGE, AND LETTING US SHARE IN THE profits, led to a golden age—but that golden age carried with it the seeds of its own destruction," former Marvel editor Jo Duffy said of the boom years of the early 1990s. "Suddenly people were making enough to buy houses and cars, and cars for their friends, and hiring professional sports-team cheerleaders to be their girlfriends. It became a sickness. The more some of these people made, the more they wanted to make. Being able to have your own apartment without a roommate, or maybe buy a little condo wasn't enough. Suddenly they were thinking in terms of rock-star and movie-star money." Stories circulated about young artists hooking up with the Image team and diving into a world of Ferraris and swimming pools and six-figure starting salaries.

But there was a problem: Image's comics weren't coming out on time. With great frequency, comic shops that had put all their chips on a heavily hyped number-one issue from Image (or, occasionally, from some tiny start-up) would see the publication date come and go, causing serious cash-flow troubles and, eventually, as the books finally trickled out, lower-than-expected sales. An intercompany crossover between Valiant and Image was reportedly only finished when the Valiant editor in chief flew out to California, planted himself in Rob Liefeld's studio, and refused to leave.

Meanwhile, Marvel's mid-selling titles were getting crushed by all the extra competition, and DC was putting its energy into big-event issues of its own. In November 1992—as Image announced that it was freeing itself from Malibu, to act as its own publisher—"The Death of Superman" racked up heavy media coverage and four million in sales, as average Joes everywhere read in their daily newspaper that *Pow! Zap! Blam!: The Man of Steel is Dying*—and *oh, by the way, here are the breathtaking prices of important comics from the past. Superman #75* sold out quickly, and went into reprintings, as everyone scrambled to hoard what would surely, one day, pay for college tuitions.

Nothing about the market was consistent anymore. In February 1993, Marvel and DC titles were shut out of the top-five sales list completely. Two months later, Marvel had only one comic in the Top 20, but DC was on its way back to the top. Superman, inevitably, returned from his much-touted demise, and stores who'd been caught by surprise by "Death of Superman" sales figures the previous November now bet the farm on DC's $2.50 and $2.95 editions. For the first time since 1987, DC Comics was the best-selling publisher of comics.

Unfortunately, the larger public had lost interest in Superman's comings and goings. "The news media realized they'd been scammed," said Tom DeFalco. "Nobody covered it, but all the retailers ordered it like they *wished* they'd ordered 'The Death of Superman.'" After initial brisk sales, backroom storage spaces became overcrowded with unsold copies of *Adventures of Superman #500*. It had been the most popular comic book since the X-Men relaunch, but it also marked the end of an era. That month, of the thirteen comics Image had solicited, only two were shipped; the non-returnable product agreement meant that stores were stuck with whatever happened to dribble in from the UPS truck that week.

The speculating tourists who'd gobbled up cases of comics had now departed, and it turned out that somewhere along the way, many of the actual comic-book *readers*, fed up with paying jacked-up prices for hologram covers, had left, too. When the comics went on the racks, no one was there to buy them. Within six months, thousands of stores would be out of business.

The glut of new launches continued through 1993—even Dark Horse had a whole new superhero universe to promote—and by summer, two new creator-owned ventures found themselves making naïvely hopeful announcements to an industry that was approaching panic. Dark Horse introduced an imprint called Legend, which would feature the work of

Frank Miller, John Byrne, Art Adams, and a handful of others. Jim Starlin, who'd helped to get Marvel's Epic Comics off the ground a decade before, and had lately been turning out a series of mega-hyped Marvel crossovers with titles like *Infinity Gauntlet* and *Infinity War* and *Infinity Crusade*, had his lawyer hammer out a deal with Malibu to do a creator-owned project for a new line called Bravura. "Quite frankly," Starlin said, "Marvel is not paying rates or royalties that are competitive with what Malibu and Dark Horse are offering." But the timing could hardly have been worse for artists and writers looking to strike out on their own, and the Bravura line, which also included work by Marv Wolfman, Walt Simonson, and Howard Chaykin, soon ran into trouble, as Malibu's finances dried up.

The industry at least made the pretense of reacting to fissures in the market. *Wizard* magazine, accused by suspicious retailers of artificially inflating the numbers in its industry-standard price guides, hired a new editor to manage the figures. Image cut loose several of the creators behind its late-appearing titles. And Marvel Comics promised a new, "back-to-basics" approach—even as its fourteen-part "Maximum Carnage" crossover ran through five different Spider-Man series, "Fatal Attractions" ran through six different X-Men titles, and X-Force members Cable and Deadpool began starring in spin-off titles.

The allegedly permanent demises of Jean Grey and Elektra had once prompted death threats to Chris Claremont and Frank Miller. But even the grim reaper, it seemed, could not grant characters immunity from cash-cow special events. A deluxe issue of *X-Men* featured the wedding of Scott Summers and Jean Grey, shortly after an issue of *Cable* revealed that Cable was, in fact, their transported-from-the-future son. In the pages of *Daredevil*, Elektra returned after nearly a decade, much to the consternation of Miller, who'd been promised that the character would not be used without his involvement. "It stings like hell," Miller told an interviewer. "But I can't bellyache too long and hard, because a generation of Kirby and Ditko didn't have the ground rules spelled out the way I did, and they got ripped off a lot worse than I did. So Marvel can drag that corpse around the block all they want."

At Marvel, the best one could hope for was to deliver a well-crafted variation on what had come before. "I was constantly butting heads with the people upstairs, trying to do different types of products," said Tom DeFalco. "If it didn't have webs on it, or a big 'X' on it, they were afraid to do it." Marvel did ax some titles that year, but the cancellations only served to clear the way for new product.

Todd McFarlane lashed out at Marvel for churning out product to please shareholders. Although Image's trouble in meeting deadlines had cost him some industry goodwill, McFarlane could rightfully claim having avoided enhanced covers and bagged trading cards. "I don't give a crap that you've got 12 *Wolverines* out there if my mom and dog are drawing them," he said. "Why don't you put your energies into *Captain America* instead of getting out six number-ones. . . . You're forgetting that what made Marvel Marvel was that they had the best quality products. Now, as the years go by, they're gonna have the most products. Not the best—the most."

Even Marvel's own letters pages began to reflect fatigue. A blurb announcing a glow-in-the-dark *Daredevil* cover read, "If you're one of the die-hard comics fans who loathes special covers, then don't despair—we're also printing a regular $1.25 edition! In this day and age of sales gimmicks and overpriced incentives, we'd like to think we still publish great ideas!"

Gone were the days when a low-selling title was grounds for experimentation with form or content. After Scott Lobdell wrote an issue of *Alpha Flight* in which a character declared his homosexuality, Marvel's PR department issued a string of *no comments* to CNN and newspapers while reports circulated that Ron Perelman had gone ballistic. Rob Tokar, the Marvel editor who'd inherited *Alpha Flight* shortly after the story was approved, was summoned into Terry Stewart's office for an explanation. Tokar's assistant extended his hand and, assuming the worst, bid him farewell.

On the twelfth floor, Tokar ranted to Stewart, Tom DeFalco, and a displeased Marvel publicist about Marvel's poor handling of the uproar and how distancing itself from homosexuality flew in the face of its historical progressiveness. "Every time I said the word *gay*," Tokar recalled,

"I saw them flinch, so I found myself saying it more, to the point where I was leaning over Terry's desk, pointing my finger in his face. Finally I ran out of steam, and Tom told me to have a seat." A phone call for Stewart interrupted the meeting, but Tokar's point was taken to heart—he never heard about the matter again. "I think Terry and Tom shielded me from higher up," he said. "They could have easily thrown me under the bus."*

Alpha Flight wasn't the only title to act as a lightning rod for controversy. In the pages of *Nomad*, Fabian Nicieza had transformed the title character into a paragon of Gerber-level absurdity: a shotgun-wielding vigilante who carried around an adopted infant in his backpack. Nicieza saw the book as his creative outlet, a venue to take chances on stories about transvestites and class warfare that he'd never be able to work into the X-Men titles he wrote for Harras. "I wanted to make Nomad HIV positive," said Nicieza. "The stigma around the disease was just colossal, but I wanted to make that part of his ongoing story. I'd already done an L.A. riots issue that we got on *Entertainment Tonight* for, I understood that there were certain buttons I could push that would not only make it stronger creatively but would generate publicity in ways that other titles couldn't." With the support of Tom DeFalco, Mike Hobson, and Terry Stewart, the idea was sent up to the top for approval.

The answer was relayed back to Nicieza: *This isn't the kind of thing we should be doing with one of our major characters.* Nicieza sent a response back up the chain of command, through DeFalco and Stewart and up-town to Bill Bevins: *But this isn't one of Marvel's major characters! This is exactly the kind of thing we should be doing with this character.* Eventually, another response filtered down: Bill Bevins—whose avoidance of the Marvel corridors meant that many employees had never seen him—would meet with them to explain his thinking.

In Terry Stewart's office, Bevins drew a bell curve that demonstrated that all titles in the Marvel Universe were off-limits to such

---

* Eventually, Marvel gave Tokar the green light to give an interview with *U.S. News & World Report* about Northstar's sexuality. "I talked to them for a half hour, with the PR person there, ready to put her hands over my mouth if necessary," Tokar recalled. "I went through all the stuff I'd been through with Terry about Marvel's history of breaking ground. When the article came out, my quote was cut down to four words: 'Superheroes are outsiders, generally.'"

experimentation. The Marvel Universe titles were the core of their sales. "No, that's not it!" Nicieza protested. "Within the Marvel Universe publishing line, you have to differentiate the importance of the characters you have, so you understand what you can or can't do with certain characters. I write *X-Men*—I write your number-one-selling title right now. I also write *Nomad*, one of your lower-selling titles. I'm not saying I want to do this with *X-Men* . . ."

"Thank you very much for your time," Bevins replied tersely. "No."

When the door had shut behind them, Nicieza turned to DeFalco and Stewart.

"They have a fundamental lack of understanding of what Marvel is," he said. "If Bill Bevins was around in 1966, when Stan Lee wanted to do the Black Panther, Bill Bevins would have said 'No.'"

Marvel's publishing department, which only five years earlier had accounted for 90 percent of its sales, now represented a mere one-third of its business. While Bevins continued to scan for acquisitions to expand the Marvel kingdom, DeFalco pushed for a broader spectrum of published product, including science-fiction magazines and novels. "They said, 'Oh, we should buy a company!'" he recalled. "I said, 'We don't have to buy a company. We already *are* a publishing company! We already have distribution to the newsstands.' But they weren't interested in that, because they wanted to buy things that would instantly add to the value of the company."

"They wanted to make us a merchandising empire," said John Romita. "They were going to sell clothing and costumes and other products, and they got to the point where they told us to our face that 'comic-book production is the minor part of this company's future.' They told us we were worth ten percent of their time."

Bill Bevins didn't have time for meetings with the troops on the ground. When Marvel's British division was running out of money, he and Stewart were summoned to London to discuss a last-ditch strategy. Shortly after the discussion began, Bevins paused to take a phone call. When he returned to the conference room, he was presented with Marvel UK's one-million-pound plan. A furious Bevins quickly interrupted. "You brought me here for a million pounds? The call I just took was a ten-million-dollar deal. Why are you wasting my time? You want the money, you got the money." He turned to Stewart, barked, "Come on, let's go," and headed out for an early flight back to New York.

Bevins's modus operandi was to pick up his phone at the Townhouse, call a Marvel executive, and solicit an opinion about buying a new company or forming a new corporate partnership. "Write me a memo," Bevins would say, and then hang up. Then he would swoop in to make the deal. There was always room for growth, even if it meant leaving old partners behind. When Bevins realized that the volume of Marvel's action figure sales was limited by an exclusive license with Toy Biz, he set up a meeting with the manufacturer's principals at the Regency Hotel in midtown.

"Listen," Bevins told Toy Biz's Ike Perlmutter and Avi Arad over breakfast, "we have 4,500 characters, and you guys are a small company. There are just so many characters you can execute. . . ."

But Perlmutter and Arad weren't about to release their stranglehold. Instead, in what would prove to be a fateful moment, they suggested that Marvel and Toy Biz strengthen their ties even further. In April, only days after *The Return of Superman* flooded into comic stores, Marvel added yet another business to its portfolio, assuming 46 percent interest in the high-grossing Toy Biz. In return, Toy Biz got the "master license" for Marvel characters—exclusive, royalty-free, and in perpetuity—and $7 million of working capital.

Arad, the toy designer who through his position at Toy Biz had served as a vocal producer of the *X-Men* animated series, joined Stan Lee as a liaison between Marvel and Hollywood; he would oversee "development of all animated and live-action television and film projects." Upstart comic companies lapped Marvel in the movie game; cameras were already rolling on *Timecop* and *The Mask*, both based on comics from seven-year-old Dark Horse. Even Rob Liefeld had a lucrative development now, with Steven Spielberg. But Arad had gotten a lot of credit for the *X-Men*, the number-one-rated kids' cartoon. It pulled in a sizable adult audience, as well, and had spun off into apparel, trading cards, video games, and fourteen million action figures and Pizza Hut meal deals. With Fox Kids already committed to a Spider-Man cartoon, James Cameron finally turning in script pages for his planned Spider-Man film,* Wesley Snipes lined up for a *Black Panther* movie, and Wes Craven set to direct *Doctor Strange*, maybe Arad would accomplish what Stan Lee had been unable to in the nearly fifteen years he'd been in Hollywood. If his track record as a toy developer was any indication, Arad figured, he would. "In baseball, if you bat .300 you are a superstar," he told a reporter. "I'm batting in the high .800s."

At the newly christened Marvel Films, Arad was as dependent on Hollywood studios as Lee had been. Perelman didn't want Marvel to get into the risky business of film production. He just wanted to license the properties and make a killing on the merchandise that followed. But by October, Arad was off to a strong start, signing a deal with Twentieth Century Fox to do a live-action X-Men movie.

Then he heard about a low-budget *Fantastic Four* film that was nearing completion. Months earlier, only three days before producer Bernd Eichinger's $250,000 option from 1986 was due to expire, *Fantastic Four* had begun shooting with borrowed cameras on a soundstage in the Venice section of Los Angeles; it was being directed by the son of Vidal Sassoon and produced by Roger Corman. Convinced that the movie would do damage to the brand, Arad called Eichinger and offered to buy back the movie for a couple of million dollars in cash. Then he destroyed every print of the film.

In late 1993, Marvel's stock began to fall precipitously, by more than 60 percent. It had been a good ride, the last two years. "When we went public, all that frenzy of media attention—of course, Stan loved it, but that's what killed us," said Mary McPherran. "Wall Street is very fickle—*Ha-ha, isn't this trendy; look at you colorful comic-book artists!*—and then their focus turns away, and we're left with all these print runs of the same comics with different covers when it crashes."

---

* Carolco paid Cameron $3 million for a forty-seven-page treatment that included pages of dialogue.

19

AMID THE CROSSOVERS AND THE ENHANCED COVERS AND THE NUMBER-ONE collectors' editions, there was one comic that seemed to please everyone, from the fickle fourteen-year-olds chasing the next hot artist to the patience-tested boomers who faithfully held out for Marvel Comics to return to the way they remembered it being when *they* were fourteen. A four-issue limited series printed on glossy paper at $4.95 a pop, *Marvels* was the creation of writer Kurt Busiek, who'd worked in Marvel's sales department under Carol Kalish before launching an erratic freelance career, and Alex Ross, a young painter who had no use for the frowning-vigilante mode of superheroes that was now in vogue. The series was originally intended as a showcase for Ross's artwork, in which the important events of the Marvel Universe would simply be retold, but then they touched upon the idea of following those key episodes through the eyes of one ordinary man, a photographer named Phil Sheldon. As the proverbial innocent bystander, Sheldon's life was affected by each development, from the 1939 creation of the android Human Torch to the early 1970s death of Gwen Stacy. While the immortal heroes marched on, hale and undiminished, Sheldon, like the real-life writers and artists behind the scenes of the comic books, became an aging witness to history.

Busiek and Ross worked on *Marvels* for more than a year, under the radar, Busiek plowing through stacks of back issues and Ross photographing models on which to base his painted figures. "We were doing an up-priced series with an artist few people had heard of, a writer nobody cared about . . . and an elderly man with one eye and no superpowers as the lead." Their editor begged them to include Wolverine, if only so the sales team would have something to work with.

As it turned out, *Marvels* was a hit anyway. Ross's photo-realistic images—inhabiting some weird place halfway between Norman Rockwell and Leroy Neiman—left readers gasping, and Busiek's sprawling, metatextual experiment carried the added charge, increasingly rare in comics, of humanism. It was comics' answer to E. L. Doctorow's *Ragtime*, a decades-spanning epic packed with guest stars—but through the character of Phil Sheldon, it also provided a poignant story of a man's helplessness in the face of unfolding history. Sheldon was forever standing on the ground, watching nervously as the Sub-Mariner attacked New York City, trembling as the mutant X-Men struck fear into the hearts of ordinary humans. As a young man, he cheered at movie-house newsreels of Captain America fighting the Axis powers; in 1960s midtown Manhattan, he watched Captain America triumphantly return, to a world of convertible sedans and gray flannel suits: "There was so much energy in New York. As if fireworks had been going off for months. The birth of the FF—Thor—Giant-Man—the return of the Sub-Mariner—and, of course, the biggest blast of all—the show-stopper that lit up the world like a dozen Fourth of Julys rolled into one—like a force of nature in chain-mail. To catch a glimpse of him—always in motion, always moving forward."

In this version of late-twentieth-century America, there was no mention of the Cuban Missile Crisis, no plague of race riots, no campus protests of the Vietnam War—even though the Marvel Comics 1960s and early 1970s had tackled political and social issues quite explicitly. Here, the great trials of the modern world were the appearance of the Sentinels (as seen in the *X-Men* in 1965) and the subsequent anti-mutant riots, and the arrival of Galactus (as seen in the *Fantastic Four* in 1966). You could choose to dismiss the story as hermetic escapism, a history void of reality—or you could admire the way it took the inherent sociopolitical metaphors always present in the comic books and fit them together into one digestible package.

Still, *Marvels'* most impressive achievement was to recapture, for a short time, the thrill that Marvel superheroes had once provided. And in this light, it was notable that the story ended shortly after Gwen Stacy fell to her death, and even re-created the sound effect that provided a sharply accented *snap!* to nail shut an era of innocence. Our protagonist, Phil

Sheldon, who'd begun to dedicate his life to photographing the "Marvels" of the world in action, gave his camera to his assistant and told her to take over his work. He'd grown weary, had lost his eye for it, wanted instead to spend time in the real world. "No more Marvels for me. Time instead," he declared, in words that could have doubled for those of the Marvelmaniacs who'd continued in vain to look for the magic they'd once known.

Jack Kirby, whose staggering number of creations and co-creations provided the bulk of the material to which *Marvels* paid tribute, might also have uttered those words dozens of times over the years. His relationship with Stan Lee had been, in later years, filled with acrimony. In 1989, two years after their awkward radio show encounter, Kirby raised the stakes in a *Comics Journal* interview. "Stanley and I never collaborated on anything! I've never seen Stanley write anything," Kirby said. "Stanley had never been editorial-minded. It wasn't possible for a man like Stanley to come up with new things—or old things, for that matter. Stanley wasn't a guy that read or that told stories. Stanley was a guy that knew where the papers were or who was coming to visit that day. Stanley is essentially an office worker, okay?" Kirby said that Lee "didn't know what the heck the stories were about" and that he had "a God complex"; he vehemently denied that his former editor had ever even asked for plot changes. "I should have told Stan to go to hell and found some other way to make a living, but I couldn't do it," Kirby told the interviewer. "I had my family, I had an apartment. I just couldn't give all that up."

Lee pushed back. "I think he's gone beyond the point of no return," he said after the interview was published. "Some of the things he said, there is no way he could ever explain that to me. I would have to think he's either lost his mind or he's a very evil person."

But at a 1993 chance meeting in San Diego, the rhetoric melted away. "Jack said something strange to me," Lee recalled. "He called me over and he said . . . and again, I felt Jack wasn't fully with it, you know . . . he said to me, 'You have nothing to reproach yourself about, Stan.' And it was such . . . kind of a strange thing for him to say. I was glad to hear it, but I didn't expect it. And that was about it. And then some people came over and interrupted us and he went away and I went away."

That encounter, more than fifty years after they'd first met, was the last time that Stan "the Man" Lee and Jack "King" Kirby—the co-creators of the Fantastic Four, the Hulk, Iron Man, Thor, the X-Men, and so many more—ever saw each other. Kirby finally retired from comics; his last published work, on a comic called *Phantom Force*, was done as a favor to a friend and, fittingly, published by Image Comics, which had often invoked his name as the prime example of industry mistreatment. He spent his days quietly with his wife, Roz, in their Southern California home until he died of heart failure on February 6, 1994. The King was dead.

After Kirby's death, Lee reached out to Roz Kirby through mutual friends and cautiously asked for permission to attend the funeral. On the morning of the services, he drove north, parked outside the chapel, greeted Roz, and quietly took a seat. Later, he made a quiet exit out a side door. Roz called to him from the receiving line, but he didn't hear her.

In June 1994, Frank Miller paid tribute to Jack Kirby, delivering a keynote speech at an industry seminar in Baltimore. "An age passes with Jack Kirby," Miller said. "I can't call it the Marvel Age of comics, because I don't believe in rewarding thievery. I call it the Jack Kirby age of comics."

Members of the Marvel staff, sitting at a table front and center, shifted in their seats as Miller declared that the only way to talk about the future of comics was to talk about its "sad, sorry, history of broken lives . . . of talents denied the legal ownership of what they created with their own hands and minds, ignored or treated as nuisances while their creations went on to make millions and millions of dollars." After noting that "seventeen years of loyal service and spectacular sales didn't buy Chris Claremont one whit of loyalty from Marvel Comics," and scoffing at Jim Shooter's claims that he'd "spent his whole life fighting for creators' rights," Miller turned the screws.

> Marvel Comics is trying to sell you all on the notion that characters are the only important component of its comics. As if nobody had to create these characters, as if the audience is so brain-dead they can't tell a good job from a bad one. You can almost forgive them this, since their characters aren't leaving in droves like the talent is.

For me it's a bit of a relief to finally see the old "work-made-for-hire talent don't matter" mentality put to the test. We've all seen the results, and they don't even seem to be rearranging the deck chairs.

Creators who complained about defections to Image and other companies, he continued, were "like galley slaves complaining that the boat is leaking." The age of company-owned superhero universes—the Jack Kirby Age—was over. "It's gone supernova and burned itself out, and begun a slow steady collapse into a black hole. We couldn't feed off the genius of Jack Kirby forever. The King is dead, and he has no successor. We will not see his like again. No single artist can replace him. No art form can be expected to be gifted with more than one talent as brilliant as his. It's a scary time because change is always scary. But all the pieces are in place for a new proud era, a new age of comics. Nothing's standing in our way, nothing too big and awful, nothing except some old bad habits and our own fears, and we won't let them stop us."

The crowd rose to its feet.

Industry sentiment against Marvel gathered steam as sales continued to plummet, dropping 36 percent in the first six months of 1994. Marvel executives, in turn, laid blame at the feet of comic retailers and distributors, who they felt were not adequately pushing Marvel product over those of smaller, more fashionable start-ups, and were even daring to publicly criticize Marvel's business decisions.

So the sales department masterminded a plan: What if Marvel cut out the middleman and sold directly to stores? It could take the money it was currently sinking into co-op advertising and promotional events with ungrateful distributors and invest instead in a team of field representatives, each of them unwaveringly committed and dedicated to Marvel policies and product. After a series of top-secret, off-site meetings, the idea went up the chain to the Townhouse. Meanwhile, the marketing department developed an initiative for an in-house mail-order venture, which would bypass not only distributors but retailers as well. Over several months, as the company quietly cast about for a distributor to purchase, it continued to evoke ire and paranoia in retailers, who were already on the lookout for ways in which they might be squeezed out. Marvel raised the price of its comics another quarter, to $1.50—representing a 100 percent increase in the five years since Perelman acquired the company. Terry Stewart revived plans for a Marvel outlet based on the Disney Store model, and announced plans for a Marvel restaurant chain and a Marvel theme park, each of which would also sell T-shirts and other items that had previously been the jurisdiction of comic shops. When ads for an in-house mail-order venture called Marvel Mart—which included promotional items that retailers had been forbidden from selling, as well as otherwise out-of-print paperback reprints—began running in the comics, one distressed distributor sent out a cautionary newsletter to retailers, suggesting that they promote other publishers and reduce the importance of Marvel sales to their business. Marvel eventually pulled the catalogs, but not before cutting off the distributor's supply of Marvel product.

The House of Ideas had, it seemed, turned into Big Brother. "Unfortunately, if people who are in the know talk about [Marvel], they will be terminated if they are an employee, or punished in some other respect if they are not," one ex-staffer told the *Comics Journal*. "There is this incredibly threatening atmosphere [at Marvel] that lets you know you just can't get away with anything." A document that required employees to report coworkers suspected of violating company policy was distributed, although Tom DeFalco reportedly rallied the editorial department to refuse to sign.

DeFalco, by now, had a target on his back. He'd had shouting matches with Stewart, had resisted when it was proposed that the marketing department begin designing the comic-book covers. The rest of the company felt that the editorial department was closing ranks, just when its cooperation was most needed. One executive characterized editorial's attitude as "Leave us alone. We don't have time to deal with you people. Creative people can't be burdened by the mundane responsibilities of the numbers. The only thing we have to worry about is if the freelancers are happy, and making good books. If the numbers are there, that's great; if not, that sucks for you."

"Tom was willing to take all the shit from management and protect editors," said Director of Sales Matt Ragone. "Tom would go to meetings and get kicked around, and just absorb it, would shield the editors from the intense pressures that existed. But people felt . . . if things were going to change, we had to change the structure, and get these guys to take ownership of the process." Stewart approached Fabian Nicieza, who had experience with sales and marketing, and told him there was going to be a change coming, and wanted to know if he had any ideas.

But Nicieza's response—an organizational chart that funneled more power to the editor in chief position—was exactly the opposite of what Stewart, and the sales and marketing departments, had in mind. They wanted to find a way to circumvent any editorial resistance, to dictate corporate goals directly to the line editors. Shortly after Nicieza's plan was rejected, Marvel rented a sports bar across the street from the offices and invited the entire staff to dinner, where Terry Stewart unveiled a strategy dubbed "Marvelution." Tom DeFalco would be promoted to a senior vice president position and replaced by *five* editors in chief, who would report to Stewart. This plan, Stewart explained with the help of a slide show, would strengthen the "sub-brands" within the Marvel brand—so that, say, Captain America and Daredevil wouldn't languish in the shadows of the X-Men and Spider-Man. Each EIC would be responsible for a family of titles: Bob Harras (X-Men); Bob Budiansky (Spider-Man); Mark Gruenwald ("Marvel Classic," which included the Avengers and Fantastic Four); Bobbie Chase ("Marvel Edge," focused on grittier characters); and Carl Potts ("General Entertainment," which consisted largely of licensed properties).

Sitting next to each other, two employees who'd been at Marvel since the 1970s watched in disbelief as someone took the microphone and hurried through more slides about reorganization. "Don't worry," said the voice onstage, "it'll all be over in a few minutes, and then we can drink afterward."

"We looked at each other at the same time," recalled one of the veteran staffers, "and we just said, 'This is the end. We're fucked.' This was such a half-baked idea. We were being sold a bill of goods."

They weren't the only ones who weren't on board. After the presentation, one naïve assistant editor made the mistake of congratulating DeFalco on his promotion. The response was a hollow chuckle. "Well, you won't have DeFalco to kick around anymore," the former editor in chief said.

The confused assistant editor stammered. "But . . . they just announced it!"

"I'm gone, kid, I didn't take it," shrugged DeFalco, who walked away.

There were other shake-ups, other reflections of power shifts within the company. In the same conference call with distributors that announced the five-editors-in-chief structure, Marvel also named Richard Rogers— the chief proponent of variant covers and double-sized issues—as the executive vice president of sales and marketing. Although the EICs reported to Terry Stewart, they were overseen on a day-to-day basis by former newsstand sales director Jim "Ski" Sokolowski, who took the title of "Editorial Coordinator"—and who himself reported to Rogers. To further grease the relationship between departments, a marketing rep was assigned to each editor in chief.

Rogers's hard-charging philosophy filtered through loud and clear. "This organization wants you to sell $160 million worth of comics," he told his charges. "Editorial can complain all they want, sales can complain all they want—you can try to be obstinate, and say you're not going to do it—but if it's not you, it'll be the next guy. So maybe a better use of your time is to try to figure out how to get there in the best possible way."

Access to Stewart became increasingly difficult. "We were supposed to meet with him weekly," said Carl Potts. "Anything we couldn't solve amongst ourselves, or anything for which we needed extra resources or input, was supposed to be discussed in these meetings. Most of the time when a decision needed to be made, Terry would defer and say, 'I'll get back to you next week.' Bobbie Chase and I kept lists of stuff that needed to be followed up on, and would bring these up, but they never got resolved. Eventually, Terry's solution was to stop having these meetings. I know he was probably under tremendous pressure from Bevins and whoever else he was dealing with up there, but I found it beyond comprehension that you would set up this system that relied on you to be the final arbiter, and then bail on that responsibility."

"What Marvelution did," recalled one former editor, "was split us apart. Aside from the occasional crossovers, we didn't really interact with Bobbie Chase that much; we didn't really interact with Bob Harras that much. We were no longer a cohesive editorial staff." Now each of the five "families" had sales marks to meet. Creative talent, already disproportionately in demand thanks to the glut of comic-book product, was now the target of competing editors. Even the characters themselves moved into their own corners, each now flush with supporting casts huge enough to support their insularity from the greater Marvel Universe. "It would have been easier," said the staffer, "to have Spider-Man team up with Superman than to have Spider-Man team up with the X-Men."

This division came at a time when the Marvel Universe was more confusing than ever. Marvel spun off facsimiles of its biggest characters, including Thor, Iron Man, and Captain America (the hammer-wielding Thunderstrike; the iron-armored War Machine; the star-spangled crime-fighter USAgent); alternate-reality variations of several characters hopped around as well. In *Fantastic Force*, the child of the Fantastic Four's Reed Richards and Sue Storm switched places with his other-dimensional adult counterpart and led a superhero group.

Meanwhile, in the pages of the Spider-Man titles, a proposed twelve-issue crossover was supposedly heading toward resolution. When "The Clone Saga" had been set in motion, Peter Parker was married to Mary Jane Watson, and they were expecting their first child. Obviously, this domesticity was going to cramp the Spider-Man mythos. The writers and editors conspired to bring back the supposed Spider-Man clone—introduced and discarded by Gerry Conway twenty years earlier*   and reveal that, in fact, *he* was the original Peter Parker, that there had been a mix-up, and that readers had been following the adventures of a gene-spliced imposter since 1975. Now calling himself Ben Reilly, the original item got back into costume as *The Scarlet Spider*. When his identity was revealed, Peter Parker (the clone) would go off into the sunset with Mary Jane and their child, and the original Peter Parker (formerly known as Ben Reilly) would swing freely once again. "As the writers grew older and

---

* When Conway left Marvel for an editorial staff position at DC in 1975, his parting gift was a story in *Amazing Spider-Man* #149 about a cloned Peter Parker battling the real Peter Parker. Just who it was that walked away from the fight was ambiguous.

got married and had kids and got mortgages, we sort of wrote *Spider-Man* that way, and wrote him away from our audience," said Terry Kavanagh, who'd first pitched the story. "This was a way to get him back to his essence organically—without divorcing him, which would just give him more baggage." Unfortunately, a combination of marketing department pressure and editorial indecision delayed the story's ending. As the Clone Saga stretched out over months, readers would point to its excessive complications as a sign of all that was wrong with what Marvel Comics had become.

But at first, it was a sensation. "Bob Harras heard about this," recalled Kavanagh, "and said, 'Oh my God, the Spider-Man books are going to rocket past the X-Men books. We have to do an event of our own.'" In the sprawling "Age of Apocalypse" crossover, Professor X's son traveled back in time to kill Magneto and set in motion a dystopian version of our world. At the behest of the sales and marketing departments, "Age of Apocalypse" kicked off with chromium covers and $3.95 cover prices before moving into eight new monthly X-titles that temporarily replaced the old ones.

"Once you're on the ride, you can't get off until it's over," said Tom Brevoort. "If the owner of the company is saying, 'We need you to exceed your budget this year,' that's your job. You have one of two options: either you accomplish that or you don't and face the consequences."

As the editorial staff struggled to handle internal demands for more product, Marvel continued its buying spree. Over the summer, it had purchased the European sticker and magazine company Panini for $158 million. In the fall, it bought the Welsh Publishing Group, which produced children's magazines. Then, as it continued its talks to purchase a distributor, word came that Malibu, the onetime publisher of the Image imprint, had been entertaining offers from DC Comics. Word went up the chain, from Terry Stewart to Bill Bevins to Ron Perelman, and came back down: *do not let that happen.* If DC purchased Malibu, Marvel would be displaced from its position as the market share leader. Perelman went out to California and met with Malibu owner Scott Rosenberg. Rosenberg asked Perelman if he had read Malibu's product.

"I don't read comics," said Perelman.

Eager to show off Malibu's digital color process, Rosenberg put a stack of comics in front of him. Just open them up, Rosenberg said.

Perelman looked down. "I don't have to read them?"

After a rash of covert meetings, Marvel announced in November that it had acquired Malibu, citing its in-house coloring system, its West Coast presence, and its pending Hollywood deals as strategic advances, but making no mention of the market-share protection that drove the decision. Steve Gerber, who'd been writing for Malibu's Ultraverse line, was taken by surprise. "If I were really paranoid," he said, "it almost seems like Marvel keeps following me around, buying up whatever I create."

Marvel, meanwhile, was suffering, the costs of the company's spending spree on full display. The comic industry might have taken the bubble burst of the baseball card market as a warning—a flood of "limited edition" product, metallic foil and holograms, and a Major League Baseball strike in August converged to kill that market. Marvel's investment in Fleer was hemorrhaging money. The comic company seemed to be hurtling toward the same fate.

Immediately after Marvel's latest extravagant Christmas party had been thrown, the company laid off the woman who'd planned the festivities, along with a few dozen other employees, including several editors, and canceled more than twenty titles. It was the first time Marvel had instituted layoffs since 1957, but it wouldn't be the last.

On December 28, Marvel announced the acquisition of the New Jersey distribution business Heroes World. The two companies had a deep history. When former Marvel president Al Landau had been fired in 1975, Landau's number two, Ivan Snyder, had been given inventory of licensed product as his severance package. Over the next two decades, Snyder had turned that inventory into a series of New Jersey comic stores, and eventually into a distributor that claimed an 8 percent share of the market. Heroes World was primarily a regional business, serving the tri-state area, but the Marvel team scouting for distributors decided that paired with a new troop of sales reps, it would serve Marvel's purposes. The top-level executives at the Townhouse never consulted the architects of the original plan. "Had I known that all we were going to have was a telemarketing staff and a warehouse," said a member of the sales team, "I would have stuck with the old plan, and let the chips fall where they may. The whole reason for Heroes World was to get people into the field. No amount of telemarketing could do that. To me, that was a fatal flaw."

Unfortunately, Marvel soon dragged the entire industry into its clumsy business strategies. On March 1, 1995, a leaked memo divulged Marvel's plan to make Heroes World its exclusive distributor, meaning that any comic store desiring access to the publisher that held 40 percent of the industry market share was forced to open an account. All other distributors, meanwhile, were left out in the cold. By the time of Marvel's official announcement on March 3, Capital City, the number-two distributor, had filed suit against Marvel for unfair termination of its distribution contract; an undisclosed settlement was reached within days. DC Comics and Image Comics also reacted quickly, announcing that they had signed an exclusive arrangement with Diamond, the number-one distributor. Capital City brought a similar lawsuit against DC Comics and then signed exclusive deals with several smaller comic publishers. Retailers panicked. Smaller distributors, suddenly denied access to the majority of their product, folded.

A week later, Marvel announced that it had purchased the trading card company Skybox—competitor to Marvel's own money-losing Fleer, and a license holder for cards featuring DC Comics and Image Comics characters—for $150 million. The reaction was one of disbelief. Marvel Comics, which had just suffered layoffs for the first time in nearly forty years, was siphoning money into the imploding card industry?

At the end of the month, a group of Marvel employees, including Terry Stewart and Richard Rogers, hit the road on a nineteen-city Marvelution PR tour, meeting with concerned distributors and retailers. "The first presentation was a disaster," recalled one staffer. "People wanted us to talk to them about what was happening, not receive a thirty-minute editorial presentation. People wanted to find out where their comics were coming from—they didn't care what was happening in *X-Men*." The presentation modified as the tour wore on, and soon Marvel was peddling a "Covenant of Partnership" with the rest of the industry and spouting contradictory logic that convinced nobody: on one hand, the contraction of the industry was caused by a "lack of available product"; on the other hand, smaller publishers were filling the racks with "clutter" that distracted customers from "reliable Marvel product." The question-and-answer sessions that followed were tense. Asked for reassurance that Marvel wouldn't squeeze out retailers the way it had squeezed out distributors, Stewart steamrolled along through his talking points.

"Does that answer your question?" he asked, winding up.

"No, not really," said the retailer.

"I'm sorry to hear that," said Stewart.

On April 2, in the midst of the tour, Terry Stewart announced that he was being promoted to a vice chairman position* and that Jerry Calabrese, a Marvel marketing executive with a magazine publishing background, would be the new president. The retail community knew Calabrese's name, and didn't like it: he had been the one behind Marvel Mart, a campaign to sell the company's product directly to readers through mail order.

The environment at Marvel itself became increasingly chaotic, with the skeleton-crew editorial staff taking on a multiplied workload, and freelancers feeling jerked around. John Romita Jr. briefly returned to draw X-Men, and then found that a popular young artist was getting his assignments. Fabian Nicieza, who along with Scott Lobdell had become a major architect of the mutant titles in the post-Claremont era, saw his relationships with Bob Harras and Lobdell deteriorate as increasingly improvisatory changes in story direction replaced Nicieza's long-term story planning. Last-minute dialogue changes, in which characters' conversations turned from light banter to grim lectures, began to chafe. Nicieza resigned from X-Men in June, declaring publicly that his sizable paychecks weren't worth "the lack of creative satisfaction and perpetuation of mediocrity." Lobdell, though now a superstar making eighty-five grand a month, wasn't immune to the micromanaging and second-guessing;

---

* The *Comics Journal* quoted Stewart as grumbling candidly from the stage, "You're moved from position to position, and you're really not sure what your job is and what your responsibilities are. . . ."

his next issue of *Uncanny X-Men* had to be rewritten from scratch, four times, before everyone could agree on a story.

In the meantime, the Clone Saga continued to play out in the Spider-Man titles, but the initial mood-lightening objective had been foiled. At what was supposed to be the story's climax, Peter Parker's Aunt May finally died, having been on her deathbed countless times in the previous decades. (Stan Lee first gave his blessing to the turn of events, and then, just as he had with Gwen Stacy's death, denied knowledge of the plan.) Then, when Peter Parker learned that he was a clone, he smacked Mary Jane in a fit of rage. Readers were appalled, but sales were good, and Marvel milked the cash cow with one-shot tie-ins that cost $4.95 a pop. A "Maximum Clonage" series that further extended the story featured a third Spider-Man clone, named Spider-Cide, and then, finally, an entire army of clones.

Spider-Man writer Dan Jurgens, who'd been hired away from DC at great cost, gave an ultimatum: unless Peter Parker was restored as the one and only original Spider-Man, he was quitting. Of course, if Peter Parker was remaining Spider-Man, the editors realized, something had to be done about Mary Jane and her pregnancy—you couldn't have a super-hero *with a kid*. Amid all-day conference calls and flurries of memos, the writers and editors of the Spider-Man books argued over who had to be responsible for giving Mary Jane Watson a miscarriage.

Jerry Calabrese quickly found, to his dismay, that Heroes World didn't have the infrastructure in place to support its business. There were billing errors, unfulfilled orders, and long wait times on the customer service line that ended with handwritten messages for someone who knew what to do. Calabrese told Matt Ragone to pack his bags for New Jersey and clean up what he could.

But much of the damage caused by the distributor wars was irreparable. Retailers who wanted a variety of publications were now forced to deal with at least two or three different distributors. "If you were a comic book specialty shop," explained Tom Brevoort, "the way your finances worked is that you'd get a discount based on total sales volume. So if your order at the distributor was $100, that qualified you for x percentage

off; if it was $200 you'd qualify for a higher percentage. Now your to-
tal order was the same, but your Marvel/Heroes World order by itself
wouldn't necessarily qualify you for the same discount, and your DC/
Diamond order wouldn't qualify you for the same discount. So suddenly
the same product at the same volume was costing a lot more, and eked
into a profit margin that made it untenable. A few bad choices on titles
that didn't move or didn't show up at all—there was a lot of egregiously
late shipping, particularly among Image titles—and you were tying up
money. That put tons of stores out of business." The number of comic
shops, which had already fallen from 9,400 to 6,400 in just two years,
soon dropped to 4,500.

Unlike Terry Stewart, Jerry Calabrese did not read comic books—he
was a "pure businessman," in the words of one Marvel colleague. Still, he
only needed a calculator to pine for the good old days of the early 1990s,
the days of *X-Force* #1 and *X-Men* #1, the days when it seemed like Hollywood might come knocking. In San Diego, Calabrese approached Chris
Claremont and asked him if he'd like to return. Claremont, who'd been
writing for Dark Horse, DC, and even—along with Len Wein and Dave
Cockrum—Jim Shooter's Defiant, declined the offer. But Calabrese had
more luck when he met with Larry Marder, the executive director of
Image Comics, and asked if any of the ex-Marvel superstars at Image
would like to take a shot at revising the origins of some of the company's
biggest characters. "Marvel knew that their core flagship properties were
ill," said Marder. "The properties that they had, had just failed over and
over again to sell to Hollywood. Think about it, you go in, and you make a
pitch that the world's smartest man built a rocket ship and then went up
with his family, and the world's smartest man forgot to shield the rocket
ship against cosmic rays. It's laughable. The idea that Captain America
was frozen in ice for 50 years was laughable in Hollywood . . . asking the
Talmudic continuity scholars in Marvel editorial to throw away the holy
litany of Stan and Jack to satisfy Hollywood was having no effect at all,
they just weren't getting anywhere."

Todd McFarlane had no interest in helping turn Marvel into a movie-
making empire, and he couldn't understand why anyone at Image would.
"Why do you want to work for your competitor?" he wondered. "I've got a

toy company; are you fucking out of your mind I would ever make a toy for Hasbro or Mattel? It would never happen." Jim Lee and Rob Liefeld, though, were intrigued. Negotiations began.

Calabrese, no fan of Richard Rogers or the changes that he had championed, wanted to undo the moves of the preceding two years. He began by restoring Marvel's editorial hierarchy. "I don't like this five editors-in-chief system," he told the five editors in chief during a meeting in his office, hinting of things to come. After the meeting, one of the editors turned to Bob Harras. "You're going to be my new boss," he predicted. Harras smiled slightly.

As supervisor of the X-Men line, Harras was already responsible for fully one-third of Marvel's sales in the direct market. "Because of X-Men revenue, Bob was exposed to a lot more corporate push and pull," said Matt Ragone. "He was willing to sit down and say, 'How can we grow this, how can we make it better?' We all had to sell our souls a little bit."

Once it was made official that Harras would be the one and only editor in chief, he told Bob Budiansky not to end the Clone Saga just yet—it would compete with the attention that Marvel hoped to gain for an upcoming X-Men crossover. Budiansky warned Harras that this move would alienate writer Dan Jurgens, who'd finally been promised a resolution to the clone madness, but Harras's word was final. Sure enough, Jurgens was furious. After a wave of screaming matches, he quit the title and returned to DC.

By now, another wave of title cancellations had been announced. Among those who lost work was Herb Trimpe, the longtime *Hulk* artist who'd been a fixture in the late 1960s Bullpen and who now was writing "I'm beginning to hate drawing comics" in his journal and, at fifty-six years of age, applying to take classes at a state college. "Went down to New York yesterday," Trimpe wrote,

All the editors either in meetings or out to lunch. Talked to human resources at Marvel today. The lady seemed embarrassed. Said maybe I should consider retiring. I told her I wasn't going to hold the gun to my own head. They'd have to shoot me themselves. With a family, I need the health care benefits and income.

Adding insult to injury, rumors were swirling about Jerry Calabrese's overtures to Image: was it true that everything but Spider-Man and the X-Men was going to be farmed out to Jim Lee and Rob Liefeld?

Stan Lee flew to New York for the official announcement. Since Avi Arad's ascent at Marvel Films, Lee had distracted himself with projects like Excelsior Comics, a modest-sized imprint of titles to be packaged from the company's West Coast offices. But most of his public appearances of late—like popping up on *Conan O'Brien* to promote *Best of the Worst*, a low-budget book of trivia and one-liners—were the extraneous gestures of celebrity life, and had little to do with current Marvel Comics business. Now he returned to his old rah-rah mode: "We're matching some of the best talent in the industry, with some of the best characters in the industry, to change the status quo and create the stuff of legends!" he beamed to the gathering of journalists at the Grand Hyatt on Park Avenue. *The Avengers, Fantastic Four, Captain America,* and *Iron Man* would now be created completely by the California studios of Jim Lee and Liefeld. The news that Marvel was removing control of its characters from its own staff and handing million-dollar contracts (plus profit sharing) to those who'd recently walked out on the company was, in the words of one editor, "catastrophic to morale."

Even the fictional world of the Marvel Universe was being disassembled. For a multi-title event called "Onslaught," the outgoing editors, writers, and artists of *The Avengers, Iron Man,* the *Fantastic Four,* and *Captain America* were charged with implementing their own obsolescence. The heroes would be destroyed, and then re-created in a "pocket universe," an alternate world where Jim Lee and Rob Liefeld's reimagined versions would take over. The "Heroes Reborn" titles, as they would be called, would be renumbered as #1 issues for the first time since the 1960s. Other titles—including *Thor, Doctor Strange,* and *Silver Surfer*—would be canceled outright.

"This is a turning point," *Marvels* writer Kurt Busiek told a newspaper.

"The Marvel reader is essentially being told that Marvel's long-term history is more or less irrelevant. It's secondary to what will make the characters more popular and what will make the company more money."

The day after the press conference, Trimpe made another journal entry:

No matter what I say or who I call or write at Marvel, I can't get assigned to another book. I've tried reason, outrage, guilt trips and begging. Nada. I haven't been able to scrounge together enough work to meet my monthly quota. The place is a shambles. When I press, they admit sales are down and so is morale. The scuttlebutt is that more layoffs are coming.

Pictures of the smiling old Marvel Bullpen now carried the weight of irony. Don Heck, who'd died of lung cancer earlier in the year, had been ignored by the company for years; when one employer asked him if he had any work lined up with Marvel, Heck barked, "You think they want their fucking grandpa working on their goddamn books?" Marie Severin, who'd given Marvel decades of service, couldn't get regular assignments as a colorist; her contract was soon terminated. Fabulous Flo Steinberg, Trimpe's old pal from the 1960s Bullpen, summed up the feeling among the veterans: "Herb, they just don't care. Don't you get it?"

John Romita and his wife, Virginia, still worked in the offices, but over the past year found the workplace turning intolerable. "Virginia had about thirty people in the bullpen working under her; I had five people working under me," he said. "We were coached by outside consultants on how to let people go. You know that movie with George Clooney? We lived that. It was the most horrible time of our life, to have to lay off people we had just given a raise to six months before, because they were doing so well. We would get them in a room and tell them, 'We hate to do this, but the company is cutting back, and we have to let you go.' And to see their faces—friends of ours, people we had worked with for years—Virginia and I just dreaded going into work." The first day after Christmas vacation, the sixty-four-year-old Romita—who'd drawn *Captain America* in the 1950s, whose artistry had delivered Spider-Man to a mass audience, who'd co-created Mary Jane Watson—put in three weeks' notice for himself and his wife.

A week later, after Marvel tallied a loss of $48 million for the year, word came that 40 percent of the workforce was going to be eliminated. On January 3 and 4, 275 Marvel employees—including Carl Potts and Bob Budiansky, who only months earlier held editor in chief titles—lost their jobs. One by one, editorial staffers were called in to Bob Harras's office, where Harras gave them the bad news. One even fainted. As Carl Potts walked back to his desk to call his wife, he passed Mark Gruenwald's open door. The perpetually upbeat and cheerleading Gruenwald had, only weeks earlier, been forced to break the news to the creative teams of *The Avengers*, *Fantastic Four*, *Captain America*, and *Iron Man* that Lee and Liefeld would soon be taking over. Although Gruenwald had kept his job, Potts recalled, "He looked like he was taking it harder than any of those getting the axe."

Over the next few days, as two feet of snowfall closed businesses and schools, the departing Marvel employees made their ways back into the office to gather the detritus of years of faithful service from their cubicles and offices. Unworn "Marvelution" T-shirts, handed out after the miserable slide show, went into trash cans. Mary McPherran, who'd been with the company since arriving as a hot-pants-and-sandals-wearing receptionist a quarter-century earlier, unpacked her desk and found, stowed away, a stack of old envelopes. She'd once mailed these envelopes from 635 Madison, where she worked beside Stan Lee and Herb Trimpe and Marie Severin and John Romita, to True Believers all over the world. "Congratulations!" they read. "This envelope contains a genuine Marvel Comics NO-PRIZE which you have just won!" The joke, of course, was that they were empty.

She put the box under her arm and walked out the door.

PART V

A New Marvel

$$\text{(20)}$$

BOB HARRAS HAD SIMPLY INHERITED "HEROES REBORN," JUST AS HE'D INHER-
ited the layoffs, and just as he'd inherited a bruised and battered Marvel
Comics, where surviving employees doubted the security of their jobs
even as they struggled with increased workloads. But the scapegoating of
the new editor in chief was nearly unanimous. Burgeoning Internet message boards buzzed that Harras—who'd given Jim Lee and Rob Liefeld so
much latitude in the early 1990s—was responsible for yanking the carpet
from underneath loyal employees and rolling it out for Those Image Trai-
tors. "I don't know if anybody from Marvel ever called me and said that I
wasn't working on *Captain America* anymore," recalled one writer who'd
been replaced by Liefeld.

Jerry Calabrese was getting an earful from critics, too—when he submitted to a CompuServe chat, retailers and readers grilled him about why
Marvel had ruined the distribution network, and why there weren't movie
adaptations. Calabrese just wanted to talk about the bright future with
Lee and Liefeld. "Marvel has a lot of unfinished business with guys who
came up through Marvel and are no longer associated with us. The door
is open and will remain open with any of them whom we can make common cause to make excellent editorial product." A message from Steve
Gerber, whose Malibu title had just been canceled by Marvel, popped up
on the screen. "As someone with whom you might like to make 'common
cause,'" Gerber wrote, "I've shied away from working with the company
because it seems Marvel is unwilling to publish anything more potentially offensive than a Jell-O commercial."

Things would get worse for Marvel. In March 1996, Bullpen fixture
Jack Abel, who'd drawn for Timely Comics since 1952 and had worked

hard to recover from a stroke in the early 1980s, suffered another stroke while working at his desk. An editor attempted CPR while the ambulances arrived, but Abel was pronounced dead at the hospital. He was sixty-nine.

The same month, sixty-year-old Sal Buscema was informed that, due to falling sales, he was being relieved of his art duties on *Spectacular Spider-Man*—his only title. "My career was essentially behind me," recalled the man who'd regularly provided the visuals for Steve Gerber's *The Defenders*, Steve Englehart's *Captain America*, and countless others. "I'd been working for Marvel for over 30 years, and here I was just shoved aside." His older brother John Buscema, who'd begun drawing for Timely in the 1940s, coauthored *How to Draw Comics the Marvel Way*, and remained in high demand, immediately decided that it was time for him to retire, too. "I think 48 years in any business is enough," he said. "If I can help it, I never want to do another comic."

Stan Lee's Excelsior line had been in the preparation stages for a year and a half. Complete issues were finished and sitting in a drawer, awaiting the go-ahead from the sales team back east. Now, finally, it was abandoned.

The other major focus of Stan Lee's efforts, Marvel Films, was in the same position: everything was always in development, never on the release schedule. And Lee was feeling more and more like he'd been pushed to the sidelines by Avi Arad, invited to fewer meetings, his commentary less welcome. Lee turned his attention to taping intros for the *Marvel Action Universe* cartoons. Except for a doomed TV pilot for an adaptation of the X-Men spin-off *Generation X*, the closest he'd come to seeing cameras roll was when he played himself in a cameo for Kevin Smith's *Mallrats*, talking up the creations of Spider-Man, the Hulk, and the X-Men. Those were just three of the dozens of Marvel projects currently with various studios, and they weren't looking good. Over the last few years, a number of *X-Men* and *Hulk* scripts had been rejected by rights-holders Fox and Universal, and *Spider-Man* . . . well, the problems with *Spider-Man* were by now legendary.

Over the decade that movie producer Menahem Golan had retained the rights for *Spider-Man*, he'd managed to involve half a dozen different corporate entities. Golan had originally bought the *Spider-Man* rights for his Cannon Films; after leaving Cannon, he transferred them to 21st Century Films. Next, he raised money by preselling television rights to Viacom, and home video rights to Columbia Tri-Star; then he signed a $5 million deal with Carolco that guaranteed his role as producer. But after Carolco assigned the film to James Cameron, Cameron refused to give Golan the producer credit, and the lawsuits began. By the end of 1994, Carolco was suing Viacom and Tri-Star; Viacom and Tri-Star were countersuing Carolco, 21st Century, and Marvel; and MGM—which had swallowed Cannon— was suing Viacom, Tri-Star, 21st Century, and Marvel.

Toy Biz's Isaac Perlmutter, who stood to profit from the impact that Marvel-related films would have on the action figures, pushed Perelman to start investing in Hollywood. "Right now, you're dying," Perlmutter said, in his heavy Israeli accent. "And if you don't do anything, I tell you again, Marvel is a bankruptcy."

Of course, one of the reasons that Marvel struggled to sell studios on its movies was that Toy Biz had already sewn up the lucrative product licenses for itself. But in July 1996, Marvel sold a chunk of its 46 per-cent ownership in Toy Biz to raise money to create Marvel Studios. Now Jerry Calabrese and Avi Arad (with the help, presumably, of Stan Lee) would assemble pre-production packages—commissioning scripts, hiring directors, casting actors—and then turn them over to studio partners for completion. No longer would Hollywood's whims hold Marvel hostage. "We are finally on the verge of breaking out," Arad told *Variety*. "This is our bar mitzvah year in a sense."

Those in New York, where a post-layoff bunker mentality had taken root, might have disagreed. Office doors stayed shut throughout the day, opening briefly only to facilitate micromanaging. ("We see writer-driven comics as an experiment that has failed," Bob Harras's assistant told one *X-Men* writer). The Spider-Man titles, mired in the Clone Saga, contin-ued to cause headaches. At Harras's insistence, the team of editors and writers was supposed to explain that Norman Osborn, the original Green Goblin, was behind the entire villainous plot; this twist was complicated by the fact that Norman Osborn had been quite memorably impaled in a

1973 issue. There was also the difficulty of eliminating Peter Parker and Mary Jane Watson's baby. In the end, Mary Jane was told by a nurse that she'd had a miscarriage, while a suspicious-looking hospital worker was shown delivering a package on seaside docks. In subsequent years, no writer has been eager to revisit the morbid question of whether Spider-Man's infant daughter was miscarried or permanently kidnapped.

Originally conceived as a four-month story, the Clone Saga lumbered on for two years, as the monthly circulation of *Amazing Spider-Man* dropped 50 percent. Now the most vital moments in the Spider-Man comics were sly references to Marvel's financial struggles. In an issue of *Spider-Man Unlimited*, a criminal businessman advises publisher J. Jonah Jameson to make a public offering. "I'd never take the *Bugle* public, Kingsley," Jameson spits, "because I know that its long-term integrity would suffer under corporate connivers like you, who dream up ridiculous little schemes which only produce short-term goals!" The *Daily Bugle* newspaper downsized. "They're laying off nearly a hundred people! I heard one poor kid fainted when he was terminated!" a secretary tells Peter Parker, before he is called in to his editor's office. "You'll still have plenty of freelance work," the editor assures Parker, in language that intentionally echoed what outgoing Marvel employees had been told, "probably more than ever!" Even Spider-Man had been put out on the street.

For the newly launched *Spider-Man Team-Up* comic, Harras told editor Tom Brevoort to bring back Howard the Duck. But when Brevoort and his assistant called potential writers, they all voiced the same concern: *I'd love to read that, but I'd hate to be the one to write it. Call Steve Gerber.*

They braced themselves, and reached out to Gerber.

After thinking it over for a few days, Gerber called back and explained that he was at work on a comic that teamed his Destroyer Duck character with Savage Dragon, a creation of Image cofounder Erik Larsen. "I want to do an unofficial crossover," Gerber said, "where we'll do these two stories—the one in that book and the one in your Marvel book—and we'll set them in the same location, but the characters won't really run into one another, they'll just kind of run back and forth across the same landscape. But if you have the two books together, you can see the larger tapestry." Brevoort, intrigued, approved the idea, on the condition that nothing in *Savage Dragon/Destroyer Duck*—over which he'd have no editorial control—was going to get him in trouble.

But when Gerber learned that Harras had been campaigning to bring back Howard the Duck not just for this specil issue but in issues of *Ghost Rider* and *Generation X* as well, he called his lawyer. There was no contesting Marvel's ownership of Howard the Duck anymore—that had been settled out of court—but Gerber was damned if he was going to unwittingly endorse a full-blown Howard revival. Gerber's lawyer called Marvel and raged. Brevoort called Gerber and told him there were no hard feelings if he wanted to walk away from writing the issue.

Gerber paused. "No. I said I was going to do this story and I'm going to do it."

*S*pider-Man Team-Up #5 featured not only the returns of Howard the Duck and Beverly Switzler, but also long-absent, off-the-wall Gerber creations like the Kidney Lady and the Elf with a Gun. The crossover, as it were, was only a matter of a few panels that overlapped with *Savage Dragon/Destroyer Duck*, in which Howard and Beverly find themselves in a crowded scrum of duck clones.

Over in that other, non-Marvel, comic, Gerber pulled a switcheroo. "They haven't got any friends over there! They're comin' with us!" shouted Destroyer Duck as he grabbed Howard and Beverly from the melee. "Anyhow, one of the clones ran out that way. They'll never know the difference!"

In effect, Howard and Beverly had been rescued from the Marvel Universe, replaced by imposters. In the remainder of *Savage Dragon/Destroyer Duck*, Gerber's beloved creations were put into a witness protection program. "They'd never know me back on the ol' plantation," says Howard, now sporting eyeglasses and green-dyed feathers. He and Beverly Switzler take the names Leonard and Rhoda Martini, and head for Buffalo, New York, far from Marvel's clutches.

*M*onths later, Gerber was sending out emails about the "Howard the Duck Death Page" that he'd posted on AOL. "That page contains my final word on the subject," he wrote, "until *Savage Dragon/Destroyer Duck* comes out. As I've been telling people: There's more than one way to skin a duck. *Dragon/Duck* illustrates Method #2."

Brevoort was furious at Gerber's deceit and certain that he'd lose his job for allowing it to happen. When confronted, Gerber explained that Brevoort had simply been "in the way of the gunfire." The editor, who said he'd always considered Gerber a "bastion of moral integrity and moral fiber, the little guy fighting the man," vowed to never work with Gerber again. "He decided that me and my life and my family, we're perfectly acceptable collateral damage to the larger point that he wanted to make," Brevoort concluded, years later.

Savage Dragon/Destroyer Duck was met with audience indifference and low presales. Gerber, heartbroken, offered to fax the twenty-page plot to retailers, but when the comic finally shipped, months late, nobody noticed.

Mark Gruenwald put his game face on and tried to raise morale, but coworkers noticed that even he was keeping to himself more than usual, his attentions seemingly elsewhere. He'd always been organized; now he became fastidious, straightening shelves and rearranging the office library. On a writer's retreat in Long Island, the team leader, the constant cheerleader, was uncharacteristically quiet as his friends joked with him.

"He loved the Marvel Universe and the characters and the publishing profoundly, but he loved the people more," said Tom Brevoort. "There were cases where a title under his purview really needed a change if it was going to recapture any sort of an audience, but in doing so, that was going to put some writer or artist out in the cold. Mark resisted doing that for the longest time because he just didn't have the heart to do it. And then when he had no choice but to do it, it haunted him." Former Marvel editor Mike Carlin, one of Gruenwald's best friends, offered him a job at DC Comics, but Gruenwald felt too invested in the company he'd helped to build over the past twenty years.

Before Gruenwald left for his weekend home on August 9, he grabbed a preview copy of Rob Liefeld's *Captain America* #1. It was Gruenwald's favorite Marvel character; until a few months earlier, he'd either written or edited every issue since 1982. On Monday morning, rumors started flying around the offices, confirmed by an 11 a.m. email from Terry Stewart. "It's with my deepest and most profound regret that I inform you that Mark Gruenwald passed away unexpectedly early today at home," the note began. The cause of death was a heart attack. A collective shock ran through the building, and, via phone calls, to freelancers throughout the country. One former colleague collapsed upon hearing the news. "It can be said without reservation," the email concluded, "that Mark embodied the spirit of what we like to think Marvel is and should be."

Gruenwald was forty-three years old, a nonsmoker who exercised regularly. But over the last year he'd been in the position of removing dozens of freelancers from titles and seeing his longtime colleagues put on the street. Those closest to Gruenwald had no doubt that Marvel's disintegration was one of the reasons for his death. In the words of one friend, "He was so attached to that place, and it had stopped being what it once was, and what he had worked so hard for it to be. It took the soul out of him."

Against all odds, things had gotten even worse at Marvel—"Mark's death just seemed to symbolize the collapse of the whole place," said one former editor. But rather than address the crumbling of the core business, the Perelman regime continued to focus on inflating the company's paper value. Before Marvel CEO Bill Bevins retired, due to his own heart trouble, he made a move to replace Jerry Calabrese, who'd only been president a year. David Schreff, a clean-cut former president of marketing at the NBA, succeeded Calabrese. And when Bevins stepped aside, Schreff had a new boss: Scott Sassa, a thirty-seven-year-old, Hollywood-connected whiz kid from Turner Entertainment Group. Although Sassa spent more time in the Marvel offices than the haughty Bevins had, his focus was on moving the company's characters into other media—clearly, the comic books weren't making much money. Sassa drew up plans for theme restaurants and Internet initiatives.

"All of the outside executives that were brought in after Stewart and Calabrese thought that they were joining Disney, that the Marvel brand was much more ubiquitous than it really was," said sales director Matt Ragone. "Marvel was not Disney. The characters have edge; the stories have violence. But they counted the number of characters and changed the tag line of all press releases to say that Marvel owned 2,000 characters, because they wanted to leverage the entire character library. Well, the reality is that only a handful of these characters—The Hulk, X-Men, Spider-Man, Captain America, Iron Man—had any identity to the general population."*

It was too late, anyway. After posting third-quarter losses, Marvel's public debt—$1.2 million in junk bonds, about 50 percent more than the stock value of the company—was downgraded, and stocks dropped. Wall Street experts expected a cash infusion from Ron Perelman, who'd just lined his pockets selling New World to Rupert Murdoch for $2.5 billion. "MacAndrews & Forbes is not going to sit by and allow its investment to slide into bankruptcy," an analyst said of Perelman's holding company.

After discussions with Ike Perlmutter and Avi Arad, Perelman finally presented a recapitalization plan: Marvel would pay $22 a share to purchase Toy Biz (Perlmutter and Arad would get $200 million and $60 million, respectively, plus bonuses); then 410 million new shares of the merged company would be printed and sold to Perelman for $350 million. The trouble with this plan, of course, was that the millions of new shares (which Perelman would purchase at a bargain price of 85 cents each) would dilute the company stock by 80 percent. And it wasn't just stockholders who were aghast; shares in Marvel had also been used as collateral to bondholders. Within days, stocks dropped again, and shareholders filed lawsuits against Perelman.

At the end of the week, Scott Sassa—who had been on the job for less than a month—announced another staggering round of layoffs. A third of the remaining 345 Marvel employees were cut.

Reports surfaced that one of Perelman's advisors had quietly met with major bondholders, who dumped their investments only days before his controversial recapitalization announcement; lawsuits followed.

There was another major bondholder, though, who didn't get a warning. Carl Icahn, like Perelman, was a corporate raider with ties to Michael Milken; he'd been one of the inspirations for the character of Gordon Gekko in *Wall Street*. If anyone was less abashed about grabbing

---

* David Schreff, who had once worked at Disney, suggested the staging of a "Marvel Macarena" production, which would feature a dancing Spider-Man.

for money than Perelman, it was Icahn, an abrupt, high-stakes gambler. Once, when asked during a congressional hearing why he'd instigated a hostile takeover, he'd responded, "Do you ask Willie Mays why he jumped a certain way for a ball?"

Now Icahn aimed to use his position as the chief bondholder (he owned nearly a third of the debt) to block Perelman's plan. And if Marvel defaulted on its bank loans, the bondholders could collect the collateral—a substantial number of (undiluted) shares. Icahn could take over Marvel.

There was an escape hatch for Perelman, however: if Marvel declared bankruptcy, the court might rule in favor of his Byzantine recapitalization plan; he wouldn't even need the approval of the bondholders. On December 27, 1996, Perelman's various holding groups, set up like Russian nesting dolls, filed for Chapter 11 protection in Wilmington, Delaware: Mafco Holdings, which owned MacAndrews & Forbes, which owned Andrews Group, which owned Marvel III Holdings, which owned Marvel Parent Holdings, which owned Marvel Entertainment Group and Marvel Holdings.

For the fourth quarter of 1996 alone, Marvel posted losses of more than $400 million. Some bar mitzvah.

At the beginning of 1997, as fleets of lawyers were shuttling from New York to bankruptcy court in Delaware, Scott Sassa and David Schreff brought in Shirrel Rhoades, a veteran of the magazine world, as vice president of publishing. Rhoades was assigned two immediate tasks, both of which involved undoing actions by previous administrations.

One was to pull the plug on Heroes World. Marvel quickly laid off all fifty-seven employees and announced an exclusive deal with Diamond Distribution, which would now have a virtual monopoly on all comic book sales. Marvel's foray into self-distribution had not only been self-sabotaging; it had also upset the balance of power throughout the industry.

Rhoades's second mission was to fly out to California and tell Jim Lee and Rob Liefeld that Marvel was canceling the "Heroes Reborn" experiment. Liefeld had seen the writing on the wall when, on a trip to New York, a pair of Marvel editors smugly reminded him that the executives who'd decided to hire him were no longer at Marvel. Although sales had increased, the degree of improvement couldn't justify the high fees. Marvel was also tired of Liefeld pushing deadlines. "The only way he'd give Marvel the pages of each issue," Rhoades recalled, "was by flying a guy to New York with instructions not to turn over the disk of finished material until we handed him a check—something like a hostage exchange. I would hold out the check, he would hold out the disk."

Marvel wasn't the only company displeased with Liefeld. The Image fraternity had fractured the previous year, after Todd McFarlane had vocalized his disapproval of Lee and Liefeld's return to Marvel. (Even Frank Miller, who'd practically been Image's patron saint, said he "felt like I'd made a fool of myself by standing up for those guys.") Then, amid allegations that Liefeld was poaching talent from his partners' studios and not paying employees, the other six cofounders told Liefeld over a conference call that he was going to be ousted from the company.

McFarlane's thick Canadian accent droned over the speakerphone. "Uh, in case we're doing something illegal here, you know, then we'll come back and do it again, but uh, we don't like you no more, and we're kicking you out of the company, and do I hear anybody disagree with me? And if I don't, then let me take a formal vote. . . . Okay, bye, is that it? Anybody else got anything to say? Nope? Okay, good-bye." The line went dead. Liefeld was out.

McFarlane went on to rant about his former sidekick in interviews. "Over my dead body," he declared, "will that kid come back to Image Comics."

Liefeld would soon be singled out by Marvel as well. "I got to California," recalled Rhoades, "and at two in the morning, I get a call from Scott Sassa, who said, 'Just make this a goodwill ambassador mission, I know you can do it, you're our Great White Hope.' What it really came down to was that Sassa and Jim Lee were both Korean-Americans, and they liked each other, and Scott didn't want to screw Jim over. So I go out and make pretty to everybody, and Jim shows me his office that looks like the deck of the Starship Enterprise, and Rob invites us in and does his self-serving little dance." As soon as Rhoades returned to the East Coast, he sent a letter to Liefeld informing him that his contract for *Captain America* and *The Avengers* was being terminated. (Jim Lee, who by now enjoyed a rivalry with Liefeld, would take over the titles until the contract ran out.)

Liefeld quickly announced plans for a comic called *Agent America*, featuring a suspiciously familiar-looking patriotic character (complete with teenage sidekick and an archenemy named the Iron Skull), into which he would rework his leftover *Captain America* plots. After Marvel threatened legal action, Liefeld abandoned *Agent America* and bought the rights to the Fighting American—the star-spangled, shield-wielding rip-off hero that Joe Simon and Jack Kirby had created in the 1950s as a riposte to Marvel's ownership of Captain America. Then, to amplify the similarities even more, Liefeld gave Fighting American a shield to throw. Marvel sued, and a judge ruled that Liefeld could continue to publish *Fighting American* only if he made specific changes. Both sides claimed victory. In a matter of months, Rob Liefeld had gone from competitor to prodigal son to pariah.

In the minds of many, Marvel's time in bankruptcy court would be reduced to a power struggle between Ron Perelman and Carl Icahn. But there were, in fact, two other major forces at work: there were the banks to whom Marvel owed money, who just wanted their hundreds of millions of dollars back, and there was Toy Biz, which wanted to protect its exclusive and nonexpiring license to make Marvel toys. Over the next several months, a head spinning number of alliances would be formed and dissolved between the four sides, in varying permutations, as teams of lawyers screamed obscenities at one another.

After the bankruptcy judge ruled in March that Icahn and the bondholders could foreclose on the stock collateral, Ron Perelman withdrew his recapitalization plan, on the condition that Icahn would not bring legal action against his team for any mismanagement of Marvel over the previous years. (Perelman did not, however, insist on immunity for Toy Biz's Ike Perlmutter and Avi Arad. If Icahn needed to squeeze them out of the company, so be it.)

By now, Ike Perlmutter was no longer on speaking terms with Perelman. "How you feel when somebody promise you and agree to pay you eighteen and a half a dollar a share, and a few months later you find you have zero?" he asked the court. "How you feel when you lose $200 million?" Perlmutter and Arad briefly aligned themselves with Icahn, until Icahn confirmed their worst fear—if he took control, he would try to nullify Toy Biz's contract for the Marvel license. So in April, Toy Biz announced its own plans for acquiring Marvel, a leveraged buyout in which the banks would receive $420 million in cash and a 28 percent share in a merged Toy Biz/Marvel company, plus proceeds from the sales of Fleer and Skybox. Icahn was furious. "I will crush your company," he told Perlmutter, "just like I did at TWA, at Texaco, and at U.S. Steel." In response, Perlmutter faxed Icahn a clutch of threatening pages from the Old Testament.

But Toy Biz second-guessed the terms of the merger after conducting due diligence and withdrew its proposal. Perlmutter instead cut a deal with Icahn, and then, just as suddenly, backed out of that, too. Toy Biz was flailing around, looking for delaying tactics.

The court, however, was ready to move forward. On June 20, the bondholders were granted control of the Marvel board, with Carl Icahn installed as chairman. The company wasn't entirely his yet, though. Marvel would remain in bankruptcy while the banks continued to wait for an acceptable proposal. At the behest of the banks, Ron Perelman would remain a fly in the ointment, doing what he could to prevent Icahn from winning ownership of Marvel. But his days with Marvel were effectively done. He'd done okay for himself, though, having lined his pockets over the years to the tune of $300 million.

"One day [Scott] Sassa was there in the center of the bullpen assuring the publishing staff that Perelman would prevail over the barbarians at the gate," recalled publisher Shirrel Rhoades. "The next day he'd disappeared, never to be seen in the Marvel offices again." The following week, employees were surprised to see retired Marvel executive Joe "the Squid" Calamari saunter into the office. Calamari, who had volunteered his consultancy services to Icahn at the rate of $1,500 a day, was the new president. "Joe Calamari shows up and says, 'I'm in charge,'" recalled another senior-level employee. "We didn't even know if it was true! It wasn't like Carl Icahn came in and called a meeting and introduced Joe

Calamari as president. It seemed like Joe just showed up on the doorstep one day."

Even more than the executives who'd preceded him, Calamari was eager to implement his own ideas for the company. Some of his strategies seemed to reflect a desire to return to past glories: Chris Claremont was hired as editorial director,* and Michael Golden, the fan-favorite artist whose early 1980s work had inspired the Image generation, was named art director. Other Calamari initiatives—like promoting Marvel's comics at hot-air balloon festivals, or creating the world's largest pizza for the Chicago Comic-Con—seemed downright quixotic. He tried, to no avail, to convince the editorial department that it should create two new universes to replace the classic Marvel one. They'd been down that road with Jim Shooter already.†

"It was a bit of a disaster," Shirrel Rhoades said of Calamari's appointment. "Calamari is ADD. He cannot hold a coherent thought for 13 seconds. You go in and ask him A, and he's off on B and G and Z, and you walk out saying, 'What did we decide?' I thought Calamari was the worst boss that I've ever had in 45 years in publishing. He meant well, but he was very ego-driven, and he wanted to screw around with movies."

Calamari had been the East Coast point person for Marvel Productions and Marvel Films during the frustrations of the early 1990s, and now he rolled up his sleeves to get things done. He wanted to make deals, wanted to hobnob with producers and directors, even if it meant stepping on the toes of Avi Arad and Marvel Studios. Unfortunately, Carl Icahn was no more excited about film investments than Perelman had been—he just wanted to flip the company and make a quick buck. Calamari's conference calls with Icahn's people were epic, hypnotic fugues: *"Fuck you." "No, fuck you." "No, no, no—fuck you!"*

---

* Before this deal was completed, there was the matter of settling Claremont's claims of unpaid royalties.

† The new-universes strategy had been introduced in the courtroom before Icahn took over. "Okay, who are these new characters going to be?" asked a skeptical lawyer for the banks. "What are these new twenty-one comic books going to be about? Zip! They have no answers. We think there will be a descent into chaos, and there will be no plan here, if these people come in."

Out in Hollywood, Marvel Studios plugged away anyhow. *Blade*, based on Marv Wolfman and Gene Colan's *Tomb of Dracula* character, was actually in production, with a respectable $45 million budget, and Nicolas Cage was eager to star in *Iron Man*. But otherwise it was the same holding pattern that Stan Lee knew all too well: Silver Surfer, Fantastic Four, X-Men, Daredevil, and Doctor Strange in various stages of development. And the fact that Marvel Studios' Avi Arad was also part of Toy Biz—which was still scheming to gain control of Marvel—meant his days serving in Icahn's administration were numbered. In October, Toy Biz met with the banks, and Arad gave a stirring speech about the value of Marvel's characters in an attempt to dissuade them from agreeing to a deal Icahn had on the table. "We live in one of the most creative countries in the world. But look around you and see how few characters have been introduced and survived. You have *Star Wars*, maybe *Star Trek*, and you'll be hard-pressed to name any other characters that survived that long." His years of pitching movie studios were paying off. "I feel certain that Spider-Man alone is worth a billion dollars. But now, at this crazy hour, at this juncture, you're going to take 380 million—whatever it is from Carl Icahn—for the whole thing? *One* thing is worth a billion! We have the X-Men. We have the Fantastic Four. They can all be movies."

A few weeks later, after Icahn heard that Toy Biz had bought some of Marvel's debt—to have a say when the banks voted on reorganization plans—Calamari finally got the green light to fire Arad from his position as head of Marvel Films.

In a quest to lure up-and-coming talent to Marvel, Joe Calamari turned to *Wizard*, the comics magazine whose ascent was, for many, synonymous with the rise of the speculator mania that had swallowed the industry. *Wizard* publisher Gareb Shamus recommended that Calamari talk to Joe Quesada and Jimmy Palmiotti, two former Valiant Comics artists who'd formed their own fledgling company. "Gareb recommended us," Palmiotti said, "because we'd done *Wizard* covers and we were throwing a lot of parties in New York, you know? We would invite every comic company. We didn't play the DC versus Marvel game. We just thought, as the comics community, we should all be drinking, partying, celebrating the books we do." But there were two other qualifications that attracted Joe Calamari to them: one, they were also drinking and partying with Hollywood, and had sold a property to DreamWorks. Calamari figured that Quesada and Palmiotti's movie industry contacts might be of help. Two, they had made a name for themselves on a low budget.

"Make me and Jimmy co-editors-in-chief of Marvel Comics," the baby-faced, spiky-haired, and earringed Quesada told Calamari, "and we'll fix your whole company." For starters, they would deliver movie director Kevin Smith to write the *Daredevil* comic, which was then on the cusp of cancellation.

They settled on revamping four titles, just as "Heroes Reborn" had—and Marvel ponied up the money for overhauls of *Daredevil*, *The Inhumans*, *Black Panther*, and *Punisher*. Not Lee and Liefeld dollars, but enough that Palmiotti and Quesada could pay for state-of-the-art digital coloring processes and attract top talent. The titles would get their own imprint, "Marvel Knights."

"We wanted to show Marvel that we could do their characters better," Palmiotti said. "It's an arrogant thing, but it was our goal, to do the best we can and show them how it should be done." Rhoades set them up in the penthouse floor of the building, to keep them within reach—but out of sight from the rest of the editorial staff. Sure enough, the resentment from Marvel veterans was instant. "They were looking at a map of the Marvel offices," remembered one editor. "It was editorial on the 10th floor, executives on the 11th floor, and then the penthouse. They were talking about how they were going to refurbish the penthouse, and Quesada made some comment like, 'At this point, all you really need is the penthouse and the 11th floor.'" Bob Harras started getting letters from his staff complaining that the playing field was not level, that Quesada and Palmiotti could use their budget to outbid the rest of Marvel for talent. "Everybody in editorial had gone through two or three consecutive years of layoffs, and a very real concern that everything would just be outsourced, and the offices would be closed down," said Tom Brevoort. "One complaint was that it was unfair in that if you gave Marvel editorial access to those same resources, we could produce the same results. But we were often handcuffed—saddled with outdated printing systems, not up to date, whereas they could use more sophisticated processes to make their books look better." Quesada made sure to visit Bob Harras's office as often as he could, to show that he was a team player. But Harras never came up to visit the penthouse.

Meanwhile, for the second time in just over a year, relaunched versions of *Captain America*, *The Avengers*, *Fantastic Four*, and *Iron Man* hit the stands. This time, a more back-to-basics approach was embraced, with traditionalists like Kurt Busiek and Mark Waid writing, and superstar artist George Perez returning to Marvel for the first time in twenty years.

The strategy was called "Heroes Return," and if it was easy to confuse it with "Heroes Reborn," which it replaced—well, everyone was starting to get whiplash. The executives who'd signed off on the latest relaunches weren't even at Marvel anymore. "It was like being in a war zone," recalled one senior employee. "You didn't know from day to day whether you were reporting to Scott Sassa, or Calamari, or Icahn, or the bankruptcy court, or who."

On the eleventh floor, Harras was attempting the Herculean task of keeping everyone on the same page. "A new person would come in at the top," said Tom Brevoort, "and they'd declare, 'We're marching left.' Bob would turn everything around, only for somebody new to come in a week later and say, 'Why the fuck are you marching left? You should be marching right.' And then he'd have to run around and do that. It was absolutely crazy. He had to deal with a company that didn't necessarily know if it was going to make its payroll. Yet it was still the best-selling comic book company in existence, and he needed to keep that machine running."

Some of the staff, though, were starting to lose faith. Harras had never been known for his directness, and now coworkers complained that he was retreating behind the closed door of his office, waiting for cues from each succeeding executive. "A real leader," said one editor, "would have seized the opportunity to say, 'There's a revolving door at the top; nobody's looking at what we're doing. Here's my opportunity to put my stamp on the entire line, and give everybody the kind of leadership they need for as long as it lasts. This house of cards may fall tomorrow, but at least let's go down doing our best.' He was paralyzed."

"Heroes Return" gave Marvel a brief sales spike, but sales were dropping for Marvel, along with the rest of the industry, at a rate of about 20 percent a year. And the problems went beyond publishing. "The licensing dried up," said Rhoades, "because nobody wanted to pay a lot of money to make a Spider-Man bed sheet if Marvel was going to go out of business. All of the revenue streams were drying up in the middle of this huge public battle."

Just before Christmas 1997, the bankruptcy court—sensing that Carl Icahn's team was failing to put together a workable strategy—named a trustee, John Gibbons, to oversee Marvel. Gibbons, looking to retain some continuity at the company, told Joe Calamari he could stay and run things while he focused on showing Marvel's paperwork to prospective buyers in a conference room in his Newark office. (Meanwhile, according to Rhoades, Calamari and Marvel CFO Augie Liguori "got it in their heads that they could snatch the company out of the bankruptcy judge's hands, and were playing their own game against Icahn, and against Avi and Ike Perlmutter.")

Jim Shooter, who'd already been part of a team that made a bid for Marvel back in 1988, found backing from yet another group of bankers, and enlisted comics retailer Chuck Rozanski to sort through the hundreds of cartons of files. "By the time I was done reading the licensing contracts," Rozanski recalled, "I came to realize that there was nothing of value left to buy in that area. Ronald O. Perelman's staff, either through ignorance, or by design, had completely ruined the prospects for Marvel to earn any substantial licensing revenues. The Toy Biz deal totally screwed up the toy rights, the lawyers had created a tangle of conflicting rights in other areas, and whatever remained had been sold cheaply in exchange for upfront cash payments."

MGM, Sony, and Warner Bros. (which owned DC Comics) each trekked out to Newark, but they didn't like what they saw, either. According to Rozanski, "It would take years before the income streams could be restored to cover even the $20 million per year in interest that a $200 million bid would entail. For Icahn and Perlmutter to be talking numbers over $400 million was simply irrational except within the context of their own fears. Icahn was terrified he would lose the $200 million he invested, and Perlmutter feared losing Toy Biz."

Perlmutter's patience eventually paid off. By February 1998, Toy Biz had put together another reorganization plan; the court finally approved it in July, over Icahn's objections. To clear the final hurdles, Toy Biz paid $3.5 million of Icahn's legal costs and granted him general release from litigation; in turn, Icahn promised not to take legal action against Toy Biz. On September 27, 1998, Toy Biz and Marvel Entertainment Group merged into Marvel Enterprises. The two-year bankruptcy was over, and Isaac Perlmutter and Avi Arad were back on top.

Toy Biz's seizure of Marvel could not have come at a more opportune moment. In early August, New Line Cinema released *Blade*; although the vampire slayer from *Tomb of Dracula* never had more than a cult following in the comics, the Wesley Snipes vehicle quickly earned $70 million, four times the intake of the much higher-budget *Howard the Duck*. *Blade* had been in development for a decade, and now, although Marvel only saw $25,000 of the profits, suddenly there was proof that Marvel Comics characters were viable as film franchises. "*Blade* was the least likely to succeed," said Avi Arad. "That was the first time it seemed clear to Hollywood that the Marvel franchise was something special."

Weeks later, more serendipity: the Marvel Knights line launched with Kevin Smith's *Daredevil*, garnering attention from the mainstream media attention—and development executives. Joe Quesada and Jimmy Palmiotti had both worked in advertising, and now they put their marketing skills into a grassroots full-court press. They traveled the country, pumped hands at conventions, signed at galleries, and showed up on MTV. "Joe and I would drive up to *Wizard* magazine," said Palmiotti, "and outline the press we wanted to do for the next six months. We'd trade favors, do art for the magazines, chatrooms, all that stuff." Before long, their own sunglasses-wearing faces were featured in the advertisements, trading on a cult of personality not seen since the early Marvel days.

"We made some good money and we threw big parties in New York," said Palmiotti. "We'd have guys coming and saying, 'I'd love to do a book for you guys.' And we'd get our next talent there." They also started meeting comic-reading filmmakers, like John Singleton and Robert Rodriguez, and going to their parties. "All of a sudden, there was a switch that went off. People were looking at superheroes differently. We had the door open for people to start thinking about comic books as films."

Many of the veterans argued that they'd already been thinking about films for a while—they just couldn't get anyone else to listen. There was still tension between the rest of the editorial staff and the shiny penny that was Marvel Knights. If Kevin Smith missed a deadline, he didn't get fired; the book just came out later. If a Punisher series failed, Quesada and Palmiotti could just launch another. "No one would have gotten that many swings of the bat, but they did," complained one editor. "It seemed as if Marvel Knights got to use more money, have more time, with less restrictions, all so that they could look good in relation to the standard editorial row."

But the penthouse lights burned until one or two in the morning most nights. "I used to come in every Saturday," said another editor, "and they were always there."

Quesada and Palmiotti restored luster to *Daredevil*, *The Inhumans*, *Black Panther*, and *Punisher*, each of which had diminished since they'd first read them as children in the 1970s. Even more notable was *Marvel Boy*, by Scottish enfant terrible Grant Morrison, who in his work at DC had revived Steve Englehart's neglected legacy of absurd metatextualism and political commentary. Although Marvel Boy was a new character, the name borrowed from a handful of short-lived heroes who'd flitted in and out of existence since the 1940s, and his violent tantrums (Morrison called them the "ultimate adolescent power fantasy") were an intentional throwback to Bill Everett's early, angry Sub-Mariner tales. An alien Kree traveler whose spaceship was shot down by a maniac industrialist, Marvel Boy trashed New York City in revenge—spelling out profanities with fifty-foot flames—and fought a "living corporation" called Brand Hex. (There was even a winking acknowledgment that Marvel itself was part of the creeping globalization: subway dwellers wore Punisher jackets and Fantastic Four T-shirts.) "I wanted my hero to be an outcast," Morrison said, "a fiery rebel with an appetite for righteous mass destruction." In another couple of years, it would be unthinkable to show such behavior in a comic-book satire, but in that tiny window at the turn of the century, playing out against the real-life backdrop of *No Logo*, the Seattle WTO riots, and *Bush v. Gore*, Grant Morrison's *Marvel Boy* revived the dual thrills of danger and relevance. Marvel hadn't taken chances like this in years.

But the company was still broke, surviving on a $200 million bridge loan that would have to be paid back soon. Perlmutter's first order of business was to terminate the expensive contracts with executives that dragged on the company's finances. Stan Lee wasn't worried when he heard the news. His $500,000 per year lifetime deal was a special case—after all, he was the face of Marvel Comics. Nor did he worry when Perlmutter summoned him to New York. "Ike greeted me like a long-lost brother," Lee recalled, "telling me how important I was to him and the company and assuring me that I'd be making more money than ever from now on. I thought to myself, Gee, why did people tell me he's such a cold fish?" Then Perlmutter presented him with a two-year contract at half his previous salary. Lee was astonished. After the royal treatment by Bill Bevins, he thought, this was like Martin Goodman all over again.

But Perlmutter had underestimated just what Stan Lee's loyalty meant to the company. Lee's lawyer began negotiating. Without a contract, Lee might contest the ownership of some of those characters for which Marvel had, on innumerable occasions over three decades, credited him as the creator. And even if Lee didn't have much of a case, the damage to Marvel's public image would be devastating. The two parties eventually settled on a salary raise to $810,000 (with generous annual increases), plus a $500,000 yearly pension for his wife, plus $125,000 for writing the Spider-Man comic strip, and a whopping 10 percent of any movie and television profits that Marvel enjoyed. Furthermore, the new contract was nonexclusive, which meant that Lee could supplement his income in other ways—in fact, by the time he re-signed with Marvel, he'd already lined up an Internet start-up called Stan Lee Media.

While Lee's lawyer played hardball, Perlmutter saved money by sacking executives. He removed Joe Calamari (who only a year earlier had personally fired Avi Arad), Shirrel Rhoades, and a half dozen others. Then he rehired former president Jerry Calabrese to put editors out on the street. In a matter of weeks, most of the staff was gone; the number of editors was reduced from thirty to six. More titles were canceled. Every Friday, members of the dwindling staff wondered which side of the going-away parties they'd be on.* Once fired, an employee was told to leave his personal belongings in a box for inspection and leave the building. If the box contained comic books on which the employee had worked, they would be removed—they were company property, Perlmutter insisted.

Speculation that Marvel would soon simply hire its competitors to produce its line of comics, entirely eliminating the need for an editorial staff, ran rampant. Smoked-glass conference room doors, etched with Spider-Man logos, had been special-ordered five years ago, at the height of success; now they were among the items the company auctioned off and shipped away.

The joke everyone muttered was that, if Ike Perlmutter had his way, Marvel would consist of one guy in an office with a phone, licensing the characters. Why waste money on anything else? Memos demanded that paper clips not be thrown away, that lights be turned off if an office was vacated for more than five minutes. "Ike was an absolute tyrant, plain and simple," said one longtime employee. "There was no negotiation, there was no meeting of the minds, If Ike said, 'Turn the computers off at 5 pm,' you turned the computers off at 5 pm. If you crossed Ike, you were gone." (Fueling the fear was the rumor that the Six-Day War veteran still carried a pistol on his ankle.) After the coffee machine and bottles of water were removed from the Bullpen, word got around that Perlmutter was pushing for a policy of urinalysis for all employees. President Jerry Calabrese, for one, couldn't take it. "After only a little less than two months," he wrote in November, "it's clear to me that it would be impossible for me to make the kind of positive impact and difference I believed possible when I accepted the task."

---

* At Halloween, a member of the sales team dressed up as the Mount Rushmore of 1990s Marvel presidents, affixing blown-up head shots of Terry Stewart, Jerry Calabrese, David Schreff, and Joe Calamari (the costume-wearer's own head took up one spot) to a piece of corrugated cardboard. Calabrese, president once again, was not pleased.

Meanwhile, Perlmutter had begun to suspect that his longtime Toy Biz ally Joseph Ahearn, who was now chief executive at Marvel, was about to make a bid for power. Against the advice of his inner circle, Perlmutter called for Ahearn's ouster. Eric Ellenbogen, formerly of Lorne Michaels's Broadway Video, was announced as the replacement. In his first days on the new job, Ellenbogen suggested that a Christmas party would help the Marvel staff's morale.

No, said Perlmutter. That was a waste of twelve hundred dollars.

Weeks later, a number of freelancers began receiving letters claiming overpayment and demanding that money be returned to the company. Steve Gerber opened his mail to find a bill for fifty-three dollars.

In a strategy that was now tradition for Marvel ownership—but ironic nonetheless, given recent history—Toy Biz repaid its bridge loan with money raised through the sale of junk bonds. In February, the dumping of Fleer and Skybox, those dual albatrosses from the Perelman years, brought in another $26 million. They were sold at a fraction of what they'd cost, but Perlmutter was glad to take the money.

An even more important transaction took place in March, when the rights to the *Spider-Man* film were finally, miraculously, extricated. After MGM's claims were rejected in a summary judgment, a series of settlements—which included Columbia Pictures waiving the rights to a James Bond series—freed the way for Marvel to resell the license to Sony, for approximately $10 million. After nearly fifteen years and countless "Tangled Web" newspaper headlines, the resolution seemed almost sudden. (Eric Ellenbogen got to announce the legal victory, and then he too was gone, after seven months, with a $2.5 million severance package. The *New York Post* reported that he'd been fired for failing to turn around and sell Marvel once the Spider-Man mess had been cleared. Others simply said he'd crossed Perlmutter one time too many, or rented one too many Porsches on business trips.)

But even as things were falling into place for the *Spider-Man* movie, more battles were under way. After Stan Lee reminisced in *Comic Book Marketplace* about his inspirations for writing an acclaimed late 1965 issue of *Amazing Spider-Man*, Steve Ditko broke his long silence. "Stan never knew what was in my plotted stories," the artist wrote to the magazine's editors, "until I took in the penciled story, the cover, my script and Sol Brodsky took the material from me and took it all into Stan's office, so I had to leave without seeing or talking to Stan." A few months later, after Lee was identified in *Time* as the creator of Spider-Man, Ditko popped up on that magazine's letters page, too: "Spider-Man's existence needed a visual concrete entity," Ditko wrote. "It was a collaboration of writer-editor Stan Lee and Steve Ditko as co-creators." This time Lee picked up the phone and called Ditko, for the first time in more than thirty years.

"Steve said, 'Having an idea is nothing, because until it becomes a physical thing, it's just an idea,'" Lee recalled. "And he said it took him to draw the strip, and to give it life, so to speak, or to make it actually something tangible. Otherwise, all *I* had was an idea. So I said to him, 'Well, I think the person who has the *idea* is the person who creates it. And he said, 'No, because I *drew* it.' Anyway, Steve definitely felt that he was the co-creator of Spider-Man. And that was really, after he said it, I saw it meant a lot to him that was fine with me. So I said fine, I'll tell everybody you're the co-creator. That didn't quite satisfy him. So I sent him a letter."

But the wording of the open letter that Lee sent out in August 1999 was a stumbling block. "I have always considered Steve Ditko to be Spider-Man's co-creator," it read, and Ditko quickly pointed out that "'Considered' means to ponder, look at closely, examine, etc. and does not admit, or claim, or state that Steve Ditko is Spider-Man's co-creator."

"At that point," Lee said, "I gave up."

Marv Wolfman had filed a suit when the *Blade* movie was released, contesting the ownership of more than seventy characters, including the titular hero, which he claimed to have created before his employment at Marvel. The trial began in November. Unfortunately for Wolfman, he did not have the backing of his peers. "My assumption for my work was that Marvel owned it," Roy Thomas said in a deposition. "I sort of thought that Marv, coming from DC, would know that." Gene Colan contended that the Blade character had only been fleshed out after he and Wolfman were collaborating on the *Tomb of Dracula* issue in which he first appeared. And John Byrne—still proud to be a company man—testified that Wolfman and Len Wein had warned him, at a 1975 Thanksgiving dinner, that the "companies own everything you do." Wolfman and Wein had expressed surprise, Byrne claimed, when Steve Gerber had sued over Howard the Duck. "How could he have a case?" Byrne said they wondered aloud. "The companies own everything!"* Ultimately, the court ruled that Wolfman had insufficient evidence of creating Blade before his Marvel employment, and that all characters he created while on staff fell under the category of work-for-hire.

Soon afterward, Joe Simon began actions to terminate Marvel's copyright transfer for the first ten issues of *Captain America*. He'd already settled with the company once, in 1969, but in the interim, the courts had redefined the rules of work-for-hire, and an April 1999 claim by the widow of *Superman* co-creator Jerry Siegel paved the way. When Marvel's *Captain America* copyright was up for renewal in December, the eighty-six-year-old Simon leaped at his chance.

"Christ, I'm doing this for my children and other creative people who should have their rights," Simon told a reporter. "I'm not doing it for myself. I'm too old to be doing this for myself, but I'm not going to quit by any means. They've spent so much money on this. Marvel must have spent a million bucks on this. I think some people would get together and back me on this."

Even Simon could see that it was movies, not publishing, where the future lay—comics, he said, were for the "masturbation generation," a parade of big guns and big breasts. "The business is going to hell in the first place, but the characters are more valuable than ever. So, we'll do the best we can."†

---

* "He was making faces whenever I'd look in his direction," Wolfman said of Byrne's appearance in the courtroom. "Because the comments I had to make referred to him, he would start to make faces. He would move up and down. There was a wall in front of him, a couple feet high where the witnesses are behind. He would, like, lower himself so I couldn't see him then raise himself up. He would start shaking his head no as if I was making a mistake, and he flustered me, because I'm trying to remember specific events. He was acting very much like a two-and-a-half-year-old child who has not had any Ritalin."

† Simon and Marvel settled out of court, once again, in September 2003.

Peter Cuneo, the third Marvel CEO to work for Perlmutter inside of a year, was a renowned turnaround king. He didn't follow comic books any more than Perelman had. Did it matter? "Whether you're selling deodorant or a wrench," he said, "you're always trying to find a way to emotionally bond to the consumer." Like Joe Simon, Cuneo had no doubt what the future held for Marvel: not just Hollywood, but the cross-marketing of video games, fast-food restaurants, and soft-drink companies. A new division, the Marvel Characters Group, was created solely to manage synergistic opportunities. "The Marvel Characters Group will be running the superheroes as brands," said Cuneo. "Think of them as agents for the characters. An agent for the X-Men says, 'I have an X-Men movie coming out in July. What special things are we going to be doing in the publishing division? What integrated promotions are we planning?'"

Coordinating all that with the comic books was easier said than done. Although the X-Men titles remained at the top of the charts, they were as much a creative battleground as ever, as a half-dozen successive writers complained of editorial micromanaging and rewriting. The editors, meanwhile, insisted that they were only listening to the fans, that letter-writing campaigns determined which characters stayed or departed. "What do the fans want?" one writer grumbled. "They want change. What happens when you give them change? It's not the change they wanted, and everybody wants things back the way they were."

It wasn't just a matter of populist rule. Within the offices, a full-fledged bureaucracy had taken root. Editor in Chief Bob Harras and Editorial Director Chris Claremont, who'd once fought for custody of the mutant characters, were now both part of the chain of command, and neither was ready to cede control. "Bob definitely stood over my shoulder a lot," said one editor. "I don't think it was good for the books, for me, or for him." Scripts were turned in, second-guessed by Harras, and then triple-guessed by Claremont, who still had emotional ties to the characters and stories. "Technically, Chris was not supposed to be involved in the X-Men books, but there was no way to keep them away from him," the editor said. "I would often say to my assistant, 'I don't think Chris really wants to write the books, but I don't think he wants anyone else to write them either.'" By the end of 1999, Chris Claremont was, once again, writing *The X-Men*.

As the pillars of Marvel's publishing business, the X-Men titles had long carried a heavy weight. Now, during an industry-wide slump, the burden was tremendous, and everyone on the creative side felt it. Perhaps Harras summed it up best. "There seems to be a perception that there's this evil corporation of Marvel dictating changes and so on, but that's not reality. It's just that everyone is watching you, inside and outside the company."

Shortly afterward, when Peter Cuneo appointed a new president of the company, it meant there was one more person to watch the X-Men franchise. Bill Jemas, a Harvard Law graduate and NBA executive, had gained experience with the Marvel brand in the 1990s, when he worked for Fleer. Now he took a look at the company's biggest properties and made his disapproval clear. There were sixty titles a month, Jemas said, and he didn't like any of them. And *The X-Men*, with its complicated story lines and overpopulation of characters, was at the top of his list. "I went to Harvard Law," he told a room of editors. "If I can't understand it, it's not because of me."

Fox's *X-Men* movie was coming out that summer, and the *Spider-Man* movie was scheduled for the following year. Each could potentially bring in a whole new audience, but only, Jemas felt, if the comics' serpentine plots were made accessible. He also blanched at how the Marvel heroes had aged, complaining that "characters who were envisioned as teenagers were walking around with goatees, beards, and children." The quickest solution was to start over from scratch. Jemas actually toyed with destroying the Marvel Universe and building it back up from scratch, but finally settled on the idea of adding a parallel "Ultimate" line of comics, filled with younger counterparts to the Marvel heroes.

Jemas, dissatisfied with the initial pitches that came through Bob Harras's office, asked Quesada to sit in on an end-of-the-day meeting about the Ultimates line and explain why it was failing. "That was one of my most uncomfortable meetings at Marvel," remembered Quesada, "because politically I'm trying to make sure everything runs smooth and there are no snags between Marvel Knights and the editor-in-chief of the Marvel staff, and Bill sort of brought me in as his hammer." Eventually charged with scouting talent for the project, Quesada called Brian Michael Bendis, a writer of crime comics who'd filled in when Kevin Smith didn't make his *Daredevil* deadlines. Bendis would bring *Spider-Man* into the twenty-first century.

The Peter Parker in *Ultimate Spider-Man* was a backpack-toting computer whiz with a skater haircut and an internship at *eBugle*, the *Daily Bugle* website. Aunt May and Uncle Ben were former commune dwellers, the same kind of baby boomers who might have been holding picket signs in the background of *Amazing Spider-Man* circa 1968. But these changes were mostly cosmetic. *Ultimate Spider-Man* recovered the angsty essence of the original Lee and Ditko stories, and livened the tug of Parker's ego and conscience—the struggles of great power and great responsibility—in a way that hadn't been done in decades.

Jemas got free samples of the comic in Wal-Marts, KB Toys, and Buster Brown shoe boxes. When the marketing blitz was done, eight million copies of *Ultimate Spider-Man* were circulating.

But the script for *Ultimate X-Men*, assigned to another writer, was rejected, and when Fox moved up the release date of *The X-Men* movie by six months, Marvel had missed its synergistic opportunity. *The X-Men* made $75 million its opening week, but sales on the comic didn't budge. "I think at the time it was the third-biggest opening weekend of all time for a non-sequel," said Jemas. "Crazy numbers. But the comic books were based on the '60s continuity. So there was no graphic novel, no TV promo. The movie was for 20-year-olds and the toys were for 10-year-olds and the toys didn't sell. We had a TV show that was from hell that didn't tie into anything and we had merchandise that was from hell that didn't tie into anything, too. So, we had a movie success and a god awful financial failure and we were broke—like, can't-make-payroll broke."

Jemas turned his attention back to streamlining the Marvel Universe proper, hammering away in meetings at the importance of stripping each character to its "central metaphor." That week, a *New York* magazine story on the *X-Men* began with Chris Claremont's editors shooting down his plot ideas. Bob Harras was among those challenging Claremont, but Jemas wanted to clean house entirely.

It wasn't a difficult mission to carry out. Perlmutter and Harras had their own tensions, owing in part to Perlmutter's draconian cost-cutting. At the end of August, Bill Jemas asked Joe Quesada if he'd be interested in the job of editor in chief.

Quesada immediately began shaking things up at Marvel. Grant Morrison, fresh from the critical success of the Marvel Knights title *Marvel Boy*, was recruited to take over *X-Men* from Chris Claremont; Claremont left his staff job as well. Quesada then recruited editor Axel Alonso from DC Comics' edgy "Vertigo" line, and Alonso in turn hired J. Michael Straczynski, the creator of the television show *Babylon 5*, to take over *Amazing Spider-Man*. Howard Mackie, who'd been regularly writing the web-spinner's adventures for most of the decade, was out.

It was not surprising, then, when Quesada's arrival caused friction with two of the more contentious Marvel veterans. Steve Englehart, working on a Fantastic Four series, complained publicly that changes to his script were made without his input; he and Quesada issued a series of competing press releases. A week later, Quesada canceled John Byrne's *X-Men: The Hidden Years*, a series set in the past, and Byrne took up the matter on his website. "Joe Quesada was not able to give me any sort of reason that made sense—killing profitable books in a failing market?—so, since I have no interest in devoting my time and effort to a company apparently intent on committing suicide, my relationship with Marvel is over."* Nearly every remnant of the old guard was gone.

Stan Lee was gone, too, except for his scant duties as a well-paid Marvel figurehead. Two years earlier, during the lapse in his Marvel contract, Lee began working with a lawyer and businessman named Peter Paul on an Internet venture called Stan Lee Media. They'd met through

---

* At Joe Quesada's request, Chris Claremont had recently agreed to collaborate with John Byrne on an alternate-reality, one-shot X-Men story called "The End." It would have been their first pairing on the characters in twenty years.

fund-raising events, and before long Paul was introducing Lee to A-list celebrities like Bill and Hillary Clinton and Muhammad Ali. "I was looking for ways to liberate him," Paul said of Lee. "He was lying fallow at Marvel."

Although its primary concern was online animation, SLM had other, ambitious plans—feature films, amusement park rides, a line of clothing featuring famous Stan Lee catchphrases—and with the power of Lee's name, it quickly attracted investors. Within a year of the company's creation, Peter Paul engineered a reverse merger with a shell company, and Wall Street money started flowing in. Six months later, when its website finally launched, stocks were changing hands at $31 a share, and SLM was capitalized in the neighborhood of $300 million. For a while, Lee continued to write his "Stan's Soapbox" column for Marvel. "Nothing short of an H-bomb could tear me from the company I love," he wrote in 1999. "I'm just setting up my own website, in my spare time, for the fun of it. Come and visit when we officially open in August, but no matter what—Marvel rules!"

But most of his time was spent breathing in drywall dust at the SLM headquarters, where he'd arrive at nine thirty each morning to find an ever-expanding office space. Even Marvel had never grown at the pace of an Internet start-up, but it suited Lee's energy. Although his level of technology savvy topped out at replying to email messages, at nearly eighty years old Lee was giving speeches at technology conferences.

To the SLM creative staff, he lived up to his legend, bouncing around and acting out scenes for new characters, even if some of those creations seemed suspiciously like pastiches of Marvel heroes; one, the Accuser, managed to incorporate a wheelchair (like Professor X), a law-practicing alter ego (like Daredevil), and an armored suit (like Iron Man). And Lee had generated a tremendous amount of goodwill among the entertainment industry over the past decades. There were partnerships on the table with Burger King, Fox Kids, the Backstreet Boys, and RZA of the Wu-Tang Clan. Michael Jackson toured the offices and pondered a team-up of mammoth proportions. "If I buy Marvel," the King of Pop asked Stan the Man, "you'll help me run it, won't you?" Lee assured him that he would.

By the summer of 2000, Lee would have certainly enjoyed putting Marvel in its place. "I was very surprised that Stan Lee was, on the inside, considered to be an outsider," recalled a Marvel executive. "Somebody to take care of—somebody we've gotta pay attention to." The "Stan's Soapbox" column, a regular feature since 1967, was discontinued; Marvel explained that it took up potentially valuable advertising space. Perlmutter had also been campaigning to remove the "Stan Lee Presents" banner from the comics, and had even insisted that Lee be scratched from the list of those who received complimentary copies of new comics. "Ike had it in for Stan like you wouldn't believe," said one editor. "Ike hated him."

Lee could afford to buy his own comics—his Stan Lee Media stock was, by now, valued at $35 million. But there were signals that he ultimately wielded no more power at SLM than he did at Marvel in the 1960s. "Stan once had a big lunch with all the artists," recalled SLM artist Scott Koblish, "and we all steered it toward our ideas for making money: CD-ROMs, publishing—we had a fistful of ideas, and Stan was jazzed about all of them, but he warned us before he left the lunch that as soon as he'd show these ideas to the execs they'd get shot down."

At the very least, Lee was not in the loop when it came to the inner workings of the business. "He would sit in business meetings and occasionally say something," one friend reported. "But mainly he'd sit there and doodle, or fall asleep." He didn't yet know that his business partner, Peter Paul, had served jail time in the 1970s for cocaine possession and defrauding Fidel Castro for $8.7 million in a bizarre coffee shipment scheme that involved plans to sink a Panamanian freighter. (Paul would later claim he was working as a CIA operative.) Paul had not put his checkered past behind him: Stan Lee Media was outspending its revenues 20 to 1, and falling behind on its bills, as Peter Paul manipulated the stock prices.

No one knew why the stocks were falling. But in a matter of weeks, the SLM staff braced for the end, backing up portfolio samples and removing valuable items from their offices. On December 15, a Spider-Man statue arrived from Germany, a birthday gift the staff had collectively purchased for Lee's birthday. As they waited for an ominous 4 p.m. meeting, they pieced together the seven-foot statue and signed a card.

When the layoffs were announced, Stan Lee collapsed. "I think of that old James Brown trick in 'Please, Please, Please,' where they gather him up because he can't go on," Koblish recalled. "They gathered Stan up and led him out, and then they gathered the rest of us up in the big room, room 145, and told us that that was it."

It had been forty-three years since Martin Goodman made him fire the Timely staff, leaving Lee alone to build from scratch. Now, half a lifetime later, he had to suffer the additional blow of betrayal. Peter Paul was gone, on his way to São Paulo, Brazil, along with $250,000 that Lee had loaned him personally. "He is like a grandfather. He is sweet and unassuming—and easily taken advantage of," said a friend. "But not anymore; he's jaded. He said to me, 'Now the only people I know I can trust are my wife and my daughter.'"

Across the country, several members of Perlmutter's team were gathered in a meeting with Bill Jemas and Joe Quesada. "A guy stuck his head in the door," recalled one attendee, "and said, 'Great news, guys! Stan Lee Media is going under!' Joe had the good sense to put his head down and not say anything. Bill made some kind of comment like he was playing along, but I don't think even he was comfortable with that. But everybody else in the room was having a good laugh about this. That was the mentality. They hated him. It was bizarre."

Bill Jemas was the kind of guy who cared more about the New York Knicks than about Nick Fury. He was proud to slay the sacred cows of the geeky world he'd entered—no more hang-ups about continuity, he liked to say, no more writing "comics about comics." He took pride in challenging the staff on what kinds of stories were off-limits: in one early meeting he suggested revealing the origin of Wolverine, which, despite the popularity of the character, had remained shrouded in mystery. The editors were aghast at his impiety.

Marvel suddenly pushed for commonsense changes that might seem blindingly obvious to anyone who wasn't entrenched in industry tradition: first pages were given to story recaps of previous issues, freeing writers from having to shoehorn clumsy exposition into the dialogue or captions. The all-capital-letters word balloons, a holdover from a time in which poor printing technology necessitated the extra clarity, were replaced by proper English. Sensing that trade paperback collections could be a vital part of the company business—and a beachhead into bookstore chains— Marvel began clearly demarcating beginnings and endings of story arcs, so that a half-dozen "episodes" could easily be packaged into a single paperback volume. When another writer-artist team came along, to continue the television show analogy, a new "season" began.

How many of these changes involved input from Joe Quesada was difficult to say, because Jemas was the strongest personality in Marvel editorial since Jim Shooter—and Jemas wasn't even technically in editorial. But Jemas and Quesada jumped with both feet into the world of online comics fandom, becoming a two-headed public persona for the Marvel Comics of the twenty-first century. Before long, they'd perfected a good-cop, bad-cop routine. Jemas had little interest in diplomacy, blaming "bad, bad books" for Marvel's late 1990s slump, and implying a network of cronyism. "In 1995, a typical Marvel *X-Men* book was selling a million copies a month," Jemas told an interviewer. "We could have afforded to hire just about any writer in the world—from John Irving to Scott Turow—but the editors hired each other, and they hired their friends."

He was no more polite to Marvel's readership. Questioned about plans to launch a category of titles he called "Bad Girls for Fanboys," Jemas shot back, "We have quite a few male readers who live in the basement of their parents' house in Queens. For them, an evening with Elektra is as good as it gets." To another interviewer, he delicately clarified what he meant by "Bad Girls": "Elektra is so bad you are going to want to spank her." Frank Miller's tragic heroine was not only back from the dead; now she was a cheesecake ninja pinup.

Thankfully, not all of Marvel's forays into more "adult" content catered so embarrassingly to one-dimensional titillation. At the end of an all-night bender, editor Axel Alonso recruited British writer Peter Milligan for a drastically reimagined version of *X-Force*, the *X-Men* spinoff that had once been Rob Liefeld's playground. The brand-new, college-aged characters resembled nothing more than spoiled members of a professional sports team, juggling talk shows, limousine rides, and endorsement deals; the group was funded by a venture capitalist. *X-Force*'s dim view of youth culture—there were characters based on Allen Iverson and Eminem, and a grisly execution scene involving a teenage boy band—made it the most gleefully acerbic title Marvel had published. In the first scene of Milligan's tenure, a character named Zeitgeist pauses from a ménage-à-trois with two supermodels to watch the "game tape" of the graphically violent super-battle he'd fought the night before; by issue's end, all but two of the team's original members are dead. The Kirbyish primitiveness of Mike Allred's art, and the primary-color palette, only accentuated the ironic corruption of old-fashioned Marvel innocence. When the issue came back from the Comics Code with a slew of objections, Jemas shrugged. Not only did Marvel publish *X-Force* without the Comics Code seal, it boasted about it: "Hey Kids!" shouted one corner of the cover. "Look! No Code!"

When *Ultimate Spider-Man* writer Brian Michael Bendis pitched *Alias*, a series about a heavy-drinking, swearing, down-on-her-luck, ex-superheroine-turned-private detective, Bendis clarified, before Quesada responded, that he was prepared to tone it down. But Jemas went for it, without hesitation, in all its profane glory. Marvel wouldn't just publish it without a Comics Code seal—it would create a whole new line of "Adults Only" superhero comics, called MAX. The first issue leaped in with both feet. "Fuck! This is—fuck! "God Fucking Dammit!" comprised the entirety of the first page's dialogue. As it turned out, though, the obscenities were just a bit of throat-clearing before the comic settled into complex, sympathetic characterization and the smart, rat-a-tat dialogue that marked David Mamet screenplays or Richard Price novels. Bendis retrofitted his bruised underdog heroine, Jessica Jones, into Marvel's history, making her an aging alumnus of the early 1980s Avengers (code name: Jewel), and her emotional interactions with Marvel fixtures like Luke Cage, Matt Murdock, and Steve Rogers simultaneously satisfied fanboys' desires for in-jokes and added dimensionality to decades-old characters. Despite its achievements, it was the reference to rough sex (between Jessica and Luke "Power Man" Cage) that got all the attention. After a printer in Alabama refused to handle the first issue, Marvel had to take it elsewhere for publication.

Jemas had no patience for moral watchdogs. He withdrew Marvel's membership from the Comics Code Authority, just like that, after nearly fifty years. The other dues-paying companies protested, but the feeling within Marvel was electric. Seemingly no one had questioned before why a publisher would continue to underwrite an outdated third-party entity that limited the content of its product.

There were other changes. Suddenly the quality of the coloring and printing improved. The practice of overprinting—through which retailers could always reorder fast-selling product, but which stuck Marvel with mounds of unsold inventory—ceased. "Bill was absolutely fearless in the way a man who does not understand the consequences of his actions can be," said Tom Brevoort, "and he bulldozed through obstacles that could not be moved beforehand, because he was heedless—courageous, insightful, and oblivious to the fact that things couldn't be done. That was very valuable to knocking out some of the calcification that had been built up."

The MAX line sent the message that Marvel was a creative haven once again. Doug Moench and Paul Gulacy returned, after twenty years, to *Shang-Chi, Master of Kung Fu*. Gail Simone, a former hairdresser who wrote feminist critiques of comics on websites, got the green light to re-vive *Night Nurse* as a former "wild chick" who was "part Elvira and part Mother Teresa." Even Steve Gerber returned, to do a *Howard the Duck* series for the MAX line, and because he didn't like the Howard redesign that had been in place ever since Disney's lawyers came calling in the early 1980s, Howard the Duck was rendered as a mouse. There was a thrilling sense of danger at Marvel once again, a sense that the creative forces of Marvel didn't have anyone to answer to.

But unhinged flights of the imagination were the exception—capturing an audience was front-and-center of the editorial strategy. No one articulated this balance of experimentation and crowd-pleasing bet-ter than Grant Morrison, whose *X-Men* pitch had read like a call to arms, a manifesto for calculated rule-breaking. "This is a *pop* book," Morri-son wrote, "as essential as the new Eminem release or the latest Keanu movie. We can rejoin the culture here and the only way to do it is to drop '80s and '90s notions of who our audience should be. The only way to get back in there is to deliver the stuff the movies and the games *can't*.

And what the mainstream audience wants from us (and I've asked a lot of 'em) is raw imagination, ready-made characters, outrageous spectacle, storming angst and emotional drama. Beautiful people with incredible powers doing startling, diverting things!" Taking a cue from the movie version, Morrison replaced the X-Men's spandex costumes with standardized team uniforms, but uniforms with a sense of fashion that could only come from an ex-raver: Day-Glo yellow biker jackets, military pants, and heavy boots. As he'd promised in his pitch, he revamped and reintroduced classic concepts like the Sentinels, the Shi'Ar Empire, and the Phoenix Force, "in such a way that it will seem as though we're seeing these concepts for the first time."

"Dead characters always return," Morrison complained of the X-Men comics of the preceding decade. "Nothing that happens really matters ultimately. The stage is never cleared for new creations to develop and grow." In a neat metafictional trick, Morrison wanted to use the well-worn elements of the X-Men mythos to explore what he saw as the central metaphor of the humans-versus-mutants theme: the ways in which older species try to stifle their newer, evolutional replacements. But even as he introduced the most off-the-wall new characters anyone had seen in a Marvel comic for years—a clumsy, virginal, straight-edge, hard-core mutant with a beak and talons; a chain-smoking, problem-drinking teen-age Latina with insect wings; a creepy set of psychically linked quintuplets named the Stepford Cuckoos; Xorn, a Chinese meditator whose iron skull contained a powerful star—he built up everything to climax with the death of Phoenix. Everything new was old again.

When it was time to hit the reset button and roll out the "Ultimate" version of *The Avengers*, Jemas and Quesada hired Morrison protégé Mark Millar and artist Bryan Hitch, who had pushed the boundaries of DC's corporate patience with *The Authority*, a pitch-black comic that imagined superheroes as part of the military-industrial complex. They brought a similar sensibility to the assured—and, some would say, cynical—*The Ultimates*. In this version of the Earth's Mightiest Heroes, Nick Fury allied with Stark Industries to organize a team of super-powered living weapons for the United States. Thor was no longer the alter ego of Dr. Donald Blake, but rather a long-haired WTO protester with delusions of godhood. Tony Stark was no longer just a rich industrialist who had different dates to every fund-raiser—he was a nihilistic, wisecracking louche. Psychodrama abounded, from Bruce Banner's suppressed rage to Henry Pym's feelings of inadequacy. It was realism in ways that only comics readers defined the term: pessimistic, violent, and more concerned with repercussions than with moments of transcendence.

Hitch's artwork—smooth and polished, filled with photographic references, and often organized in horizontal grids that approximated CinemaScope grandeur—gave readers the sense that they were peeking at beautiful storyboards for an unproduced blockbuster. Where Busiek and Ross's similarly lifelike *Marvels* had reserved its full-page big moments for tableaux of wonder, the Millar-Hitch synthesis gave the widescreen treatment to spectacles of destruction.

Its cinematic qualities were, of course, no accident—*The Ultimates* was intended as a demonstration of how *The Avengers* franchise could be transmogrified into a megaplex attraction, a floppy comic book that could be handed over to a Hollywood producer as an all-in-one pitch souvenir. Captain America's likeness was based on Brad Pitt; Iron Man's on Johnny Depp. And Nick Fury, no longer a greatest-generation relic, was transformed into a dead ringer, visually and verbally, for Samuel L. Jackson in his monologue-inclined Tarantino mode. If *The Ultimates* were ever made into a movie, the casting précis was already complete.

"I'd much rather be an actor than a writer," Stan Lee once told French auteur Alain Resnais. He'd had a brief moment onscreen as a hot-dog vendor in the *X-Men* movie; when cameras rolled on Sam Raimi's $140 million *Spider-Man*, he was assigned a role as a curbside vendor of cheap sunglasses. He even got some dialogue: "Hey," he shouted to a potential customer, "how about these? They wore 'em in the *X-Men*!" The week before *Spider-Man*'s release, he appeared, as himself, in a guest spot on *The Simpsons*.

Lee took full advantage of the publicity machine surrounding the movie. In countless newspaper, magazine, radio, and television interviews, which always included mention of his teeming seventy-nine-year-old energy, he not only told his familiar tales—about coming up with the idea for Spider-Man, about his years toiling for Martin Goodman—but he looked to the future. Avoiding conversation about Peter Paul or Stan Lee Media, he announced yet another start-up, POW! Entertainment, for which he'd already created an animated Pamela Anderson vehicle called *Stripperella*. He promoted a biographical DVD called *Stan Lee's Mutants, Monsters & Marvels*, and, a quarter-century after he'd signed a contract to write his memoirs, proudly mentioned that Simon & Schuster was finally publishing *Excelsior: The Amazing Life of Stan Lee*. (The introductions to each chapter in his autobiography, worded in the third person, gave an idea of how he felt about the recent successes of the Marvel films: "Stan thought Avi did quite well in his new task. Of course, he had a great ballpark to play in. It would be difficult not to do well when you controlled characters like The X-Men, Spider-Man, The Hulk, Daredevil, and so many additional heroes who had been popular for decades, and were offering them to studios that were hungry for proven characters that could be franchised.")

This was Lee's moment in the spotlight, and he wasn't going to let any opportunity go to waste. On April 23, a press release announced that he was taking his file copies of Marvel publications out of storage and putting them up for sale. The auction house predicted they would take in about $4 million.

Six days later, at the *Spider-Man* premiere party in Westwood, Los Angeles, Adam Sandler, Cuba Gooding Jr., and Will Smith were Lee's red-carpet compatriots, along with stars Tobey Maguire and Kirsten Dunst. The film grossed $39 million on opening day—a new world record.

Spider-Man ran 121 minutes. Both of Stan Lee's lines were cut.

(21)

"I HAVEN'T MADE A PENNY FROM SPIDER-MAN," READ A LONDON *TIMES* HEAD-
line in June 2002, for an article in which Stan Lee good-naturedly explained that he wasn't seeing any profits from the movie. "People naturally
assume that I have. They read that the movie will make half a billion
dollars so they figure I'll get about a third of that, but no." When the
journalist expressed his surprise, Lee waved it aside. "But I've had a great
life," he assured him. "I've enjoyed it and I have formed a new company
and things look very promising."

Still, it seemed that there were subtle ways in which he was distancing himself from his old company. "If I had done that movie there would
have been less destruction," he said of the myriad explosions that ripped
across the screen in *Spider-Man*. When another reporter informed him
of a Nick Fury series—part of Marvel's adult-readers MAX line—in
which the crusty colonel strangled an enemy with his own entrails, Lee
responded, "I don't know why they're doing that. I don't think that I would
do those kinds of stories."

Lee had long outgrown an interest in keeping up with new superhero
adventures, and now he'd even sold his comic book collection. Even as he
insisted that he held no regrets, in conversation he returned to the idea
of what might have been. "I wish I had come to Hollywood and been a
screenwriter," he mused. "I wish I had the time to be a novelist. I think I
could have done better. I mean, I would have loved to have written a great
novel. I would have loved to have written a great bunch of screenplays. I
would have loved to have written a Broadway show. I didn't have any big
compulsion to write comics. It was a way of making a living."

On November 12, 2002, citing the provision in his 1998 contract that

416

called for "participation equal to 10% of the profits derived during your life by Marvel (including subsidiaries and affiliates) from the profits of any live action or animation television or movie (including ancillary rights) production utilizing Marvel characters," Stan Lee filed a $10 million lawsuit against Marvel Enterprises and Marvel Characters.

By the time of *Spider-Man*'s release, Avi Arad and Peter Cuneo had renegotiated Marvel's Hollywood deals so that the company would receive a percentage of gross, rather than net, profits. It was an impressive feat, and fortuitously timed, since the company's heroes were now hot property. *Blade 2*, which opened at number one at the box office on Easter, was still in theaters when *Spider-Man* was released, and by then big-budget adaptations of *Hulk* and *Daredevil* were already in production, and Fox had given *X-Men 2* a release date.

Almost overnight, superheroes were the apple of the public's eye. The weekend that *Spider-Man* opened, thousands of comic shops around the country participated in Free Comic Book Day, an idea hatched by a California retailer who'd noticed the long lines at Baskin-Robbins Free Scoop Night. Timed to piggyback on the movie's buzz, the event included giveaways from all the major publishers, who hoped to lure new audiences to the endangered art form.

After seven straight years of decline, Marvel had finally stopped the bleeding, with a combination of Hollywood hype and the influx of fresh ideas. But even as direct-market sales began to turn around—and they were still only a quarter of what they'd been a decade earlier—publishers watched helplessly as newsstand exposure shrank. A whopping 85 percent of sales now came from comic stores, and nobody was likely to wander into a comic store unless they were already looking for comics.

Marvel continued to talk about the importance of attracting new readers, but appealing to younger children wasn't part of that strategy. "I think the 8-year-old comic reader is a myth," Joe Quesada told a reporter. "It's not a concern to me. A year ago, when I took that job, that's what I was concerned with. I heard comic-store owners saying, 'Where are my 8-year-old readers?' You know what? I don't think they were ever really out there." Instead, Marvel wanted to court teenagers, a demographic that had been nearly eradicated by competition from television and video games. The syndicated *Buffy the Vampire Slayer* TV show became Jemas's shorthand for what he was looking for—a continuing series with young, attractive stars and a rich backstory that nevertheless was accessible to a new audience. (According to one writer, at the height of Jemas's *Buffy-mania*, there were three female-monster-killer series simultaneously in development at Marvel.)

"There has been a perpetual push and pull over whether each project should target the loyal 'core' market of dedicated comic fans ('fanboys') or the broader audience of Marvel fans in the 'mass market,'" Jemas wrote, and it was clear that he relished his role in antagonizing the pimply nerds of the base readership. In fact, it started to seem like chasing away die-hard customers was a primary goal. After a series of public debates between Quesada and writer Peter David about the low-selling *Captain Marvel*, Jemas stepped in with a challenge. "Peter is a talented writer maybe two or three issues of the year," Jemas announced to the press, "but the rest is just inside jokes for fans who have been reading his stuff for 20 years. He's just feeding off his old work. I feel that he needs to make his stories accessible to new readers or it's doomed." In a contest dubbed "U-Decide," sales of David's *Captain Marvel* would be judged against a new title called *Marville*, which Jemas himself would write. Whichever title sold least would be canceled.*

Politically incorrect, attention-getting trash talk was business as usual for Jemas and Quesada. ("They have Batman and Superman, and they don't know what to do with them," Quesada once said to a reporter about DC Comics. "That's like being a porn star with the biggest dick and you can't get it up. What the fuck?") The difference was that, with *Marville*, the dog-and-pony show seemed to dictate the content of the comics. It had been trumpeted as a demonstration of the storytelling techniques Peter David had failed to learn, but its first issue perpetrated precisely the crimes Jemas had denounced. *Marville* was a directionless string of satirical set pieces so filled with inside jokes that a text feature on the

---

* A third title, the Batman-and-Robin pastiche *Ultimate Adventures*, written by frequent Howard Stern guest Ron Zimmerman, was later added to the contest. Peter David's *Captain Marvel* was the winner.

first page of each issue was necessary to spell out each reference. In the first issue, the Superboy-like KalAOL, son of Ted Turner and Jane Fonda, is sent back in time from 5002 A.D., where he meets a sexy redheaded cab driver named Mickey and a sexy brunette cop named Lucy. There were jabs at Ron Perelman, but also at Peter David. Iron Man showed up and, after bloodying a few bystanders, spouted, "I know, I destroyed the local economy. But you can pay Mexicans a dollar an hour and they still work like N—" at which point he was interrupted by the Black Panther: "People would think poorly of you if you said a bad word." Spider-Man and Daredevil's old enemy the Kingpin turned out to be Spike Lee in a Malcolm X cap. The politics of *Marville* #1 might have been deemed offensively incendiary, if only they weren't so bewildering. At its most coherent, *Marville* #1 simply came off as an extended screed against superhero comics and the culture that had grown around them.*

Worst of all was the cover, which uncomfortably melded Marvel's post–Comics Code embrace of prurience with its interest in the teen market. The front of the first issue prominently featured Mickey's crotch, as she sat in the driver's seat of her taxi, clad in a bikini and high heels. (She was a dead ringer for *Buffy* star Sarah Michelle Gellar.) On the next issue's cover, she appeared at a front door, smiling at the reader, her nakedness barely hidden by the housewarming gifts that filled her arms: pizza, a six-pack, video games, and porn on VHS.

Meanwhile, within the actual pages of *Marville*, a godlike being towed KalAOL, Mickey, and Lucy through the ages, leading Platonic dialogues about the relative merits of creationism and evolution. During parts of these lectures, they all skinny-dipped. In the sixth issue, KalAOL returned to the twenty-first century and pitched a comic-book executive on the series itself. "This thing," the executive finally said, "will never sell."

"Because I'm president of Marvel," Jemas wrote in an open letter on the issue's last page, "I could ignore the bean counters and publish Marville without regard for minimum sales projections and margin

---

* Jemas offered the job of scripting *Marville* to Steve Gerber, who declined because of the book's portrayal of DC's Paul Levitz. "I wasn't prepared to participate in the character assassination of someone I'd known for thirty years and whom I value as a personal friend," Gerber wrote later.

requirements. But that's just me. Let's talk about you." With this, he announced he was bringing back the Epic line, not as a creator-owned imprint, but as "Marvel's *Project Greenlight*," an open-submission contest for novices. A seventh issue of *Marville* was published, but there wasn't a story, just twenty-five pages of text: Jemas's storytelling advice and rules for submissions.

Marville only lasted six months, but the dreadful and bizarre legacy of its front covers continued. A cover for *Thunderbolts*, which featured a *Fight Club*–like network of villainous wrestlers, depicted a young woman, glistening, covered in bruises and smiling, sitting on the floor of a gym shower. Along the top ran the words "Bling-Bling • Booty • Boxing • Bars" (Jemas pushed his editors to adopt the attention-grabbing cover lines of magazines like *Cosmopolitan* and *Maxim*). Another series, *NYX*, was about young mutants on the street, in the tradition of Larry Clark's *Kids*; the young teenage girl on the cover of the first issue fingered her bikini strap, a pacifier hanging from her parted lips. And *Trouble*, which relaunched the Epic line, made a bid to revive romance comics—by imagining adolescent, sexually active versions of Peter Parker's Aunt May and Uncle Ben.

To the outside eye, it may have seemed that Bill Jemas had a free hand to do whatever he liked—but that would be discounting Ike Perlmutter and Avi Arad. Perlmutter was the most hands-on owner Marvel ever had, as the employees were reminded repeatedly. A conference-calling executive might be interrupted from his negotiations by an angry Perlmutter, waving a thirty-dollar invoice in his face, asking why so much money was being spent. "He used to wander the hallways and stand in your doorway," recalled one editor, "and stare at you until you got uncomfortable and then he'd leave. He always had a notebook in his hand, like he was writing notes about you." Once, when Perlmutter heard that some employees were involved in a Fantasy Football league, the staff returned from a meeting to find all computers confiscated. Social, frivolous lunchtime activities—a half hour of watching television, or playing Dungeons & Dragons—were banned from the offices.

For a while, Jemas held sway with the Israeli boss, even bypassing the CEO in the chain of command. "Bill reported to Peter Cuneo," re-called one observer, "but it was just a façade for the investors. Bill really reported to Ike. They screamed at each other, but Ike listened to him for some reason. 'He's smart,' Ike would say to me, maybe because he stood up to him."

But Perlmutter's longtime ally Avi Arad, who was trying to put to-gether movie deals on the West Coast, had an agenda that was often at cross-purposes with Jemas's chance-taking. Arad felt like he was stuck on damage-control duty with Hollywood stars who'd gotten eyefuls of over-the-top blood and guts. Michelle Pfeiffer walked into his office and told him she wouldn't take her son, an *X-Men* fan, into comic-book stores because of the gratuitous violence. George Clooney pulled out of talks to portray Nick Fury after he laid his hands on the issue in which the hero choked an enemy soldier with his own intestines.

Arad began paying closer attention to the comic books; he and Je-mas were increasingly at each other's throats. Occasionally, when a MAX series about an old character—Deathlok, say, or Shanna the She-Devil—was scrapped at the last moment, the scuttlebutt would be that the envelope-pushing content had been deemed a threat to already-in-the-works movie deals. Marvel's plans to feature a back-from-the-dead Princess Di in *X-Statix* caused outrage in the British press, but some claimed that it was Arad's displeased Hollywood friends who ultimately nixed the issue.

"Publishing was where it all started, and it was great source," Arad said. "You had readymade storyboards to look at, to understand how to lay out stories. But the big deal for the company was merchandising—everything from cereals to shirts to videogames to shoes, you name it. That's where the serious revenues were coming from."

If the comic books damaged the brand, it would all come crashing down.

As his conflicts with Arad mounted, Jemas also increasingly sparred with staffers, who complained that he was quick-tempered and prone to shift-ing mandates. "Bill was the smartest guy in the room in most rooms he went into," said Tom Brevoort. "But as the success got greater, Bill started to think he was the smartest guy in every room." When the writer of *The*

Fantastic Four resisted the idea of moving the group to the suburbs and giving them day jobs, Jemas took him, and the artist, off the title. Then he typed up a two-page treatment and hired a playwright to take over.

Grant Morrison grew frustrated with Jemas's lack of interest in his proposals for new series, which he wanted to load with complex ideas about religion and mind-melting imagery—a revisiting of the "cosmic comics" of Starlin and Englehart. A sequel to *Marvel Boy* would devote an entire issue to the Kree bible "in full-on Prog Comics style"; *Silver Surfer: Year Zero* would depict the character in the way that Jack Kirby had always intended, he said: not as a Christ figure, but as an avenging angel, screaming through the starways. "I decided that movies were doing comics so well, there was no point in doing comics to look like movies any more," Morrison said. "Let's make this stuff really crazy . . . so that special effects have to *keep up* with *us*. I foresaw a new demand for intricate bizarre psychedelic comics and was eager to oblige. Cycles whip and twist faster all the time and pop culture's threshing tentacles are flailing into an ultraviolet magic goth phase for a little while before the lights come on and the kids all look really weird in the sunshine. Time for the comic books to get crazier again."

But tensions between Jemas and Morrison rose, climaxing with an angry phone call in which Jemas's top-of-lungs screaming rattled nearby Marvel staffers. Quesada called Morrison to smooth the ruffled feathers. Morrison assured him it was water under the bridge.

Morrison had given up on the idea of winning over Jemas, though, and during the San Diego Comic Convention that summer, DC Comics announced that it had signed Morrison to an exclusive contract. Shortly after the announcement, a blindsided Joe Quesada cornered Morrison on the convention floor, where, according to one account, Morrison briefly fell into a panicky trance before railing against Jemas, whom he called "the biggest arsehole I've ever met."

"It's over, it's over!" Morrison spat. "The Marvel era is done!"

With no Marvel booth to return to—Perlmutter had refused to pay for one that year—a shaken Quesada headed over to sign comics at the *Wizard* magazine setup. Just as he was wondering how to replace Morrison, *Buffy the Vampire Slayer* creator Joss Whedon walked into view.

Whedon was an avowed Marvel Comics fan—Buffy, in fact, had been largely based on the character of the *X-Men*'s Kitty Pryde. Quesada offered Whedon the job writing *The X-Men* on the spot.

Enlisting Whedon was exactly the kind of coup for which Bill Jemas was always advocating. But Jemas left before Whedon turned in his first script. "We were having a lot less fun," Jemas said when asked about the reasons for his departure. "The money started piling up and the heads started swelling."

Grant Morrison's remaining issues of *X-Men*, published after he'd departed for DC, played out like a white flag, waving resignedly to the status quo. In "Planet X," Morrison revealed Xorn, whom he'd introduced two years earlier as an iconoclastic hero, to be just another of Magneto's disguises. The other characters' mixed reactions might have stood in for those of fans old and new. "What's wrong with you these days? What happened to the brilliant, charismatic mutant outlaw I fell in love with?" asked one. Another muttered, "I miss Mister Xorn . . . when is he coming back?" ("He was a fiction," Magneto snapped. "How often must I explain?") Magneto murdered Jean Grey, and then Wolverine beheaded Magneto. Was there any doubt that everyone would come back?

"The 'Planet X' story," Morrison said later, "was partially intended as a comment on the exhausted, circular nature of the X-Men's ever-popular battle with Magneto and by extension, the equally cyclical nature of superhero franchise re-inventions. I ended the book exactly where I came on board. . . . 'Planet X' is steeped in an exhausted, world-weary, 'middle-aged' ennui that spoke directly of both my own and Magneto's frustrations, disillusionment and disconnection, as well as the endless everything-is-not-enough frustrations of a certain segment of comics' aging readership." For Morrison, whose early manifesto for *The X-Men* trumpeted the necessity of evolution, this was a strange kind of climax.

A new title, *Astonishing X-Men*, was launched to commemorate Joss Whedon's participation. Whedon brought his longtime favorite, Kitty Pryde, back to the fold, and returned Colossus to life. "Nothing has changed," were Kitty Pryde's first words when she arrived at Charles Xavier's mansion in *Astonishing X-Men #1*. "The place was destroyed, and now it looks like nothing happened. No time has passed. Of course the professor would have it rebuilt this way. Give everyone a sense of stability. Continuity." At Marvel's request, the uniforms that Morrison had designed were retired, and the X-Men returned to their old costumes.

By 2004, Marvel was employing statistical analysts to feed information about creator and character performances into algorithms that determined launches, cancellations, and frequencies of publication. The company embraced the concept of crossovers as never before, with a relentless chain of big-event story lines that determined the course of multiple other titles. In turn, each of these massive arcs—which included prologues, epilogues, and entire spin-off series—fed into the one that followed. Major characters were torn in half, died in explosions, sacrificed themselves, lost their memories, regained their memories, lost their powers, or were revealed as shape-shifting Skrull aliens who'd posed as the real thing for years while the original hero was kidnapped on a spaceship.

These stories were conceived at "creator summits," periodic conferences at which a core brain trust of writers (including Hollywood screenwriting veterans Jeph Loeb and J. Michael Straczynski) gathered with Marvel editors and hammered out the next six months of the company's publishing strategy, comics' version of the writers' room of a television series. The level of craftsmanship was high, with special attention paid to the beats of every story pitched. And none of the new breed of writers—Brian Michael Bendis and Mark Millar, and, later, Ed Brubaker and Matt Fraction—complained publicly about editorial interference, or about a lack of equity. They'd made their names with odd, ambitious projects for smaller publishers, but at Marvel they knew the game going in. In the twenty-first-century comics industry, those who fared best were those who held no illusions about the relative priorities of commercial viability and personal expression. (For their contributions, they were each rewarded with the opportunity to publish creator-owned material through Marvel, under a new imprint called Icon. Promoting these titles was left entirely to them.)

The heavily photo-referenced look of *The Ultimates* became au courant as the Marvel Universe moved closer to real life, or at least to what could be imagined as a CGI adaptation. And, in a kind of return to Stan Lee's early 1970s stories about campus riots and LSD, many of Marvel's big events nodded at headlines without getting too caught up in taking a political stand.

INTERVIEWER: Were you looking to have the story be a forum for the discussion of capital punishment or . . . preemptive capital punishment?

BRIAN MICHAEL BENDIS: It's a discussion among the characters, but nothing is being preached, because I don't have an opinion about it, myself.

In *Secret War* (whose very name acknowledged the granddaddy of Marvel crossovers), Manhattan was attacked in retaliation for covert operations that S.H.I.E.L.D. director Nick Fury had undertaken in Doctor Doom's homeland of Latveria. In *Civil War*, the U.S. government responded to potential dangers by passing the Superhuman Registration Act, which led to a rift between those supporting heightened security (such as Iron Man) and those supporting civil liberties (such as Captain America).

By the end of *Civil War*—which, when it was finally collected into paperback reprints, spread over two dozen books—Iron Man was the new director of S.H.I.E.L.D., Captain America had been assassinated, and Spider-Man had revealed his identity to the world. None of those developments would last.

"There is an old joke about death in the comic-book world," noted the *Wall Street Journal* editorial page upon learning of Captain America's death. "No one stays dead except Bucky, [DC's] Jason Todd and Uncle Ben." But the so-called Bucky Clause no longer held—all of those characters had, in recent years, returned. It was revealed, in fact, that Bucky Barnes had been a bionic-armed Soviet assassin in the decades since World War II. Now he became the new Captain America, and Steve Rogers, the original Captain America, was out of the picture—for a while, until it turned out he'd been shot with a gun that simply "froze him within space and time."

And when Spider-Man unmasked himself, it wasn't much of a threat to the status quo, because Marvel's creative summits had already hatched a *diabolus ex machina* to get out of it. To save the life of his Aunt May,

Spider-Man made a deal with the demon Mephisto, which also erased the public's memory of his identity and undid his albatross marriage to Mary Jane. For a while, the idea of bringing Gwen Stacy back from the dead was once again batted around.

For those who weren't central to Marvel's story-planning committee, the misdirections and interdependencies of the Marvel Universe could be daunting. "Everything is so connected that I can't get my head around it," Joss Whedon said, when he decided to leave *Astonishing X-Men*. "I kind of like it when the Hulk's doing his thing, and Cap's doing his thing, and you buy it once a month and get excited. . . . There are definitely characters I like, but I have no idea if they're going to be dead, rebooted, Ultimated or be wearing a black costume by the time I get to them."

During a conference call in April 2005, Marvel Studios announced that it had settled the lawsuit with Stan Lee. Lee received $10 million and would continue to collect his yearly salary. "Our settlement with Stan terminated all rights to future profits," Peter Cuneo told investors. "Both sides felt that we wanted to settle not only the past, but the future."

That future was the real reason for the call. For the past year, Avi Arad and Chief Operating Officer David Maisel had been working on a plan for Marvel to produce its own movies, through a unique deal structure in which Merrill Lynch would put up $525 million for Marvel to make its own films of ten characters. Budgets would range from $45 million to $165 million, and Marvel would put up its own movie rights as collateral. To some, it looked like a big risk.

Arad felt differently. In the past seven years, the company had become a virtual IP farm club for Columbia (*Ghost Rider* and the two *Spider-Man* films), Fox (three *X-Men* films, *Daredevil*, *Elektra*, and the upcoming *Fantastic Four*), and New Line (three *Blade* sequels), with studios raking in $3.6 billion worldwide. For *Spider-Man* and *Spider-Man 2* alone, Columbia pulled in nearly $1.6 billion; Marvel saw only $75 million, and nothing from DVD releases. "Nobody knows better than us how to make our characters come alive for audiences," Arad said. "We just want to get paid for it."

The strategy was to corner the market on films about the individual members of the Avengers: they'd get back the rights to *Iron Man* from New Line; roll out *Captain America* and *Thor*; they'd even redo *The Hulk*, which had been a disappointment for Universal in 2003. And then, for the coup de grace, they could build on brand familiarity with the Avengers and combine the franchises into a monster-sized team-up movie.

But after the deal was in place, Arad and Maisel clashed about how quickly to produce the films, how to allot the budgets, and which characters to use. Just as Ike Perlmutter had once favored Arad over Stan Lee and Bill Jemas, now he put his faith in Maisel. Less than a year after Marvel Studios had gained its independence, Arad quit. He cashed out his stock and walked away with $59 million.

Iron Man, the first self-financed film from Marvel Studios, took in nearly $100 million in its opening weekend. After the credits rolled, there was a preview of what was to come: Nick Fury (Samuel L. Jackson, just like *The Ultimates* had imagined) showed up in Tony Stark's apartment to talk about "the Avengers Initiative." The circle was closing. The interweaving intricacies of the Marvel Universe, in all their glory, would be replicated as synergistic Hollywood franchises.

On the first weekend of May 2012, *The Avengers* broke the record for the biggest box-office debut in movie history. A week later, it had grossed more than $1 billion worldwide.

"When kids were creating comics, they were happy to get their job," Arad mused in 2012. "A movie is made, it's successful, and all of the sudden they say, 'Wait a minute, what's in it for me?' It's human nature. If a creator wants to create a book, and self-publish it, and make a big success of it, which is what McFarlane did, that's their prerogative. If they want to work for a company and be guaranteed so many pages a month and so on, that's a different business. So there are people who feel that they did this, therefore they deserve that, and . . . I don't remember any of them on a journey to try and make a movie out of these things. And believe me, it's far tougher to make a movie than publish a comic book."

Some of the journeys of those happy kids, who were now middle-aged men, were tougher than others. When former *X-Men* artist Dave Cockrum wound up in a Bronx veterans' hospital with pneumonia, Neal

Adams approached Marvel and suggested they do something to help the creator of Nightcrawler, Storm, and Colossus, and writer Clifford Meth brought attention to the matter on a comics website. Marvel's lawyers were nervous about setting a precedent. "They wanted to get Dave to sign a piece of paper and not show anyone what was on that piece of paper," Adams told the *Comics Journal*, which reported that Cockrum would receive $200,000. Cockrum said he was "very happy that so many people cared about my work and about me. It feels like one big family again."* Cockrum died in November 2006, due to complications from diabetes.

In 2007, Gary Friedrich, who'd been a Marvel editor with Roy Thomas in the mid–1960s, sued Marvel over the copyright renewal rights of Ghost Rider. Although Roy Thomas and artist Mike Ploog also claimed credit for aspects of the character's creation, it was Friedrich who'd been given a "conceived and written by" acknowledgment on the opening page of the first Ghost Rider story, and who'd been named in the "Bullpen Bulletin" as having "dreamed the whole thing up." But Marvel maintained that Friedrich had signed away his rights, first on the back of a check, and again on the 1978 work-for-hire agreement; the company also filed a countersuit against Friedrich for selling unauthorized autographed Ghost Rider merchandise. A U.S. district judge ruled for Marvel. The destitute Friedrich—unemployed and suffering from a liver ailment—agreed to pay Marvel $17,000 in punitive damages.

Roy Thomas wrote occasionally for Marvel Comics through 2007 but spends most of his time as editor of *Alter Ego*, a glossy update of the comics fanzine he edited before he became a professional writer.

Steve Gerber died in February 2008, of idiopathic pulmonary fibrosis. "There were some people who could only write, that's all they could do," said Mary Skrenes, his former writing partner and girlfriend. "Steve, unfortunately, was one. And people should know comics are a place to start and then move on. But he didn't like animation, and he didn't like television. He liked comic books."

Steve Ditko continues to create low-budget black-and-white comic

---

* Shortly afterward, Meth wrote that the royalties had stopped, but in a 2011 email he stated that "every dime" of the "generous settlement was paid by Marvel to Dave Cockrum." The terms remain confidential.

books from his Manhattan studio. In 2008, the original artwork for *Amazing Fantasy #15*, the first appearance of Spider-Man, was anonymously donated to the Library of Congress. A reporter for the *Chicago Tribune* reached Ditko by telephone. "I couldn't care less" was his only comment.

In early 2009, Len Wein, who created Wolverine with John Romita, attended the premiere of *X-Men Origins: Wolverine*, starring Hugh Jackman. "I have not seen a dime off of any Marvel stuff, nor do I have a credit on the Wolverine film," said Wein. "Hugh Jackman is a lovely man, and at the premiere he told the audience that he owed his career to me and had me take a bow. It was very gratifying and very nice. I would have preferred a check."

Todd McFarlane, Marc Silvestri, Erik Larsen, and Jim Valentino continued as partners in Image Comics. McFarlane, the onetime major-league baseball prospect, acquired the home-run balls of Mark McGwire, Sammy Sosa, and Barry Bonds, for a total of $3.7 million.

Jim Lee sold his studio, Wildstorm, to DC Comics, and continued to oversee the studio's line of comics. In 2010, he was named co-publisher of DC Comics.

Chris Claremont continued, off and on, to write various X-Men related series. Recalling his days as a Marvel intern in the late 1960s, he said, "I remember seeing Jerry Siegel, then working as a proofreader, hustling around the office and trying to get writing jobs. I said to myself, I'm never going to be one of those guys. Now I look on the stands and see comics of all these characters I created, and Marvel won't let me write them." In 2009, Claremont began writing a series called *X-Men Forever*, an alternate-universe story with the conceit that the characters were exactly as he'd left them in 1991. It was canceled in 2010.

Marv Wolfman, Steve Englehart, Jim Starlin, Jim Shooter, Frank Miller, and John Byrne continue to write and draw comics for various publishers—but not Marvel.

On August 31, 2009, after months of negotiations, the Walt Disney Company announced that it was purchasing Marvel Entertainment for approximately $4 billion. Isaac Perlmutter was set to receive nearly a third of that.

Within weeks, Jack Kirby's son and daughters served forty-five notices of copyright termination to Marvel, as well as to Disney, Sony Pictures, Universal Pictures, Twentieth Century Fox, Paramount Pictures, and others, for concepts that Kirby had created between 1958 and 1963. The lawyer for the Kirby heirs collected declarations from Jim Steranko, Joe Sinnott, Dick Ayers, and Neal Adams; Marvel called Roy Thomas, John Romita, Larry Lieber, and Stan Lee to testify. Among the documents produced was a contract that Jack Kirby signed in 1972, which granted copyrights for all his works. (Why Kirby would have signed such an agreement two years after he left Marvel remains unclear.)

"It is important to state what this motion is not about," U.S. district judge Colleen McMahon of New York wrote in her 2011 decision. "Contrary to recent press accounts . . . this case is not about whether Jack Kirby or Stan Lee is the real 'creator' of Marvel characters, or whether Kirby (and other freelance artists who created culturally iconic comic book characters for Marvel and other publishers) were treated 'fairly' by companies that grew rich off the fruit of their labor."

It is about whether Kirby's work qualifies as work-for-hire under the Copyright Act of 1909, as interpreted by the courts, notably the United States Court of Appeals for the Second Circuit. If it does, then Marvel owns the copyright in the Kirby Works, whether that is "fair" or not. If it does not, then the Kirby Heirs have a statutory right to take back those copyrights, no matter the impact on recent corporate acquisition or on earnings from blockbuster movies made and yet to be made.

The judge, however, ruled "that there are no genuine issues of material fact, and that the Kirby Works were indeed works for hire within the meaning of the Copyright Act of 1909." The lawyer for the Kirby family announced that they would file for an appeal.

In recent years, Stan Lee has appeared as himself on episodes of *The Big Bang Theory* and *Entourage*, and in 2006 he hosted a reality show called *Who Wants to Be a Superhero?* He has also filmed cameos for nearly every theatrical release from Marvel Studios. In 2011, at the age of eighty-eight, he received a star on the Hollywood Walk of Fame. On the eve of the *Avengers* release, he was asked if he felt the comic book industry had been fair to its creators. "I don't know," he replied. "I haven't had reason to think about it that much."

After a pause, he continued. "I think, if somebody creates something, and it becomes highly successful, whoever is reaping the rewards should let the person who created it share in it, certainly. But so much of it is . . . it goes beyond creating. A lot of people put something together, and nobody knows who really created it, they're just working on it, you know?"

The writing and art work of Marvel's line is, across the board, more sophisticated than ever before, an especially impressive feat considering that it is overseen by a relatively small group of editors, working from a smaller office space than in the past. The Marvel "Bullpen" is a series of small cubicles with glass partitions, from which employees shepherd computer files through the production process. Visitors to the office must sign a nondisclosure agreement before passing the reception area.

Comic books have reentered the public consciousness, and trade paperbacks and deluxe hardcover reprints finally fill bookstore shelves. But the publishing industry grows increasingly endangered, and Marvel Comics has yet to find a solution to the long-standing challenge of capturing a wider audience. In 2011, the company's two best-selling issues were those featuring the death of the Ultimate version of Spider-Man (167,000 copies) and the death of the Human Torch (144,000). The attendant media coverage of such events is likely to have diminishing returns if Marvel continues to cry wolf with its characters' demises.

The average age of the monthly Marvel comic consumer now hovers at around thirty, which means that most readers have watched the narrative cycles repeat multiple times. Fans complain about the deaths and rebirths and crossovers, but in collective fits of repetition compulsion, they vote affirmatively with their dollars (the cheapest titles are priced at $2.99 each). This points to the central challenge of a narrative-driven commercial franchise, a challenge that existed long before Stan Lee told his editors and writers that he only wanted the "illusion" of change: Stories that are told with freely wandering imaginations jeopardize not only the integrity of corporate trademarks, but, in the eyes of dedicated readers, the sacred tapestry that has been woven over the decades, by hundreds of hands. Comics that exist independently of the overarching framework, of crossovers, are at an economic disadvantage. To the hard-core Marvel reader, those stories don't count; they're "imaginary" diversions from the canonical saga. "I wish it weren't the case," said Axel Alonso, who succeeded Joe Quesada as editor in chief in 2010, "but the fact of the matter is, the surefire way to spike a monthly title is to tie it in. The zeitgeist of the day is determined by the man or woman who goes into the comics store on Wednesday, and they want to know [the story] counts. And the only way they know it counts is for other people to say it counts because it's tied in to the bigger title."

At a certain point—it's impossible to locate precisely—decades of continuity exceed the capacity of the human brain. So the Marvel Universe chugs forward, and backtracks, and takes detours. The movie adaptations mix and match from various past interpretations of the Marvel characters, add their own inventions, and, in reaching larger audiences, ultimately supplant the "official" versions of the mythologies. Multiple manifestations of Captain America and Spider-Man and the X-Men float in elastic realities, passed from one temporary custodian to the next, and their heroic journeys are, forever, denied an end.

Stan Lee and Jack Kirby in 1965.

ACKNOWLEDGMENTS

MUCH OF THIS BOOK IS BASED ON THE PERSONAL RECOLLECTIONS OF MORE than 150 individuals, and relatives of individuals, who worked at or with Marvel Comics and its various parent companies between 1939 and the present day. I'm deeply grateful for the generosity of the following people, as well as those who chose to speak with me on the condition of anonymity.

Leonard Ackerman, Marcia Amsterdam, Avi Arad, Lou Bank, Marcia Ben-Eli, Irwin E. Billman, Charles Brainard, Tom Brevoort, Eliot R. Brown, Frank Brunner, Steve Buccellato, Rich Buckler, Bob Budiansky, Paul Burke, Roger Burlage, Kurt Busiek, Mary Mac Candalerio, Mike Carlin, Rusty Citron, Chris Claremont, Gene Colan, Gerry Conway, Peter David, Tom DeFalco, J.M. DeMatteis, David DePatie, Buzz Dixon, Jo Duffy, Matt Edelman, Scott Edelman, Steve Englehart, Lloyd Feinstein, Danny Fingeroth, Linda Fite, Frank Fochetta, Matt Fraction, Stuart Freedman, Bruce Jay Friedman, Josh Alan Friedman, Mike Friedrich, Chuck Fries, Jim Galton, Peter Gillis, Stan Goldberg, Iden Goodman, Roberta Goodman, Alan Gordon, Bert Gould, Steven Grant, Robin Green, Glenn Greenberg, Bob Hall, Larry Hama, Ed Hannigan, Arnold Hano, Bonnie Hano, Dean Haspiel, Glenn Herdling, Michael Z. Hobson, Henry Homes, Richard Howell, Donald Hudson, Nanette Jacovitz, Al Jaffee, Marie Javins, Bill Jemas, Arvell Jones, Barry Kaplan, Nancy Shores Karlebach, Terry Kavanagh, David Anthony Kraft, Tony Krantz, Alan Kupperburg, Tina Landau, Sven Larsen, Batton Lash, Stan Lee, Steve Lemberg, Jason Liebig, Irwin Linker, Margaret Loesch, Lavere Lund, Ralph Macchio, David Mack, Howard Mackie, Arthur Marblestone, Elaine Markson, Frances McBain, Don McGregor, Mary McPherran, Will Meugniot, David Michelinie, Al Milgrom, Bobby Miller, Frank

Miller, Michael Minick, Doug Moench, Bobby Moore, Stuart Moore, Nancy Murphy, Fabian Nicieza, Annie Nocenti, Amy Kiste Nyberg, Denny O'Neil, Patrick Daniel O'Neill, Jimmy Palmiotti, Rick Parker, Ann Picardo, Nancy Poletti, Carl Potts, Mark Powers, Ivan Prashker, Joe Quesada, Devon Quinn, Benjamin Raab, William Rabkin, Matt Ragone, Shirrel Rhoades, Diane Robbens, Jean Robbins, Mike Rockwitz, John Romita, Bob Rosen, Steve Saffel, Jim Salicrup, Mary-Jane Salk, Peter Sanderson, Mike Sangiacomo, Andy Schmidt, Diana Schutz, Stu Schwartzberg, Jim Shooter, Ed Shukin, Carl Sifakis, Steve Skeates, Evan Skolnick, Mary Skrenes, Roger Slifer, Ivan Snyder, Jim Starlin, Flo Steinberg, Jim Steranko, Amy Goodman Sullivan, Sheri Sunabe, Roy Thomas, Rob Tokar, Herb Trimpe, Chris Ulm, Ellen Vartanoff, Irene Vartanoff, Mark Waid, Len Wein, Alan Weiss, Marv Wolfman, Gregory Wright, Nel Yomtov, Ron Zalme.

For sharing documents, research, and/or advice, I'd like to thank the following:

Jim Amash, Vinnie Bartilucci, Robert Beerbohm, Blake Bell, Daniel Best, Nick Bowler, Massimiliano Brighel, Scott Brown, Norris Burroughs, Nick Caputo, Thom Carnell, Todd Casey, Clark Collis, Caleb Crain, Sloane Crosley, Bill Dineen, Brad Elliott, Michael Feldman, Stephen Fishler, David Folkman, Nikki Frakes, David Gaddis, Aileen Gallagher, Thom Geier, Jason Geyer, Ian Gittler, Glen David Gold, Aaron Goodman, Gary Groth, David Hajdu, Jim Hanley, Mark Harris, John Hilgart, Gina Hirsch, Timothy Hodler, Erin Howe, Gary Howe, Valerie Howe, David Hyde, Christopher Irving, Dave Itzkoff, Nat Ives, Steve Kandell, Arie Kaplan, George Khoury, Wook Kim, Carrie Klein, Jeff Klein, Chuck Klosterman, Ernie Knowles, Peggy Knowles, Claudine Ko, Seth Kushner, Batton Lash, Edgar Loftin, Heidi MacDonald, Melissa Maerz, Clifford Meth, John Jackson Miller, Greg Milner, John Morrow, Frank Motler, Noel Murray, Will Murray, Dan Nadel, Evie Nagy, Sean O'Heir, Vince Oliva, Barry Pearl, Leonard Pitts Jr., Ken Quattro, Jordan Raphael, Phoebe Reilly, Eric Reynolds, Steven Rowe, Chris Ryan, Marc Schuricht, Mark Schwartzbard, Rob Sheffield, Nancy Sidewater, Gabe Soria, Alexis Sottile, Matthew Specktor, Tom Spurgeon, Tucker Stone, Tim Stroup, Peter Terzian, Maggie Thompson, Stephen Thompson,

Steven Thompson, Derek Van Gieson, Dr. Michael J. Vassallo, Lou Vogel, Michael Weinreb, Douglas Wolk, and Josh Wolk.

Kira Garcia, Joe Quigley, Cat Tyc, and Shawn Wen provided transcription assistance. Thanks to Cheryl's Global Soul for the use of the office space, and to Roger's Time Machine for the use of the library.

Although this is not an "official" account of Marvel's history, Marvel's Arune Singh, and Jeff Klein at DKC were invaluable in arranging interviews and a pleasure to work with. Thanks go to Gregory Pan for the amiable exchanges.

My virtuoso agent, Daniel Greenberg, encouraged this project from the very beginning, and provided sage guidance and good humor throughout. Thanks to him and his team, especially Monika Verma, at Greenberg-Levine. At HarperCollins, my graceful editor, Tim Duggan, applied laserlike focus to an unwieldy manuscript; his contributions were indispensable. Tim's assistant, Emily Cunningham, navigated the many changes to the book's moving parts with terrific cheer and efficiency. Rakesh Satyal and Jonathan Burnham were immediate champions of the project; I'm hugely indebted to them for their enthusiastic support. Milan Bozic designed the mind-bogglingly perfect cover. Thanks also to David Koral, Tom Pitoniak, Beth Silfin, Kate Blum, and Katie O'Callaghan, and to Jaime Wolf at Pelosi Wolf Effron & Spates.

I'm hugely lucky to have had a brain trust of genius correspondents and early readers in Andy Greenwald, Joe Gross, Andrew Hultkrans, Jonathan Lethem, Alex Pappademas, Brian Raftery, Gabriel Roth, Gabe Soria, and Chris Sorrentino.

The brilliant Emily Condon spent more time with this book than should be expected of anyone but its credited author; the ways in which she helped give it shape are nothing short of miraculous. For her devotion, patience, and inspiration, I am forever in her debt.

Finally, I thank my parents, who set me on this journey, and whose shining examples continue to steady my course.

NOTES

Author's note: Unless otherwise noted, all quotations are from personal interviews, conducted between 2008 and 2012.

PROLOGUE

2　"It took a few days": Stan Lee, with George Mair, *Excelsior!* Fireside, 2002.

2　"Marvel was on its ass": Gary Groth, "I've Never Done Anything Halfheartedly," *Comics Journal* 134, February 1990.

4　"Marvel often stretches": "O.K., You Passed the 2-S Test—Now You're Smart Enough For Comic Books," *Esquire*, September 1966. The list of "28 People Who Count" appeared in the September 1965 issue.

4　"It isn't generally known": "Bullpen Bulletins," February 1966.

5　"It seems to work out well": Letter to Jerry Bails, January 9, 1963.

1

9　Eastern soon fell apart: Martin Goodman's earliest days in the magazine business have been documented with varying degrees of accuracy. Les Daniels's *Marvel: Five Fabulous Decades of the World's Greatest Comics* (Abrams, 1991) was one of the earliest published works to tackle the subject; Will Murray's astonishingly researched introduction to the *Golden Age Marvel Comics Omnibus* (Marvel, 2009) provided several corrections and integrated new discoveries. Blake Bell and Dr. Michael J. Vassallo's *The Secret History of Marvel Comics: Jack Kirby and the Moonlighting Artists at Martin Goodman's Empire* (Fantagraphics, 2012), which focuses on Goodman's pulp publications, extends the scholarship.

10　"If you get a title that catches on": "Big Business in Pulp Thrillers," *Literary Digest*, January 23, 1937.

11　"little beehive of nepotism": Joe Simon, *Comic Book Makers*, Vanguard, 2003. Information about the origins of American comic books comes from Robert Lee Beerbohm and Richard D. Olson, "The American Comic Book: 1929–Present," *The Official Overstreet Comic Book Price Guide*, Gemstone, 2008; Bradford Wright, *Comic Book Nation*, Johns Hopkins, 2001; Mike Benton, *The Comic Book in America*, Taylor, 1989.

14　Timely's first comic book was published: Matt Nelson, "Marvel #1 vs. Motion Picture Funnies Weekly #1: The Chicken or the Egg?," Classicsincorporated.com.

14　sold 800,000: Arthur Goodman shared this information in conversation with Stephen A. Fishler in 1983.

16　Simon . . . was earning: Simon, *Comic Book Makers*.

16　"My mother once wanted": *Hour 25*, radio program, circa 1986.

16   "I would wait behind a brick wall": Unpublished Leonard Pitts interview.

18   "I stayed up all night sketching": Simon, *Comic Book Makers*.

18   "We can't keep putting out this crap": Ibid.

18   "He didn't like them very much": Jim Amash, "Simon Says," *Alter Ego* 76, March 2008.

19   On Shores's first day: Mark Evanier, "Jack FAQs," *Jack Kirby Collector* 44, Fall 2006.

19   "seemed to be made entirely": Stan Lee, *History of Marvel*, unpublished draft, late 1980s.

19   fired from a menial job: Lee, with Mair, *Excelsior!*

19   Descriptions of the Timely office interiors are taken from author interviews, as well as Jim Amash, "A Long Glance At Dave Gantz," *Alter Ego* 13, March 2002, and Amash, "Simon Says."

20   "This is my nephew": Amash, "Simon Says."

20   "And when the script came back": Amash, "Simon Says."

21   "Jack sat at a table": Stan Lee panel, San Diego Convention, 1975.

22   "We just stayed": Roy Thomas interview with Bill Everett, published in *Timely Presents: Human Torch*, Marvel, 1999.

22   slept in shifts: Jim Steranko, *Steranko History of Comics*, Supergraphics, 1970.

23   "You guys must be": Simon, *Comic Book Makers*.

23   "The next time I see that": John Morrow and Glen Musial, "More Than Your Average Joe," *Jack Kirby Collector* 25, August 1999.

24   "No matter how many new titles": Quote from Al Jaffee in Gary Groth, "Face Front, True Believers: The Comics Industry Sounds Off on Stan Lee," *Comics Journal* 181, October 1995.

25   In less than two years: Figures are taken from the following sources, via Bradford Wright's *Comic Book Nation*: "The Comics And Their Audience," *Publishers Weekly*, April 18, 1942; "Superman Scores," *BusinessWeek*, April 18, 1942; "Escapist Paydirt," *Newsweek*, December 27, 1943.

25   "Sometimes we'd put": Jim Amash, "I Let People Do Their Jobs!," *Alter Ego* 11, November 2001.

26   "We always had backlog": Amash, "I Let People Do Their Jobs!"

26   He moved into a room: Blake Bell, *I Have to Live with This Guy*, TwoMorrows, 2002.

26   "Like you see in the movies": Jordan Raphael and Tom Spurgeon, *Stan Lee and the Rise and Fall of the American Comic Book*, Chicago Review Press, 2003.

26   "I was in love": David Anthony Kraft, "The Foom Interview: Stan Lee," *Foom* 17, March 1977.

26   "I had three secretaries": Kraft, "The Foom Interview: Stan Lee."

27   90 percent: Bradford, *Comic Book Nation*.

27   They moved out of their: Edward Lewine, "Housing History: Sketching Out His Past," *New York Times*, September 9, 2007.

28   "No thanks, maybe later": Bruce Jay Friedman, *Lucky Bruce*, Biblioasis, 2011.

28   "Every so often": Michael Vassallo, "A Timely Talk with Allen Bellman," Comic-artville.com, 2005.

30   Ayers donated: David Hajdu, *The Ten-Cent Plague*, Farrar, Straus & Giroux, 2008.

31   "Talk was no longer": Jules Feiffer, *The Great Comic Book Heroes*, Dial, 1965.

32   "It was the toughest thing": Hajdu, *The Ten-Cent Plague*.

32   "If Stan Lee ever calls": Jon B. Cooke, "John Romita: Spidey's Man," *Comic Book Artist* 6, Fall 1999.

33   half-dozen artists: Per the research of Dr. Michael J. Vassallo, they were: Dick Ayers, Dan DeCarlo, Al Hartley, Jack Keller, Morris Weiss, and Joe Maneely.

33   Steve Ditko, a quiet thirty-year-old: Blake Bell, *Strange and Stranger: The World of Steve Ditko*, Fantagraphics, 2008.

35   "Jack never liked": John Morrow, "Would You Like To See My Etchings?," *Jack Kirby Collector* 10, April 1996.

35   "I would much rather": Mark Evanier, *Kirby: King of Comics*, Abrams, 2008.

35   "It's like a ship sinking": Roy Thomas and Jim Amash, "To Keep Busy As A Free-lancer, You Should Have Three Accounts," *Alter Ego* 31, December 2003.

2

38   "We are trying": Letter to Jerry Bails, August 29, 1961.

41   When Lee asked Steve Ditko: Steve Ditko, "A Mini-History: 13. 'Speculation,'" *The Comics*, 14 (August 2003). More discussion of the Spider-Man/Fly connection appears in Joe Simon, *Comic Book Makers*. In a 2010 videotaped deposition for Marvel's suit against the Kirby estate, Stan Lee stated that Spider-Man was not, to his knowledge, based on Kirby's Fly character.

43   "The poor guy only has": Letter to Jerry Bails, January 9, 1963.

44   He worked from a varnished-pine room: Neal Kirby, "Growing up Kirby: The Marvel Memories of Jack Kirby's Son," *Los Angeles Times*, April 9, 2012.

44   "That was a lot of stuff": Richard Howell, "An interview with Don Heck," *Comics Feature* 21, November 1982.

44   "We seem to exist from crisis": Letter to Jerry Bails, January 9, 1963.

45   "My job was mainly": Dwight Jon Zimmerman, "Sol Brodsky Remembered," *Marvel Age* 22, January 1985.

45   "Martin Goodman started pressuring": Jim Amash, "I Wrote Over 800 Comic Book Stories," *Alter Ego* 90, December 2009.

45   "I have to go to": Gerard Jones, *Men of Tomorrow*, Basic, 2004.

46   Rousso, weary of: Mark Gruenwald, "George Roussos," *Comics Interview* 2, April 1983.

46   sixty-five dollars a week: Dwight Jon Zimmerman, "Fabulous Flo Steinberg," *Comics Interview* 17, November 1984.

50   "Stan wanted": Mark Evanier, *Kirby: King of Comics*.

50   "Don Heck drew": Letters pages of November 1965 issues.

51   "like digging into": Daniels, *Marvel*.

52   "The problem . . . was": Mark Evanier, "Jack F.A.Q.s," *Jack Kirby Collector* 39, Fall 2003.

53   "the most depressing exchange": Ethan Roberts, "The 1964 New York Comicon: A Personal Reminiscence," *Alter Ego* 7, Winter 2001.

53   "This isn't the first time": Bill Schelly, *Sense of Wonder: A Life in Comic Fandom*, TwoMorrows, 2001.

53   "the tendency to take": Ditko via Bell, *Strange and Stranger: The World of Steve Ditko*.

54   "Stan treated it like": Mark Evanier, NewsFromMe.com, October 12, 2005.

55   "I don't know what": Steve Duin and Mike Richardson, *Comics Between the Panels*, Dark Horse Comics, 1998.

56   "We had to write down": Jon B. Cooke, "Absolutely Fabulous," *Comic Book Artist* 18, March 2002.

57   "You have no idea": Jim Salicrup, "John Romita," *Comics Interview* 89, 1990.

58   The details of Roy Thomas's hiring come from Roy Thomas, "Two Weeks With Mort Weisinger," *Alter Ego* 50, July 2005; and Rob Gustaveson, "Fifteen Years at Marvel: An Interview with Roy Thomas," *Comics Journal* 61, Winter 1981.

60   "Marvel Comics are the first": Sally Kempton, "Spiderman's Dilemma: Super-Anti-Hero in Forest Hills," *Village Voice*, April 1, 1965.

60 McClure featured: Bhob Stewart, Potrzebie.blogspot.com, November 13, 2010.

61 "We wrote an unbelievable contract": Adam McGovern, "Marvel Man," *Jack Kirby Collector* 41, Fall 2004.

61 "living comic books": Josh Alan Friedman, "Mel Shestack Lives!," *Black Cracker Online*, March 8, 2010.

61 "They'd come in and giggle": Dwight Jon Zimmerman, "Fabulous Flo Steinberg," *Comics Interview* 17, November 1984.

61 "Mario Puzo would": Jon B. Cooke,, "Absolutely Fabulous," *Comic Book Artist* 18, March 2002.

62 "I was just kidding him": Bell, *Strange and Stranger: The World of Steve Ditko*; Nat Freedland, "Super Heroes with Super Problems," *New York Herald Tribune Sunday Magazine*, January 9, 1966.

65 "It's almost like I was watching Laurel and Hardy": "The Mighty Marvel Bullpen Reunion 2001," *Alter Ego* 16, July 2002, p. 17. Lee's account of *Herald* fallout from Ro Ronin, *Tales To Astonish*, page 104.

66 "I've had theories advanced": Duin and Richardson, *Comics Between the Panels*.

66 "Not until Goodman": Bell, *Strange and Stranger: The World of Steve Ditko*.

3

70 "I came in one day": From Mark Evanier, "Jack FAQs," *Jack Kirby Collector* 44, Fall 2005, p. 13.

75 "wasn't going to have to be paid back": Jim Amash, "Roy Thomas Interview," *Jack Kirby Collector* 18, January 1998.

76 "I never saw his collection": Jim Amash, "The Privacy Act of Carl Burgos," *Alter Ego* 49, June 2005.

77 "We've had movie offers": *Fantastic Four* 50.

77 "Simon said he created Captain America," Simon, *The Comic-Book Makers*.

77 "I felt that whatever I did": Sworn statement from Jack Kirby, posted in "*Marvel Worldwide, Inc. et al v. Kirby et al.*—Jack Kirby's 1966 Statement," *20th Century Danny Boy*, April 3, 2011.

78 In February 1956: "Admit Stealing 25 Cars in State," *Gettysburg Times*, February 6, 1956.

78 "None of the things": Robin Green, "Face Front! Clap Your Hands, You're on the Winning Team!" *Rolling Stone* 91, September 16, 1971.

80 "The kids were unbelievable": McGovern, "Marvel Man."

80 "sold 50,000 printed t-shirts": "O.K., You Passed the 2-S Test—Now You're Smart Enough for Comic Books," *Esquire*, September 1966.

80 "Marvel often stretches": "As Barry Jenkins, Ohio '69, Says: 'A Person Has to Have Intelligence to Read Them,' " *Esquire*, September 1966.

80 shaving cream and cars: Leonard Sloane, "Advertising: Comics Go Up, Up and Away," *New York Times*, July 20, 1967.

81 "I couldn't believe that a guy": Roy Thomas, "Fifty Years on the 'A' List," *Alter Ego* 9, July 2001.

82 Lee himself was asking for changes: "An interview with the Romitas," Mike Harris, *Comics Feature* 22, December 1982.

82 *Women's Wear Daily*: "Original Art Stories: John Romita," *20th Century Danny Boy*, October 21, 2010.

82 "goddamn automobiles and skyscrapers": Roy Thomas, "An Avengers Interview—Sort Of—With John Buscema," *Alter Ego* 13, March 2002.

84 "a lonely sort of guy": "1966 Kirby Keynote Speech," *Jack Kirby Collector* 43, Summer 2005.

84 "share ideas, laughs": "Meet Jack Kirby," *Merry Marvel Messenger*, 1966.

84 "Marvel's been very kind": "1966 Kirby Keynote Speech."

86 "I'm not going to give them another": Mark Evanier interview in Jon B. Cooke, "The Unknown Kirby," *Comic Book Artist Special Edition*, December 1999.

87 clicked his heels: Green, "Face Front! Clap Your Hands, You're on the Winning Team!"

88 While DC's forty-eight titles: Leonard Sloane, "Advertising: Comics Go Up, Up and Away," *New York Times*, July 20, 1967.

88 "eventually outstrip us": Gene Reed, "A Conversation with Arnold Drake," *Comic Reader* 192, July 1981.

90 "I guess I treated the whole thing": David Anthony Kraft and Jim Salicrup, "Stan Lee," *Comics Interview* 5, July 1983.

91 "Good evening": Otto Friedrich, *Decline and Fall*, Harper & Row, 1970.

92 roughly the amount that the company: *Variety*, June 28, 1968.

92 "Stan, . . . I'll see to it": *Excelsior!*

92 "We're going to make a fortune": Chris Welles, "'Post'-Mortem," *New York*, February 10, 1969.

93 "They didn't believe": Dwight Jon Zimmerman, "Fabulous Flo Steinberg," *Comics Interview* 17, November 1984.

93 In May, instead of: John Morrow, "A Tale of Two Contracts," *Jack Kirby Collector* 41, Fall 2004.

93 Thomas . . . returned to a lecture: Roy Thomas, "So You Want A Job, Eh?," *Alter Ego* 6, Autumn 2000.

93 "He was predictably thrilled": Timothy Wylie, *Love Sex Fear Death: The Inside Story of the Process Church of the Final Judgment*, Feral House, 2009.

94 When makereadies: Roy Thomas, "'Echh' Marks the Spot," *Alter Ego* 95, July 2010.

94 "the fact that the heroes": David F. Nolan, *The New Guard*, June 1966.

95 "People were congratulating me on this particular issue": Jon B. Cooke, "John Buscema Interview," *Jack Kirby Collector* 18, January 1998.

95 "We had one sequence": From *The Dick Cavett Show*, May 30, 1968; printed in Jeff McLaughlin, ed., *Stan Lee: Conversations*, University Press of Mississippi, 2007.

96 "Our thinking": Speech at the 1968 Comic Art Convention.

97 Lee had an assistant: Alan Hewetson, *Skywald! The Complete Illustrated History of the Horror-Mood*, Headpress, 2004.

97 "You implied that the Panther": *East Village Other*, April 23, 1969.

98 "sort of a Sidney Poitier": Don Allen, *The Electric Humanities*, Pflaum/Standard, 1971.

99 "I started thinking about": Jim Amash, "Writing Comics Turned Out to Be What I Really Wanted to Do with My Life," *Alter Ego* 70, July 2007.

100 "You lose the very young kids": Saul Braun, "Shazam! Here Comes Captain Relevant," *New York Times*, May 2, 1971.

103 "You fellas think of": Shel Dorf, "Speak The Language of the '70s," *Jack Kirby Collector* 42, Spring 2006.

103 "I can't understand" Conversation with Alain Resnais recorded by Stan Lee, May 14, 1969.

104 "I'm out": "Ackerman Decides to Shun Limelight of Corporate Life," *New York Times*, March 20, 1969.

104 set himself up with: "Ackerman Named Adviser at Perfect," Robert E. Bedingfield, *New York Times*, August 26, 1969.

105 "Magazines were dying": Jon B. Cooke, "John Romita: Spidey's Man," *Comic Book Artist* 6, Fall 1999.

105 So in a cautious: Mark Evanier, post to Crisis on Infinite Comics forum, November 1, 2009.

106 The next time Carmine Infantino: *Jack Kirby Collector* 46, p. 68.

106 "the bullpen had become": Green, "Face Front! Clap Your Hands, You're on the Winning Team!"

107 provides visual evidence: Jon Riley, *We Love You Herb Trimpe*, 1970.

107 When artist Barry Smith visited: Jon B. Cook, "Alias Barry Windsor-Smith," *Comic Book Artist* 2.

108 "Jack's on line two": "1997 Kirby Tribute Panel," *Jack Kirby Collector* 17, November 1997.

108 "Are you crazy?": "John Romita," *Jack Kirby Collector* 33, November 2001.

108 "I thought they were going to close up": Jon B. Cooke, "John Buscema Interview," *Jack Kirby Collector* 18, January 1998.

108 "Marie Severin made": Dave Sikula, "Wondercon: Kirby, King of Comics," *Comic Book Resources*, February 28, 2008.

4

111 "frenzied, frantic and frenetic": Stan Lee letter to Ken Koch.

111 moving his family: *Marvelmania* 6, August 1970.

112 He made plans with the poet: WNYC interview, October 15, 1970.

112 "meets up with a New Orleans": *Comic Fandom Monthly* 3, November 1971.

113 "when his contract is up": *Newfangles* 39, September 1970.

113 "The comic book market": Speech delivered at Lamb's Club, New York, January 20, 1971, printed in *National Cartoonist Society Professional Report* 1, no. 2, March 1971.

114 "The Monster Maker is": A. H. Weiler, "Alain Resnais: La Garbage Est Finnie?," *New York Times*, May 2, 1971.

117 "probably has more": *Comics Fandom Monthly* 3.

117 script sold for $25,000: Raphael and Spurgeon, *Stan Lee and the Rise and Fall of the American Comic Book.*

118 "I don't have the feeling of repression": Bruce Hamilton, *Rocket's Blast Comicollector* 81, 1971.

119 "near-paranoid delusions": *Comic Fandom Monthly* 3, November 1971.

119 With the Marvelmania fiasco: "Marvel Comics to Go Audiovisual," *Billboard*, Oct. 16, 1971.

120 A slide show spilled: Bob Lardine, "Superheroes May Sandwich America," *New York Sunday News*, January 2, 1972.

120 "While the Surfer scored highest": Don Geringer, "The Hulk Is Searching for a Place in the Sun," *Palm Beach Post-Times*, January 29, 1972.

121 "But who's going to become the editor?": Gustaveson, "Fifteen Years at Marvel."

121 "Stan tried to give": Ibid.

122 He started to line up: Michael Kustow letter to Stan Lee, July 12, 1972.

122 Lee also turned: Will Eisner letter to John Doe, February 20, 1973.

123 "All the other people": Jon B. Cooke, "Comix Book: A Marvel Oddity," *Comic Book Artist* 7, February 2000.

124 "If we even talked about": Daniels, *Marvel.*

124 "The waiting room was": Mike Baron, ". . . and Now Spider-Man and the Marvel Comics Group," *Creem*, April 1973.

126 "You must help me": "Marvel Bullpen Profiles: Steve Gerber," *Foom* 5, Spring 1974.

126 "I'd wish them well": Duin and Richardson, *Comics Between the Panels.*

5

130 "Martin Goodman always thought": "Stan the Man & Roy the Boy," *Comic Book Artist* 2, Summer 1998.

130 "There were some people at Marvel": Gustaveson, "Fifteen Years at Marvel."

131 "It's kind of a shame": Daniels, *Marvel*.

131 "much of Cage's jivin' slang": *Foom* 2, Summer 1973.

134 "I was always too academic": David Anthony Kraft, "The Foom Interview: Steve Gerber," *Foom* 15, September 1976.

135 "For years": *Captain America* 157, January 1973.

137 "The idea that the three": Scott Brick, "Who Really Killed Gwen Stacy?," *Comics Buyer's Guide* 1647, November 2008.

138 "I told them not to kill": Jim Magill, "POW! Stan (Speaker-Man) Arrives," *Daily Collegian*, December 10, 1974.

139 "The office was flooded": Kraft, "The Foom Interview: Steve Gerber."

146 "By the time we finally": David Smay, "Jim Starlin," *Amazing Heroes* 98, July 1, 1986.

146 "I got five issues into it": Peter Sanderson, "An Interview with Steve Englehart," *Comics Feature* 5, September 1980.

146 "I swore up and down": Ibid.

149 "When you're used to": Tom Spurgeon, "John Romita," *Comics Journal* 252, May 2003.

149 "too much like a vacation": Gustaveson, "Fifteen Years at Marvel."

150 "By becoming publisher": Ibid.

150 "Roy was very open to ideas": Peter Sanderson and Peter Gillis, "Marv Wolfman," *Comics Feature* 12/13, September–October 1981.

151 "unethical, immoral": Gustaveson, "Fifteen Years at Marvel."

6

154 Cockrum, who filled: Tom DeFalco, *Comics Creators on The X-Men*, Titan, 2006.

155 "It was just another book": Jim Amash, "Alienation Was What the X-Men Were All About," *Alter Ego* 24, May 2003.

156 "I'm looking at this book": Richard Howell and Carol Kalish, "An Interview With Bill Mantlo," *Comics Feature* 17, June 1982.

156 "The problem at Marvel": Richard Howell and Carol Kalish, "The Mind of an Editor: Len Wein," *Comics Feature* 6, October 1980.

157 "There was a definite hierarchy". Howell and Kalish, "An Interview with Bill Mantlo."

158 "It's not that I think": Jon B. Cooke, "The Heir Apparent," *Comic Book Artist* 2, Summer 1998.

160 "I never liked Mantis": Glen Cadigan, "The Man Who Loved Comics," *Alter Ego* 78.

160 When Englehart received: Sanderson, "An Interview with Steve Englehart."

160 "Basically, Mantis was": Diana Schutz, "Steve Englehart," *Fantaco's Chronicles Series* 4, August 1982.

160 "to be a slut": Jon B. Cooke, "Marvel's Third Wave," *Comic Book Artist* 18, March 2002.

160 "By the end": Jon B. Cooke, "Marvel's Third Wave," *Comic Book Artist* 18, March 2002.

161 "The Beast was a product": Sanderson, "An Interview with Steve Englehart."

161 "He got older": David M. Singer, "I Deliver the Goods," *Comic Times*, 2, September 1980.

164 "We never had a fight": *Rocket's Blast–Comicollector* 114, October 1974.

164 "I came up to the office": Marie Severin at San Diego Comic-Con, July 19, 1997. Transcribed in John Morrow, "The 1997 Kirby Tribute Panel," *Jack Kirby Collector* 17.

164 "Whatever I do at Marvel": Nicholas Caputo, "A Shocking Story," *Jack Kirby Collector* 10, April 1996.

165 "Stan told me": Robert Gustaveson, "Gerry Conway Talks Back to the Comics Journal," *Comics Journal* 69, December 1981.

166 "This doesn't really work": Craig Shutt, "The X-Men: A 'Cool Concept,'" *Alter Ego* 24, May 2003.

166 "really didn't feel": Gustaveson, "Gerry Conway Talks Back to the Comics Journal."

166 "I'm not all that great": Howell and Kalish, "The Mind of an Editor: Len Wein."

167 "Len was taking a lot of tranquilizers": Peter Sanderson, *The X-Men Companion I*, Fantagraphics, 1982.

167 "We're presently undergoing": *Comic Reader* 129, April 1976.

167 "I was just speaking to our printer": Scott Edelman, "Bullpen Bull," *Comics Journal* 43, December 1978.

168 the publisher's Los Angeles distributor: *Comic Reader* 113, December 1974.

169 $300,000 of Marvel's sales: *Comics Journal* 64, June 1981.

170 there would be no more Marvel Comics: Chuck Rozanski, "Evolution of the Direct Market VI," milehighcomics.com.

170 "I think by June 30th of the year": Daniels, *Marvel*.

170 "The first thing I had to do": David Anthony Kraft, "Jim Galton," *Comics Interview* 1, February 1983.

171 "If *Celebrity*'s attitude": James Monaco, *Celebrity: The Media as Image Makers*, Dell, 1978.

171 Now Lee enjoyed: "Super Stan the Comics Man," *Cue*, 1974.

171 "What's this—why is this here?": *Marvel Age* 8, November 1983, p. 15.

171 not to make major changes: Howell and Kalish, "The Mind of an Editor: Len Wein."

171 "not by Stan Lee as the top": Singer, "I Deliver the Goods."

7

174 "My father had a beat-up old car": Christopher Irving, "Jim Shooter's Secret Origin, in His Own Words, Part One," NYCGraphicNovelists.com, July 20, 2010.

175 "You know who my inspiration was": David Anthony Kraft, "Gerry Conway," *Comics Interview* 13, July 1984.

175 he cruelly berated: David M. Singer, "Chatting with Jim Shooter," *Comic Times* 4, 1980.

175 "He caused a kind of": Harry Broertjes, *Legion Outpost* 8, Summer 1974.

176 By the time a couple of: Ibid.

176 "young, strange looking, and dressed": Jim Shooter, "Marvel and Me," *The Comic Book Price Guide*, 1986.

178 "I said, 'What's with this duck?'": Mark Singer, "The Underestimated Duck," *New Yorker*, February 7, 1977.

179 "one of the best written comics": "Wise Quacks," *Howard the Duck* 5.

179 "gruesome": *Comic Reader* 129.

179 "I was working at that particular time": Sanderson, "Marv Wolfman."

180 "Thor, the fine fool's gold": *Avengers* 137, July 1975.

180 "Don and I used to be": Kim Thompson, "An Interview with Marv Wolfman," *Comics Journal* 44, January 1979.

180 "I *believe* in the fairy tales": *Jungle Action* 20, March 1976.
181 "When a writer is specifically told": Thompson, "An Interview with Marv Wolfman."
181 He was arguing: Amash, "Writing Comics Turned Out to Be What I Really Wanted to Do with My Life."
181 He was publicly predicting: *Comic Reader* 129, April 1976.
182 "It was a job that was just impossible": Sanderson, "Marv Wolfman."
182 "It was like being caught": *Comic Reader* 147, p.13.
184 He immediately called: *Comic Media Showcase*, Conway letter.
185 "I tried to read the 'good' stuff": Gary Groth, "Pushing Marvel into the 80s: An Interview with Jim Shooter," *Comics Journal* 60, November 1980.
186 "It seemed like the thing to do for the bicentennial": Sanderson, "An Interview with Steve Englehart."
186 "I found myself": Singer, "I Deliver the Goods."
186 "I just said": Sanderson, "An Interview with Steve Englehart."

8

189 "I think in most cases": *Comic Reader* 147.
189 based part of his onstage costume: Gene Simmons, *Kiss and Make-Up*, p. 65, Random House, 2002.
189 Aucoin's VP went ballistic: David Leaf and Ken Sharp, *Kiss Behind the Mask: The Official Authorized Biography*, Grand Central, 2003.
190 "the first bit of sophisticated ad copy": Gary Groth, "An Interview with Steve Gerber," *Comics Journal* 41, August 1978.
190 "I wonder if the basic idea": Letter to Richard Kane of Marden-Kane agency, December 1, 1976.
191 Shooter, the perpetual second in command: Letter from Sol Brodsky to Barry Kaplan, April 20, 1976.
191 Goodwin, furious: Bell, *I Have to Live with This Guy.*
191 royalty payments for reprinted stories: Memos, courtesy Scott Edelman.
191 a letter from Sheldon Feinberg: Joe Brancatelli, *Eerie* 87, October 1977.
192 "I'm the most famous": Jerry Lazar, "A Duck Is Born," *Circus* 154, April 28, 1977.
194 "We felt, or maybe Stan felt": Quoted in Gary Picariello, "The Equation for Success," *Jack Kirby Collector* 41, Fall 2004.
195 Roger Stern had to rewrite: John Byrne, post to Byrne Robotics forum, July 28, 2006.
196 "I was supposedly": Video interview at Virginia Tech, November 1977.
196 the Kiss special sold: "Newswatch," *Comics Journal* 45, March 1979.
196 "For a while": Groth, "An Interview with Steve Gerber."
197 "I don't want to say anything bad": Sanderson, *The X-Men Companion I.*
197 "the phoenix-force": *The Official Handbook to the Marvel Universe* 14, March 1984.
197 "quite active in the New York City demimonde": Cat Yronwode, post to alt.magick, June 8, 2003.
198 "I made it known at Marvel": Peter Sanderson, *The X-Men Companion II*, Fantagraphics, 1982.
198 "John was the heir apparent": Jim Amash, "We Kicked the Whole Thing Around a Lot," *Alter Ego* 24, May 2003.
198 "I had become obsessively": Roger Slifer, "Len Wein," *Comics Journal* 48, Summer 1979.
199 He told Wein that he would: Kim Thompson, "Roy Thomas Leaves Marvel," *Comics Journal* 56, June 1980.
201 "Among other things": Gustaveson, "Fifteen Years at Marvel."

201 Lee took Shooter out to lunch: *Marvel Fanfare* 1, March 1982.
201 "I helped clean out his office": Dwight Jon Zimmerman, "Danny Crespi," *Comics Interview* 9, March 1984.

9

205 "Stan wants me": Kim Thompson, "An Interview with Marvel's Head Honcho," *Comics Journal* 40, June 1978.
205 "Everything that has": Gary Groth, "Birth of the Guild," *Comics Journal* 42, October 1978.
205 sales of the *Hulk* comic: Jean-Paul Gabilliet, *Of Comics and Men*, University Press of Mississippi, 2010.
206 Gerber's lawyer informed: Groth, "An interview with Steve Gerber."
206 "I would just say": "Marvel Fires Gerber," *Comics Journal* 41, August 1978.
206 "Once I was gone": "Souped Up," *Village Voice*, September 4, 1978.
207 "imaginative but undisciplined": Hoy Murphy's account of the Moncon II convention appeared in *Comics Reader* 157, June 1978.
207 "The editorial staff . . . had": Jon B. Cooke, "Starlin's Cosmic Books," *Comic Book Artist* 2.
208 an editor went through: John Byrne post to Byrnerobotics.com, July 28, 2006.
208 "I didn't really get a shot": Howard Zimmerman, "Kirby Takes on The Comics," *Comics Scene* 2, March 1982.
208 The poster for the Comics Contract Meeting is reproduced: Gary Groth, "The Comics Guild," *Comics Journal* 42, October 1978.
209 "If we really want": "John Byrne: The Interview," *Comics Feature* 27, January–February 1984.
210 "I was tempted to throw": Sanderson, *X-Men Companion II*.
211 margin notes: "John Byrne in Dallas," *Comics Journal* 76, October 1982.
211 "Chris' idea of a perfect": Mitch Itkowitz and J. Michael Catron, "John Byrne," *Comics Journal* 57, Summer 1980.
211 "To me, . . . the fights are": Margaret O'Connell, "Chris Claremont," *Comics Journal* 50, October 1979.
211 "He used to call": Lou Mougin, "Jim Mooney," *Comics Interview* 103, 1991.
213 "Confidentially": Dave Olbrich, funnybookfanatic.wordpress.com, December 18, 2008.
213 "In five years": Gerard Jones and Will Jacobs, *The Comic Book Heroes*.
213 "His position was unique": *Avengers* 175, September 1978.
214 "I was in the unique position": *Avengers* 176, October 1978.
214 Stan's salary: Raphael and Spurgeon, *Stan Lee and the Rise and Fall of the American Comic Book*.
214 "On his wrist": Barbara Rowes, "Stan Lee, Creator of Spider-Man and the Incredible Hulk, Is America's Biggest Mythmaker," *People*, January 29, 1979.
214 "Comic books are like": Jim Dawson, "Hello, Culture Lovers! Stan the Man Raps with Marvel Maniacs at James Madison University," *Comics Journal* 42, October 1978.
215 "I didn't know we had any Russian superheroes": "Stan Lee Replies to Eric Leguebe," 1978, published in Jeff McLaughlin, ed., *Stan Lee: Conversations*, University Press of Mississippi, 2007.
215 "Sol Brodsky got pictures": Shutt, "The X-Men: A 'Cool Concept.'"
215 "I should have gotten": Ira Wolfman, "Stan Lee's New Marvels," *Circus*, July 20, 1978.
215 They convinced Cadence: Video interview at Virginia Tech, November 1977.

215 a budget was set: Ro, *Tales to Astonish*.

216 "With a new approach": *Comic Reader* 128, March 1976.

216 Marvel's nonreturnable sales: "Marvel Hires Specialty Sales Manager," *Comics Journal* 54, March 1980.

216 he was now supplying: *Comics Journal* 37, February 1977.

217 The company was missing: Chuck Rozanski, "Tales From the Database," mile-highcomics.com.

217 Within months, Marvel announced: "Spectacular Sales Prompt New Projects," *Comics Journal* 52.

217 "With the other editors-in-chief": Groth, "Pushing Marvel into the 80s: An Interview with Jim Shooter."

218 "*To: Anthony Stark*": *Iron Man* 127, October 1979.

218 "I don't want to continue working": "Magazine Line Reorganized; New Editor Hired," *Comics Journal* 50, October 1979.

218 Lee stepped in: "Gene Colan Leaves Marvel," *Comics Journal* 63, Spring 1981.

219 anonymous staffers grousing: "Superheroes' Creators Wrangle," N. R. Kleinfield, *New York Times*, October 13, 1979.

219 "garbage": "N.Y. Times Article Blasts Marvel," *Comics Journal* 52, December 1979.

219 The direct-sales market: "Direct Sales Boom," *Comics Journal* 64, June 1981, and Rozanski, "Tales from the Database."

219 "The old Marvel needed": Joe Brancatelli, "The Comic Books," *Eerie* 110, April 1980.

220 "Fourteen years ago": Peter Sanderson and Dean Mullaney, "Comics Feature Interview: Denny O'Neil," *Comics Feature* 4, July–August 1980.

220 Marvel's most popular title: "TCR Top 100 Comic Books," *Comic Reader* 175.

221 "When I brought in the one": Amash, "We Kicked the Whole Thing Around a Lot."

222 "They said, 'let's do'": "Wizard One-on-One with John Romita Jr.," wizarduniverse.com, December 23, 2006.

222 "At one point Casablanca": Richard Howell and Carol Kalish, "Dissecting the Dazzler," *Comics Feature* 7, November 1980.

222 "I swore that I": Ibid.

223 he scanned *GQ* and *Playboy*: Frederick Marcus and Dean Mullaney, "Comics Feature Interview: David Michelinie and Bob Layton," *Comics Feature* 2, May 1980.

225 Roy Thomas, also in Los Angeles: Negotiations between Shooter and Thomas were outlined in both an interview with and a letter from Roy Thomas, in *The Comics Journal* 61.

228 "Having a character destroy": *Phoenix: The Untold Story* 1, April 1984.

228 "Shooter wanted Jean punished": Sanderson, *The X-Men Companion I*.

228 It was the first time: Peter Sanderson, "The Many Alternate Fates of the Phoenix," *Comics Feature* 4, July–August 1980.

229 So was Perez: Heidi MacDonald, "The George Perez Interview," *Focus on George Perez*, Fantagraphics, 1985.

10

230 "Unfortunately . . . you come": Sanderson, *The X-Men Companion I*.

230 death threats: Diana Schutz, "X-Men: Chris Claremont Interview, Part II," *Comics Collector* 2, Winter 1984.

230 cash registers rang: TCR Top 100 list, *Comic Reader* 184, October 1980.

230 Shooter asked Jim Starlin: *Comics Feature* 5, September 1980.

231 "twenty developmental": Ibid.

231 "We figured if people": David Schwartz, "Marvel Goes Hollywood," *Marvel Age Annual* 1, 1985.

231 asked to work up a presentation: Peter Sanderson, "Steve Gerber," *Comics Feature* 12/13, September–October 1981.

231 "Stan was responsible": Steve Gerber letter published in *Comics Journal* 57, Summer 1980.

232 "derivative media work": "Gerber Sues Marvel Over Rights to Duck; Comes Out Ahead in First Legal Skirmish," *Comics Journal* 62, March 1981.

232 Among the other prospective: "New Gerber Creation on ABC," *Comics Feature* 4, July–August 1980.

232 "For me it was almost": Tom Field, *Secrets in the Shadows: The Art & Life of Gene Colan*, TwoMorrows, 2005.

232 "I've got fans": Mitchell Itkowitz and Michael J. Catron, "John Byrne," *Comics Journal* 57, Summer 1980.

232 "You get to hang out": Howell and Kalish, "An Interview with Bill Mantlo."

232 "Rarely will you find": Diana Schutz, "X-Men: Chris Claremont Interview, Part II," *Comics Collector* 2, Winter, 1984.

235 he volunteered: John Byrne, "The Fantastic Four: A Personal Recollection": *Fantastic Four Chronicles*, 1982.

236 30 percent of Marvel's sales: *Comic Times* 3, November 1980. Wein and Wolfman take Byrne to task in Jay Zilber, "Interview: Len Wein and Marv Wolfman," *Fantastic Four Chronicles*, 1982.

239 "Some friend of John Byrne's called": Roger Green, "Questions and Answers with Jack Kirby, Version Two," *Fantastic Four Chronicles*, 1982.

239 "Yeah, . . . sounds like fun": John Morrow, "The Other Duck Man," *Jack Kirby Collector* 10, April 1996.

11

240 "After I got mugged": Michael Catron, "Devil's Advocate," *Amazing Heroes* 4, September 1981.

240 "I like to play into very daily fears": Peter Sanderson, "The Frank Miller/Klaus Janson Interview," *The Daredevil Chronicles*, February 1982.

241 "probably the most Christian": Richard Howell and Carol Kalish, "An Interview with Frank Miller," *Comics Feature* 14, December 1981.

243 "In the country of the blind": Richard Howell and Carol Kalish, "Looking Ahead at DC: Roy Thomas," *Comics Feature* 11, August 1981.

243 Dave Cockrum created: *Comics Feature* 11, August 1981.

243 A sort of West Coast X-Men: Peter Sanderson, *The X-Men Companion II*, Fantagraphics, 1982.

243 "I wanted to handle it": DeFalco, *Comics Creators on The X-Men*.

244 "We poke fun at ourselves": Geoff Gehman, "Captain America: When A Musical Won't Fly," *Morning Call*, March 27, 1988.

244 "ads for toys": Howard Zimmerman, "Kirby Takes on the Comics," *Comics Scene* 2, March 1982.

245 "I've created a number of characters": Robert Greenberger, "Marvel Turns 20," *Comics Scene* 1, January 1982.

245 "I have, of late": John Byrne, "On Creator's Rights," *Comics Scene* 2, March 1982.

246 "most definitions of that word": Letter from Donald S. Engel to Stuart J. Freedman, December 16, 1981.

246 *X-Men* selling over: Kim Thompson, "Marvel Announces Royalties Plan," *Comics Journal* 70, February 1982.

246 "It's me and Frank Miller and": Sanderson, *The X-Men Companion II*.

247 "I think they're the best two": Howell and Kalish, "An Interview with Bill Mantlo."

12

251 "I didn't give a damn": Zimmerman, "Danny Crespi."

252 With Marvel's comic sales rising: Kim Thompson, "Marvel Miscellania," *Comics Journal* 79, January 1983.

252 "How soon 'til we see": "Marvel's Professional Fannishness," letter from Matt Feazell, *Comics Journal* 84, September 1983.

254 "There are writers and artists": "John Byrne at Dallas," *Comics Journal* 75, September 1982.

255 "No female character": *Spider-Woman* 48 letter column, February 1983.

257 "He works eight hours": Robert Greenberger, "Creating the Comics Part B: Inking," *Comics Scene* 6, November 1982.

257 "one of the most traumatic": Kim Thompson, "Miller, Day, Sienkiewicz Drop Marvel Titles," *Comics Journal* 76, October 1982.

257 "drastic, sweeping changes": "Moench Goes Freelance," *Comics Scene* 7, January 1983.

258 "I could kill off": Cat Yronwode, "Fit to Print," *Comics Buyer's Guide* 461, September 17, 1982.

258 "I never told": Hal Schuster, "Doug Moench, Jim Shooter, and Death in the Marvel Universe," *Comics Feature* 21, November 1982.

258 "None of them": Ibid.

258 "Jim had an idea": "Moench Goes Freelance," *Comics Scene* 7, January 1983.

259 "When I was talking": Ibid.

259 "My guess is that someone": Jim Shooter, Comment on "Superman—First Marvel Issue!," JimShooter.com, October 11, 2011.

259 "He had been writing": Diana Schutz, "Chris Claremont—Superstar," *Comics Scene* 11, September 1983.

259 "a rhetorical example": September 1982 WAIF radio interview by Chris Barkley; a transcribed version was published on booksteveslibrary.blogspot.com on March 24, 2006.

260 "Gene was a creature": Doug Moench, "Gene Day: Dweller by a Dark Stream," *Comics Scene* 7, January 1983.

260 "Gene Day Left *Master of Kung Fu*": Gary Groth, "Marvel's War with the Press," *Comics Journal* 79, January 1983.

260 "I'm a big Marvel supporter": Mark Shainblum, "The Last Interview," *Orion* 2, 1982.

13

262 "I came back the afternoon": "Shop Talk: Jack Kirby," *Will Eisner's Spirit Magazine* 39, February 1983.

262 "I don't know whether . . . or not": Jim Salicrup, "Stan Lee," *Comics Interview*, July 1983.

263 "I said, 'I want to do a god'": Leonard Pitts interview with Stan Lee, circa 1984.

263 Jenette Kahn and Paul Levitz took Jack and Roz: Ro, *Tales to Astonish*.

264 "In essence": Jim Salicrup, "Marvel Super Heroes Secret Wars," *Comics Interview* 14, August 1984.

264 In August 1983: "Cadence Proposal to Take Firm Private Set by Top Managers," *Wall Street Journal*, August 8, 1983.

266 "Why don't you do": Mitch Cohn, "Fred Hembeck," *Comics Interview* 22, June 1985. Direct market increases reported in Kim Thompson, "Marvel Miscellania," *Comics Journal* 79, January 1983, and Kim Thompson, "Marvel Miscellania," *Comics Journal* 86, November 1983.

268 "If the comics are good": "Bullpen Bulletins," February 1983.

270 "Why would a being": *Secret Wars* 9.

270 When the final issue: Renee Witterstaetter interviews with Beatty and Zeck, *Comics Interview* 72, 1989.

271 "The Fire Marshal shut it down": Dan Johnson, "Black and White and Read All Over," *Back Issue* 12, October 2005.

272 "elimination of an irritation": February 21, 1984, letter from Jim Shooter to Joe Calamari, posted to JimShooter.com on August 26, 2011.

14

273 "I proposed that we do a Big Bang": Dan Johnson, "Sparks in a Bottle: The Saga of the New Universe," *Back Issue* 34, June 2009.

273 "It sold through the roof": Duin and Richardson, *Comics Between the Panels*.

274 "Since I don't have a lettercol": Tom Heintjes, "Secret Wars: The Memo and the Plugs," *Comics Journal* 97, April 1985.

277 "The letter was basically two sentences": Paul Power, "Chic Stone," *Comics Interview* 121, 1993.

277 "I got a very short note": Chris Knowles, "Jim Mooney over Marvel," *Comic Book Artist* 7, February 2000.

277 "Shooter . . . knows full well": "Behind the Lines: Special Report," *Marvel Age* 19, October 1984, quotes from the interview in the British fanzine *Chain Reaction*.

277 "They don't give a shit": Tom Heintjes and Kim Thompson, "Marvel's Original Art Vault," *Comics Journal* 92, August 1984.

278 "I wouldn't cooperate with the Nazis": Tom Heintjes, "Marvel Withholds Kirby's Art," *Comics Journal* 100, July 1985.

278 "We've never tried": Tom Heintjes, "Shooter Speaks Out on Kirby Art," *Comics Journal* 104, January 1986.

278 "I saved Marvel's ass": Unpublished Leonard Pitts interview with Jack Kirby.

279 "I don't know much of what Jack is talking about": Leonard Pitts interview with Stan Lee.

279 "Let's be honest": http://paulhowleysstory.blogspot.com/2009/12/part-70-79.html.

279 Shooter told reporters: Hal Schuster, "Marvel Superheroes Secret Wars," *Comics Feature* 29, May 1984.

284 The first plot that Gerber submitted: Tom Heintjes, "Gerber pulls Howard Script," *Comics Journal* 101, August 1985.

284 "I'm of the opinion": David Smay, "Jim Starlin," *Amazing Heroes* 98, July 1, 1986.

284 "I got tired of writing stories": Peter Sanderson, "Steve Englehart," *Comics Journal* 100, July 1985.

285 "one Bernhard Goetz": Kim Thompson, "Frank Miller: Return of the Dark Knight," *Comics Journal* 101, August 1985.

287 "It would really be a cheat": Peter Sanderson, "The Many Alternate Fates of the Phoenix," *Comics Feature* 4, July–August 1980.

289 They holed up in a Manhattan hotel room: Brian Cronin, "Comic Book Legends Revealed #204," ComicBookResources.com, April 23, 2009.

289 Forty-five years earlier: Roy Thomas, "Fire and Water," *Timely Presents: Human Torch*, February, 1999; Steranko, *Steranko's History of Comics*.

290 "Continued to snipe": John Byrne, Byrnerobotics, September 17, 2007.

292 That summer: Sholly Fisch, "The Wedding of the Year," *Marvel Age* 54, September 1987.

293 "If the movie is as good": Dwight Jon Zimmerman, "Steve Gerber," *Comics Interview* 38, 1986.

294 "bloody awful": December 16, 1985, letter from Jim Galton to Golan.

294 "The young, hip, fun-loving": "Stan's Soapbox," *Marvel Age* 51, June 1986.

296 screamed threats of a class action lawsuit: *Back Issue* magazine, with Warlock on cover. See *Wizard* 142 for more, including "Fuck you."

299 "He had helped build Marvel": Ro, *Tales to Astonish*.

300 CompuServe messages: Kim Fryer, "Jim Shooter Fired," *Comics Journal* 116, July 1987.

15

303 "He gave you a title": Letter reprinted in "Vinnie Colletta's Exit 'Conversation,'" *20th Century Danny Boy*, April 29, 2007.

304 "I didn't consider it merry": *Earthwatch with Robert Knight and Warren Reece*, WBAI, August 28, 1987.

307 "Originally we weren't going to": DeFalco, *Comic Creators on X-Men*.

310 "He didn't know what": John Lustig, "Boaz Yakin," *Comics Interview* 76, 1989.

312 "find an undervalued company": Peter Hood, "Roy Cohn Called Them the Perfect Couple" *Spy*, January–February 1988.

312 "mini-Disney in terms of": Marvin R. Shanken, "Ron Perelman," *Cigar Aficionado*, March 1995.

313 $300 million portfolio: Hood, "Roy Cohn Called Them the Perfect Couple."

313 who'd met Perelman at: Phyllis Furman, "Perelman's Tangled Web," *Crain's New York Business*, April 28, 1997.

313 "We exchanged pleasantries": Lee, *Excelsior!*

16

319 "It wouldn't have been my choice": Len Wong, "Spider-Man Artist: Todd McFarlane," *Amazing Heroes* 179, May 1990.

319 "Uh . . . I don't really consider": Ibid.

320 "Right now, I still feel good": Ibid.

320 "As long as I get Spider-Man": Patrick Daniel O'Neill, "Writing & Drawing the Web-Head," *Wizard* 1, September 1991. Liefeld note to Harras published in *Marvel Age* 81, November 1989.

321 "Bob said, 'Let's call him'": Patrick Daniel O'Neill, "No Holds Barred," *Wizard* 10, June 1992.

321 "would do square windows": DeFalco, *Comics Creators on The X-Men*.

321 "The books were suddenly being used": *Wizard Special Edition: X-Men Turn Thirty*, 1993.

322 One Los Angeles store: John Jackson Miller, "June 2010 Flashbacks: McFarlane Spider-Man #1 at 20," blog.comichron.com, July 13, 2010.

322 Estimated as an $8000 promotion: Lou Bank, *Comics Retailer* 58, January 1997.

323 The manufacturing department's five months of experiments: Sven Larsen, "What Spider-Man Can Teach Us About Interface Design," *From Bogota With Love*, February 2009.

324 Marvel giddily noted: Floyd Norris, "Boom in Comic Books Lifts New Marvel Stock Offering," *New York Times*, July 15, 1991.

325 "I thought it was the worst idea": DeFalco, *Comics Creators on The X-Men*.

326 "He would change plots": Paul J. Grant, "Poor Dead Doug, and Other Mutant Memories," *Wizard Special Edition: X-Men Turn Thirty*, 1993.

326 1988 Bob Harras interview: Dwight Jon Zimmerman, "Bob Harras," *Comics Interview* 62, 1988.

327 "It just happened that Bob hated": George Khoury, *Image: The Road to Independence*.

328 "an outright knock-down drag-out fight": Steve Darnell, "Proceed With Prudence & Caution: Chris Claremont Drives Outside the Lines," *Heroes Illustrated* 12, June 1994.

329 "What you have is a corporate": Kim Thompson, "Chris Claremont," *Comics Journal* 152, August 1992.

329 "abrupt, rude, and disrespectful": Tom DeFalco, *Comics Creators on The Fantastic Four*, Titan, 2005.

329 "The X-Men . . . are going to pay": Patrick Daniel O'Neill, "Mutants Aren't Everything," *Wizard* 4, December 1991.

330 "Years later . . . I was told": DeFalco, *Comics Creators on The X-Men*.

330 "Your title *X-O Manowar* is": M. Clark Humphrey, "Does X-O Sound Like X-Men?," *Comics Journal* 146, November 1991.

331 "You sell a million, I'll listen to you": Kim Howard Johnson, "Spawn," *Comics Scene* 2, no. 27, June 1992.

331 "There's no reason for me": O'Neill, "Writing & Drawing the Web-Head."

332 In the past two years: 1991 prospectus.

332 which, according to Marvel: *Amazing Heroes* 186, December 1990.

332 In March 1991: Kate Fitzgerald, "Marvel Leaps Into 900 Promo," *Advertising Age*, March 18, 1991.

333 the money raised would not: Furman, "Perelman's Tangled Web."

333 "revenue growth depends on": Nancy Miller, "Spider-Man Makes Super Wall St. Debut," *USA Today*, July 17, 1991.

334 "We've been accused of": Sean Piccoli, "Comic Meister Extraordinaire," *Washington Times*, October 25, 1991.

336 "More artists writing": Letter printed in *Comics Buyers Guide*, August 1991.

336 "Quitting one at a time": Kim Howard Johnson, "Spawn" *Comics Scene* 2, no. 7, June 1992.

336 "Marvel Comics felt they could lose": Duin and Richardson, *Comics Between the Panels*.

337 "That's the wrong thing to say": Ibid.

337 "There'll always be somebody": Michael Dean, "The Image Story," tcj.com, October 25, 2000.

337 "Terry basically said": George Khoury, *Image: The Road to Independence*, TwoMorrows, 2007.

338 "Jim and a couple": Duin and Richardson, *Comics Between the Panels*.

17

339 a two-page article that warned: Douglas A. Kass, "Pow! Smash! Ker-plash! High-Flying Marvel Comics May Be Headed for a Fall," *Barron's*, February 17, 1992.

342 "If the Punisher appears": Jim Starlin, *The Art of Jim Starlin: A Life In Words and Pictures*, IDW, 2010.

343 "The editors are as trapped": Peter David, "X'd Out," *Comics Buyers Guide*, March 5, 1993.

344 It was through this maneuver that Marvel: Furman, "Perelman's Tangled Web."

345 There were eight thousand comic-book stores: Gabilliet, *Of Comics And Men*.

345 converted to comic sales to fill the void: Eric Reynolds, "Industry Sales Records in 1993 Shadowed by Collapse of Speculator Boom," *Comics Journal* 166, February 1994.

346 "The founding creators": Gary Groth, "Marder for the Cause," *Comics Journal* 170, August 1994.

346 "Everyone had expense accounts": Sean T. Collins, "The Amazing! Incredible! Uncanny Oral History of Marvel Comics," *Maxim*, September 2009.

346 "We have to take our shot now": Alex Chun, "Image Enhancement," *Amazing Heroes* 202, June 1992.

346 two of the principals: Carolyn M. Brown, "Marketing a New Universe of Heroes," *Black Enterprise*, Nov. 1994.

347 "I had my turn": Duin and Richardson, *Comics Between the Panels*.

347 "There's nothing to differentiate": Patrick Daniel O'Neill, "Claremont Returns with the Write Stuff," *Wizard* 22, June 1993.

18

351 "Quite frankly": Michael J. Catron, "Starlin Takes New Project To Malibu," *Comics Journal* 161, August 1993.

351 "It stings like hell": Thom Carnell, "Walking the Streets of Sin City," *Carpe Noctem* 2, 1994.

352 "I don't give a crap": *Amazing Heroes Interviews* 2, 1993.

354 Marvel's publishing department: Eric Reynolds, "Marvel in Flux," *Comics Journal* 170, August 1994.

355 "Write me a memo": Furman, "Perelman's Tangled Web."

355 Marvel added yet another business: Paul Noglows, "Marvel's plan: Toys are must," *Daily Variety*, April 22, 1993.

355 It pulled in a sizable adult audience: Gaile Robinson, "The X-Men Want the Night Too," *Los Angeles Times*, October 27, 1993.

356 *Fantastic Four* film: Robert Ito, "Fantastic Faux," *Los Angeles,* March 2005.

19

359 "Stanley and I never": Gary Groth, "Jack Kirby," *Comics Journal* 134, February 1990.

359 "I think he's gone beyond": Duin and Richardson, *Comics Between the Panels*.

359 "Jack said something strange": Ro, *Tales to Astonish*.

360 After Kirby's death: Duin and Richardson, *Comics Between the Panels*.

361 36 percent in the first: Tim Jones, "Holy Competition, Batman!," *Chicago Tribune*, August 25, 1994.

366 Perelman went out to California: Scott Rosenberg, talksaboutcomics.com podcast interview, by Joey Manley and Scott Kurtz, June 29, 2006.

367 "If I were really paranoid": Eric Reynolds, "The Rumors Are True: Marvel Buys Malibu," *Comics Journal* 173, December 1994.

368 The presentation modified: Eric Reynolds: "Marvelution: The Art of the Deal," *Comics Journal* 176, April 1995.

369 "You're moved from": Tom Spurgeon, "Witness at the Marvelution," *Comics Journal* 177, May 1995.

369 "The lack of creative satisfaction": Fabian Nicieza post to rec.arts.comics.xbooks, June 2, 1995.

369 eighty-five grand a month: Alex Foege, "The X-Men Files," *New York*, July 17, 2000.

370 rewritten from scratch: Marc Shapiro, "The Wizard Q&A: Scott Lobdell," *Wizard* 65, January 1997.

371 The number of comic shops: Gary Groth, "John Davis," *Comics Journal* 188, July 1996.

371 "Marvel knew that their": Heidi MacDonald, "Larry Marder," *Comics Journal* 201, January 1998.

371 "Why do you want to work": Khoury, *Image: The Road to Independence*.

372 Herb Trimpe journal entries: Herb Trimpe, "Old Heroes Never Die, They Join the Real World," *New York Times*, January 7, 2000.

373 "This is a turning point": "The End of the Marvel Age," *Oregonian*, December 21, 1995.

20

379 "I don't know if anybody": Matthew Senreich, "The Wizard Q&A: Mark Waid & Ron Garney," *Wizard* 72, August 1997.

380 "I'd been working for Marvel": Jim Amash, *Sal Buscema: Comics' Fast & Furious Artist*, TwoMorrows, 2010.

380 "I think 48 years in any business": Greg Stump, "News Watch," *Comics Journal* 190, September 1996.

381 By the end of 1994: Michael A. Hiltzik, "A Tangled Web of Deal-Making," *Los Angeles Times*, August 29, 1998.

381 "Right now, you're dying": Raviv, *Comic Wars*.

381 one of the reasons that Marvel: Gary Levin, "A Marvelous Post," *Daily Variety*, October 24, 1996.

381 Now Jerry Calabrese and Avi Arad: Nancy Hass, "Investing It: Marvel Superheroes Take Aim at Hollywood," *New York Times*, July 28, 1996.

381 "We are finally on the verge": Michael R. Goldman, "Marvel sets a new agenda," *Daily Variety*, October 1, 1996.

382 the monthly circulation of *Amazing Spider-Man*: Furman, "Perelman's Tangled Web."

382 "I'd never take the *Bugle* public": *Amazing Spider-Man* 416, October 1996.

382 "I want to do an unofficial crossover": "Brian Bendis Presents Tom Brevoort," Wizarduniverse.com, January 8, 2007.

383 "That page contains my final word": Message relayed to rec.arts.comics.marvel.universe by Michael R. Grabois, November 6, 1996.

384 offered to fax the twenty-page plot: Steve Gerber to rec.arts.comics.misc, October 2, 1996.

386 "MacAndrews & Forbes is not going to": *Hollywood Reporter*, October 23, 1996.

387 "Do you ask Willie Mays": Connie Bruck, *Predators Ball*, Simon & Schuster, 1988.

388 "The only way he'd give": Rhoades, *A Complete History of American Comic Books*.

388 "felt like I'd made a fool": Tom Russo, "The Wizard Q&A: Frank Miller," *Wizard* 59, July 1996.

388 "Uh, in case we're doing . . .": Hart Fisher, "Rob 'n' Todd," *The Comics Journal* 195, April 1997.

388 "Over my dead body": "McFarlane Blasts Liefeld, Lawsuit," *Wizard* 65, January 1997.

389 "How you feel when": Raviv, *Comic Wars*.

390 "I will crush your company": Ibid.

390 "One day [Scott] Sassa": Shirrel Rhoades, *A Complete History of American Comic Books*, Peter Lang, 2008, p. 146.

391 "Okay, who are these new": Raviv, *Comic Wars*.

392 "We live in one of the most": Ibid.

395 "By the time I was done reading": Chuck Rozanski, "How Could We Possibly Make a Bid for Marvel?" milehighcomics.com, October 2002.

395 "It would take years before the income": Chuck Rozanski, "Our Bid for Marvel Was Never Placed," milehighcomics.com, October 2002.

396 "*Blade* was the least likely": Susanna Hamner, "Marvel Comics Leaps into Movie-Making," *Business* 2.0, May 2006.

397 "No one would have gotten": Richard Johnston, "Waiting for Tommy: Jason Liebig," DynamicForces.com, September 3, 2003.

399 "After only a little less than two months": *Comic Book Net Electronic Magazine* 189, November 20, 1998.

400 Meanwhile, Perlmutter had begun: Raviv, *Comic Wars*.

400 "Stan never knew what": Steve Ditko letter published in *Comic Book Marketplace* 63, October 1998.

401 "Spider-Man's existence needed": Steve Ditko letter published in *Time*, December 7, 1998.

401 "Steve said, 'Having an idea . . .'": Jonathan Ross, *In Search of Steve Ditko*, 2007.

402 "He was making faces": Michael Dean, "Post Mortem: Marv Wolfman Talks About His Day in Court," *Comics Journal* 239, November, 2001.

402 "Christ, I'm doing this": Robert Wilonsky, "Custody Battle," *Dallas Observer*, Thursday, April 19, 2001.

403 "Whether you're selling deodorant": Michael Dean, "Meet Marvel's New Boss," *Comics Journal* 218, December 1999.

403 "What do the fans want?": Matthew Brady, "Army of Darkness," *Wizard* 72, August 1997.

404 "There seems to be a perception": James Busbee, "Danger Room," *Wizard* 90, February 1999.

404 "characters who were envisioned": Jonah Weiland, "Ultimate Bill Jemas & Joe Quesada, Part I & II," *Comic Book Resources*, November 4 and 5, 2008.

405 "I think at the time": Ibid.

406 he and Quesada issued a series: James Busbee, "Fantastic Four: Big Town," Fandom.com, November 8, 2000.

406 "Joe Quesada was not able": John Byrne post to JohnByrne.com, November 15, 2000.

407 "I was looking for ways to": Raphael and Spurgeon, *Stan Lee and the Rise and Fall of the American Comic Book*.

407 stocks were changing hands: Michael Dean, "If This Be My Destiny: The Stan Lee Story Reaches Chapter 11," *Comics Journal* 232, April 2001.

407 "If I buy Marvel": Michael Dean, "How Michael Jackson Almost Bought Marvel and Other Strange Tales from the Stan Lee/Peter Paul Partnership": *Comics Journal* 270, August 2005.

408 "Stan once had a big lunch," and subsequent Scott Koblish quotes: Dean: "If This Be My Destiny."

408 "He would sit in business meetings": Laura Rich, "The Trials of a Comic Book Hero," *Industry Standard*, March 19, 2001.

408 No one knew why the stocks were falling: Carl DiOrio, "Stan Lee Selloffs Persist," *Daily Variety*, November 29, 2000.

409 "He is like a grandfather": Rich, "The Trials of a Comic Book Hero."

410 "In 1995, a typical": Rutgers interview.

410 "We have quite a few": Jennifer M. Contino, "Your Media-Man at Marvel," *Sequential Tart*, February 2001.

410 "Elektra is so bad": Andrew Goletz, "Gray Haven Interviews Bill Jemas of Marvel Comics," *Ain't It Cool News*, August 17, 2001.

412 "Part Elvira and part": Jonah Weiland, "Gail Simone announced as new 'Deadpool' Writer," *Comic Book Resources*, August 17, 2001.

414 "I'd much rather be an actor": Conversation with Alain Resnais recorded by Stan Lee, May 14, 1969.

415   "Stan thought Avi did": Lee, *Excelsior!*

415   The auction house: Don Kaplan, "Spidey Tag Sale," *Daily News*, June 23, 2002.

21

416   "People naturally assume": Andrew Billen, "I Haven't Made a Penny From Spider-Man," *Times* (London), June 17, 2002.

416   "I wish I had come to Hollywood": Raphael and Spurgeon, *Stan Lee and the Rise and Fall of the American Comic Book.*

417   A whopping 85 percent: James Adams, "Code Red in the New Comicdom," *Globe and Mail*, May 2, 2002.

417   "I think the 8-year-old": Sridhar Pappu, "The Next Action Hero," *New York Observer*, April 29, 2002.

418   "There has been a perpetual": Jim McLaughlin, *Marvel Year in Review: 2000–2001.*

418   "Peter is a talented writer": "Bill Jemas vs. Peter David!! The Marvel vs. Captain Marvel!!," *Ain't It Cool News*, April 2, 2002.

418   "They have Batman and Superman": Sridhar Pappu, "The Next Action Hero," *New York Observer*, April 29, 2002.

419   "I wasn't prepared": Steve Gerber "New Comics Ideas—2002," SteveGerber.com, July 20, 2006.

421   some claimed that it was: "Marvel's Version of Kill Bill," ICV2.com, October 13, 2003.

422   "I decided that movies": Hector Lima, "Catching Up with Professor M," *Comic Book Resources*, August 7, 2003.

422   "the biggest arsehole": Rich Johnston, "Lying in the Gutters," *Comic Book Resources*, July 27, 2003.

422   Just as he was wondering: "Getting Reloaded with Quesada & Marts," *Newsarama*, March 2004.

423   "The 'Planet X' story": Jonathan Ellis, "Grant Morrison: Master & Commander," PopImage.com, 2004.

425   "Were you looking to have the story": Matt Brady, "Bendis on House of M," *House of M Director's Cut* 1, 2005.

425   "There is an old joke": Jonathan V. Last, "Captain America, RIP," *Wall Street Journal*, March 13, 2007.

426   For a while, the idea of bringing: Jonah Weiland, "The 'One More Day' Interviews with Joe Quesada,' Pt. 2 of 5," *Comic Book Resources*, December 31, 2007.

426   "Everything is so connected": Richard George, "Interview: Joss Whedon" IGN Comics, March 2, 2007.

426   "Our settlement with Stan": "Marvel Enterprises: Conference Call Notes," *Motley Fool*, April 28, 2005.

426   $3.6 billion: Hamner, "Marvel Comics Leaps into Movie-Making."

426   "Nobody knows better": Ibid.

427   He cashed out his stock: Devin Leonard, "Calling All Superheroes," *Fortune*, May 23, 2007.

428   "They wanted to get Dave": Michael Dean, "Marvel Makes Dave Cockrum an Offer He Can't Refuse," *Comics Journal* 260, May–June 2004.

429   "I couldn't care less": Robert K. Elder, "Donation Spotlights Comic Book Dispute," *Barre Montpelier Times Argus*, September 8, 2008.

429   "I have not seen a dime": Collins, "The Amazing! Incredible! Uncanny Oral History of Marvel Comics."

429   acquired the home-run balls: "This Day in Sports: McFarlane Spawns Monster Bid for Bonds' Ball," ESPN.com, June 25, 2010.

429 Isaac Perlmutter was set to: Ben Fritz, "Disney tells details of Marvel Entertain-
     ment acquisition in a regulatory filing," *Los Angeles Times*, September 23, 2009.
431 "I don't know": Alex Pappademas, "The Inquisition of Mr. Marvel," *Grantland*,
     May 9, 2012.
432 "I wish it weren't the case": "A Few Questions with Marvel Editor-in-Chief Axel
     Alonso," *Beat*, January 13, 2011.

INDEX

ABOUT THE AUTHOR

Sean Howe is the editor of *Give Our Regards to the Atomsmashers!: Writers on Comics*. He is the former editor and critic at *Entertainment Weekly*, and his writing has appeared in *New York*, *The Los Angeles Times*, *Spin*, *The Village Voice*, *The New York Observer*, and *The Economist*. He lives in Brooklyn, New York.